The Wyvern Revenge

Bob Warren

authorHOUSE®

AuthorHouse™ UK Ltd.
500 Avebury Boulevard
Central Milton Keynes, MK9 2BE
www.authorhouse.co.uk
Phone: 08001974150

© *2010 Bob Warren. All rights reserved.*

No part of this book may be reproduced, stored in a retrieval system, or transmitted by any means without the written permission of the author.

First published by AuthorHouse   11/3/2010

ISBN: 978-1-4259-8792-3 (sc)

This book is printed on acid-free paper.

Author's note: Many technical terms, generally unknown words and species of African flora and fauna are used in this story. In addition, there are many references to historical fact, some accurately recounted, while others have been fictionalised, to suit the story. For the interested reader, these have been marked and included in glossaries at the end of the book.

Bob Warren
Berkshire,
United Kingdom

FOREWORD

   This novel is dedicated to the people of Rhodesia/Zimbabwe, both black and white, who understand the injustice of what happened to that country; to the many who died or were maimed on both sides, sometimes in terrible and gruesome circumstances; to the many innocents who didn't understand, who were coerced, brainwashed by dialectic poison and who today have lived and died or lost all in a vicious self-serving reign of fear and downward spiralling anarchy, and to the many who for their own and safety of their families, took 'the gap', forsaking their lives and history.
   This story seeks to celebrate the spirit of man, the bravery of so many who fought against the totalitarian inhumanity that has overcome those poor people who have survived. In this I am mindful also of the millions of young Zimbabweans who have grown up knowing nothing but tyranny.
   In writing this story, I have used a large number of facts, woven into a saga of pure imagination.
   No apology is made to the megalomaniac Mugabe clique, who in my mind, have destroyed what was once a wonderful country, brutalised a wonderful people and brought misery, poverty and the threat of starvation to millions.
   I do apologise to those to whom this story may in places be a little

too close to the truth, but ask that you understand that it is a depiction, as close as I can imagine it, of the reality of power in Africa and what happens when it all goes wrong.
   Bob Warren,
   September 2010.

THE WYVERN REVENGE

I was led into this mortal existence,
blind, ignorant, following a path laid not by myself,
but by tradition, by others.
They whom, motivated by admirable sentiments perhaps,
Had no idea what that course would bring.
For in youth I did not know.

Thus when, as each step brings greater clarity,
I discover that the path chosen for me by fate is wrong,
have I the courage, the vision,
to change the direction, to take another road? Or,
do I continue, plodding, led by the nose?
For in truth I do not know.

ZIMBABWE
(Previously Southern Rhodesia then Rhodesia)

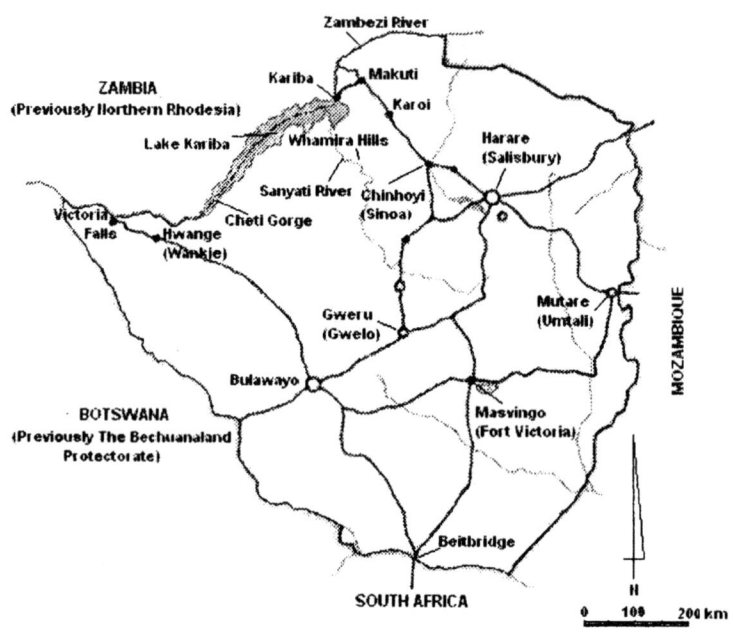

BOOK 1 – TRIAL AND REALISATION

CHAPTER 1

*T*he man entered the Prince of Wales pub in Stoke Lane most evenings at around 6:00 pm. The girls behind the bar, who knew everybody, didn't even know his name, let alone where he lived in Bristol. It must have been somewhere in Westbury, because he always walked. He had been seen climbing the hill up Great Brockeridge. They had no clue where he came from. He just appeared in the autumn of 2001.

He had a slight West Country accent, maybe Somerset, but somehow it was purer and softer with a slight twang, almost as if he had spent a long time abroad. Generally conservatively dressed in corduroys, collared shirt and a sweater, he'd been coming in for some months and he never varied his routine. He would drink two pints of Fosters Lager. Someone said that they'd heard him say that he couldn't stand real English beer anymore. Then he would leave.

He seldom spoke to anyone, except to politely order his drinks, choosing to nurse his beer while sitting on a stool in the small alcove at the rear of the pub, just in front of the door leading to the beer cellar. Occasionally he'd be in the way and when necessary, would move with deferential courtesy. The other punters left him alone.

"If he wants to be by himself, why doesn't he just stay at home and drink," was one of the cutting remarks made. The fact is that everyone, including the Bristol rugby supporters who came in every Saturday evening after a match, just ignored him. They refrained from taking the piss, because they didn't know how he would react, and they were a friendly bunch. Most of all, it was probably his eyes; they were dead or scornful, depending on the moment. When he looked at anyone, the piercing blue moroseness seemed to induce a desire to just leave him alone.

That and the thin sunburnt scar, which started in the middle of his tanned forehead just under his hairline and ended up just above the end of his left eyebrow. Another thing was his nose. It had been broken somewhere along the way suggesting that he'd been a fighter in his youth.

It was these visual elements, despite the way he carried his slim 5 foot 10 inches in a slouch that set him a little apart.

In point of fact, the punters recognised that he was a troubled man. In his mid fifties now, he had returned to England to start his life anew, to forget the past and let go his bitterness. What the punters didn't notice about him was the hidden alertness that could only be apparent to the closest observer. Sometimes if the bar got really crowded, he wouldn't finish his drink. He would get up abruptly; pick up his coat and scarf, normally bundled at his feet, and leave immediately. Even he recognised that it was stupid, but he couldn't help it. He just had to get out.

He'd walk from there back to his room. Once there, he generally sat down for a while in an old deep lounge chair facing the window. Everything about the room, soft, beautiful and female, was alien to him. He was used to the hard edges of his previous existence. His only additions to the room were three gilt-edged framed photographs, which he'd set up on the bedside table. There was one other thing of his that was visible. On the small table in the bay window, lay a large crudely carved hippopotamus tusk.

After a while his mother, now in her eighties but still fit, would come in, bringing him a cup of tea and would then herself sit quietly in her favourite chair. He would just stare out of the window over the River Trym valley not really taking in the view of rooftops and the horizon of trees that marked the edge of Blaise Castle Estate. It took three months and then he started talking. It really all started back in 1972. He'd just turned 27 years of age.

The touchdown was flawless, a perfect example of hand-eye co-ordination. The right nose-up attitude, airspeed bled off to the exact number, and on the runway numbers, if there had been any.

But the right wheel of the light aircraft hit the newly built anthill;

almost exactly square on. The right hand main gear olio[1] and strut collapsed instantly bringing the right wing down to the ground, all lift and ground effect lost. Within a fraction of a second the wing caught in the soil and grass initiating a sudden and violent slew to the right as the aircraft rushed forwards.

The imparted slew immediately turned into a violent spin, which caused both the left hand main gear and the front undercarriage to collapse as the aircraft veered off the grass strip. This caused the new aluminium compound propeller to strike the ground. All three blades buckled immediately. The forces were enormous, causing the engine[2] to overstress and seize.

In the meantime the aircraft continued spinning off into the sparse woodland. The screeching and tearing of the aluminium hull against the exposed pebbles and rocks created a fearful noise. But if anyone had been looking, they wouldn't have seen anything anyway; there was so much dust and debris flying around.

The occupants were helpless as they were tossed and spun about in the machine.

One final event occurred which finally put paid to the fate of the aircraft. The V-tailed empennage[3] hit a large Mopane[4] tree growing at the edge of the strip, and the entire tail-plane broke off. At last it ended as the aircraft, a Beechcraft Bonanza BE 35[5] came to rest in a cloud of dust, flying grass and clods of earth.

Then there was virtual silence contrasting with the loud clashing and screeching seconds before, just the sporadic crackling of the broken engine cooling down. The scene cleared, heavy particles settling, the lighter dust blowing away in the gentle breeze. The only movement visible was the dry, brown grass, stems waving in unison in the heat, oblivious of the catastrophic event that was to bring people trampling all over them.

To the pilot, Harry Andrews, the whole thing, or what he could remember of it, seemed to happen in slow motion. The only jarring he could recall feeling was as the aircraft had come to a final halt. He released his grip on the woman sitting tightly strapped into the seat next to him and in a daze sat up to take stock.

He was aware of pain and it built up rapidly. Excruciating pain, the likes of which he'd never experienced, started to pulse through his body. It started in his arm. He looked down at his left hand, almost idly noticing the odd way it looked. It was covered in blood, as were his previously immaculate navy blue trousers and white shirt. His addled brain noted that his pilot's shirt was ruined and the flying wing insignia pinned to his left breast had disappeared. It gradually dawned on him that he couldn't see out of his left eye. It didn't hurt but his forehead was burning.

He came fully to his senses with a start. Got to get out of here, he thought. Forget the pain, this 'plane could go up at any minute. He looked across at the woman. He couldn't remember flinging his right arm across in front of her.

"Are you alright, Mrs. Fischer?" he asked, his speech slurred and hesitant, his concern invisible through the blood on his face. Her own plumpish face looked agonised, but her screwed up eyes were peering out over the bottom edge of the window as if to see what was going on.

"What happened?" she asked.

"I'm afraid we've crashed the aeroplane," he replied. Before he could ask her again whether she was all right, he caught a movement out of the corner of his right eye and everything went black for a moment. He felt as if a brick had hit him.

"You bloody fool, Andrews," shouted the male passenger sitting in the back. He threw back his fist to strike Harry again. "What the hell haf you done? You haf nearly killed us," his guttural accent reflecting his fear and rage.

Harry turned and looked at Mr. Fischer, whose enraged face was red and bloated, and he just managed to duck down as the man's fist came at him again. Blood from his head splattered across the control column and instrument panel in front of him.

"Christ, Mr. Fischer, get a hold of yourself!" Harry shouted back, momentarily stopping the attack. "At least until we're out of the aircraft. I must try and open the door and get us out of here in case there's a fire." Bloody hell, that hurt. Fischer was a burly man, strong and work hardened. His short-cut ginger hair over the coarse sun browned face gave him an intimidating, almost menacing air. All I need now is a scrap with this guy, Harry thought. He'll finish me!

With difficulty, he leaned across Fischer's heavily pregnant wife to open the door, in the process dripping blood all over her frock. He flipped the handle but despite the evident click as the lock disengaged, the door didn't swing open.

'Damned airframe's bent,' he muttered. Putting his agony aside, he cradled his left arm in his right hand. He wiggled around, bringing his legs up out of the rudder well and onto the seat. For a moment he crouched on the seat waiting for a spell of dizziness to pass. Then he lent back and squeezed his feet over and in front of the woman, for a second getting them entangled in the co-pilot control column. She feebly pushed at his legs with her hands but he ignored her and leaning with his back against the other side of the cabin he kicked out hard. The door flew open viciously. That seemed to bring her to life and she started to complain as she began to focus on her surroundings.

"OK, everybody out," said Harry. Breathlessly he manoeuvred his feet back off Marie Fischer. Her disdain and efforts to brush him off actually helped him get back into a kneeling position on his own seat. The agony of the activity was getting to him as waves of nausea swept over him. But, doggedly he unbuckled the woman's safety belt with his right hand.

"Can you move?" he asked her, his voice now very strained. She at last turned and stared at him, her thick lips hanging open in horror and shock. She didn't move an inch but let out a terrified scream. She actually focussed on him for the first time and all she saw was an apparition, masked in blood, opening and closing its mouth.

God, I must look a sight, he thought.

"Come on, Ma'am, you must try and get out." He turned to look back at Fischer and only then did it register that the rear of the aircraft had gone. Behind Fischer there was nothing, just dry grass, the stalks leaning with the wind, small eddies sending up occasional wisps of dust. Within the jagged hole that remained of the tail of the machine, three avionics units, normally located on the back hat shelf, hung rocking to and fro on their own electric cables. It was eerily quiet, just a low-pitched wind sound, like when one blows into a milk bottle.

"Get out, Mr. Fischer, and help me lift your wife out of here," he ordered, leaning back between the front seats and shaking Fischer's knee.

"Undo your seat belt, come on!" After his initial outburst Fischer was subdued, a glazed look in his eyes. He focussed slowly on Harry,

"I'll get you for this, you bloody maniac."

In slow motion, Fischer gripped the buckle, released it and rolled to the right, squeezing himself out of the aircraft through the low loading hatch onto the rough ground. He picked himself up and stepped up onto the wing. Leaning in, he took a strong grip on his wife's upper arm while Harry, half kneeling tried to lift her up from inside.

Suddenly she came to life.

"Leave me alone you monster," she spat at him, and moving nimbly, as large people are often capable of doing, and with her husband's help, she sprang up and out of the machine. Fischer put his arm around her shoulders and led her away leaving Harry kneeling on the pilot's seat.

Christ, this is what you get when you play the Good Samaritan, he thought to himself. Bloody long grass, we never had a chance. Must have hit a land mine or a rock or something. What a fuck up! He leaned sideways against the seat and felt the pain wash over him.

Must shut down the aeri[6], he said to himself. He turned and awkwardly using his right hand, he flipped off the main switch and the ignition key. He couldn't get to the fuel-flow switch and had to turn and face the rear of the aircraft to enable him to reach down with his right hand in front of the pilot's seat and move the lever to "closed". The pain and weakness resulting from his efforts were now making it hard for him to focus.

His second-last conscious thought came as he heard the sound of a vehicle in the background. Thank God she's OK; they can take her into Karoi[7] Hospital from here. He had one last thought sequence before he passed out. How could this have happened to me? Two thousand hours on Gloster Javelins, and now this. Oh well, two down, two to go.

"Arrest that maniac!" shouted Fischer at the two policemen who'd arrived. He waved and screamed at them, not even waiting until they'd gotten out of their vehicle. The two policemen, immaculate in their British South Africa Police uniforms, climbed out of the Land Rover.

"Arrest whom?" asked the white Chief Inspector. Turning to the smart black Sergeant he said, "Sergeant Ndlovu, get the fire extinguisher out of the back and take it to that aeroplane." He pointed in the general direction of the wreck. "But don't go too close, I'll come in a moment."

Looking back, he interrupted the still-shouting Fischer and repeated, "May I ask again Sir, arrest whom?"

"The bloody pilot, man, he nearly killed us, and my wife's pregnant, can't you see?"

"Yes, Sir, but where, may I ask, is the pilot?" he asked politely. He looked at the woman. Despite the perspiration beginning to form on her face from standing in the sun and some blood smears on the front of her dress, she looked none the worse for wear.

"In the aeroplane, you fool," replied Fischer.

"Good Lord, you left him there?" The question was rhetorical; he was already running towards the wreck.

"What about my wife?" Fischer called after him, "She needs to be taken to a hospital." The policeman ignored him and while running, he warily searched the ground for evidence of fuel spillage. There appeared to be nothing. He could smell the heat of the engine but there was no petrol smell. He could see a man slumped in the front.

"Sam, please hand me the fire extinguisher, then go and call for an ambulance. Tell the duty officer exactly where we are and that it appears that one person has been seriously injured in an aeroplane accident. Also call the farmhouse and find out where the hell Chris Swan is. The farmers chat frequency is 123.4. Tell him to get down here fast."

"Yes, Sir." The Sergeant handed the Chief Inspector the extinguisher and ran back to the vehicle. The Chief Inspector glanced back and noticed that the other man had opened the door of the Land Rover and had put the woman into it. The Sergeant ran around to the driver's side to access the radio.

The Chief Inspector shouted across to the man, "Excuse me, Sir, how many people were there on board?"

"Two, me and my wife," Fischer called back.

"And the pilot?"

"Yes, and that bastard!" he spat.

Turning back to the wreck the Inspector primed the extinguisher, climbed onto the starboard wing and peered at the man inside. The pilot was unconscious or dead, half lying and kneeling, facing back across the seat. His right arm was skewed behind him and hanging down into the pilot's foot well. The left arm that hung over his thigh looked queer and was very swollen; it was clearly broken. There was blood splattered throughout the front of the cockpit, drips of it coagulating on the windshield. The flies were beginning to gather already.

Putting the extinguisher on the roof, he knelt down and reached across to feel for any pulse at the man's throat. After a moment he found a strong throbbing. Sighing with relief, he grasped the man firmly around the waist.

"Right, fella, let's get you out of here before this machine goes up in smoke." He raised him up backwards with some effort and finally hugging the man's back to his chest, he dragged him onto the wing.

"Sam, first aid kit, now," he called over his shoulder.

"Yes, Sir. And, Sir, there's no one at the house."

"OK." Under his breath, he asked himself, "Odd? Then why has this plane tried to land here?"

The man was quite slim, and with no real effort the policeman was able to lift him up and trudge a safe distance away from the wreck. He moved to the triangle of shade cast by the tailplane, which was lying on its side about 40 yards from the main wreck.

Laying him down, the Chief Inspector felt again for a pulse on the man's neck. Satisfied the man was alive he opened the first aid kit handed down to him by the Sergeant and began to apply his not inconsiderable skill to the task of making the man more comfortable. He swabbed away as much of the blood from the man's head as he could revealing a vicious gash. He poured some iodine into it and then quickly and expertly applied a field dressing.

"There now, that cut's not too bad." Cleaned up a bit, the man didn't look much better, but he'd live. Even though the dressing hid his fine black hair, his tanned square jaw and pugilists nose, gave him a little of the look of a buccaneer. The Inspector looked at the strong hands and noted a signet ring on the broken hand.

"I'd better take that off you; otherwise your finger won't get any blood to it." He gently grasped the man's left hand and slowly and carefully worked the ring off. Dropping it into the pocket of what was once an immaculate gabardine bush-jacket, he rose and went in search of a splint for the arm. He could find nothing suitable lying around and eventually decided to use his Sergeant's rubber truncheon. Folding the man's fingers over the rounded end, he gently bound the broken arm to it. Placing the now bound lower arm against the man's chest he created a sling by winding a crêpe bandage repeatedly around the arm and up around the man's neck. By the time he'd finished his hands, jacket and the highly polished leather webbing were badly smeared with blood. He climbed to his feet again, took another look at the man slumped against the twisted metal of the tail-plane, and went back to the wreck.

Retrieving the extinguisher from the roof, he climbed into the front of the aircraft and checked the "main" switch. It was in the "off" position. He then searched for the fuel switch and within seconds found it on the floor in the "closed" position. Obviously the pilot had had the sense to shut down the aircraft after the accident. Satisfied, he climbed out taking the pilot's flight bag with him.

He'd already noted the swathe of gouged up soil and grass leading back past the lone Mopane tree. He squatted down near the aircraft and swept his eyes over the wreck. He missed nothing. He noted that the wing flaps were down, so the aircraft was probably under control at impact. The tail had probably broken off as a result of impacting the tree.

He screwed his eyes up against the glare of the sun and looked at the build up of the clouds. There would be rain in an hour, he thought. I'll have to prepare a description of the accident now, before the rain washes away all the evidence. He made his way back along the trail of wreckage and bags, one of which had broken open: clothing spewed out, flapping around in the light breeze. The trail of turned up twigs, flattened grass and exposed rocks went back towards the end of the grass strip.

Coming finally to the start of the trail, he stopped and looked at a newly exposed termite colony. He knelt down and watched the termites scurrying about, frantically trying to rebuild their broken mound. He glanced back to a wheel and strut lying about 30 yards away. There was a short skid mark, the grass flattened. This ended where the anthill had been sheared off. Touching the remains of the termite mound he ran his fingers across a smooth six inch deep rounded indentation near the lip, and then back along the skid mark. He glanced back again and saw the top of the mound lying some 10 feet away. He walked over to it, nudged it over with his foot and saw that it had been crushed on one side, the frantic termites running around on it in confusion. He looked back past the remains of the mound and noted that the grass was about 18 inches high.

"Poor bugger, he couldn't have seen it," he said quietly to himself. Clear in his mind now he walked rapidly back to the Land Rover.

First he washed his hands under the small tap of a canvas water bag draped over the front grill of the Land Rover. He then leant into the vehicle and took out an official police "Vehicle Accident Report" pad. He found his ballpoint pen on the dashboard and putting the pad on the front mudguard of the vehicle he flipped through and inserted two pages of carbon paper.

"Why does everything have to be done in triplicate?" he asked himself. He started to write.

CHAPTER 2

"I demand that you take us immediately to the nearest hospital, Inspector," said Fischer, approaching the policeman around the front of the vehicle.

"There's an ambulance on its way, Sir." The policeman didn't even look up.

"Inspector, we can't wait for the ambulance, it might take hours." Fischer was shouting now. He was incensed. Grabbing the policeman's shoulder, he twisted the policeman around, "I insist that you take us now."

"Please remove your hand, Sir." Fischer looked straight into the policeman's eyes and realising that this man wasn't in slightest bit worried, he dropped his hand and stepped back.

"I'll bloody have you too, you swine," he said under his breath. As Fischer opened his mouth and let loose with more invective, the policeman took a pace towards him, pushed the peak of his cap up slightly and looking mildly at him, said,

"Sir, you will go around to the other side of this vehicle and stay there with your wife. Do not move until I tell you to, or I shall place you under arrest for interfering with an officer of the law while in the course of his duty. Do I make myself clear?" His eyes bored into Fischer, a slight smile on his face. "You and your wife are fine, Sir, it's the pilot I'm worried about, now push off."

Fischer broke away and muttering under his breath he walked away around to the other side of the vehicle.

"Sergeant?"

"Sir?"

"If that gentleman moves as much as three feet, handcuff him to the door handle."

"Sir." The Sergeant moved around to the shady side of the Land Rover and squatted down on his haunches next to the rear wheel, as only African men seem capable of doing without moving for hours. He was within five feet of Fischer.

"And if you don't mind, Sir," the policeman said quietly across the bonnet of the vehicle, " my rank is Chief Inspector, not Inspector. And my name is Templar." He spelt it out. "And that is Sergeant Ndlovu. Make sure you get them right when you lodge your complaint." Fischer just glowered at him and said nothing.

The Chief Inspector concentrated hard and wrote rapidly for about 10 minutes. Then he turned to a new page, repositioned the sheets of carbon paper and walked off to the place where he identified the aircraft had touched down. He started pacing forwards and every time he got to a spot where there was some debris or other observable feature he stopped and made notes on a plan of the crash site he was drawing. Finally he got to the aircraft itself and pacing everything out, he slowly drew that onto his plan. Happy at last, he called the Sergeant over and went through the entire report with him, pointing out the features on the ground.

"Do you agree with me, Sergeant?"

"Yes, Sir, I think that everything is correct."

The Chief Inspector then walked back to the Land Rover. All this had taken about 40 minutes. Now I must deal with this ugly fellow, he thought. I wonder what it was that made him so antagonistic against the pilot. His reaction is totally out of keeping with the situation. Surely he must realise that it wasn't really the pilot's fault? He shrugged, maybe he's had a run in with this pilot somewhere before. His mind continued to search for answers as he approached his vehicle. Lifting his boot up on the front wheel-bearing cap, he once more leant down over the mudguard.

"Right, Sir, while we wait for the ambulance, may I start taking down the details? What is your name?"

Harry Andrews heard talking and through the haze of pain he slowly focussed on his surroundings. At first he was only aware of the dry brown veldt grass gently moving in the hot breeze right in front of him. Little brown ants were scurrying up and down the stems of the grass and he concentrated on them for a few minutes wondering where he was. He tried to orientate himself and painfully looked around. He saw the wreck off to his left. It took a moment for it to register.

He turned his head the other way and saw a policeman leaning over the front mudguard of a Land Rover talking to Fischer. His forehead was throbbing and he discovered that his head had been bandaged up. He looked down at his heavily bound left hand. Must be broken, he thought and groaned. The heat was soporific. Hell I've really blown it this time.

Spitting a fly out of his mouth, he put his right hand down onto the ground. I must get a drink, he thought. Supporting himself on his hand, he slowly rolled onto his knees and climbed unsteadily to his feet, leaning on the metal structure behind him. He lasted less than a second and collapsed again in a heap, sliding supine down the ruddervator.

The Chief Inspector heard him fall and without wasting a second ran to the crumpled heap. The only movement he could see was a tuft of the man's hair blowing up occasionally in the fretful hot dusty thermals. He propped the man's head up,

"Hello old boy, can you hear me?"

"Hi." After a moment Harry asked, "Have you got any water?" The words came out as a whisper.

"Sergeant, bring some water" the policeman called out. He turned back to Harry. "Hold on, we'll get you some now."

"Where am I?" He struggled to speak coherently.

"You've been involved in an aircraft accident. We're waiting for an ambulance to come from Karoi; should be here shortly."

"Oh yes, that's right, Karoi. Who are you? Where's Chris Swan?"

"I am Chief Inspector Peter Templar. You just relax; we'll have you out of here soon. Thanks, Sergeant." He took the cork stopper out of the canvas water bag and tipped the spout into Harry's mouth. The water poured out and gagging, Harry managed to swallow a small amount. Some of the water spilt down onto his chest. It felt marvellous.

"Thanks, Peter, I'll be OK now. By the way my name's Harry Andrews."

"Pleased to meet you, Harry. Chris Swan and the family are not at the house. Do you know where they'll be, Harry?"

"He must have gone to Salisbury. I was diverted here to pick up the boy; he's got appendicitis. Please look after my flight case an..." He never finished the question, but groaned and passed out again.

Two minutes later the ambulance arrived from Karoi. The young ambulance attendants were fairly efficient. They bound Harry's left arm to his chest, laid him out on a stretcher and put him in the back of the old converted Land Rover. When invited to climb into the back as well, Marie Fischer reacted violently.

"I'm not getting in the back of that thing, especially with that monster on board." Despite all the cajoling and gentle tugging, she became quite hysterical, and with tears streaming down her fleshy face she collapsed to the ground. Oh my God, thought Templar, here we go! He went forward to help Fischer pick up his wife off the ground.

"All right, Sergeant, you go in the ambulance. Mrs. Fischer, you get into my vehicle, and you, Mr. Fischer, will climb in the back of my Landy. Come on, let's get her up." Chief Inspector Templar's voice carried such authority that none of them argued any further and it was done.

It was only five miles or so along the main road to Karoi and they arrived at the small district hospital in twenty minutes. Marie Fischer was taken into the maternity ward while Harry was made comfortable on a bed in the out patients section. A flustered young doctor appeared.

"Hello Pete, what have you got here?" He shifted his glasses further up his nose and took a pencil-thin flash light out of his pocket.

"Victim of an aircraft accident, Doc; doesn't appear too badly injured, just the arm and a nasty gash on his forehead. I'll need a blood sample and I want my truncheon back. Can I leave him with you?"

Using his left thumb the doctor lifted the right eyelid and shone his flash backwards and forwards. The left eye was still caked in dried blood.

"This lad is badly concussed," he said to nobody. Then he started taking the patients pulse.

"Hang around a few minutes, Pete, our x-ray unit is down again; arrangements may have to be made to get him into Salisbury. Next of kin, anybody?" the doctor cut away the bandage holding Harry's arm still and started inspecting the arm.

"No, just his boss. I searched his flight bag. I reckon it's a good thing I was driving past the farm when it happened. One of his passengers is ready to murder him." The doctor grunted, concentrating on his examination.

"Be a star and get hold of his boss. This lad must be taken into Salisbury immediately. He needs a brain scan amongst other things. Tell his boss what happened and ask him where he wants us to send the lad. Pulse is good, he'll be fine, but the arm is bad. A fracture of the wrist I think. What's his name?"

"Harry...." He paused. "Actually according to his pilot's license, it's Henry Andrews. Can I use your phone?"

The doctor nodded. "Through there," he said.

The Chief Inspector moved off to find the phone while the doctor carried on his examination. On his way he encountered Fischer, sitting on a bench in the corridor.

"Mr. Fischer, how's your wife?"

Fischer glowered at him.

"I don't know. She's in there," he said shrugging in the direction of a door to his right, "but if anything happens to her or the baby, I'm going to sue the pants off you and that maniac."

"Mr. Fischer, it wasn't his fault..."

"'Course it was his fault," cut in Fischer, "he just bloody crashed the aeroplane, he shouldn't be flying. What was he doing trying to land in that field anyway?"

"Look, the aircra..."

"Bugger off and leave me alone," Fischer was starting to go red with anger. "I'll sort you and that dickhead out later." He turned away and stared down the passage. Templar looked at him and shrugged; clearly

15

the man wasn't going to listen. Andrews must have had a run in with him before. He turned away and went on to find the phone.

"Trans Afrique Air?" The Chief Inspector got through quickly having identified himself to the telephone operator. He thought that with the district party line telephone systems still in place, this was good going.

"Good Afternoon, Sir. Who would you like to speak to?"

"This is Chief Inspector Templar, BSAP[8]. There's been an accident involving one of your aircraft," said the policeman.

"Please stand by, Sir. I'm putting you through to Jim Leonard, the owner." The woman on the switchboard wasted no time. In seconds a voice came on the line.

"Hello, Chief Inspector Templar, I'm Jim Leonard. What's this about an accident?"

"Good Afternoon, Sir. This morning a V-tailed Bonanza of yours, registration ZS-IBU, piloted by Harry Andrews crashed while landing at Swan's farm near Karoi."

"Oh Christ! Any fatalities?"

"None, Sir, but Andrews has a broken wrist and a cut on his head. He's badly concussed and needs to be sent into Salisbury to hospital. The purpose of the call is to find out where you want him to go."

"What happened?"

"I cannot discuss that Sir. It is the duty of the Investigating Committee to reveal what happened."

"OK, well, it must have been under control at impact, otherwise they'd all be dead. Chief Inspector, can you have him sent into St. Anne's?"

"I'm sure that can be arranged, Sir. I'll deal with it straight away."

"Well done, Chief Inspector. You seem to know a bit about aircraft?"

"A little, Sir. I once started pilot training but gave it up. Too dangerous." Leonard laughed.

"Tell Harry I'm flying up to Salisbury tonight; I'll see him in the morning."

"I can't, Sir, he's still in a coma."

"Shit.., OK Chief Inspector thanks a lot. Hopefully I'll meet you in due course."

"Cheerio Sir."

"Bye, Chief Inspector, thanks for calling."

Chief Inspector Peter Templar walked back into the corridor and once again stopped in front of Brad Fischer.

"Mr. Fischer, I'll require you to come down to the Police Camp to finish giving me your statement. You've got 24 hours and don't leave town until you've seen me, is that clear?" Fischer looked up at him, the look on his face evil.

"Who're you ordering around, Chief Inspector? I'm not one of your Sergeants. I'll come when I bloody well like." He turned away from the policeman's gaze.

"You'll see me before the weekend, Mr. Fischer, because if you don't I'll issue a warrant for your arrest." With that he turned and went on.

Jim Leonard put down the phone and immediately shouted through for his secretary. She was there in seconds.

"Binny, Harry's been hurt. He pranged 'IBU in Karoi."

"Yes I overheard." He looked at her quizzically.

"You don't miss a thing do you? Bloody huge great shell like ears!" he laughed. "Binny, get me David Jenson's in Johannesburg now. And get me on the 5:30 to Salisbury, even the jump seat if I have to. If bloody Harry has gone and totalled 'IBU we could be in shit up to here." He gestured about 6 inches above his head. Anyway he's still in a coma, so I'm having him admitted into St Anne's. Send some fruit."

"Yes Jim." She almost ran out of his office. Typical of the man, she thought. Sinking in a quagmire of problems and he laughs.

He paced around for the next few minutes, worrying about what this meant to his business and literally jumped when the phone rang.

"Yes."

"It's Miss Stevenage at Jenson's, Jim."

"Thanks, Binny, put her through." A couple of clicks. "Hello, Miss Stevenage?"

"Yes, Mr. Leonard, may I be of assistance?"

"Yes you can. We've crashed ZS-IBU in Karoi. Can you get your accident assessors up here and fax me a claim form? Bulawayo[9] 62 731" Jim never wasted time on small talk on the phone.

"I'll start the ball rolling immediately, Sir. You are insured through us?"

"Of course I'm bloody well insured through you. Why else would I phone you?"

"Were you flying the aircraft?"

"No, Harry, that's Henry Andrews;" he shuffled through the papers on his large untidy desk; "here it is. Yes, Henry Andrews: RSA[10] Airline Transport Pilots License No. TA 18182. You get that?"

"Repeat the number please."

"TA 18182. Look you've got all this shit on your files and anyway DCA[11] in Pretoria have the expiry date." Jim was exasperated. " Look it up in your bloody files or ask them!"

"Thank you Sir. I'll phone you back shortly." Jim smashed the phone down.

"Shit, that's all I need, two prangs in a month. Bloody insurers are going to give me a hard time on this one." He gazed out of his window at the apron outside the hangar. The guys were servicing one of his two remaining aircraft; an old Douglas DC3 Dakota. It was due to fly to Pietersburg in South Africa that night to fetch a haul of aircraft tyres and helicopter rotor blades for the Air Force. He was making a fortune out of sanctions. He wondered where it all went.

"Cup of tea Jim?" He nearly jumped out of his skin again. He whipped around.

"Oh, it's just you. Thanks, Binny, you gave me quite a start."

"Sorry about that. You can pick up your ticket at the airport. Shall I send someone to get a bag for you?"

"No thanks, I still haven't unpacked this one yet. It'll do." He'd just got back from a trip to Pretoria. He sat down. "Anyway I'll be in Salisbury for the next few days. When the tyres and blades get here, phone Mick at Kentucky and tell him to send someone, with a cheque! We're going to need every cent we can find."

Harry's first conscious thought as he woke up was, angels, I'm surrounded by angels. Through the slowly clearing mist, he could see the figures of angels moving around him. I must have died. He laughed inwardly to himself. Don't be stupid, if you were dead, Andrews, you'd be in hell.

THE WYVERN REVENGE

"Look, he's coming out of it," said Nurse Whitworth. "Let's hope he's not brain damaged, all he's been able to say so far is 'Two down, two to go.' He repeated it over and over again while he was under. I wonder what it means." She was addressing a nurse on the side of the room counting syringes in a big bowl.

It means, he mused, that we've now crashed two aeris and my boss has only got two others and I'm probably out of a job. Harry tried to move his hand, which he saw was suspended above his head in a sling tied to a thin metal gantry hanging over his bed. He became aware of a powerful ache emanating from his arm. He squinted through the clearing haze over his eyes at the nurse hovering over him.

"You're the most beautiful sight I've ever seen, but where am I?"

"Oh, you're awake are you?" Nurse Whitworth said. "Now don't move. You must rest. You're in St Anne's Hospital in Salisbury. And while I appreciate the compliment, flattery is not going to get you anywhere!" She was dressed in a plain white frock and a perky white nurse's cap and Harry thought she was gorgeous. She tidied the edge of his bed and was just turning to go and report to the matron when he called her back.

"Nurse, how long have I been here?"

"Two days, now just relax, you've had a nasty accident."

"You're telling me," was his rejoinder. "Oh well, two down, two to go." But his mind was on her. He appreciated the swing of her hips as she walked off down the ward. Harry couldn't keep his eyes off her. Everything about her was exquisite. Each time she walked into his ward, it was as if the room brightened and he felt light enough to float off the bed. He could see a wisp of wavy auburn hair hanging down next to her cheekbone, almost as if it had purposely escaped the hair clip that should have kept it in place. As she leant over when tidying the bed, the smell of her was intoxicating. Eventually he plucked up courage to ask her name.

"Annie Whitworth, and I know yours is Henry Andrews," she pouted. He shivered with pleasure.

"Harry, Annie, Harry, not Henry."

"That's not what the chart says," she teased. Her big blue eyes sparkled with hidden amusement. Harry was in love; she was gorgeous.

Nurse Whitworth was only to learn later what his "two down…" comment alluded to.

CHAPTER 3

It was a week later and his arm throbbed mercilessly in its sling. The doctors said that he'd suffered a bad fracture of the wrist and severe concussion. He'd be out of action for at least six weeks. But as he sat there in the corridor outside the Aircraft Accident Investigation Committee Room at the Division of Civil Aviation office in the "Avenues" in Salisbury, all he could think about was Annie Whitworth. He gazed adoringly at her signature on his plaster cast, touching it lightly with the forefinger of his right hand. He was woken from his reverie with a start. He jumped to his feet so quickly that he jerked his arm and nearly cried out in pain. He fell back down onto the rigid wooden bench again.

"Sorry to surprise you, but I repeat, Mr. Andrews, will you come in and please take the stand?" Colonel McIlwain, Chairman of the Accident Investigation Tribunal looked down at him.

"Yes, Sir." Harry got up carefully and followed the elder man into the room. He made his way forward through the rows of brown wooden upright government service chairs to the front and sat down at the seat indicated as reserved for witnesses. Leaning forwards he rested his right elbow on the table in front of him and looked expectantly at the man who had called him, clearly the chairman. His eyes took in that there were three other members of the Tribunal and looking around he noted the austere drabness of the room. A black board on one wall had been used to display a number of photographs. Those are of the accident scene, he thought. God, I'd rather be back in hospital.

"You are Mr. Henry Andrews?" the man who had fetched him asked.

"Yes, Sir."

"Were you the pilot in command of a BE 35 with a South African registration ZS-IBU on the 24th March 1972."

"Yes, Sir."

"This committee is convened in terms of the Civil Aviation Act to investigate the cause of the accident involving that aircraft on that date. I am Colonel McIlwain, chairman, and these gentlemen are Mr. Bissett," he said waving to the man on his left, "and Mr. van Tonder." He pointed at the thin weasely looking man to his right. He didn't introduce the fourth person, a woman, who he saw on closer inspection, was merely taking minutes. "Mr. Andrews, are you prepared to take an oath that you will tell the whole truth and nothing but the truth?"

"Yes, Sir." God, I sound like a stuck record, Harry thought.

"Mr. Van Tonder, would you be kind enough to administer the oath?" McIlwain turned to his right. The thin man came around his desk and came right up to Harry, carrying a small volume of the Bible.

"Please stand, raise your right hand, and place your left on the Bible." Harry looked at him, watching the man's long beak bobbing up and down, frowned and then actually giggled. He couldn't stop himself

"What is so funny Mr. Andrews?" Harry stopped laughing and just smiled down at the flustered little man in front of him.

"I'm sorry sir, no disrespect intended, but how do you propose I do that Sir? I can't move my left arm." Mr. van Tonder looked at the sling, then back at Harry's face, and then back at the plaster, totally nonplussed.

"Raising your right hand will suffice Mr. Andrews," interceded the chairman, "It will still represent a solemn oath." Mr. van Tonder looked relieved and recited,

"Do you swear to tell the whole truth and nothing but the truth, so help you God?"

"Yes, Sir." The man turned around and went back to his seat. Harry could feel the enmity in him and thought, you stupid twit Andrews, now you've created an enemy and the hearing hasn't even started yet.

"Mr. Andrews, please be seated. Now, in the light of the evidence before us, before we ask you to go over the events leading up to and during the aircraft accident of the 24th March 1972, in which you were pilot in command, it would please this tribunal to go over your background first. Would that be acceptable to you?"

"Yes, Sir," replied Harry. What's this all about?

"Mr. Andrews, I understand that you were previously a Squadron Leader in the Royal Air Force. Is that correct?"

"Yes, Sir." Might as well have a recording. Just press the 'play' button to get "Yes, Sir" every time, Harry mused.

"You resigned your commission in the Royal Air Force on the 23rd August 1970. Is that correct?"

"Yes, Sir." Using his right forefinger, he automatically pressed an imaginary 'play' button into the desk in front of him.

"Why did you resign, Mr. Andrews?" The penny dropped. He wants to establish whether I was kicked out.

"I served in 47th Regiment, based at RAF Odiham, near Basingstoke in Hampshire, United Kingdom. We were equipped with Gloster Javelins, Mark 6's. These aircraft, classed FAW, Fighter All Weather, were due to be scrapped when we received orders to deploy in Lusaka, Zambia. We arrived there in January 1969. It was a major cock-up…, excuse me, Sir…, but we had no spares, fuel, nothing. Our aircraft couldn't even be serviced there. Our quarters were bug infested and initially we just sat around wondering what to do with ourselves. We spent most of the time playing squash and golf at the Country Club."

"So you resigned?"

"No Sir. That came later…"

"Will you get to the point Mr. Andrews," the question was put by the thin little man sitting to McIlwain's left. Now, there's a prize runt, thought Harry.

"I'm getting there, Sir, if you'll allow me to continue." Harry looked straight at his inquisitor. You're not going to get much out of me I'm afraid. He sat back.

"Before you continue, Mr. Andrews, why was your squadron sent to Zambia, do you know?" asked McIlwain.

"Before continuing, Sir, I must advise that what I am about to reveal is probably still secret in this country."

"Only the findings as the cause of the accident are made public by this committee, Mr. Andrews. Otherwise everything you say is dealt with in confidence. You'll notice that there is no one else in the room except the stenographer." Harry looked at her.

"Very well, Sir. Would you repeat the question please?"

"Certainly, Mr. Andrews, why was your squadron sent to Zambia?" repeated the chairman.

"It was to protect the Zambian Government from attacks by the Rhodesian Forces."

"I see, yes, well carry on, Mr. Andrews." The scrawny man was scribbling something down at a frenetic pace. Careful pal, you'll break the nib, Harry joked to himself as he continued.

"Well Sir, suddenly we, the aircrews, were all given secret individual orders to fly to Rhodesian Air Force Base, Kentucky, at Salisbury; a single but different aircraft each time. We were ordered to take our ground engineers with us but to identify our missions to the Lusaka Military Air Traffic Control as night exercises and patrols. Under no circumstances were we to reveal that we were flying to Salisbury. We were generally airborne at dusk and landed dark at Salisbury 38 minutes later. Dark, that is, without lights Sir," he explained. "We used frequencies known only to us, and the Rhodesian Air Force. When we landed there we were required to taxi straight into an assigned hangar. The hangar doors were immediately closed shut behind the aircraft as we rolled to a halt."

"Are you telling me, young man, that you and other pilots in your squadron, were conniving with the Rhodesians?" The scrawny man glared at him.

"Yes, Sir. We would stay overnight until 0400 hrs, be airborne, low level, by 04:30 hrs and then be well back over the border before dawn."

"Surely the Zambians could pick you up on radar?"

"No Sir, We went low level through the Zambezi valley, and only come up off the deck when we were well into Rhodesian airspace. This wasn't because we were afraid of the Zambians. We were more afraid of a South African counter-strike. Their early warning systems could pick us up before we crossed the border southbound, and they could have scrambled their Mirages[12] based at Louis Trichard[13] so fast, they could have hit us before we reached Salisbury. Besides the Zambian radar installations were already unserviceable." The Committee was clearly staggered and for a brief moment there was a stunned silence.

"Assuming this is all true, what were the purposes of such flights?" The question again came from the runt.

"Whilst we slept in a mess room adjacent to the hangar, the Rhodesians assisted our engineers to service and refuel our aircraft."

"What? This is preposterous!" shouted the runt. "He's making this all up."

"Well, why don't you check this out with Squadron leader Mick Glover at Kentucky Air base?" responded Harry. "He was assigned to deal with us. I met him several times."

"I suggest you're trying to hide the fact that you were kicked out of the Royal Air Force," said the runt. "And in view of that I don't think that your evidence before this committee can be trusted." He turned to the chairman. "Colonel McIlwain, I move that we strike out the evidence being given by this man as being unreliable and subject to doubt."

"Why, Mr. van Tonder? He hasn't told us what happened yet," replied McIlwain.

"Well you heard what the previous witness, Mr. Fischer, had to say yesterday about him and the accident. Clearly he's just trying to cover his backside."

Ah, so that's what this is about, thought Harry. I wonder what Fischer did have to say, and why the hell has Fischer got it in for me? I really would like to know. He sat back in his seat while the committee went into a huddle and listened. McIlwain had his way and soon turned back to Harry.

"Mr. Andrews, we'll certainly call on Squadron Leader Glover, G L O V E R did you say?" He spelt it out and wrote the name down as he spoke, "and we'll have him confirm your statement. In the meantime please continue your story, however improbable my colleague might find it." Harry took his eyes off the PWD green walls and looked at the runt. You prick, he thought, turning back to the chairman. McIlwain's face looked as if it was about to explode, almost as if he sensed what Harry was thinking.

"Thank you, Sir. I served in Zambia until October of the same year and was then sent home on leave. When I got back to Odiham, I immediately resigned."

"Why?" The runt again.

"Surely it's obvious Sir. There we were, the Great British, ostensibly with the Rhodesians as our enemies, battleships enforcing an oil blockade on your ports, imposing sanctions against you, beaming propaganda at you through Francistown in Botswana, and here you were helping keep our aircraft in the air. I was disgusted, I mean, wars are games politicians play, aren't they? I wanted no further part in it."

"What did you do then?" The question came from the quiet man, Bissett.

"Well Sir, I flew to South Africa and approached the Rhodesian Chargé d'Affairs Office in Pretoria and applied for a Rhodesian Residence Permit. The rest is history. I came up here and got a job flying in the charter division of Trans Afrique Air, my present employers." He remembered the day well, when he arrived in Salisbury and refused to let the Immigration officer stamp his passport. He was nearly arrested but eventually they agreed to stamp a separate piece of paper, which, now along with dozens of other similarly stamped slips, he kept in his passport. The British government under Harold Wilson had declared that any British citizen found going into the rebel state would be arrested and tried for treason.

"Right, now lets look at your flying record and your licences." From there they progressed to the flight itself.

"I flew from Bulawayo to Binga."

"Why Binga?"

"Mrs. Fischer lives there. Her husband runs a fishing camp on Lake Kariba, just south of Chete Island, in the Chete Gorge."

"You still haven't answered the question Mr. Andrews," the runt. "Why Binga?"

"I was ordered to casevac Mrs. Fischer to hospital in Salisbury. She was heavily pregnant and was to have her baby in Lady Chapman Hospital. It was complicated by the fact that I was diverted to Karoi, to the Swan strip, to pick up their son. He apparently needed to go into hospital as well, for an appendix op. I have no idea as to whether or not either he or Mrs. Fischer are all right."

"Well if anything has happened to either of them, you will take the blame for it Mr. Andrews," said the runt. Harry jerked upright in his chair and stared at the man.

"How's that Sir? Have you already found me incompetent and guilty of crashing that aeroplane?" He leaned right forward, the angry scab on his forehead changed shape as blood began to seep from it. Staring at the man, his face betraying nothing of his thoughts, he felt in his pocket, withdrew a handkerchief and held to his forehead gently, so as not to pull on the stitches.

"Steady on Mr. Andrews, I'm sure that my colleague doesn't mean it that way," interjected McIlwain. Harry then lent back in his chair, careful not to bump his bad arm. His look became casual, almost uncaring.

"Well how does he mean it, Sir?" It came out slowly and quietly. Harry was angry now and wasn't going to be denied. McIlwain knew that look and realised that this young man in front of them was not to be messed with.

"That's quite enough, Mr. Andrews." He turned to van Tonder. "Mr. Van Tonder, as chairman of this committee I insist that you withdraw that remark."

As he looked at Harry now slouched there, it slowly dawned on Mr. van Tonder that here was a very dangerous man, a beast, and it would be well not corner him. He would always come out fighting.

"Apologies, Mr. Chairman, my mistake," said van Tonder. Harry could see the smirk on the man's face, but he let it drop.

"I'm sure that the boy is all right and I do know that Mrs. Fischer had a healthy boy in Karoi Hospital on Monday, so don't concern yourself about them, Mr. Andrews. Are you all right, Mr. Andrews? Would you like to take a break?"

"I'm fine, Sir."

"Very well. Would you please continue with your explanation of the flight," said McIlwain authoritively.

"Sir, I picked up the woman and her husband on schedule and then flew to Karoi. I buzzed the farmhouse; it's about two miles away, and even did an inspection fly-past at 300ft AGL[14] and then set up to land using the prescribed techniques. I know that strip like the back of my hand, Sir. I've landed there dozens of times. If anything, the only unusual thing on that occasion was that I had to land on runway two seven[15]. Normally the wind is from the west and we use zero nine, the reciprocal runway."

"Well what happened when you brought the aircraft into land, Mr. Andrews?" again a pertinent question from the third man, Bissett.

"Yes, well I crossed the fence at seventy five knots, thirty five degrees of flap, cut the power and brought her down onto the numbers. Well, where the numbers would have been. It's an easy approach, no trees, and very little crosswind. Only then everything went haywire, it seemed as if something hit us. I thought it was a Sam Seven missile; or that we'd triggered a land mine. That's all I remember, Sir."

The hearing dragged on until 12:30 pm. They covered all the ground and it was clear to Harry that they'd been to the site and done a very careful analysis of the accident. They confirmed payloads, distribution of weight, fuel on board etc. Harry had explained the accident as he understood it and eventually was granted leave to go. As he entered the corridor outside, he put his hankie into his pocket; the bleeding seemed to have stopped. Then he noticed Chief Inspector Peter Templar sitting on the bench.

"Hey, you're Chief Inspector Peter Templar aren't you?" the policeman grinned. "They got you going in there as well?"

"Hello, Harry, how are you doing? Besides the broken arm, the bloody stitches across your forehead, the black eye and your skew nose, you look well." They both laughed. "Have those lovely nurses at St. Anne's been looking after you?" replied Peter Templar.

"I'll say. They're absolutely gorgeous. I'm going to ask one of them out."

"If I might interrupt, gentleman," it was Colonel McIlwain. "Chief Inspector Templar?"

"Yes, Sir."

"I'm afraid you'll have to carry on this discussion another time. We're ready for you now." He turned to Harry. "Mr. Andrews, I'd be grateful if you'd make yourself available at 9:30 tomorrow morning.

You'll need to sign the transcript of your evidence. We should be able to wrap it up by then."

"Yes, Sir." As the policeman turned to follow McIlwain in, Harry called after him. "Peter, I'm staying at Fife House, feel like a drink later?" Peter turned and with a broad smile on his face said,

"Sure, I'll see you in the pub at five thirty." With that he entered the room and Harry wandered morosely off down the corridor. He was thinking about what Fischer may have told them. I'm sure I didn't do anything wrong. What's with the guy anyway? As he stepped out into Speke Avenue it occurred to him that there was something funny about Brad Fischer.

Just as he was leaving the building, Chief Inspector Peter Templar was nearly bowled over by the heavyset man coming through the same door Harry Andrews had gone out of two and a half hours earlier.

"I'm awfully sorry," said the man. "Are you alright?"

"I'm fine Sir," said the policeman picking his attaché case off the floor. "You must be Mr. Leonard?"

"Good Lord! How do you know that?" Leonard looked at the man. He recognised a hard man when he saw one, and a BSAP Chief Inspector to boot.

"I spoke to you on the telephone the other day, Sir, and I never forget a voice."

"Chief Inspector Templar?"

"Yes, Sir."

Leonard smiled and stuck out his paw.

"Pleased to meet you, Police Inspector. Let me buy you a cup of coffee. Little place round the corner in Jameson Avenue, if you've got the time. They finished with you in there?"

"Yes, Sir, and I'd love a cup of coffee, they never even broke for lunch. I'm not due back at the 'Camp' until three thirty."

"Good, my business here can wait and I've already given the Aircraft Log Books to the Tribunal."

They sat in 'Nancy's Cup and Spoon' surrounded by society women dolled up to the nines, not that the policeman minded. They spoke briefly about Harry.

"What happened, Chief Inspector? I went out to Karoi on Sunday but your guards wouldn't let me onto the farm, let alone take a look at the accident site. Is there any problem?"

"We cannot allow anyone near the scene of the accident until the tribunal have concluded their investigation and made their findings. Well, that's not quite true. Only the insurance assessor is allowed to view the wreck. He's due over the weekend, I believe. Also I'm not supposed to discuss the accident until then."

"Chief Inspector, you've given your evidence, what harm?"

The policeman thought for a moment and concluded that it wouldn't hurt.

"My opinion, and this is strictly between you and me; it all has to be confirmed by the committee of enquiry in due course, is that the aircraft struck an anthill on touchdown, cart wheeled, hit a tree and broke in half."

"Good Lord man! Did that idiot land short or something?"

"No Sir; from my measurements on the site I'd say that he touched down in exactly the right spot. It wasn't his fault. He couldn't have seen the anthill; it was hidden in the long grass."

"Thank you, Chief Inspector, I never doubted it. Harry's a brilliant pilot, cuts it fine sometimes, but none the less, good. And it buggers me because I've now got no reason to fire him." He looked out the window of the deli into the street. The jacarandas were still losing their flowers and the ground and cars parked under the trees were covered in the fallen purple blooms.

"Lots of rain this year," he mused.

"How's that?"

"Jacarandas are still flowering." He said almost in a whisper. The Chief Inspector could see that Leonard was a worried man.

"Fire Harry?"

"Yes, Chief Inspector. If the insurers don't pay out, this accident is likely to put me under. The insurance underwriters probably won't insure my operations any more. This is the second prang we've had in a month, and you'll understand that the South African insurers are starting to say that aviation operations in Rhodesia are just too dangerous."

"Wow, is that why Harry looks so unhappy?"

"Probably seen the writing on the wall, like the rest of us." He called for the bill. "Well Chief Inspector, nothing for you to concern yourself with. The local Standard Bank is considering acting as aviation insurance underwriters because of the problem, so maybe it'll all turn out OK in the end. Thanks for your help. We need all we can get in this business."

"What business is that, Sir?"

"Sanctions Busting." The intonation suggested a question along with his raised eyebrow. With that he rose from the table, threw a R$2.00 note onto the table, shook hands again with the policeman, walked out the door and strode briskly off. The policeman still had half a cup of coffee left. He sat there idly looking at all the beautifully turned out women, and wondered about this man whom he'd agreed to meet for a drink that evening. Bit of a pirate it seemed. Since the advent of punitive economic and trade sanctions that had been imposed by Great Britain, a lively business in 'Sanctions Busting' had developed in the former Crown Colony of Rhodesia. Many organisations which previously had been involved in export and import had turned their hands, aided and abetted by the regime, to breaking the trade boycott Britain had imposed on the country. A window to the world still existed through the Republic of South Africa and while the average Rhodesian mildly despised the folk 'down south', they made good use of the friendly 'Apartheid' State.

Peter sat there thinking about it. What a bloody mess. Rhodesia have had a qualified universal franchise since 1934, you'd hardly be able to call Rhodesians racists. Certainly not in the same breath as you'd talk about the average white South African. The 250 000 whites in Rhodesia had brought this country of 7 million into the late twentieth century through guts and sheer hard work. Sure, the indigenous peoples provided all the manual labour, but many of them had risen above it, had created businesses, become productive farmers, gained the 'vote' and were fully integrated members of the modern technocratic society that had developed. The emergent middle class of black white-collar workers was growing rapidly and they had carved a large piece of the action for themselves.

As he swept a lock of hair that had fallen forward over his face aside, Peter sighed. And now this! What the hell have we done to warrant this? Why the sanctions, the terrorist war? Why are we the polecats of the world? All we want to do is make sure that this country doesn't go the same way as the rest of Africa; destroyed economies; mass genocide of anyone who dares to disagree; the breakdown of medical and education services; autocratic thieving murdering dictators; institutionalised nepotism and all the rest. All we did was tell the socialists in Britain, who know bugger all about the situation here, to get lost. But no, couldn't have that could we? Can't have a small band of dissident white ex-patriots telling the British Government where to get off, can you?

Peter thought back trying to think of any occasion that he'd come across a case of blatant racism and had had to deal with it. He couldn't. OK, so the two cultures do live separately, not by law, but naturally. But surely that was all right? What the Americans and British themselves practice and call ethnicity. But hell, because we live the same way, it's called racism. Because we're a minority in a nation of people who, in reality for the meantime, are incapable of governing themselves properly, maintaining the high standards of government, education, health, production and financial service. So the world has come down on us like a ton of bricks. Well, maybe history will prove us right, who knows.

You know, he thought to himself as he got up from the table to leave, I am and always will be a Royalist. I should have thought all of us are, we've fought for Britain through two world wars, lost an extremely high proportion of our men, but now we're rebels. Shit, none of us wanted it to come to this. And sure as God made little green apples, it's going to get worse. The American War of Independence all over again, but we're on a hiding to nothing!

CHAPTER 4

Nurse Annie Whitworth got the surprise of her life when the gigantic bunch of flowers arrived for her at the nurse's home behind St Anne's Hospital. The other nurses teased her mercilessly.

"Who's the man then?" She blushed and ran to her room with the flowers. She locked the door behind her, laid the flowers on the dressing table and opened the envelope attached to them. He'd naively written,

"My dear Nurse Whitworth,

This verse is the least I could do, to show my great appreciation for you.
You made me well, I know it took a while,
But more, you brightened my days with your smile.
Your hair, your laugh, your tease,
Remain in my heart and mind too much to ease.
I have to see you, take you out, although you think I'm just a lout.
I think I'd die if you turned me down,
But will you see me before I leave town?
So please say yes when I make the call;
Because if you don't, I'll go up the wall.
Harry Andrews."

Annie threw herself onto her bed and lay there, on her stomach, feet in the air, ankles crossed. She read the simple poem over and over again. She thought of him and his quick wit. The way he'd accepted his fate, never complaining of the pain, always smiling as he lay in his hospital bed. His hands were the thing she remembered most. They were not big, but were well shaped and strong and the middle finger of his right hand had a slight kink in it, from some old injury. She rolled a little to one side and hugged her pillow to her breast and closed her eyes. Yes, Harry Andrews, I will go out with you, you old rogue. Yes he is a rogue; you can see it in his eyes. For a moment she couldn't remember the colour of his eyes. Were they blue? Yes pale blue and his hair is black. She remembered the pale smooth quality of his skin against the almost leathery tan of his face and arms. I wonder where he's from... She'd started to get goose bumps and she'd become very warm. Barbara Forester, her roommate, breezed in, taking in the flowers immediately. She threw her nurse's cape and bag on her bed.

"Hi Annie, what's this?" Annie, hardly moving, reached out a white arm. The creases from the pillow could be seen imprinted on her skin, so tightly had she been hugging the pillow. She waved a piece of paper. Barbara snapped it out of her fingers and read.

"Oh, oh, here we go. Annie, you're not going to see him are you?"

"Yes."

"Well you'd better ask him if he's got a friend," said Barbara. "I couldn't bear it if you got a man and I was left here by myself all the time." She plonked herself down next to Annie on the bed and kicked one of her working shoes over to her side of the room.

"Annie Whitworth, telephone!" The strident call came across the loud speaker at the end of the passage outside her room. Her dream shattered, Annie jerked back into reality, jumped up almost throwing Barbara to the parquet floor and rushed out the door, nearly knocking over two girls walking past. They whistled at her and jeered; the whole place knew she'd got flowers from someone.

"Hey, Annie, who's the lucky guy?" She ran past, the colour rising up her neck.

"Hello, Nurse Whitworth speaking."

"Hi, Annie, it's Harry Andrews."

"Oh, it's you is it? You didn't waste any time did you? Thank you for the flowers, they're beautiful."

"They suit you," he replied.

"I suppose you tell all the girls that," she pouted.

"Annie, cross my heart, I've never sent flowers to anyone before."

"You're such a fibber and if you knew what embarrassment they've caused me." She giggled. "I'm the laughing stock here now; all the girls are teasing me!"

"Let me make it up to you," he responded. There was a pause, almost an embarrassing vacuum, he couldn't think of what to say. So he blurted out, "You've got me so flustered I didn't even ask you how you are."

"I'm fine." She thought, he's sweet but I mustn't make it too easy for him or he'll realise how flustered I am. "But your poetry is awful, without structure, no imagination, no imagery."

"I can't write either," laughed Harry. She laughed with him. That broke the ice. "When can I see you?" he asked.

"I'm off tomorrow at four."

"Great, I'll be there at six. There's so much I want to tell you."

She hesitated. "You know there was a policeman in to see you when you were still under. Are you in trouble?"

"Good Lord no! Who was he?"

"Didn't give his name, but he did say that he saw you at the accident and thought he'd come in and see how you were doing. And he was looking for a missing truncheon. Did he have to beat you with it? Is that how you got your black eye?"

Harry laughed.

"No, he didn't. Anyway, that's Peter Templar; he's a Chief Inspector or something. Funnily enough, I'm seeing him at five thirty this evening so I can buy him a beer to say thanks for his help."

"He's a really nice guy Harry Andrews. He was very worried about you." His heart sank. Shit, she's after him. Silence… She giggled, "No, not for me you fool, but he's perfect for my friend Barbara."

"Whew! You had me going there for a moment, Annie."

She laughed. This guy was like putty, she thought, watch it though, he's a bit fragile.

"Do you think he's married or anything?"

"I shouldn't have thought so. I think he's stationed in Karoi. Must be or he wouldn't have arrived at the accident site so quickly." He thought for a moment. "Ok, is your friend Barbara also free tomorrow evening?"

"Yes." She thought, safer if we go out as a foursome.

"I'm not going to regret this am I?" Harry asked.

"No, she's lovely!"

"OK, I'll ask him."

After the call, her first thought went to her clothes. What am I going to wear? Must wash my hair, what perfume should I wear? I wonder if I can get some nail polish and so on. She rushed back to her room to find that Barbara was still reading the poem, only now she was on her stomach, feet waving in the air. They immediately got into a huddle while Annie told her everything.

"You're so lucky. He sounds so romantic," said Barbara. "I've never met anyone in the Surgical Ward in the five months I've been there, they're always under anaesthetic. Is he really nice?" Barbara was also attractive and slim. They were the best of friends and the envy of the other girls. They never seemed to mind night duties and some of the more distressing sides of nursing and as a result were doing well in the hospital. Annie had been in Intensive Care for about six months and like Barbara, was highly regarded by the Sister General.

"He's gorgeous, he's a pilot and he'd just had an accident."

"Not him, idiot, the Police Chief Inspector! What's his name again?"

"Oh! Peter Templar. Well he's big, well over six foot, but he's got soft brown eyes, like a puppy. Very rugged outdoor type but he speaks very quietly. Isn't that what you've been looking for?"

"Um, if he's horrible, Annie, I'll never speak to you again. When will your Harry let you know?"

"I don't know, but don't worry, we'll know soon enough. And he's not my Harry, not yet anyway." She pouted and then giggled. "I feel like a teenager."

"Always a bad sign!" said Barbara, being contradictory while laughing at the same time. Annie's excitement was actually becoming infectious. "How did the accident happen, did he tell you?"

"Well, Peter didn't say anything, but Harry said he didn't remember too much. He was landing his aeroplane and they were either hit by something, or a land mine blew up making them crash."

"Wow, was he badly hurt, is he going to be all right?"

"He broke his wrist and has a big gash on his forehead. He was badly concussed and in a coma for two days which is why they admitted him to ICU. He looks like a pirate because he's got a broken nose also. After he woke up, we kept him under observation for three days and then released him. It was as if he'd never been injured. He said he had to appear before an accident tribunal. Oops, I've forgotten those flowers." She leapt up and fished around under the basin for an old green quart beer bottle that had its neck cut off and sand blasted. It made an ideal vase. She half filled it with cold water and then sorted the flower stems out and placed them in it. She set the vase on the dressing table.

"There, that's rather pretty." She could barely see herself in the mirror, so moving the arrangement to one side a bit; she moved the flowers around a little until she was happy.

"They're lovely," said Barbara.

The chatter didn't stop. Annie and Barbara carried on talking through dinner and late into the night, generally preparing for Annie's big night out the following evening and, with a bit of luck, Barbara's also.

Harry in the meantime was beside himself with joy. He almost ran from the phone at the reception desk to his room. He grabbed his towel and toilet bag and headed for the bathroom whistling 'It's Been a Hard Day's Night'. As he couldn't very well shower yet, he ran a bath, propped his plaster cast arm up on the edge of the bath and lay there, slightly askew, wallowing in the hot water. He'd never been so happy in all his life, despite his problems. The pain in his wrist was now just a continuous throbbing ache, but with the painkillers the doc had given him he felt OK. Actually lying there, it was his bruised backside that ached the most. He supposed that was from the Tetanus shot and all the penicillin they'd pumped into him. Even the itch of the wound on his forehead didn't worry him. If it itches, it's getting better, he told himself.

Jim Leonard had also been very understanding. It was he who booked Harry into Fife House and he'd told Harry not worry about work until he felt better. They'd work out if he could fly later. But Harry was a tiny bit niggled. Not all was well, but he couldn't place his finger on it.

He carefully washed around his cast and managed a reasonable shave by propping up his shaving mirror at the end of the bath. Using a face flannel, he dabbed away bits of the blood caked around the wound on his forehead. Looking at his reflection he realised that he really was an ugly sight. "Well, if she likes me like this, I'm home and dry," he said aloud. The hard part was getting the towel to stay around his waist, so that it wouldn't fall off between the bathroom and his room. Eventually he just held it in place with his right hand with his bag hanging from tightly-curled third and little fingers. He draped his clothes over his plaster cast. Although there was absolutely no use in his left hand, only the tips of his fingers and thumb stuck out of the plaster, he wasn't particularly incapacitated.

He was dressed in twenty minutes, took his pipe, tobacco and box of Lion matches out of his bag, stuffed them into his right trouser pocket and went down and across the quad to the bar. Harry normally only smoked when he was having a drink. It was one of the great luxuries of life to him, a cold Castle Lager, no real English beer here, and a nicely burning briar loaded with Ridgeback tobacco. Peter Templar was already there sitting outside on the patio reading 'The Herald'. Harry would have walked right past him if the Chief Inspector had not hailed him.

"Hey, Harry!" Harry looked at him.

"Good Lord, Peter, didn't recognise you with your clothes on." He came over and pulled back a chair. "How are you?" They shook hands.

"Fine, yourself? Take a pew, or do you want to go inside?"

Harry looked round. There were three good lookers sipping G and T's two tables away under a trellis covered in a blooming Bougainvillea.

"Hell no, best time of the day to be out on the veranda, besides we can watch the birds better from here."

"Feathered or double breasted variety?" Peter was watching a Pied Wagtail, tail bobbing up and down, searching for grubs next to the fishpond in front of him. Harry laughed.

"Both," he said. He beckoned a bar steward over, "what'll you have?

"Castle, thanks, Harry," said Peter. He folded his paper, dumped it on the concrete deck next to him and picked up a packet of 'Texan' plain cigarettes.

"Twelve volt man, heh?" Harry said as he put the makings for his pipe on the table. Peter smiled

"Best cigarettes in the world." He lit his smoke while Harry ordered the beers.

"Peter, first of all, many thanks for your help in Karoi. That arsehole Fischer didn't exactly make things easy for me. In fact I'm considering charging him with assault." He relaxed back in his seat, supported his tobacco pouch in his lap and then concentrated on the one-handed packing of his pipe.

"What do you mean?"

"Crikey, after the prang I was trying to help his wife and he smacked me from the back seat, calling me a bloody maniac. I think it actually knocked me out for a moment. That's what gave me this black eye, I reckon. In fact he took another swing at me but missed, before I was able to shout loud enough about the danger of fire. That brought him to his senses."

"Hells bells, Harry, I didn't realise that. I wouldn't put it past the guy. He's a nasty piece of work."

"You can say that again."

"And it won't do you any good filing a charge. It's your word against his, and his wife." Harry looked at him and nodded acknowledgement.

"Tell me Pete.., can I call you Pete?"

"Yeah, everybody else does," Peter waved the question away.

"Tell me Pete, what hit us? You inspected the site and must have reported your findings to the investigation committee." Peter burst out laughing.

"What's so damned funny?" Harry was a bit nonplussed. He looked across the table at Peter, who in turn looked as if he was about to collapse to the ground, he was laughing so much.

"You mean to tell me, ha, ha, that you still think that something hit you?" He wiped his eyes.

"Yes, I'm more than a little confused. I thought it must have been a Sam 7 missile or a land mine as we touched down."

"Nothing quite so spectacular I'm afraid. Your right wheel hit an anthill as you touched down."

"Shit, is that all?" He reflected for a moment looking a little sheepish. He propped a box of matches on the metal surface of the patio table, struck a match across it and busied himself with lighting his pipe, sending billows of smoke wafting into the fading light. The bar steward arrived with the beers saving him from having to say anything else. He reached into his pocket, "it's mine." He paid the steward, sucked furiously on his pipe and then started pouring his beer. He took the pipe out of his mouth and looked into the bowl.

"Well it's nothing to laugh about, I must have undershot the runway. Now I really am in the cactus; no wonder Jim Leonard wasn't so pleased to see me."

"Relax Harry, you did nothing of the sort. I identified exactly where you touched down. It was exactly six feet inside the end of the runway. There were some old white washed bricks set in the ground, not that you could have seen them."

"Did I? Thank goodness for that. Cheers and thanks to you as well!" he raised his glass. Relieved, he leant back and surveyed his surroundings. The girls had noticed them and had gone into a huddle. Bet they're trying to decide who's going to get who, thought Harry looking at them. Got bad news for you ladies, I'm not available.

"Cheers Harry." They both took a long swig.

"How did you get to the scene of the accident so quickly?"

"Actually we were on our way back from Makuti, that's in my district as well. We'd stopped half a mile down the road to buy some mealies (*corn on the cob*) from a guy on the side of the road when we saw you coming in. We heard you land and realised immediately that something had gone wrong. Made a hell of a noise."

"Thank God you were there!" Harry cradled his beer glass in his right hand and relaxed

"By the way, I have to appear tomorrow at nine thirty as well," said Peter. "I'm sure that they'll clear you of any liability, despite what Fischer may have told them. If it was anything like the statement he filed with me in Karoi they'll soon see through him."

"Let's hope so. Next thing is to see if I've still got a job." Harry took another swig. "Wow, this going down like nectar, I'd almost forgotten what a beer was like. This is my first in two weeks. I've been flying so much. Waiter!" he called out to the lurking steward, "two more please."

"I had a cup of coffee with Leonard today," said Peter.

"Oh, I didn't know you knew him." Peter told him about the call he made from Karoi Hospital and then the accidental meeting at the DCA.

"I am under the impression that your company is in a bit of trouble. Well, that's what he led me to think anyway."

"It's true," said Harry. The whole general aviation industry in this country, that's privately owned stuff, is in trouble. We can't get spares, insurance is a problem; we've got very few aircraft maintenance staff. The Air Force has swiped them. Hell, we have to fly down to Johannesburg to get things done and there we get seriously ripped off." He flattened his beer while the steward poured the second for him.

"I'll tell you this, if the insurance doesn't cough up on this aeri, Leonard's finished, me alongside him. I imagine I'm finished with him anyway; he's got too many pilots. We'll soon know because the insurance company accident assessor is arriving tomorrow morning."

"That's more or less what he told me," said Peter as lightly as he could. He lit another smoke. "If you do get the chop, what are you going to do?"

"I don't know, go wherever there's a job I s'pose," Mumbled Harry. Peter leant forwards in his chair.

"Harry, I nearly took up flying you know." Harry perked up. Aviators are notoriously self-centred; they eat, sleep and drink aeroplanes.

"Is that so. Why did you pack it up?"

"Because I realised that you guys are mad. It's too bloody scary for me." Harry started laughing.

"Rubbish, it's a doddle!"

"No, it scared me shitless, really. Anyway I was going to do it because the police are starting up an air wing. The general consensus is that this war is not going to last too long now, Smith's about to give in to Harold Wilson and sign a peace treaty. The word is that they're setting up another battleship or something, to continue the talks. And then the

Air Force won't be able to carry out police missions. BSAP have decided to beef up their Air Arm. They've already bought a couple of Cessna 206's and a 210. Why don't you think about joining the BSAP?" Peter sat back and watched Harry closely. Harry didn't even flinch, which was good from Peter's point of view.

"Pete, I was a Squadron Leader in the Royal Air Force and I'm not a Rhodesian citizen. Firstly I doubt if they'd take me at all and secondly, I should say that I wouldn't be too keen to go back into a service at a lower equivalent rank."

"Give it a try."

"Hell, I wouldn't even know where to start."

"Here, I know the guy you should 'phone, Chief Superintendent Huxley." He took a notepad and a pen out of his pocket and wrote down a name and number. He tore off the page and passed it over to Harry.

"'Phone him next week. In the meantime I'll give him a call and fill him in. Interesting: if you get in, the equivalent rank in the police is about Chief Inspector, so you'd be on the same scale as me."

"Gee, thanks Pete, bloody good of you."

"That's what friends are for."

"Hey, I like that. By the way are you married?"

"Good Lord no! Are you?"

"Negative. Are you around tomorrow?"

"Yeah, I've got to be back in Karoi on Sunday evening. While I'm here, I'm staying up at the Police Camp in North Avenue."

"Doing anything tomorrow evening, there are these nurses from St Anne's I'm taking out." The twinkle in Harry's eyes really sparkled.

"You don't waste any time do you? I'm available. What are you going to do?"

"Well, I thought we'd go to Highlands Park Hotel. The Nicholson's put on a good dinner with dancing. And I get a discount because I often fly the odd contraband in for them."

"Hey, I didn't hear that."

"Aw, nothing serious, things like Angostura Bitters, odd bottle of scotch. I often stay there so it helps."

"Harry, I can't be a friend if you're into the black market."

"Hell no. We're squeaky clean. We do a lot of work for the government. If we put a foot wrong they'll nail us."

"Yes, Leonard told me you guys are into Sanctions Busting."

Harry frowned. "He did, did he? Not very discrete of him. Shucks, and he's always telling me to keep my mouth shut." Bloody hell, what else does this guy know? Shouldn't worry, he's an OK guy. "You got a car Pete? I'm not allowed to drive because of the concussion; in fact I'm not even supposed to drink."

"No, but I'll borrow my old man's, it's an old Chevy. I've got it here now in fact." Peter Templar glanced at his watch. "Wow, look at the time, I'm in cactus, I was due at their place at seven thirty. My old girl will murder me." Harry laughed out loud at his discomfort.

"Women control our lives Pete."

"That's rich coming from you," said Peter, downing the last of his drink. "You're the one with his mind between his legs." More laughter. "Harry, if I don't see you at the hearing, I'll see you here at say seven tomorrow evening."

"Hey Pete, we have to be at St Anne's at six.

"So be it. Be here at five forty five. Got to run, thanks for the beer." With that he ran quickly out the gate.

Harry got up and thirty seconds later was dialling the nurses' home again.

CHAPTER 5

It was precisely 7:00 am. A man got out of his car, looked around to see if anyone was watching and then briskly opened the passenger door of the car parked next to his in the car park of the Enterprise Road Drive-in Restaurant.

"Sorry I'm late, the plane was delayed in Johannesburg. Have you ordered breakfast yet?" The man sitting behind the wheel of the car shook his head and said,

"Go ahead, I'll have bacon and eggs, toast and coffee. The meals they serve on the aircraft these days are inedible and the coffee tastes like ground up baked beans." The smiling black face of the waiter appeared at the window and the driver ordered two standard breakfasts with coffee.

"Well, have you got something for me?" asked the visitor. He looked across at the driver. He wasn't prone to pass judgement on people, but this guy was a prick of note.

"Yes," was the reply. "But how much?"

"Show me the papers first."

"How much?"

"Well, are you sure there's something I can use?"

"Certain."

"OK." The visitor paused and looked out the far side window noting idly, "another bloody perfect day in Africa." He turned back to the driver. "OK, there's two thousand Rands in it for you."

"Christ! You promised four."

"Ya, well the boss has changed his mind. The figure is now two, take it or leave it, suit yourself." He turned to look out the window again. The waiter was already on his way back to the car with two trays of food. "Christ, what do they do? Precook the eggs and bacon?" He wound down his window leaving an inch or so for the tray support clip.

"You buggers are dishonest, you know that?" whined the driver.

"Ya, well go tell the cops." The visitor put his tray on his lap and started buttering his toast. He then lifted the eggs using the knife and slipped the toast underneath.

"Well give me the money," said the driver. The visitor put his knife down, reached into his jacket pocket and extracted a thick white envelope. He held it out.

"And the report?" The driver reached round and felt around down on the floor behind his seat coming up with a brown envelope.

"Here." The visitor slipped the report down the side of his seat next to the gearbox and continued eating. The other man opened his packet, looked inside to check his money.

"You were only going to pay me two grand all along, weren't you?"

"So sue me," he visitor said forking some bacon into his mouth. "Besides I haven't seen whether the report is of any use to me yet." Silence for a few minutes while they ate. Then the visitor put his plate back on the tray, wiped his mouth with a paper napkin and then picked up the envelope, extracted the report and began reading.

"Fischer's testament is what you'll want to read most," said the driver. The other man grunted and continued scanning through the papers, knowing that he couldn't take them with him. He had to find an avenue for claim refusal otherwise he wouldn't get paid by the underwriters. He read for about five minutes occasionally stopping to take a sip of coffee.

"Christ, this is a crock of shit. I can't use anything here," he exclaimed when he had finished.

"What do you mean, you can't use anything? Fischer has testified that the pilot was totally reckless."

"Oh, do me a favour, that's not going to stand up. It's his word against the pilot's. No, you're going to have to give me something else." He thought for a moment. "Have you got access to the Airfield Registry?" The driver nodded.

"Well can you cook up something that shows the field to be unregistered, unlicensed or something? Can it be invalidated because of the anthill? You know, failure to maintain or something?"

"I suppose so, I'll look into it, but I can't do it today, I'm due back at the hearing at nine. It may take all day."

"You can always stay at the office late. If anyone asks, you've got a lot to catch up, hearing and all."

"Very well. Where are you staying?"

"Meikles, room twenty, old wing. I'm going out to Karoi on Saturday night for two days and won't be back. I'm flying straight home to Johannesburg. Phone me at seven thirty, I'll make sure I'm in my room." With that he opened the door and climbed out. He closed the door gently so as not to shake off any of the crockery. Leaning down over his breakfast tray he said through the open window, "Make sure you do, otherwise you've got a problem. My people take a dim view of bleaters that take their money and don't deliver the goods. I will visit your offices formally on Saturday morning at nine thirty, during the normal course of my investigations. You can confirm the airfield situation then." He climbed into his car and drove slowly away, well satisfied with his morning's work. "God, I love this job," he said laughing to himself and feeling his pocket where he had pocketed the other R2000. "Bloody wanker!" he turned on the radio and settled down for the drive to Pioneer Street. He knew a great whore there who was happy to indulge in his fetishes.

At the same time some three miles away Jim Leonard and Harry were sitting down to breakfast in the Fife House dining room. Although old, it was gracious and the meals were good. The atmosphere was typical of those old colonial hotels found in the tropics across the globe, including the white-jacketed waiters wearing tasselled red fezzes. There were large silver tureens on the service counter where they helped themselves to beef sausages, bacon, scrambled egg, tomato and toast. The waiters moved about efficiently removing plates and topping up tea and coffee cups.

Jim ate in silence for a while, Harry waited for his boss to speak.

"Look Harry, if there's any problem with the insurance, I'm in the shit you know that?"

"I know, and I understand that you'll probably have to fire me."

"Hell's bells, Harry, not only you, just about everybody. I'll have to sell one of the Daks to pay the outstanding lease settlement amount on IBU and that leaves me with one aeri. What else can I do?" He was being incredibly apologetic, and obtuse, and Harry knew it. He swallowed another mouthful of scrambled egg, and said,

"Jim, I'm not a fool. Even if the insurers pay out, you're stretched to the limit and in any case you've got too many pilots on full time pay." Jim let him continue. "Look, don't feel bad about it, I've seen the writing on the wall for some time." The relief on Jim's face was dramatic. The worry lines disappeared almost instantaneously and turned into the humour creases that made him the popular man he was.

"I'll tell you what," said Harry, "Peter Templar is..."

"The Chief Inspector fellow?" Jim interrupted.

"Yes, well he is putting me in touch with a Chief Superintendent Huxley. Apparently the police are keen to start up an Air Wing and Pete thinks I might just be the guy to get it going."

"Hell, you have been cozying up, haven't you?" Jim laughed. "No, but honestly, Harry, I don't want to lose you, you're a bloody good pilot, and discreet," his breakfast forgotten.

"Well look, if it looks good, I'll tell you immediately and then maybe I'll be able to leave pretty well straight away. Whatever, we can make a plan," said Harry. He was nervous, but felt it was better that he made it easier for Jim. He hid his agitation by stuffing some more of his breakfast into his mouth.

"Harry," Jim leaned back and looked appreciatively at the man opposite him, "that took a lot of courage and I'm really thankful. You realise that this makes my life very much simpler. Have you ever had to lay off someone you like? It's hell."

"Jim, these last two years flying for you have been magic, but it's not too serious, I've got a couple of quid stashed in the UK and if a push comes to a shove I'll swap some for Rhodesian Dollars on the black market. No sweat."

"Come to me, I'll give you a better exchange rate than anyone you'll find."

"You're on."

"Chief Inspector Templar tells me you'll be exonerated this morning, I know the whole story."

"Yeah, he told me he'd seen you."

"But it's another thing getting the insurance to pay out."

"Yeah, bloody accountants."

"No, bloody crooks, they'll go to any lengths to avoid paying out and there's not a heck of a lot us Rhodesian aircraft operators can do about it." Jim turned away and thoughtfully looked out of the window. "Great day, lets have coffee on the brazza and you can light up that stinking pipe of yours." Ordering the coffee they got up and walked outside. Jim put his arm around Harry's shoulders,

"Thanks Harry, you're a bloody star! After coffee and when you're ready I'll run you up to DCA."

Police Chief Inspector Peter Templar came out of the back gate of the Salisbury Police Camp driving his father's 1957 Chevrolet Bellaire. He loved this old car with its two-tone white and gold bodywork. It was the first of the post 'spaceship' cars although the designers were still seriously into their chrome. It was a left hand drive to boot, which made it very exciting.

He drove almost directly across the Enterprise Road into the 'drive-in' restaurant, and carefully parked near the rear of the parking area and close to the exit. He liked to park away from the other cars. He took his uniform cap off and tossed it onto the wide vinyl seat. Reversing the ignition switch he then switched on the radio and began to tap his fingers on the big plastic steering wheel in time to the music. Jerry Sullivan came on and cracked his usual inane breakfast jokes and then played more music.

He read the menu posted up in bold letters on a big board above the serving hatch and when the waiter arrived, ordered a mixed grill with orange juice and coffee,

"And bring the coffee now please." He was reaching into his bush jacket pocket for his 'Texans' as he said that and coincidently looked across to see a man get out of the passenger side of one car and slip into the drivers seat of another. The car started and the man drove off, coming right past where he was parked.

"Gays," said Peter under his breath while at the same time making sure he had a good look at the chap. Maybe it was his training but once he'd seen a face he never forgot it, especially one with a smirk on it like that. He lit up a smoke, the first of the day and enjoyed his coffee while he waited for his breakfast.

It was just luck really that his breakfast arrived at exactly the same time as the driver of the second car drove out. He looked up and got the surprise of his life.

"Van Tonder," he said aloud. He thought for a moment. He wouldn't have guessed that van Tonder was a closet gay. In fact he was pretty certain he wasn't, which made this morning's encounter much more interesting.

He munched away at his breakfast, his professional curiosity now aroused. His mind was working ten pence to the dozen. What would van Tonder be doing talking to a strange man in the seclusion, or so they thought, of a 'drive-in' restaurant, especially as he was engaged in confidential work. Who was that other guy? He remembered the car, a blue Daihatsu, registration number H 346 UP. Probably a 'hire' car. He got out his notebook and wrote the number and vehicle description down. Amazing, once a cop, always a cop, he thought. How he'd remembered the number he didn't know, it was automatic.

"Thank you for attending, Mr. Andrews. Before we advise you of our findings I would be grateful if you would take the time to read a transcript of your evidence of yesterday and confirm that it is correct." Colonel McIlwain passed him a sheath of several typed pages.

"Certainly Sir." Harry got a hint of malevolence emanating from the runt but ignored it. He turned round and there was Fischer, sitting near the back of the room, also staring at him with thunder on his face. He nodded in greeting and smiled at Pete who was also reading several sheets that were clearly his statement. He sat down and started reading carefully. The others in the room were doing the same thing. There was no need really. The transcript was verbatim of his interview from the previous morning. Paging quickly through it, he looked up.

"This is fine, Sir."

"Very well, will you initial every page and then sign the last page at the place indicated? Have you got a pen?"

"Yes, Sir." Harry went through the necessary, handed back the papers and then sat down. McIlwain collected transcripts from the other relevant parties and after a few moments while he sorted out his papers, he cleared his throat loudly and said,

"Gentlemen, this Accident Investigation Committee has found as follows:

'In the matter of the accident which occurred on the 27th March 1972 involving an aircraft Type-BE 35: Registration ZS-IBU: Pilot-in-Command - Captain Henry Andrews, ATPL No. TA 18182: Pax on board - 2: Fatalities - nil: that the accident was caused when the starboard main wheel struck a termite mound immediately after a correctly executed touch down. This caused the starboard main strut to collapse and disintegrate following which the aircraft spun out of control, leaving the runway so causing further structural damage and disintegration, and to finally impact a tree which in turn tore off the empennage. The committee finds that the Pilot in Command could not have foreseen the existence of the termite mound, which as such was obscured by the existence of long grass and could not have taken evasive action. The following findings have relevance,

1. Air Worthiness Certificate: Valid and on board.
2. Aircraft Manual: Current and on board.
3. Signal Strips and F.A.K (first aid kit): Checked and found serviceable.
4. Seat belts: Serviceable and in use on impact.
5. Pilots License: Valid and type rated.
6. Pilots Alcoholic Content: tested approx 2 decimal 5 hours after the accident and found to be nil. Tested also for other drugs and or debilitating agents: Test result - negative.
7. Other extenuating circumstances: Nil.
8. Accreditation of blame: Nil, however it is a recommendation of this Committee of Inquiry that the Director of Civil

Aviation issue a directive to the effect that in future all registered airfields are to be inspected and found to be serviceable on a daily basis by owner/operators. Established failure so to do should lead to immediate removal from the Civilian Airfield Register and necessitate full reapplication procedures.'

Thank you, gentlemen, this then concludes this hearing. Let it be recorded that the Committee concluded business at 08:45 hrs Zulu[16] (10:45 am local time) on the Friday, 3rd April, 1972." The whole room stood up almost as one.

"Well, that's that," said Jim beating Peter to shake Harry's hand. "Let's go and find a pub that's open and celebrate. Harry looked around to find that both his antagonists had already gone.

"Sorry, Sir, but I'm on duty until four this afternoon and must now get back to Salisbury Central. I'll be celebrating with Harry tonight anyway, so I'll say good bye now Sir." Peter Templar held out his hand, which was quickly grasped by Jim Leonard.

"Chief Inspector, I don't know how to thank you for your help," said Jim.

"Nonsense, Sir, just doing my duty." They shook hands vigorously.

"Cheers, Harry, see you this evening."

"Look forward to it. See you, Pete," answered Harry. "Jim and I had a chat this morning at breakfast. I could be very interested in that proposition you put to me last night."

"I'll make a point of having a natter to C.S. Huxley sometime today," pre-empted Peter. "I'll speak to you when I see you."

"OK. You're a star Pete, thanks a stack." Peter left and Harry turned to Jim.

"Jim, I can't drink yet, I've got to go out to St Anne's for a check-up at two. Can I take a rain check?"

"Sure. You know, you and that policeman look like you've really hit it off. He's a great guy. OK, lets go around the corner, have some coffee and check out the society dames, and I'll tell you a little secret."

"Yes, Sir." They went off into Jameson Avenue and Jim sat down in the same chair as he'd had the previous day. Harry, his mind still in a bit of a state after hearing the decision of the Committee, didn't really notice much around him. He woke up with a start.

"I am very good friends with the Prime Minister, Harry."

"Smithy?"

"Yeah, we flew Spitfires together during the second world war. I'm having dinner with him and Janet tonight at the Prime Minister's Residence."

"Jim, you're moving too fast for me. Are you bragging or has this got some relevance?"

"Let me assure you, Harry, it's relevant." Harry couldn't stand it when Jim started pontificating.

"So?"

"So, I'm going to have a word with him about this Police Air Wing thing and suggest that Huxley gets you on board." Harry sat there in silence for a moment and gazed out the window. Crikey, when things start happening, they really get moving, he thought. Jim obviously feels bad about things. Well take what you can get.

A man sat in the bar of the Jameson Hotel in Jameson Avenue, sipping his Johnny Walker Black Label and sighed.

"Yes, life is good," he said to no one in particular. The bar was fairly full but he had no interest in anyone there. "Bloody arrogant colonists", he muttered sotto voce, "well we'll soon see about that. You bastards are finished. It's not a question of if, just a question of when. Then this country will become another client state of the Union of Soviet Socialist Republics. Then we'll see how you know-all white men will manage." He looked around himself, and considered his situation.

It had been easy.

Broderik Axel Volker, alias Brad Fischer of Donsdorf, Baden Württemberg, West Germany, was born on the February 20th 1944 in Furstenwalde, a major industrial and agricultural city some forty miles south east of Berlin. He never knew his mother and father. Rolf, his father had been killed at Stalingrad, and on his first birthday, the Russians shipped his mother off to Siberia. Brod was sent to a children's home in Nizhniy Novgorod, some two hundred miles east of Moscow.

The Russians treated him well. By the time he was six years of age, it was recognised that this strong clever young German had it in him to serve the state well. He was transferred to a small Military Academy close to his birthplace, which was run by the notorious 'Stasi', the East German secret police. From then on his fate was sealed.

His upbringing from thereon out was essentially one within strict militarist communist doctrine, except that he was also required to learn English and German to a level of perfect fluency. At the age of eighteen he graduated from the college with honours and sent to study Politics and African Affairs at the University of Leipzig, where again his performance was virtually flawless.

Brod was initiated into the Stasi and after his induction was trained in the ways of espionage, military strategy and insurgency operations. He was then sent as a young Haptbahnfuhrer into the border guards wherein he spent the next five years as an intelligence officer in East Berlin, tasked primarily to train young East Berlin graduates of the Brandenburg Military Academy in anti-insurgency and interrogation techniques. Whilst there, he also trained many southern Africans in terrorist operations, weaponry and political indoctrination.

So impressed was he of Broderik Volker's ability, a political commissar of the Zimbabwe African Nationalist Congress, a man, who later was to become their leader, asked for Volker to be assigned on training duty to their training bases in Zambia.

Armed with an infallible alias, he arrived in Zambia as Brad Fischer and went straight to work at the insurgency training base, 'Kiev' located on the escarpment overlooking the wide Luangwa valley some sixty miles north east of the capital Lusaka. After serving there for fourteen months, he was sent back to Berlin for further training and deep cover development. Whilst there he met and married Maria Schneider, a cipher clerk in the signals group attached to his Directorate. Accompanied by Maria, he arrived in Rhodesia, via South Africa in October 1968. In accordance with his instructions, he acquired a licence for, and rapidly established, a new fishing camp on the shores of the newly formed Lake Kariba. He called it the Chete Gorge fishing camp. As a tourist fishing camp it was an immediate success. He paid his taxes and got to know the local District Commissioner who frequently made use of the camp for weekend fishing trips.

Butter wouldn't have melted in his mouth. Brad Fischer was the perfect host and worked hard to cultivate an image of geniality and competence. His camp was well organised and the beer was cold. He possessed five comfortable fishing boats, which he hired out on a daily basis to his guests, either to go out fishing or merely to view the vast numbers of wild animals and birds that frequented the shores of the lake. Each evening, after the fishing boats had beached, the catch weighed, photographs taken, and the guests had taken time to shower and change, they were invited to imbibe copious quantities of ice cold lager beer while sitting in the 'boma[17]' looking out over the lake and bragging about the day's fishing.

What the guests and the authorities did not know is that this was all a front for the most sophisticated arms and terrorist smuggling operation ever to function within the borders of Rhodesia. Chete Island, 300 yards away across the gorge was Zambian territory, and provided the perfect staging location for these activities, whilst Fischer's fishing boats provided the perfect transport.

Brad Fischer was now a happy man. Here he was in Salisbury, a proud new father, and he was going to meet the aircraft accident assessor this evening who had promised him R2000.00 if he could give him the dirt on Harry Andrews and the accident. Brad Fischer couldn't remember when he had felt so good.

CHAPTER 6

*H*arry Andrews had managed to get a Devon bred dog in September 2001, shortly after arriving back in England. He carefully nurtured and trained her during his ample free time. She was an unusual breed, a Soft Coated Wheaten Terrier. He had named her Bonnie after the Bonanza he'd crashed back in Rhodesia so many years ago. At first she hated the leash, but after a while her brain grasped the fact that if she behaved herself and obeyed orders, then her master would take her for short walks along the road. By January 2002, the man started to extend the walks into a few miles. The dog's day began and ended with her walks out into an amazing new world of sights and smells.

In March he started walking all the way from Great Brockeridge up to Blaise Castle. These walks took several hours for it wasn't enough for the man to just go there and back, as if to see how far it was; he explored every nook and cranny of the park and after a while was able to let the dog run free, so used had she become to obeying his every command.

On a clear day his favourite spot was a bench up on top of the hill, just to the east of the fort. Not a fort, as such it was reported, just an imposing rich man's folly. Here the view out over the bare forest was glorious. The yellow lichen, which looked a little like spring buds, covered the trees closest to him, providing a stark contrast to the drab winter scene. After it had rained and it was wet, he could clearly see all the pigeons in the forest, perched in pale grey relief against the wet darkened bark of the bare trees. He once counted over two hundred of them in various parts of the forest. The sound of Hazel Brook spilling through the old mill hundreds of feet below was a whispering comfort that blocked out the other sounds of the city. When the wind was from the west, all that could be heard was the noise of the traffic on the M5 motorway. Sitting here he also had advanced notice of anyone that approached and it comforted him to know that he was always ready, although he knew it was silly because he was in no real danger. At times, he would involuntarily clench his fists inside his workman's fleece lined over-shirt.

While he sat there his dog would snuffle around in the undergrowth, looking for rabbits, squirrels and other animals of interest. However, Bonnie would come immediately she heard his eerie whistle, just two long low whew, whews. It had been their family whistle and if he thought about it at all, tears would come into his eyes.

Generally though the man would just sit there and daydream, perpetuating his anguish. Sometimes he would actually sob quietly as the pain became too great to bear. Sometimes he would actually smile inwardly to himself as he remembered some of the happy times. No one could ever have imagined the love Harry Andrews had for Annie. One evening he started to tell his mother about their first date.

On the last day of the hearing he remembered getting back to the hotel at four, where he whipped out a one pager to his folks back in the UK, to let them know what was happening to him. He delivered that for posting to the hotel reception and then had his bath, shampoo and shave. He'd never been so excited in his life. Even Mr. Dixon, the old codger down the passage, who was half deaf, could hear him singing and came through to the communal bathroom to find out what the commotion was about.

"I say, old chap, going to a party then?" he said to Harry.

"Mr. Dixon, I've got the date of a lifetime this evening. She's gorgeous." He ran the old Gillette safety razor down his left cheek and then flicked the razor under the hot tap.

"What's that?"

"Switch on your hearing aid you old busybody."

"I heard that young man. Don't you tell me I'm dizzy! I shall have to complain to the manager." But not even Dixon could destroy his mood. Harry leant over towards him, dripping shaving lather onto the bare concrete floor, and shouted in Dixon's ear,

"She's about six foot six, brunette, got a body to die for, smells delicious and I'm in love. On top of which I won my court case today and I even may have a new job. Do your worst!"

"Well, how about a drink then?" suggested Dixon, known throughout the establishment as being capable of flattening a bottle of gin in one sitting.

"Not tonight, Mr. Dixon, not tonight." Mr. Dixon went off Mumbling under his breath.

Harry was ready and leaning against the bar at ten past five and was just settling into a cold 'Castle' when Peter arrived.

"Couldn't wait hey?"

"No. Nothing will get in my way tonight. Another 'Castle' please, Mr. Barman," he called to the bar tender, who was having a chat to one of the waiters in the scullery. "How're you Pete?"

"Fine, this doll better be OK, otherwise as I said, I'll brain you." They laughed together. "What's her name again?"

"Chief Inspector Templar, you've got a brain like a sieve, I've already told you its Barbara Forester!"

"So have you, it seems."

"How's that?"

"Well, you've forgotten to put your sling on."

Harry held up his left hand showing the plaster cast that all but covered his fingers.

"Nah.., don't need it, as long as I don't move it too quickly. Besides it gets in the way." He stood away from the bar and twirled around holding out his arms as if dancing with an imaginary woman.

The banter carried on through their beer. Harry signed a chit for the drinks and they left. They got into the car and cruised off northwards along Moffatt Street towards Avondale.

"Bit funny peculiar sitting on the driver's side with no steering wheel," said Harry, his trepidation growing, as they got closer to the Nurses Home.

"Relax, Harry, your butterflies are because of your date, not because you're in a LH drive vehicle." Peter laughed. "Truth is I'm quite excited myself. I haven't been out with a girl for years." They chatted nervously as they went but needn't have worried. The instance they saw Annie and Barbara the mantle of doubt fell away.

"Hi, Annie."

She looked totally stunning, in a fresh summer frock that billowed out framing her full figure. Harry had to force his jaw shut. She smiled at him,

"Hello Harry, this is Barbara," she said turning slightly to bring Barbara into the frame.

"How do you do Barbara? Girls this is Peter Templar," answered Harry waving Peter forwards with his right hand. Any awkwardness was immediately lost when both Barbara and Peter smiled at each other.

"Hi," they said simultaneously, and everyone burst into laughter and then started talking all at once while the boys ushered the two women carefully to the car. Harry insisted that Barbara sit up front with Peter and almost ran to open the left rear door for Annie. Anyone watching would have laughed themselves silly at the comedy. With the girls in the car Peter and Harry crossed behind the car on their way to their respective sides.

"She OK?" asked Harry in a whisper.

"Bloody marvellous!" said Peter, wink, wink.

The girls were momentarily now in the car by themselves. Barbara immediately turned around.

"He's fantastic." She mouthed the words and looked admiringly at Peter as he climbed into the car.

"Where to, Harry?" asked Peter as he started the Chevy.

"Annie, would you like a drink first. I thought we could go to Brett's first, Archie Silanski's playing there, and then we could go to Highlands Park for supper." Harry wanted so much for her to say yes.

"Well it's a lovely evening, why don't we just go to Highlands Park, rather than going to Brett's. I've heard it's lovely to sit out on the veranda there. Brett's is always so stuffy and crowded and I can't stand all the smoke." Annie looked across at Barbara who, turning her head, nodded in agreement.

"Sure," agreed Peter, "that's fine. Barbara, are you happy with that?"

"Sounds wonderful, I've never been to Highlands Park, but I hear it's super."

"Harry knows the owners, he supplies them with illegal contraband, so we'll probably be well looked after." Peter was already laughing.

"Don't believe a word. He's talking nonsense, but I do have a little present for each of you." They looked on incredulously as Harry slipped two slim packets of Yardley's nylon stockings out of his inside jacket pocket and handed the women one each. The two women enthused over the stockings and thanked Harry profusely. He waved their excitement away.

"Mum's the word, Pete; don't ask me where I got these."

"So this is how you charm the chicks, is it?" smiled Peter.

"Well there are certain compensations for having to go to South Africa so often at the behest of the Rhodesian Government."

"Remember what I said Harry."

"Ah, relax Pete and keep your mind on the driving. I've never made a cent from importing illegal goods. It just makes good business sense to have a small stock of unobtainable gifts for friends and clients. Most of the time I declare the stuff anyway."

"You've lost me," said Barbara.

"Well what Pete alluded to was the fact that I'm often involved in flying essential commodities in from the RSA. It also gives us the opportunity to make money on the side bringing in illegal stuff in like whiskey, brandy, canned tuna, perfume, women's' stockings and so on, and flogging it. It's a no, no, though, because if we did and were caught, the government would cancel their contract with us and at the same time they'd shut us down and put us all in gaol."

"Is it a big business, Peter?" asked Barbara.

"It is a big problem because the country's losing a lot of currency through illegal dealings. There's a huge black market developing."

Annie had thus far done little more than secretly scrutinise Harry across the dimness of the back seat. She liked what she saw. An assuredness and intelligence by no means afraid of admitting what he was doing. Internationally he would have been classed as a criminal, aiding and abetting the Rhodesian regime against the effects of international punitive sanctions. He wasn't particularly good looking but she warmed to him quickly.

"Anyway, we didn't go out tonight to discuss what I do," said Harry turning to Annie. "You're from England, Annie?"

"Yes, we're both from Taunton in Somerset. We went to Nurses training college together and then both came out here together on a two-year contract with the Roman Catholic Mission. They own St Anne's."

"Thought I recognised that West Country Ahrrr! It's quite a coincidence meeting up with you; I'm from Wedmore near Cheddar. My old man's a dairy farmer there."

"You're a farm boy? So am I," said Annie.

"Could have fooled me," said Harry.

"No silly, I mean I'm from a farm as well; my mother and father live at Halse Manor in the Vale of Taunton Deane. It's actually about eight miles west of Taunton. My father has sheep and a small dairy herd."

"Good Lord, what a coincidence! How long have you been here then?"

"It's about nine months now isn't it Barbara?"

"Closer to ten Annie," said Barbara from the front seat. "We arrived on the fourth of May last year."

"Are you also a farm girl Barbara?" asked Peter.

"Good Lord no, although I'd love to be. My folks live in Taunton. My father's an Architect. When we were at school I used to spend most of my time at Annie's place, riding her horses round the countryside. Oh Annie! I was just thinking of those wonderful out-rides that we used to do up into the Brendon Hills and the Quantocks. Sometimes we'd ride 25 miles in one day. Anyway, that's enough of my reminiscing. Where're you from Peter?"

"Born UK and bred Rhodie. My folks are English, came here in forty six. He's a quantity surveyor in a big mining company here. Spends a lot of time down in South Africa and up in Zambia. So I'm lucky, I've still got a British passport tucked away."

"You go to Prince Edward Boys High School then?" asked Harry.

"No way, my dad wouldn't have me anywhere near him. And besides he is often away and takes my mom with him, so they organised for me to go to a senior school called Plumtree. It's a boarding school down on the Bechuanaland[18] border the other side of Bulawayo."

"Pretty rough place I heard," said Annie.

"Yeah, well, I suppose they really did sort out the men from the boys. But Plumtree is right out in the sticks and that's where I got my love of the wilds and the countryside. I'm certain that when I give up the police I'm going farming."

"Funny you should say that. That's what I want to do," said Harry. Almost as one the two women murmured their love of the wilds and countryside as well.

They arrived at the turn off the Dombashawa Road and climbed the hill up to the Highlands Park Hotel. The car park was quite full.

"Must be something on," said Peter.

"Well it's Friday night and The Rick Carson Combo are playing, so maybe we'll even get in some dancing." Harry's mind moved forwards in anticipation. It'll be great if there is dancing. Best way to break the ice. They went up onto the veranda where the head steward took them to the last empty table. The place was pumping. They ordered drinks and relaxed taking in their surroundings. The Hotel was in a beautiful setting some eight miles from Salisbury. The main road out of town passed about a hundred yards in front of the main buildings, down a steep sided and heavily wooded river valley. These were a group of old homestead buildings converted into a hotel complex, with lime washed walls and thatched roofs. The owners had extended the veranda out under several large Jacaranda and Syringa trees to create a large patio, popular as a watering hole for many of the people in the district. Paul Nicholson, obviously on duty and already as rotund as his father, came over.

"Harry, how're you doing? Haven't seen you round in a while." Paul stared at the stitches and wound on Harry's forehead and then looked down at the plaster cast covering Harry's hand. "Crikey! What happened to you?" Harry stood up.

"Hi Paulus, how are you? How're the folks?"

"Well, well, Mom'll want to see you, I'll tell her you're here."

"Paul, first let me introduce you to my friends. Folks, this is Paul Nicholson, he's kind of been forced to run the place. His old man's got this huge horse whip." They all laughed. Harry made the introductions, girls first.

"Christ Pete, how're you?" shouted Paul suddenly. Smiling, Peter came round the table and they shook hands vigorously. Peter turned back to the others,

"Paul and I went to school together at Plumtree," he said without letting go Paul's hand. "Trouble was, he was in the wrong house."

"Oh, all you Milner House guys are snobs. Great seeing you! What are you doing with yourself, Pete?" asked Paul.

"I'm in the police."

"Wow, a policeman and a pilot. How could you two possibly meet?" Paul had already begun to suspect a link between Harry's injuries and the relationship.

"Pete saved my life," said Harry. The women looked on enthralled by this exchange.

"Oh, bullshit! I just happened to be there, that's all."

"Be where?" asked Paul.

"I pranged an aeri," said Harry.

"You did what? Jesus, Harry, why didn't we know? My Mom'll kill you."

"Look it's a long story and I promise I'll give you all the gory details. More important right now, can you organise us a table for dinner?" asked Harry.

"Of course, you can use our table. I'll set it up. For what time?" Paul asked. The Nicholson had their own table reserved in the restaurant, which had a commanding view of the entire establishment. Normally they ran affairs from there, but when it was very busy, they gave it up and moved around.

"Seven-thirty, OK?"

"Fine, Phinius'll come out and tell you when it's ready." Paul rushed off.

"Guy's, we're in trouble," said Harry, "that's just the start. Wait until Mrs. Nicholson finds out." They all laughed and Peter and Harry sat down after sorting out the drinks. Little did Peter and Harry know, but that was only the half of it. They sat there chatting away and getting to know each other on subjects moving from weather, through sport to fashions. This was a dead loss because the men didn't have a clue. Neither of them had worn anything but uniforms and when they went mufti, it was shorts, shirt and flip-flops.

The accident assessor picked Fischer up at his hotel just after dark.

"Hop in, lets go and have a drink, I know a great pub just out of town. We can have a quiet chat there and nobody will know us."

"Ya, what is your name again?" asked Fischer as he climbed into the hire car.

"If you've forgotten it, pal, it isn't important, just call me Cedric."

"Ya, what I don't know I can't tell eh?"

"Something like that. But hang on until we get there. I don't want to be stopped by the cops." Lestering drove carefully keeping strictly to the speed limit hopeful that they wouldn't be stopped in any of the many roadblocks randomly established by the police around the city every night. They went through one, but peering at them from behind a torch, the patrol officer merely waved them on without checking their papers.

"Just two beers hey?" said Lestering rhetorically as they drove into the pub car park. "I have to drive out to the crash site in the morning."

"Suits me. Can I catch a lift back to Karoi with you? I have to get back to my wife," answered Fischer.

"Is that wise? We shouldn't be seen together."

"Agh, what harm can it do? All I'm doing is getting a lift from you."

"True," as they walked into the pub. They found a corner table where they could talk without being overheard and ordered a couple of beers.

"OK, I'll fetch you at seven thirty tomorrow morning. Be ready, hey?"

"Sure." The two men were clearly a little leery of each other. Each tolerating the other, because of what they were up to. In truth Lestering was more than a little scared of this rough German and would rather not have to deal with him. *I won't be able to screw this one out of money,* he thought.

"OK, down to business," he said. "This is what I want from you. A signed affidavit, you can get it attested by the doctor at the hospital."

"Ya, what must I say in it?"

"Don't worry about that. After I've looked at the crash, I'll write it out tomorrow night for you to copy on Sunday."

"Hey, I don't want to incriminate myself."

"You don't have to worry about that. It's for the Insurance underwriters only, and they're in Johannesburg, so you're safe." Lestering sat back well satisfied with Fischer's reaction to that bit of information and thought again, God I love this job.

Peter got up. "Please excuse me for a moment; nature calls." he wandered off in the direction of the toilets. Harry concentrated on the girls and then Mrs. Nicholson arrived, plonking her not inconsiderable self down in Peter's seat. Harry ordered her a drink and another round and told her the whole sorry story, which was the first time Annie and Barbara had really heard it also. Peter reappeared and was very agitated, saying quickly,

"Ladies, please excuse me. Harry, it's important you come with me now, quickly!" He almost lifted Harry out of his seat. "I have to show you something." He was very emphatic. "Please excuse us, ladies, won't be a moment but this may be critical." The three women looked at each other askance and then huddled together to discuss this new development.

Peter led Harry quickly through the tables of people enjoying the warm evening, into the entrance foyer and then into the toilet.

"What's the matter?" asked Harry a little prickly, a little put out by Peter's abruptness and insistence. Peter continued through the toilet and then eased another door open at the other end. The door led into the pub and pointing through the slightly open door he asked Harry,

"Have you seen that man before?" Harry peered slowly through the crack in the door and sucked his breath in.

"Well, well, well," he said. He stepped back. "The plot thickens. That man talking to Fischer is David Lestering, an aircraft accident assessor from Johannesburg." He reflected on what he'd seen for a moment. "He's obviously been sent up by David Jenson's, the aircraft insurance brokers. I can't see that there's anything wrong though. He's just doing his job. I suppose he has to interview people related to the accident."

"I agree with you," said Peter, "except that I saw him at seven this morning at the 'Drive-in' restaurant on the Enterprise Road. He was in the company of Mr. van Tonder, one of the board of enquiry Commissioners. I saw him get out of van Tonder's car. And that I do have a problem with. Interesting, Harry. Not a word; leave this with me. There may be nothing in it." He frowned and took out his notebook.

"A copper is never without a pencil and a piece of paper. What did you say his name was?" Harry spelt it out while Peter wrote it down, made some notes, looked at his watch, jotted down the time and then he grabbed Harry's arm.

"Right, until I say otherwise, this never happened, OK?" Harry smiled as they made their way back to the table. After a prolonged apology from Peter in which he gave them all a cock and bull story about identifying an unknown witness, they all settled down again. Mrs. Nicholson was equally interested in Peter after having been told by Paul that they'd been to Plumtree together.

The evening progressed well. The food was excellent and the band wasn't too loud. They danced and it wasn't long before each of the men was holding their partners hands between dances, body language indicating strong attraction. There is nothing like dancing to enable a man to whisper sweet nothings in a woman's ear, it's just legalised public foreplay isn't it? Each time the women went off to the toilet, they went together and obviously gave each other a blow-by-blow account of how it was going. The two men did exactly the same when they were left sitting at their table. Pretty soon, what had been a party of four turned into a pair of couples who just happened to be sitting at the same table. Every now and then one couple would get up and disappear outside leaving the floor clear for the other to talk privately.

It was a wonderful evening and they all hated to end it. Plans were laid for the following evening and even a picnic to Mermaid's Pool on Sunday. What started as an exploratory date for each of them ended in blossoming romance for all. On their way home after dropping Annie and Barbara off, Harry couldn't contain himself and started singing at the top of his voice, the Sinatra refrain,

"Come fly with me, come fly, let's fly away,

If you could use some exotic booze,

There's a bar in far Bombay.."

For a while Peter kept the rhythm by thumping the steering wheel with his fingers, but after a while he realised that Harry couldn't sing.

"Hey Harry, can you whistle?" he interjected.

"No, and I can't hum either," responded Harry, "but I'm over the moon. She's wonderful. What do you think of Barbara?"

"Bloody marvellous, you came out tops there."

"Brilliant." They arrived at Fife House and as Harry got out Peter said that he'd be there at one thirty pm. They'd arranged to go and watch rugby at the Police Ground that afternoon before cleaning up for their joint date the following evening.

"Gokay, see you then, and gratzie, Pedro."

"It was entirely my pleasure, let me assure you," replied Peter slipping the car into gear and cruising off.

CHAPTER 7

Peter Templar didn't go home. He turned right into 2nd Street and went west as far as Speke Avenue and turned right again. Two blocks down, he turned into the Central Police Station vehicle yard, parked and identifying himself to the Constable on duty at the Charge Office desk, he moved through and up the stairs, turning left at the top. This brought him to the door of Chief Inspector Raymond, CID. The light was on, so he knocked and entered. Raymond wasn't there but an Inspector Sturrock, who Peter knew reasonably well, was there. His feet were up on a heavy wooden desk, paging through a banned Playboy magazine.

"Hi Pete, what brings you into the corridors of power so late on a Friday night," he said, tossing the magazine aside.

"Hello Bill. Any nice dollies in this month's Playboy?"

"Nah; no fanny on show. Can't understand why the hell it's banned."

"Moral fibre of society and all that. They seem to think that you can't have the munts[19] gazing at white females in the flesh. Censorship is ridiculous isn't it?"

"Yeah; right, Pete, what can I do you for?" The word order reversal of 'you' and 'for' indicated to Peter that he should relax.

"Listen, Bill, I want to run something past you and then you decide whether anything should be done about it and whether we should open a docket or not, OK?"

"Fair enough, fire away," answered Bill Sturrock, hooking his feet up on the desktop again and leaning back so that he was perilously but comfortably balanced on the two rear legs of the chair. Peter tossed him a smoke, lit one for himself and then tossed the matches over. He pulled a seat away from the wall and straddled it, arms crossed on the backrest. Hauling out his notebook, he told Sturrock the story of the prang, the hearing and his witnessing of the two surreptitious meetings. The whole saga took three cigarettes.

"Could be something in it, Pete. Not worth putting resources into it but I'd be grateful if you provide me with a written statement. I'll open a stand-by docket and if anything develops then at least we'll have covered the ground."

"OK, Bill, I didn't know if I was being a bit paranoiac, because I really like this guy Harry Andrews and I was worried that my own feelings were making me think irrationally."

"No sweat, you did good."

"If that insurance guy goes back to the RSA, can we still reach him?"

"Yeah, the South African Police will bundle him up and deliver him to the front door, no problem."

"Good, I'll let you have something on Sunday. I've got to be back in Karoi on Sunday night, we're starting a gunja[20] sweep first thing Monday morning."

"That's fine. I won't be on duty but sling it in my tray. I'll pick it up in the morning."

"Thanks Bill," said Peter getting up. He put the chair back against the wall, shook Bill's hand and left.

Annie and Barbara were also over the moon. Lying in their beds, lights out, they continued talking until the early hours of the morning.

"Thanks for arranging the date with Pete," said Barbara. "I think he's wonderful and from the way you were behaving with Harry, I think we're both in a bit of trouble, don't you?"

"Well, I don't think I've ever been so struck by a guy so quickly before. He's quiet, but you can see he's very together. He considers everything carefully while at the same time he puts on such a carefree air."

"All pilots are like that Annie. They have to appear casual. They're supposed to be unflappable."

"No, actually I think he is. I don't think anything would worry him. I feel very safe with him there. Did you see the way he looked at those guys that were drunk. They just stopped in their tracks and crawled back to their table."

"That was a combination of both of them. Together they'd make a formidable team."

"Well that may happen, they seem to like each other a lot. I must say I do like Peter as well. He looks very strong."

"Hey, hands off! He's mine."

"No, don't worry, I like what of I've got. Barbara do you think Harry would make a good husband?"

"Annie, not already?!"

"Well when we were dancing he told me outright he's going to marry me."

"Good Lord, doesn't waste any time our Harry, does he?"

"He's not our Harry. He's my Harry," pouted Annie, curling herself into an even tighter ball.

"But you told me he wasn't your Harry yesterday," laughed Barbara.

"Well I've changed my mind," responded Annie, picking up the humour in it, "and I'm going to keep him."

"I feel the same way about Pete. Wouldn't it be funny if we get married together?" Barbara rolled over and switched on the bedside light on the dresser between their beds. "Oh Annie, wouldn't that be wonderful?"

Annie uncurled herself and sat up. She looked across at Barbara. Saying nothing for a moment, she just looked intently at Barbara.

"That's exactly what we're going to do Barbara," she blurted out. "And we're going to do it in Taunton."

"What, have you gone mad, Annie? I haven't even decided if I like Pete yet."

"Yes you have. One second you're thinking about marriage and the next minute you're saying you don't know if you like him. You're just saying that. I know you've been lying there wondering what he'd be like in bed. I admit, so have I, about Harry I mean."

"Annie Whitworth, you're incorrigible!"

"I don't care," laughed Annie. "Now switch out the light and go to sleep. I'm on duty in four hours. Night, night."

"Nightie, night Annie, sleep tight," said Barbara obeying the command.

The weekend ended up as the most incredible experience for all of them. They went dancing again on Saturday night and on Sunday sunbathed, swam and picnicked out at Mermaids Pool, some 35 miles north of Salisbury. A restaurant had been built adjacent to a natural 50 yard wide swimming pond at the bottom of a waterfall there. The beauty of the site and the resort's main attraction was a natural 100 ft high rockslide that disappeared straight into the pool. The Domboshawa River flowed over the rockslide so perfectly that the favourite sport was to carrier down it on a large inner tube, often encased in canvas, and shoot straight across the pool. Many people had injured themselves doing it, but it was all good clean fun. As a picnic spot it was idyllic. Beautiful large indigenous hardwood trees surrounded the whole site providing ample shade against the harsh midday sun.

The highlight of the weekend came with great mirth because Harry got his plaster cast sopping wet and had to be taken into the outpatients at St Anne's that evening to have it rewrapped and plastered. Because the two women were nurses there, Harry and Peter were given royal treatment and ushered through to a laboratory where the plaster cast was sorted out. Needless to say the two men were scrutinised by everybody and there were a continual stream of different personnel who for some reason or another had to come by the laboratory.

"This place is really busy," said Harry sitting there next to a stainless steel table his arm holding the attention of a large middle-aged nurse. Annie, Barbara and Peter looked on with interest.

"We'll have to call him 'Pirate'," said Peter.

"Why do you say that?" Harry put a hurt look on his face. It made him look ridiculous.

THE WYVERN REVENGE

"Well look at you, your face looks like a truck hit it, your arm's all plastered up, your nose is buckled to the point of no return and you can't keep that ridiculous grin off your face."

"I'm happy that's why. Crikey, this place is busy." Several more nurses had come through, sidling glances in their direction and one of the nuns appeared and shooed them off.

"No, it's not," said Barbara with an embarrassed laugh, adding "everyone is just coming through to check you two guys out."

"Guys, I hate to be a damp squib, but it's now six thirty and I have to take Harry home, then get my kit at the police camp and then I have to drive to Karoi," said Peter looking at his watch.

"Aw, can't you go tomorrow morning?" asked Barbara, clutching his arm possessively.

"Unfortunately not. The drug squad is already there and we're doing a gunja sweep starting at 5:00 tomorrow morning. Even more important, I've got to check with Sampson Ndlovu, my Sergeant, who is actually in Karoi on foot patrol until ten tonight. If there have been any arrests I'll have to go through the charge sheets tonight so that any detainees can be sent to Chikarubie Prison first thing tomorrow morning."

"Well you two go off outside," said Annie, "I'll finish up here with Harry and we'll meet you by the car. Ten minutes, OK?" Barbara and Peter took the hint and disappeared and Annie helped the laboratory nurse finish up with the wrapping. She came very close to Harry, her whispering touch and smell intoxicating.

"When are you going back to Bulawayo?" she asked.

"There's a Dak coming up on Wednesday so it'll either be then or Thursday morning." Harry lent close to her so that they could talk secretively enough for the other nurse not to hear, and she swayed slightly forward, her breast touching his shoulder lightly. He could feel himself getting hard.

"Can I see you tomorrow?" he whispered, his rough cheek just brushing hers. He couldn't resist touching her ear with his lips. Not a kiss, just a touch. She shivered slightly with pleasure.

"Harry Andrews, you need a shave," she admonished loudly, but simultaneously she gripped his arm strongly, keeping him close.

"Lunch? I'm on night duty."

"Fetch you at twelve." He hopped down from the table he'd been sitting on, thanked the laboratory nurse and taking Annie's hand headed off towards the car park. They approached the car quietly and could see Barbara and Peter kissing and hugging on the front seat. Harry stopped and drew Annie close.

Peter eventually arrived in Karoi at about 11:30 that night and after checking in at the Charge Office, got in his Land Rover again and went off to find Sampson. He found the Sergeant and a Constable by driving down one of the sanitary lanes, which ran parallel to the main street. They were behind the local hotel talking to a man who, from his dress, was clearly a waiter at the hotel.

"Hello Sampson," he said quietly through the vehicle window. He could see Sampson's face light up in a smile in the glow cast by the light outside the back storeroom of the hotel.

"Good evening Sir, welcome back."

"Thanks my friend, hop in and tell me what's been going on."

"Yes, Sir! Constable, take down this man's name and address and then continue your patrol."

"Yes, Sergeant," replied the Constable.

The Sergeant turned to the waiter. "The Constable will take your name and address because if what you have told me is important, we may have to take a statement from you, is that OK?"

"Yes, it's OK," said the man.

"Very good. Good night, Constable." And with that Sampson got into the Land Rover and Peter drove off.

"Something very funny happened at the hotel tonight Sir," he said to Peter.

"Oh, what was that?" Peter passed over a packet of 'Texan' and a box of matches. "Light me one too."

"Well Sir, remember that big man with the fat wife where the aeroplane crashed?" Sampson went through the process of lighting the two cigarettes, turning the exercise into a ceremony.

"Yes?" Peter's interest was immediately aroused.

"He was here tonight talking to another man, and Zephron, that's the waiter, saw the other man give him plenty money," said Sampson after passing over a cigarette to Peter.

"Interesting..." Peter stopped the vehicle in the main street about 50 yards down from the hotel. "Did he describe this man?" he took a pull on his cigarette and found what he was looking for, a blue Daihatsu parked outside the hotel. "No, Sir, only that he is from South Africa."

Peter leaned across and picked up his notebook, which had been lying on the dashboard. He groped around and located his torch on the floor, flicked it on and shining the beam onto the notebook he started paging through it with his other hand. There it was, registration number H 346 UP.

"Is he staying at the hotel tonight?"

"Yes, Sir, he apparently arrived just after lunch."

"Well, well, well, let's go and talk to the night porter." He got out, shut the door gently and crushed his cigarette on the road.

"Can you tell me what's going on, Sir?" asked the Sergeant getting out on the other side of the vehicle.

"Well, I don't really know, Sampson, but I'm suspicious because this man, whom you say, Zephron saw giving money to Mr. Fischer, also met with somebody else he really shouldn't have been talking to. Also, he has met with Mr. Fischer already, on Friday night in Salisbury. Let's see if the night porter has the hotel register."

They walked along the street, opened the front door of the hotel and entered the dimly lit foyer. A neatly dressed black man was sitting behind the counter writing something in the light of a lamp. He looked up and immediately rose to his feet.

"Good evening, Sir," he greeted Peter, at the same time nodding at Sampson.

"Good evening," said Peter. "We're doing our rounds and saw the light on. Is everything alright?"

"Yes, Sir, everything is quiet." The night man looked a little relieved.

"Have you had any late arrivals?" asked Peter leaning on the counter while searching for the register. It was there on a desk immediately behind the counter.

"Yes, Sir, a family just on their way home from Kariba." Peter pointed at the register,

"Mind if I take a look at the register?"

"No Sir, certainly Sir." The response was immediate. He placed it on the counter so that Peter could read it and stood back. Peter ran his finger down the first column and found the entry, 'D. G. Lestering'. The man had even put in a complete Johannesburg address. He got his notebook and jotted down the details.

"What time has room four asked for tea in the morning?" he asked casually, as if feigning complete boredom. The night man turned and referred to a roster hanging over a clipboard on the wall next to him.

"Oh, he's an early departure, Sir, I have to wake him at five o'clock for sure. When I came on duty, I was told he has to catch an aeroplane to Johannesburg from Salisbury at half past eight tomorrow night and has to leave here by five thirty at the latest."

Peter said nothing but started writing furiously in his notebook, trying to get down everything he had learned, dates, times and activities.

"Thank you for your help, we'll carry on now," he said finally snapping his notebook shut. "Good night. Come along, Sergeant." The two policemen turned and left. The night porter was really none the wiser as to why they'd come into the hotel at all. As they got outside Peter turned to Sampson and said,

"Do you know that guy, Sampson?"

"Yes, Sir, he's my wife's brother."

Peter laughed out loud. "God, Sampson, I should have known it." He clapped Sampson on the back. "You are related to just about everybody in this village." Sampson smiled back at Peter.

"Yes, Sir. But, there is this young maiden in the location[21]. Her name is Beauteous; I'm not related to her!" Peter crumpled up laughing. When he came up for air, there were tears streaming from his eyes. At last he blurted out,

"Sampson, you randy old bugger." He stopped for a minute trying to recompose himself. "Well you're not the only one. I've met a nurse in Salisbury. She's wonderful."

"How! The Chief Inspector is in love also?" The Sergeant looked at his boss with admiration.

"Yes Sampson, I am, and it hurts."

"Then you understand Sir that there is only one way to relieve such pain."

"How's that?" Peter looked at his Sergeant.

"You must empty your balls in her honey pot." Peter couldn't take it; it hurt too much to laugh any more. As he choked in the agony of excruciating laughter, he grabbed his friend and put him into a bear hug.

"No wonder you guys breed so fast. You reduce everything to basics." He couldn't stop giggling as the thought of Barbara naked in his arms struck him.

"Well that's because we are sensible, Sir. You Malhungus[22] are stupid to only have one wife." Peter, blinded with laughter, collapsed on his seat, dropped his cigarettes on the floor and so just sat there shaking, head in his arms on the steering wheel.

"Oh God, I haven't laughed so much for ages. Sam, you should have been a comedian." Slowly the humour subsided and he said, "Listen, Sampson, Tuesday morning, you take this Landy[23] and fetch both the night man and the waiter and bring them up to the Police Camp. I want statements from both of them, understand?"

"Yes, Sir."

"Good, now let's go home, I must get some sleep. I start at five on the Gunja sweep."

Jim Leonard listened to the head of David Jenson (Pty) Ltd, Aviation Insurance Brokers explain that the underwriters had denied his Insurance claim. He felt the anger and disbelief growing inside him.

"Furthermore Mr. Leonard, I'm afraid that the underwriters have withdrawn the cover on the other aircraft in the Trans Afrique Air fleet for all flights within Rhodesian airspace."

"What?" exploded Jim. But he'd known it was coming. "Can you tell me why?"

"As a matter of fact, it wasn't just that your company has had two aircraft accidents. There has been increasing pressure from their principals in London to deny insurance cover to all aircraft flying in Rhodesia. Indeed there is talk that they will deny cover to any aircraft operating company that has anything to do with Rhodesia." David Jenson was almost apologetic.

"Well, will you continue to find me cover for all operations outside this country?" Jim asked. He looked out of his office window directly into the interior of his operations hangar. There was a beautifully maintained Douglas DC3 parked in there being worked on by his ground crew, He thought that this issue is something he must bring to the attention of the government; or more precisely, the Prime Minister, when he next had the opportunity to see him.

"Yes, I'm sure we can sort that out, provided they are aircraft registered in South Africa."

"Well you know damned well that's the situation in my case," said Jim, "make sure it happens and I expect a refund and substantial rebate on my premiums."

"We'll sort that out, Sir. When will you be in Johannesburg to sign the papers?"

"Wednesday. Now tell me why they specifically refused my claim on IBU."

"A copy of the letter is on its way to you, but in a nutshell there are two reasons. The first is that the Swan strip is unregistered and…"

"That's bullshit, and you know it," interjected Jim.

"No, it's true. The investigator found that the registration had expired."

"I don't believe it, but carry on."

"Secondly, the investigator has concluded that your pilot acted irresponsibly in two respects, (a) that he shouldn't have landed in the long grass, but should rather have diverted to another strip, and (b), that the onboard patient was not properly secured in the passenger cabin of the aircraft."

"Crikey, David, both of the reasons are spurious and you know that too."

"Look, Mr. Leonard, you asked me to relay to you the reasons why the claim was turned down. There's not a hell of a lot that I can do about it. If you do disagree with them, you'll have to take it up with the insurers through your attorneys. I don't recommend that though, because it'll have an adverse influence on further applications for cover."

"Christ all bloody mighty," shouted Jim. "So they think they've got me over a barrel, do they? Listen, David, find me another underwriter, get me covered now on the basis that my operations are all confined to territories outside Rhodesia, and international airports in Rhodesia and I'll sign on Wednesday afternoon or Thursday morning, when I'm down there. In the meantime I'm going to get going with my attorneys and I am going to get them to sue for the amount claimed for IBU."

"OK Mr. Leonard, I'll see you on Wednesday."

Jim put the phone down, told Binny to get his attorney in Johannesburg and started thinking about what he was going to have to do to salvage his company.

That phone call dealt with, he then called Harry at Fife House.

"Hello Harry, bad news."

"Binny already told me, Jim. But don't worry; I've got an appointment with the police tomorrow morning at nine thirty. I'll let you know what transpires."

"That's uncommonly decent of you, Harry. Listen, I did speak to Smithie on Friday night and he said that he would have a word with Chief Superintendent Huxley this morning. It will probably help, although Smithie said he wouldn't insist on anything. It was not his place to seek favours for his friends."

"Thanks Jim, all contributions gratefully accepted."

"In the meantime I'm off to Johannesburg on Wednesday morning to sort out the insurance stuff and I want to organise some more supplies for Glover. Apparently Safari Air has a whole lot of parts that he can use. They're trying to reduce their inventory."

"Good luck. Are you going to have a go at the Insurers?"

"Bloody right I am. By the way while you're up in Salisbury do you think that you can get hold of Chris Swan?"

"Sure, why?"

"Look, the insurers are claiming that his field is unregistered and that's the principle reason that they're not paying."

"Well the current NOTAMs (Notices to Airmen) indicate it as registered. Your attorneys will be able to use that," advised Harry.

"Good point and good thinking Harry. Nonetheless, check it out."

"Leave it to me. See you Thursday night."

"Cheers Harry, and thanks hey!"

CHAPTER 8

"D. I. Bill Sturrock please," said Peter into the mouthpiece of the archaic phone that he had to use at the Karoi Police camp.
"Yes, Sir, may I say who is calling?"
"P. C. I. Templar."
"Yes, Sir, you're going through."
"Sturrock!"
"Hi Bill, Peter Templar."
"Hello Pete, what's up? Hell this line is terrible."
"You're not wrong, Bill, so I'll speak up." Peter spent the next 10 minutes explaining loudly what had happened.

"Furthermore, Bill, I had a beer with Chris Swan, the owner of the airstrip where the accident happened, and he says that Harry Andrews told him that the Insurers have refused the Aircraft Operating Company's claim on the grounds that the field is unregistered. Well it is registered; he's got the Licence at the farm. So maybe something has been going on between the Assessor and that little shit van Tonder at DCA. Allegedly Harry Andrews phoned him to find out about it. Trans Afrique Air is apparently going to sue the insurance company."

"Listen Pete, not a word to Andrews or Swan. I'll speak to the super after lunch. This sounds like a pretty serious case of fraud. Firstly, when can you get the witnesses statements down to me?"

"They'll be sent down with the next dispatch. There's a truck coming in this afternoon with prisoners, mainly thieves."

"Good, have them addressed for my personal attention. Secondly, where can I find Andrews and Leonard? I may need to talk to them." Peter gave him the information he needed.

"Well done, Pete, I'll get onto it. This is great; we're actually doing what the country employed us to do instead of trying to find bloody freedom fighters in the bush the whole damned time. Makes a change doesn't it?"

"Yeah, you can say that again. Cheers Bill, I'll be out in the districts for the next two days so you'll only be able to get me on Friday if you need me."

"OK Pete, see you."

At much the same time on Tuesday morning, exactly 9:25 am to be precise, dressed as neatly as he could, Harry Andrews presented himself at police headquarters. A smiling black corporal behind the charge office counter ushered him through to chief Superintendent James Huxley's office. Public Works Department's green walls made the wooden capstand, desk, chairs and bookcase look awfully drab. An old picture of The Queen hung on one wall, while another was almost entirely covered by a map of the country at a scale of 1:250 000. There were pins with little squares of different coloured paper flags slotted onto them, stuck seemingly randomly all over the map.

"Andrews, nice of you to come. I've heard all about you."

"Hope it's not all bad, Sir."

"On the contrary, I hear you're a bit of a hot shot pilot with lots of short bush strip experience."

"Been into a few over the last few years, Sir. Recently, not so successfully." Huxley smiled and shrugged.

"You must have a few friends around the show Andrews?"

"Sir?"

"Well, I've had all sorts of people phoning me to tell me to give you a job."

"I truly regret that, Sir, I asked them not to, preferring to be appointed on nothing but my own merits." Harry looked very contrite as he handed across an envelope. "That's my CV, Sir, which, I must explain, has large gaps in it because of the official secrets act; the British one that is." Huxley took the slim two-page document out and spent the next few minutes reading through it carefully.

"Reading between the lines and from what I know and what you said at the hearing, I'd say you were suitably qualified for the job. Can you handle giving up your allegiance to Great Britain and signing our official secrets act?"

"You'll know, Sir, that I think the war is a farce anyway. I believe it just a matter of time before this government is forced to capitulate. In any case, this is a flying job in the police, not the Air Force." Harry fidgeted a little because he wasn't quite sure what he was expected to say. I'm blowing this, he thought.

"Relax Andrews." Huxley looked sternly at him. "Besides I understand you're concerned that your British citizenship will be a problem."

"Yes, Sir."

"Don't be. Off the record, I have a British passport as well." Harry sat impassively and listened while Huxley explained the job and what he wanted done, how the air wing would operate and so on.

"Our aircraft are hangared and maintained at Kentucky and you can take accommodation at the single quarters there or at the Salisbury police camp, whichever you prefer." Huxley looked intently at Harry. "Are you still interested, Andrews?"

"Very much so, Sir." He didn't mention that he really had no choice in the matter; he was going to be out of a job shortly anyway. I'll be able to see Annie every day I'm in town, he thought.

"Very well; I'm prepared to recommend that you be appointed at the rank of 'Chief Inspector of Police (Flight Operations)', but you'll have to undertake a intensive three month induction course while you set things up at the base. I'll have the police training college sort out a course specially for you. Andrews, it won't be easy; you'll have to work bloody hard because although you'll really only be involved in organising and flying in the air wing, I can't have police officers running around who are not trained, you understand?"

Harry nodded in acquiescence.

"Until you pass the requisite exams, you will officially remain a civilian in police employ, so initially your rank will be honorary."

"Yes, Sir, I understand, but I'm sure I'll manage."

"Yes I'm sure you will. Your military training will be of great help. Right, I'll get the paper work sorted and I'll see you next week, same time, same place, if that's convenient?"

"Yes, Sir." Stuck record again Andrews, thought Harry, but it looks like I'm in.

"In the meantime I'll have someone take you out to the base and show you around, give you a feel for the place. I understand that you can start pretty well immediately?"

"Yes, Sir." Don't know what else to say, do I? Harry berated himself, Smithie must have spoken to him, otherwise how would he know that? So Jim's come up trumps again, the bugger.

"I'm supposed to be back in Bulawayo on Thursday evening," he continued.

"That's fine. I'll arrange for you to stay out at the base until then, if you like? Give you lots of time to get acquainted with things. Can you be back here to start on Monday morning?"

"Yes, Sir." Crikey, I'll have to move my arse. I'll have to drive up on Sunday.

"Good, you'll report to the duty chief Superintendent at the Salisbury police camp at six hundred hours on Monday morning for induction and instructions. He'll also send you down to the quartermaster to get kitted out. When does your arm come out of that plaster?"

"Another four weeks I'm afraid, Sir."

"No problem, you'll have plenty to do in the meantime," said Huxley standing up. He put out his hand and said, "Welcome to the British South Africa Police, Mr. Andrews."

"Thank you, Sir," said Harry jumping to his feet and shaking Huxley's hand firmly, "I'm really looking forward to it."

"That's that then, Andrews. Come with me." Huxley led Harry out and down the corridor to another tiny office near the rear of the building and introduced him to the duty officer sitting there surrounded by files and papers.

"Hicks, you look like you could do with a break. This is Chief Inspector Harry Andrews." Hicks leapt to his feet and shook Harry's hand warmly. Hey, Chief Inspector, that doesn't sound too bad, thought Harry.

"How do you do, Sir?" Harry shook Hicks' outstretched hand.

"Pleased to meet you, Sergeant Hicks," he replied.

"I want you to swear him in, Official Secrets Act, identity card, clearances for here, Kentucky and the police camp and all that," continued Huxley, "and then take him to get his kit wherever he's staying. I'd be grateful if you'd then take him out to Kentucky, settle him into the single quarters and give him a detailed tour of the base. Chief Inspector Andrews will be taking over the Police Air Wing. Got that?"

"Yes, Sir," nodded Hicks.

"Anything he wants, he gets understood?"

"Yes, Sir." Shit, I'm not the only one who spends his life saying 'Yes, Sir', thought Harry. But this boy Huxley's obviously the main man around here. Harry turned to say thank you and goodbye, but Huxley had already disappeared. Harry turned back to face Sergeant Hicks and then nearly jumped out of his skin as Huxley stuck his head around the door again.

"And Andrews, try not to pull a stunt like that with one of our aeroplanes will you?" Huxley winked at Harry.

"Also, Harry, once you've seen what's going on, you might start an inventory of what you're going to need. Although God only knows how we're going to get the stuff."

"That shouldn't be a problem, Sir." Shit, he's already calling me Harry. More relaxed than the military obviously, thought Harry.

"Oh, how so?"

"Well the company I was with gets a lot of stuff in for the Air Force. Squadron Leader Glover, Sir. I'm sure we can make a plan." Huxley looked questioningly at Harry, his face screwed up in thought.

"You know Glover?" Huxley asked slowly.

"Yes, Sir."

"You and I are going to have some fun, Harry." With that he turned away and stalked off down the corridor.

"Yes, Sir," said Harry after him. Wow, that was easier than I thought it would be, he thought as he left the building. And he's already calling me Harry. Must tell Annie, I can't believe it! The jumbled thoughts continued to fill his mind as Hicks took his photograph and made him sign several forms in triplicate.

"Your ID and badge will be ready for you on Monday morning at the camp, Sir," said Hicks, carefully cataloguing the papers and placing copies into a large brown paper envelope. "Retain possession of this lot, Sir and if anyone wants to know anything, just give them the envelope."

"Thanks, Hicks." It had all taken about half an hour. Shortly after that, they left and Hicks drove him along Angwa Street towards the park and Fife House. When they got back to the hotel, the first thing that he did was to call the hospital, but Annie couldn't take the call, so he left a message saying that he couldn't make lunch, but would call her when he could. He then called Jim Leonard in Bulawayo.

"Jim, you're a star. Your natter with Mr. Smith worked a treat."

"Nonsense, Harry, you would have got the job anyway. Well done! And listen, I can't tell you how relieved I am also. When do you start?"

"Officially Monday, but I've already signed the official secrets act and so on; and I'm off to the air base at Kentucky just now. And Jim, guess what? You'll be getting plenty of business from us also. We're going to have to build up an inventory of spares and so on. Apparently they've got nothing."

"Hell's bells, you don't waste time do you. But that's great; we'll get things sorted out at this end on Friday."

"I'm going to check out of Fife House immediately Jim, what do I do about the bill?"

"Just sign for Trans Afrique Air as usual. They'll send the account. OK, cheers, boy, got to run."

"Cheers, Jim and thanks again."

Within the hour, Hicks delivered him to the single quarters at the Kentucky Air Base. Harry signed-in, put his kit into a small but well maintained bedroom with a view across the base swimming pool. Hicks started to show him around the living quarters.

"Don't worry Hicks, I know the form around here. Stayed here dozens of times while flying…," He shut his mouth. "Lets just say, I know my way around."

"That's fine sir, I understand. Well in that case I'll take you to the Police Air Wing hangar."

"Great," said Harry, looking at his watch. It was 11:45 am. "But stand by a few minutes, I need to make a phone call." Harry walked through to the pay phone in the mess, fished some ten-cent pieces out of his pocket and dialled St Anne's hospital nurses' home again.

"Hello, nurses home."

"Hi. Is Annie Whitworth there, please?"

"Please hold on, I'll call for her." Harry stood there for three minutes, becoming more and more agitated. The voice came back on the line.

"I'm sorry she's out, do you want to leave a message?"

"Yes please. Please tell her that Harry phoned cancelling lunch today. But I've left that message already. Can you tell her that I'll call again tomorrow?" The woman on the other end of the line said that was fine and rang off.

Mr. and Mrs. Fischer left Karoi with their new baby on the Wednesday following the hearing. They drove to Salisbury in a hire car and then flew Air Rhodesia Vickers Viscount to the Victoria Falls. There they were picked up by their manager and taken down to Mzuma for the motorboat ride down through Devil's Gorge and onto the lake and M'bezi, the little fishing lodge near Binga. They stayed there the night before going on by boat to Chete Gorge. They sat together at the rear of the boat, close to the two large roaring outboard motors. The boat was up on the plane and with the warm wind strong in their faces; they were able to talk without any fear of being overheard. Fischer put his arm around his wife's shoulders while she sat there cuddling her baby against the wind. This is the life, he thought. So nice here in a hot climate. His mind turned to the events of the last few weeks. That bloody arrogant man, Andrews, and as for that policeman Templar. Well, I've buggered Andrews, lost his job didn't he? Bloody cowboy, he nearly had us killed. These colonial types, stupid. Except that guy, Lestering. Clever boy that, and generous. He patted his pocket, and felt the comforting bulge of bank notes. Well those guys will never work out how I shafted them. Think they can mess me around. And I'll get that cop as well, somehow, lots of time for that.

"Well, all in all a successful trip," he shouted in his wife's ear, making himself heard above the noise of the motors and the wind. He ignored the beautiful scenery as they raced down through the gorge.

"Brad, how can you say that?" she shouted back, clearly angry. "It's been nothing but a disaster!" He laughed at her.

"No it wasn't. I got that bastard pilot. I believe he's been fired and the charter company is going to go under."

"And how did you manage to do that, Brad Fischer?" she asked disbelievingly. He just smiled and patted his pocket again. After a moment, he said,

"Just you wait, you'll see," he said holding his hand over the money, his fingers tracing the edge of the bundle.

"What have you got in your pocket?" she asked suspiciously.

"Nothing." He jerked his hand away. "Just a little heartburn. Look at this wonderful scenery, aren't you happy here? Better than the cold of Europe, nyet?" He waved towards a rocky promontory where two crocodiles slid off the rocks into the water as the boat sped past.

"Ya, Brad, I am happy."

That same morning Jim caught the SAA Viscount to Johannesburg and so began his long legal battle against the insurance company.

CHAPTER 9

"*I* nearly lost her you know.*"* Harry was addressing his mother. They were sitting in the parlour enjoying a rare sunny evening in late winter, curtains open. The garden looked bare but neat. He could make out the Henbury golf course fairways across the Trym valley and commented,

"It wouldn't be half a view you'd have here if the weather was like this more often."

"Yes, it is pleasant, isn't it?" she said rhetorically, glancing briefly out of the window herself. She served him another piece of spinach quiche lorraine and sat down on her side of the small table. "Lose who?"

"Annie," he said between mouthfuls. "This quiche is delicious, did you bake it?"

"No, I bought it at Felix van den Bergh's Deli in the village. Madeleine makes them at home."

They sat there quietly together for a while, sipping their tea and finishing off the quiche, until Bunty couldn't contain her curiosity any longer.

"How?" she asked. He knew immediately what she was referring to but said nothing for a while. He continued to stare out of the window and once reached down and ruffled the hair around Bonnie's neck. He gave her a small piece of the pie that was left on his plate.

"You know you shouldn't spoil her, Harry," said Bunty.

"You're right, but I can't help it." He paused before continuing. "Well, after I got the job with the BSAP, I was so busy, it started off badly. Although I phoned often enough, she frequently didn't get my messages and had difficulty believing that I had actually phoned. I was lucky to see her once or twice a month for the first year." Bunty kept her silence and when she'd finished her tea she stared intently at the bottom of the cup as if to divine what the tea leaves were telling her. She decided that she was going to get a letter from afar.

"I had gone back to Bulawayo, packed up and then unexpectedly Jim gave me a golden handshake."

"Oh, I didn't know that."

"It was incredible. There he was, just about to go under, and he gives me a severance cheque for one hundred and twenty thousand Rhodesian dollars. I couldn't believe it. And I must tell you that in those days a Rhodesian dollar was worth about ten bob. It's worth nothing today, something like three hundred to one."

"Golly Harry, that's sixty thousand pounds."

"That's right." He paused. "Well I already had about forty thousand Rhodesian dollars stashed away there and what with the money I had here and my Air Force pension, I felt that I had enough to buy a farm, which, as you know, is precisely what I did eventually."

"But?"

"But Annie was, I suppose, understandably getting upset with me because she thought I was avoiding her. Barbara was seeing Peter virtually every weekend and used to take Annie out with them. I seldom if ever made it. Annie thought that because I now had all this money, I didn't want her anymore."

"What was taking up all your time?" Bunty asked sensitively.

"Hell Mum, when I got back to Salisbury that Sunday night, it was the last time I saw Annie for three months. From then on I worked all day, every day, out at the air base setting the air wing in motion. Then 'til late at night, I had to go to classes at the police camp. Every morning from five to six thirty, I had drill and weapons training and then weekends I had to go into the police camp for more drill, exercises, classes, a course in basic Shishona[24], and to top it all every time I had anytime off I had to help Jim and his attorneys with his court case. He used to set things up so that the instant I knocked off, there'd be an aircraft there to fly me to Bulawayo or

Johannesburg. Most of the time I just slept, I was completely knackered… Excuse me."

"Henry Andrews!"

"Sorry Mum. I meant that I was exhausted."

"I know what you meant. But carry on."

"It eased up a bit after I finished the three month induction programme; but not much, because then when my arm had healed and I'd got the strength to use it again, I had to re-do all my flying licences and get Rhodesian certification, and besides by this time I had forty eight people working for me at the base. Engineers, pilots, dispatchers, fuelers, storekeepers, drivers, guards, the lot. We had to have at least one meteorologist there at all times to give us weather briefings, another to co-ordinate flight planning with police HQ and the Air Force and the civilian ATC's. Then to top it all we started to get involved in casevacs and pretty soon there was a medical team assigned to the wing full time." Harry stopped, looked out into the gloom and sighed. He got up and moved to the sideboard, which served as a drinks cabinet. He gave Bunty a medium cream sherry as usual, and poured himself a stiff scotch. Sitting down carefully, so as not to spill his drink, he continued.

"Within three months we had six aircraft fully operational and were flying up to fifteen missions daily. I had to employ cooks to prepare onboard food and drink for the flight crews. That was just in Salisbury. I had to set up depots with fuel and beds and so on in Bulawayo, Victoria Falls and Umtali[25]. Then there were housekeepers at the base because we were all too exhausted most of the time to do our own washing and ironing or to keep the place tidy. OK for me, I had my own batman[26], but the others needed help as well. I really got chewed out by the chief super for the state of the base. He arrived one day out of the blue with some politicians. I thought he was going to fire me. So I ran myself ragged."

"But what could you have been doing, doing so much flying?" Bunty clearly had no idea what a small police air wing would involve itself in.

"Shucks Mum, our missions ranged from spotting for ground patrols and mobile units, chasing cattle rustlers, car thieves, hit and runners, smugglers, and escapees, to flying the top brass around, doing photographic runs, foot and mouth disease cordon runs, food and medical supply drops, casevacs[27], border patrols and so on. We fought hard to maintain our non-political role although occasionally we were forced to assist in security operations. Our non-political stance was considered extremely important in order to retain the trust and cooperation of the people." Harry took a sip of his whisky, twirling the warmth of it around in his mouth.

"Also I had to organise supplies and spare parts and aero-engines from RSA and pretty soon I was the liaison man for the Air Force. Mick Glover, he was the Squadron Leader of the chopper squadron, whenever he wanted something, used to just come to me. I knew him from the days that I was in the Raf, and when I was with Jim Leonard. We used to run his stuff in for him from the Republic." He stopped for a deep breath and Bunty was able to interject.

"Slow down Harry, do you mean to tell me that this was all more important than seeing Annie."

"No Mum, but when I was off, which was seldom, I really was just too tired to do anything, and I chose to just stay and relax at the base more often than not. Getting drunk in the mess became a bit of a habit I guess, but it was the quick and easy way to unwind."

"How long did this carry on, Harry?"

"For about fifteen, eighteen months, I don't know. My life was a mess. I think that Pete Templar was a little miffed at me because I was promoted to Superintendent before he was. So I wasn't seeing that much of him. Thank goodness that changed when he was subsequently promoted. Ridiculous isn't it? But that's the way it seemed at the time. In the meantime he and Barbara had got engaged. Annie was barely speaking to me and had become very distant."

"Goodness Harry, it sounds as if you nearly blew it."

"That's true, but then everything changed."

"Why?"

"Well, three or four things happened." He looked down at his glass. "This is good whisky," he said, taking another mouthful. "Firstly, van Tonder and Lestering, the insurance assessor, were arrested for fraudulently falsifying government records amongst other things. They were the reason it took so long for Jim Leonard to get paid out for the aeroplane I broke. Oh, van Tonder was that guy I didn't get on with at the accident investigation hearing, I must have told you about him?"

"Is that little man that gave you a hard time?"

"Yes. I didn't even know that the police were building a case against them, apparently started by Peter who put two and two together shortly after the hearing and managed to get CID to open a case docket. Lestering was arrested in the country. He was in Umtali trying to pull the same sort of stunt again."

"But how did that affect you?"

"Well the third person involved, the man who, with his wife, was in the aircraft when I pranged it, disappeared and we were called out to provide air support for the ground search."

"Did you catch him?"

"No, but we knew he and his wife took a boat over to the Zambian side of the 'lake' and we thought that he had started running a lodge over there. We were wrong. He was involved in other things that I didn't know about until much later. But that's another story I'll tell you another time."

"What else happened?"

"Well, Pete purchased a farm at Karoi, I got engaged to Annie and then nearly had my foot taken off by a crocodile and to crown it all I got Malaria." Harry sat back, his eyes almost shut and fiddled with the signet ring on the little finger of his left hand.

"Go on Harry. And I have to ask you why we weren't told of all of this when it all happened?" The sun was starting to set off to the west and the whole of the Trym valley was in shadow. Harry got up and went to the drinks cabinet.

"I don't know, I suppose I didn't want you to worry. Mum, would you like another sherry?"

"No thanks." She hesitated then said, "Well perhaps I will. I take it this is a long story?"

"Yes!"

Peter met Harry on the veranda of their favourite watering hole, the Avondale Hotel. The two women were due to join them in an hour or so, and so they settled down to catch up on what they'd been doing and watching the passing parade. The only people in the place who knew that they were policemen were the management, so they were left alone to enjoy their own company.

"Howzit going, Pirate?" said Peter, the nickname had stuck and everybody called him that now. Peter wasn't smiling and there was an edge to his voice.

"Aw, I'm buggered Pete, I need a holiday. Shucks, if I'd have known what this bloody job entailed I would never have taken it on." Harry stoked up his pipe while Pete lit one of his revolting Texans. He gazed intently at Harry and saw the weariness; his face was drawn and he'd lost weight.

"Why don't you take a vacation then, you bloody twit?"

"Hell, I haven't got the time."

"That's balls, Pirate, nobody is indispensable." He looked across at Harry. "Look, I've got to ask you something?"

"Yeah, what, and what are you so up tight about?"

"I am up tight, Pirate, but first answer this question. Am I your friend?"

"Of course you are!" Harry said indignantly.

"Well, will you take it amiss if I give you some free advice?"

"Nooo," said Harry warily. Wait for it Harry boy, you're going to get a mouthful. He leaned back, taking a sip out of his beer.

"Pirate, if you don't sort things out with Annie, you're going to lose her." Harry sat up slowly, and Peter could see the danger signals.

"What do you mean?" Harry's voice was soft and menacing.

"I'm your friend God dammit, Harry. Can't you see what's going on? You're never here, you miss dates, when did you last make an effort to cement your relationship with Annie? Every time you do see her, you're buggered. She misinterprets that and thinks you're giving her the bums rush and I wouldn't be surprised if she tells you to bugger off one of these days." Peter looked at Harry and saw the tension drain out of him as he sat back in his chair. In an instant he looked like a lost little boy.

"Pirate, the only reason she's coming to see you this evening is that Barbara and I have convinced her that you love her and that it is merely your work load that's keeping you away. She agreed to come on one condition, and that is unless you promise her that things will change, she's going to give you the push."

"Hell's bells, have I been that bad, Pete?

"You've been worse than bad, Harry, you've been a complete wanker!" Harry sat there in silence for a while, looking surprisingly composed, but it was the pipe puffing away in his mouth that did it. Inside he was in a turmoil.

"Pirate, that's not all I've got to say to you. I must tell you that I've resigned. And I've bought that farm at Karoi you and I have discussed. I'm going farming."

"Shucks Pete, why didn't you tell me?"

"When Harry? You're never bloody around to tell anything to."

"Oh, Crikey, I'm sorry, Pete, I've really mucked up haven't I?"

"Well, I don't think that it's too late to sort it out Harry."

"Pete, that's wonderful news about the farm. When do you start?"

"Two months time. Look, I've got some leave I have to take before I leave the police, why don't you take some time off and let's go to Kariba or something? Barbara's taking leave also so maybe you can get Annie to do the same? It'd be great if we could all go away and play, so to speak."

"You're on, Pete, if Annie says yes."

"Brilliant. Now the last thing I wanted to say," Peter said, fishing in his pocket, "is that I was the one who took your signet ring off your finger."

"What? Wow! I thought it had been swiped at the hospital. I assumed that they'd cut it off."

"No way, José. I took it off when I found you at the prang, because I thought that it may block the blood flow to your finger." Peter held out his hand. In his palm was Harry's ring. "Sorry it took so long for me to return it to you. I meant to give it back to when your plaster came off. I kept it in my cuff-link box and every time I've seen you, I'd forgotten to bring it."

"Crikey, Pete, you're a superstar." Harry took the ring and placed it on the little finger of his left hand. "Hell it doesn't fit any more, I'll have to get it made smaller."

"No don't, Harry, you don't realise it but you look like hell. You've lost weight; in fact you look positively scrawny at the moment."

"Wow, how about that?" exclaimed Harry looking closely at the ring.

"Hello." The soft voice came from behind Harry giving him quite a jolt. He leapt to his feet in embarrassment.

"Hello Annie, how are you?" he looked at her sheepishly and quickly stepped around his chair to usher her into the circle of chairs around the table.

"I'm fine, but you look positively scrawny, Harry Andrews." Harry giggled.

"Are you all in cahoots against me? That's exactly what Pete has just said."

"Well you are. You're working too hard."

"Yes I have been but that's all changing as of now. Hi Barbara, thanks for bringing Annie."

"What do you mean? I didn't bring her."

"I know you did, Pete has told me everything, and I'm very thankful." They all sat down and Peter ordered drinks for the women. Harry sat forward and took Annie's hand. Looking at her intently in the eyes, he said,

"Annie, I know now that I've been a complete arsehole. Will you please forgive me and let me make it up to you?" His voice was very low and as he said it his voice cracked.

"That's the second time you've asked if you could make it up to me, Harry Andrews," said Annie. She looked a little disappointed.

"Annie, I couldn't bear to lose you." The tears were welling in his eyes.

"Hey guys, we'll see you two later," said Peter in embarrassment. He got up, grabbed Barbara's hand and was about to drag her away. "We'll leave you two to talk."

Harry turned to him, wet eyes flashing in the light. "You bloody stay put," he said fiercely. "I want you two to see me do this, because I've been as much of an arsehole to you, as I have been to Annie." Peter and Barbara promptly sat down again and busied themselves sorting out the drinks, which had just arrived. "Annie, I promise to never ever again ignore you or to bury myself in my work at your expense again." He was actually choking back the tears as he said it. Annie couldn't believe what she was seeing and hearing. She broke down herself.

"Oh, Harry!" she cried and threw herself at him, scattering her handbag onto the floor and knocking over Harry's beer. "Oh, my dear Harry, how could I have doubted your love?" She couldn't stop herself from sobbing into his chest. He gripped her firmly to him, he was now crying openly. Everyone around, including Peter and Barbara, seeing what was going on, turned away in embarrassment. After a while he gently placed her back in her chair and while Peter ordered him another beer, he wiped the tears from her face with his handkerchief, wiping his own eyes on his shirtsleeve.

"I haven't finished yet," he said.

"What?" said Peter, "you mean that there's more to come? You'll have us all crying in a moment, Pirate." He laughed trying to inject an element of levity into the sombre moment.

"No I'm not finished and it's not funny." Harry hadn't even turned to look at him. Instead he gazed passionately into Annie's eyes and said, "Will you marry me." Well that elicited another flood of tears, only Barbara was crying now as well. A man sitting about two tables away got up and came over, concern written on his face.

"Are you two girls alright?" he asked.

"Of course we're alright," blurted Annie looking at the man venomously. "Mind your own business." The man got a hangdog look on his face and turned away. Looking again at Harry, barely visible through the tears running down her face, she asked, "Are you sure, Harry Andrews?"

"Yes, I'm sure Annie Whitworth, I want you to be my wife." Smiles now, everybody started to cheer up. Annie laughed.

"Look what you've done to my make-up, I must look terrible. Yes, I will marry you, you darling man." She found her handbag on the floor and managed to extract a bundle of tissues, with which she started wiping her face. While she was doing that, Harry got his signet ring out of his pocket and got on his knees in front of her. She didn't see him for a moment, so when she did eventually take the tissue away from her face, there he was.

"Annie, I haven't got an engagement ring, but will you accept this signet ring instead?" Unopposed, he took her right hand and slipped the ring onto her third finger. It was a little loose.

"Harry, what do you think I am, a washer woman, it's too big." She cried out in delight. Harry, relieved to see that she was not being serious, laughed with her.

"I know, but Pete only returned it to me ten minutes ago, I haven't had time to have it altered." Everyone was laughing now, including all the people at the tables around them. Someone called for champagne, which duly arrived, despite the fact that the Rhodesian variety was virtually undrinkable. Imports of the real stuff had ended years before.

Annie and Barbara disappeared to the 'Ladies' for a good twenty minutes and Pete couldn't stop grabbing Harry around the shoulders and hugging him.

"Hey, Pete, cut it out, everybody'll think we're tail gunners."

"Who cares," said Peter. Looking at the smiling faces all around him he waved his three quarters full beer tankard at them all and said loudly, "Have you ever seen anything like it, folks?" Cheers and whistles and Harry simpered in embarrassment.

After a while things settled down, the girls came back and the subject turned to the wedding. The two women had it all planned already, and Harry and Peter just looked at each other, shrugged, clinked their glasses and continued drinking too quickly.

"I see from the paper that van Tonder was arrested last night, for fraud," Harry said carelessly, just a throw away line.

"So I see," said Peter, looking absently into his beer glass.

"You can't bullshit me, Pete, what's it all about?" Peter sighed and sat back, took a swig, lit up a smoke and then took another swig. "Come on, Pete, I can read you like a book. What did you have to do with this? Is this about my prang? Come on, split?" Harry looked carefully at his friend, searching for signs that he was going to lie to him.

"Pirate, I cannot tell a lie." He recited what had happened at the beginning of the case and then told them what D. I. Sturrock had established once he'd received the 'operators copy' of the airfield registration folio from Chris Swan. "Bill waited until van Tonder was away, some meeting in Bulawayo or something and then went into the DCA headquarters one night with the ex-Director, who sort of knew where everything was kept. Apparently it took them no more than five minutes to locate the airfield register and to find that the Chris Swan strip entry had been deleted with 'typex' and a new entry inserted over it. The receipt/licence form pad was also found, in the bottom drawer of his locked desk. The relevant folio copy had been torn out with a note stapled in its place to the effect that that particular folio had been removed due to an error and had been reissued." All three of them sat there opened mouthed listening to this litany of cover-ups.

"Bloody amateur, surely he would have known that he would have been found out?" asked Harry.

"Not necessarily. He was the boss and he no reason to suspect that we were investigating him."

"Sounds to me that if it hadn't have been for you, Pete, nothing would have been investigated. Does Jim know about this?" Harry gazed blankly into the distance as he said it. Maybe there's a chance Jim will be paid out now, he thought.

"No, and he's not to be told, this is all still sub-judice." Peter took another swig of beer. "I might add that there's a warrant of arrest out for Brad Fischer as well."

"And?" piped in Annie. Harry looked at her adoringly and put his hand out to touch her arm. The response was immediate. She took his hand in hers, pulled it to her lips and kissed it lingeringly, then touched the back of his hand to her cheek. "Love you too," she whispered glancing quickly in his direction.

"Well he seems to have disappeared. CID seems to think that he might have got wind of his impending arrest."

"What's that?" asked Harry.

"Fischer, he's disappeared."

"Oh yes, sorry, I got side tracked," said Harry, a sheepish grin on his face. "Well to hell with Fischer and that mob, tell us about your trip to Kariba. He looked again at Annie. "If they let us come with them, will you come?"

"Oh Harry, how could you think that I would go off with you on a dirty weekend?" She paused, watching the look of dismay come over his face, and then laughed. "Of course I'll come, silly, in fact I've already applied for the leave to coincide with Barbara's."

"Ewww, you're a cruel woman, Annie Whitworth," said Harry giving her hand a gentle squeeze. They all burst out laughing. "Somehow I think I'm being played like a fiddle." He lent over and kissed her and whispered in her ear, "You little vixen." She rested her hand on his thigh and feeling a delicious tremor run through him, she actually blushed as her mind switched quickly to a double bed somewhere with her curled up naked in his arms.

"Friday week," said Peter again. Harry and Annie came back to reality.

"Yeah, I'm sure I can swing that," said Harry. "How long?"

"Well how about the whole of the following week, that'll give us about ten days in the valley[28]. And look, don't worry about the accommodation cost. My buddy, Johnny Walker, at Kariba Breezes, says we can use his place and one of his boats. We have to pay for the use of the boat."

"Hell, who could turn down an offer like that?" said Harry.

"Yeah, all we have to worry about is food and booze and fuel for the boat and getting there and back." Peter leant forward, elbows on his knees. "Johnny's place is magic, right up on top, near Kariba heights, beautiful views, cooling breezes, great patio and all that. I've stayed there before." He paused. "Also, he's got all the fishing gear we might need."

"We'll organise the food guys, you organise everything else," said Barbara.

CHAPTER 10

Harry got back to the air base at about 2:30 am the following morning, parked his old Renault Dauphine in the car park outside the single quarters and went in. He got to his bedroom door and found a note stuck to it with a drawing pin. Its contents were pretty straight forward advising him that URGENT orders had been received and would he come down to the despatch office ASAP.

He was slightly under the weather and dog-tired, so he stripped, grabbed his towel and had a quick shower, put on some fatigues and wandered into the dispatch office nonchalantly paging through a sheath of operational data that had been left for his attention, on the desk in his room. The police Sergeant holding the fort, leapt to his feet.

"Good Morning Sir, thank goodness you're here, Sir."

"Oh, is it morning already?" Harry asked rhetorically, letting out a huge yawn simultaneously. "What's the problem, Sergeant?"

"Both the telephone and the radio have been going berserk, Sir. The whole world wants to know where you are."

"Where is this URGENT order, Sergeant?" asked Harry, ignoring what the man had said. The Sergeant reached out to his 'in-tray' and lifted the top folio off it. Handing it over, he said,

> **Harry,**
>
> **Please lay on air support for a ground search for:**
>
> **Vehicle Description: 1967 Ford Cortina GT,**
>
> **Colour: White,**
>
> **Registration no: F 946 SY,**
>
> **Registered Owner: B. Fischer.**
>
> **Location: Binga and area thereabouts**
>
> **Date of Action to be taken: 12th Sept '73 until otherwise ordered.**
>
> **Priority: URGENT URGENT URGENT**
>
> **Liaison: Officer to report to DCI Sturrock, Binga Police Camp.**
> REF: CID/F/72/936
> ORIGIN: **D.C.S. HUXLEY**

"Here it is, Sir." Harry took the order and casually threw it down onto his desk. He scratched his head, stretched, and then bent over and opened the drawers of his desk one by one. Eventually he found his spare pipe and tobacco and he stood there gazing out into the hangar while he slowly filled his pipe. Making sure that it was properly stomped down he then began a search for some matches. The duty officer stared at him, in amazement that his commanding officer could be so casual about an urgent order. Eventually, his pipe burning away happily, Harry sat down at the desk, leaned back, threw his legs up onto the desk and read.

Bob Warren

Folio No. 0015

OPERATIONS ORDER

BRITISH SOUTH AFRICA POLICE (CID), Central Police Station, <u>Speke Avenue, Salisbury.</u>

Send to: BSAP (Flight Ops.),	From: D. Ass. C. HUXLEY
Attention: **Sup. H. Andrews**	Date: **12th September 1973**
Office location: **Kentucky Air Base**	Office location: **CID HQ.**
Telephone number: **62 4356**	Phone number:

Total pages, including cover: **1**
Comments:

Harry read the order twice and sagged a little. He perched himself on the edge of the duty officer's desk. He thought, what's all the panic about? Bloody typical, everybody gets their balls in a knot over nothing. He looked up at the Flight Operations Schedule on the wall and in an instance absorbed the current situation. Turning back to the Sergeant, he said,

"OK, now who's after me? Give me the 'Coms. Record' please?" the Sergeant handed over the journal.

"Firstly, DCI Sturrock was patched through on the radio, Sir. He was calling from Binga. He wanted to know what the status is on the air support he's requested. Then Assistant Commissioner Huxley called, Sir. He wanted to know, excuse me, Sir, where the hell you were. That was at ten this evening. Then there were two other calls which I redirected, and then D.C.I. Sturrock called again and ordered me to find you."

"OK, OK Sergeant, relax. Give me a message pad." Taking the pad and supporting it on his knee, Harry wrote out a message, and then handed it back to the Sergeant. "Send that off to Sturrock now, then call dispatch, tell them I want FSW fuelled and ready for take off at.., what time is sunrise?"

"Five forty five, Sir," said the Sergeant glancing briefly at yet another table on the wall.

"Take off at three hundred hours zulu. Put into that message, ETA Binga at zero four thirty hours. Then file a flight plan with New Sarum and Kentucky, copy everything, the message and flight plan to Huxley, and then come and wake me up at 4:30 am with a cup of coffee and some sandwiches. OK Sergeant, got all that?"

"Yes, Sir, good night, Sir."

"And, Sergeant?"

"Yes, Sir."

"If anyone else tries to get hold of me, tell them to get lost, I'm sleeping. Good night." With that Harry disappeared out the door, leaving the duty Sergeant standing there open mouthed.

The instance they were dropped off, Annie phoned her parents back home in the village of Halse, Somerset, to give them the news.

"When am I going to meet this man?" asked her father grumpily. He was not amused to be woken in the middle of the night, but Annie's happiness was infectious.

"We are unlikely to get across to England before the wedding Daddy."

"And when have you got in mind for that."

"I've already told Mummy and this call is costing me a fortune, daddy. But it'll be just after Easter next year. Barbara and I haven't finally decided yet."

"What's Barbara got to do with it?" asked her father.

"Daddy, you're the pits, you don't remember anything. I told you we're having a joint wedding."

"Oh, my God!"

"Bye, Daddy, I'll write tomorrow. Love you!" She didn't even wait for his answer and burst out laughing.

"I can just see his face, Barbara." The two of them talked excitedly until the early hours. Finally a thought came into her head.

"Do you know, Barbara, I bet you Harry will forget to tell his folks. I'll have to phone them too." The following morning that's exactly what she did, putting the two families together. Preparations had begun.

The seemingly one good deed David Lestering did, came only after he had been arrested. He told his lawyer to phone Brad Fischer and advise him that he and van Tonder had been arrested.

This proved to be more difficult than it appeared at first sight. The Chete Fishing camp didn't have a telephone, but relied on daily radio communication, via a relay located at a small government settlement some thirty miles away called Binga. This transmitted the call to the camp's booking agent in Salisbury.

So, three things worked against Fischer. The first was that it was 24 hours before the lawyer, through perseverance, was able to locate the agent to pass on the message. The second was that it was only the following morning at 6:00 am, as Fischer was making his daily call and after he'd seen off all the fishermen on their daily fishing trip that he found out about the arrests. Finally, unknown to Fischer, all his, and other's, radio calls were monitored by the police.

So DCI Sturrock, about to execute the Fischer arrest warrant, within 5 minutes of the radio call, knew that Fischer knew. Sturrock promptly instructed their roadblocks at Binga and Milibizi to arrest him, should he try to make a run for it. Unfortunately both the police patrol boats were up the other end of the lake. But rather than asking the army, who had a rubber duck patrol craft at their base at Milibizi, to blockade the approaches to the fishing camp, he did nothing. He thought that he could get to the camp before any of them. In this he was right. So instead, he went to the aerodrome, arrest warrant in hand, to await the arrival of Harry Andrews.

"Binga traffic, Victor – Fox Sierra Whisky, Charlie two ten, calling one-nine-nine decimal five, inbound from Salisbury, now on five mile final, runway two seven. Estimate touch down in two minutes. Other traffic, please advise." Harry made his second approach call as he throttled back and began his 'before landing' routine. It was precisely 6:18 am and the dawn had just broken in the eastern sky behind him. There was no reply for a moment then, after waiting for the other non-existent traffic to reply, Sturrock pressed the transmit button of his portable radio.

"V-FSW, this is Bill Sturrock at the Binga field. Hi, Harry, all clear here, stop mucking about up there and come on in. The water's fine."

"Hi, Bill, what's the plot?"

"No time for breakfast I'm afraid, we're going straight on to Chete. Prepare for immediate turn around after boarding a party of two pax. Do not, repeat, do not shut down. Sturrock."

"Copy two pax, no shutdown, immediate turn around, FSW now short final Binga runway two-seven," replied Harry. The aircraft hadn't even come to a halt when Sturrock ran out with his ever-attentive askari. They climbed on board, buckled up and Harry started the long backtrack to his touch down point. While he did this and his pre-take-off checks, Sturrock briefed him on the situation. He told Harry to fly him straight to the camp in the hope of surprising Fischer before he'd had the time to do anything. He estimated that he would be at Fischer's doorstep by 7:15 am at the latest.

They were in the air for 9 minutes, landed at Chete and alighted from the aircraft at exactly five past seven. They were too late.

Fischer's nose twitched, He knew the game was up. He wasted no time at all as his years of excellent training took over. Within twenty minutes he was pushing a boat into the water. On board were his wife and child, and their bags, pre-packed and ready were just such an emergency. They had just raced, full-throttle across the Chete gorge and were at that point in time creeping very slowly around Chete Island, hugging the rocky bank wary of submerged rocks, trees and sand banks. They heard and saw the aircraft approaching their airstrip from the east. They'd made it by the skin of their teeth.

Brad and Marie Fischer abandoned their boat in the safe keeping of staff at Sinazongwe Mission station and hitched a lift up to Lusaka where he took her straight into the Department of Immigration offices on Cairo Road. Surprisingly they both looked reasonably neat, both in khaki bush gear. He'd even managed to get in a shave on the way, which tended to soften his features somewhat. He presented their West German passports at the front desk. It was 9:30 am.

"Good morning, we wish to claim political asylum."

"Wha..? I.. ah.. Good morning, Sir, Madam," said the immigration officer sitting in front of them. He looked backwards and forwards between them noting that the woman was carrying a small baby on her hip. He was completely confused. "Ah.., yes, Sir. Please will you sit down over there and I will call my superior."

They sat down where indicated and waited while the man, his confused but smiling black face contrasting beautifully with his smart white uniform, raced off down the passage to his right. Two minutes later an older man, his short curly hair already white with age, appeared.

"Good morning, Mr. Fischer?"

"Yes."

"And this is your wife?" He paged through the passports as he spoke.

"Yes, Sir," replied Fischer, showing almost grovelling humility.

"And this is your child?"

"Yes."

"Do you have any papers for it?"

"No, Sir, only his birth certificate."

"I see, well I am Superintendent Mogali, Immigration. You will please come with me."

Fischer and his wife rose and followed the old man through to a cell like interview room at the rear of the building. They were supplied with a cup of tea each and Marie was instructed to feed her child if she wished.

"What, here?" she retorted, open-mouthed.

"This is Africa, Madam; we do not have any problem with mothers breast feeding their babies in public." Marie fidgeted a while and then realising that this man was no longer interested in her, she undid the buttons down the front of her bosom, eventually managed to extract one of her breasts and presented the nipple to the child.

The immigration officer had already started the questions. They went on for two hours and only stopped when Fischer eventually mentioned the name Motswadi. Fischer and his wife had rehearsed their cover story well and Mogali could find no fault with it. They did not disclose that they were wanted by the Rhodesian regime for a criminal offence or for all Fischer knew, for harbouring freedom fighters and gun-running at their fishing camp. But when Fischer mentioned the name Motswadi, the interrogation stopped instantly and they were left alone. Thirty minutes later, three police officers were ushered in and totally ignoring Fischer and his wife, the old man and the senior of them conversed for several minutes in their own language. Then a policeman, acting as if Fischer was a stranger, turned to Fischer. Fischer, in turn, feigned no recognition.

"Mr. Fischer, I am Police Superintendent Motswadi. I am obliged to inform you that your case will take several days to process. Until that is done you will be held in custody. Please bring your family and follow me.

"I apologise for the deception," said Superintendent Motswadi as soon as they had entered the small police safe house. "But it is important that as few people as possible know who you really are."

"Agh, that is fine, Superintendent, I understand and am thankful."

"Also I must apologise for this simple accommodation," said Motswadi waving his hand around. I hope you will settle in all right and relax. It is acceptable for you?"

"It's fine, Sir, thank you. Can you tell us how long we'll be here?" Fischer asked.

"Well that rather depends on your controllers, Mr. Fischer. I shall be in contact with them immediately. I imagine they'll want to debrief you without delay."

"Ya, I await my orders."

"I believe that it shouldn't be long because I understand plans already exist for such an eventuality." Motswadi looked dispassionately at Fischer. "But there is something that you can do for us in the meantime."

"I'll do anything to help Sir."

Motswadi thought to himself that Fischer was too ingratiating, but he was supposed to be an excellent operative. He smiled to himself. No inducements were going to be necessary and better that Fischer became operational quickly and voluntarily, rather than fret away the time waiting for clandestine meetings to be established with the East German Embassy, and then delays while the whole matter was referred back to Berlin.

"We need someone to help us keep an eye on the expatriate community here. We'd like to keep our finger on the pulse of things, if you understand my meaning?"

"Of course, how can I assist you?" Fischer was no fool and saw clearly where this was heading and licked his lips in anticipation.

"Mr. Fischer, you have experience in catering and the resort management business?"

"Yes, Sir, besides my more serious duties, I have run a bush lodge and fishing camp on the river for the last four years."

"Precisely my point, Mr. Fischer. How would you like to take over the management of the Lusaka Country Club? Could you manage that?"

"Certainly, Sir."

"Good! And would you keep your eyes and ears open and inform us of everything you see and hear at the club?"

"Of course, Sir, that'll be easy."

"Thank you, Mr. Fischer. Right, I shall convey your cooperation on to my superiors. I'm sure we'll have you out of here in just a few days."

"Thank you, Sir, I'm much obliged."

Motswadi got up and turned to leave. Turning back for a moment he said, "Mr. Fischer, I will brief you more fully on what we expect from you in due course, but in the meantime not a word to anyone, is that understood?"

"Of course, Sir."

"From now on also your code name in our communications will be 'Claude'."

"Yes, Sir. Claude." Fischer repeated.

CHAPTER 11

At the time, the 180 mile long and 50 mile wide Kariba Dam was the largest man made lake in the world. The first glimpse the four of them got of it was about 10 miles after they turned off the Great North Road leading to Zambia. There, the road starts winding its way through the heavily forested escarpment down off the central Rhodesian highlands. Harry stopped his Renault by the side of the road and they all clambered out and admired the view. In front of them the lake stretched away to the horizon.

"When it was built," said Peter, "it was supposed to be one of the largest engineering feats in the world. Over one hundred Italian workers lost their lives building it and it took three years to fill up.

"It's magnificent," said Annie. "I'm so glad we came."

"I need to go to the loo," said Barbara. "Peter, please come with me and stand guard. She took the toilet roll out of the car and she and Peter disappeared scrambling down low embankment next to the road into the Mopane and Mountain Acacia forest.

Annie snuggled up against Harry and whispered in his ear, "Are you going to have your way with me here, Harry?" He shivered, put his arm around her and said nothing. They leant against each other for a while, Harry with his back against the car.

"I'm still a virgin you know," she whispered biting his ear. He felt a stirring in his loins and broke away, clearly very embarrassed.

"Time to press on, it's still another fifty miles to Kariba village." He looked woefully at Annie and she just giggled and hung onto his arm even tighter.

"You're a coward, Harry Andrews," she said into his ear, this time biting it quite hard. He turned to her again and drew her close, hugging her tight. She could feel the hardness of him pressing her lower stomach and shuddered with pleasure.

"You don't know what you're getting into here, young lady," he said kissing her ear, knowing full well already that she couldn't take it. She tried to wriggle away, but he held tight and she was helpless in his grip. He bent down and starting gently he explored her mouth with his. Her tongue met his almost electrically. He groaned and kissed her passionately, his hands moving on her body. He strayed down and up, pressing her breasts, not so much with his hand, but more with his body.

She felt the back of his neck, the soft hair of it. She became intoxicated by his strength, his smell; the faint scent of pipe tobacco. She felt a heat building in her crotch and hugged him to her. She moved her hips slightly so that his thigh pressed between her legs. He bent his knee slightly increasing the pressure on her crotch. She moved slowly up and down at the same time gripping his head with her hands and kissing him fiercely. She let one hand roam down and soon found his manhood, straining hard against his shorts and underpants. Tracing the outline of him with two fingers her excitement grew.

He forced a hand between the two of them and pulling her blouse out from under her belted jeans, he moved his hand upwards under her blouse. The fact that she wasn't wearing a bra inflamed him further as he caressed her breast, exploring her taught nipple.

The pleasure of it added to the wonderful sensation she was feeling in her loins unconsciously made her move more frenetically against him. Suddenly she lost it and whimpered, almost a mewing sound, squirming in his grasp as an uncontrollable orgasm hit her. Her breath quickened and she dug her fingers into his back as she climaxed.

He crushed her to him, overwhelmed with emotion. Her hand grasping the outline of his penis through his shorts was too much for him to bear and he also succumbed, shuddering as waves of exquisite sensation came over him. She felt his penis swell and pulsate and his wetness penetrate the material of his clothing. She held her hand there stroking him as he jerked repeatedly in ejaculation. When it was over she let out quiet moan and shuddered again, sagging away from him. She looked up at him.

"Oh my God, Harry Andrews, I love you. That's never happened to me before, do you mind?" The tears in her eyes; the flush of her face and her hair all awry said it all. She was breathing incredibly heavily

"Mind, goodness, never, that was the most wonderful experience I've ever had. I'm shattered by your love," said Harry softly, still gazing at her intently and holding her so tight.

They stood, sagging against the side of the car for a long while and it was only an old bus, full of smiling black faces peering out, that came trundling past them that woke him to the problem facing him.

"Only trouble is I'd better clean up and disguise this lot. And they've taken the toilet roll. Have you got some tissues handy?"

She laughed and stepping quickly to the door of the car she leant in and fetched a handful of tissues from her handbag. Harry managed to sort himself out just in time to greet Peter and Barbara as they climbed back up onto the road. He didn't even notice how flushed they were, so great was his own embarrassment and effort to hide the front of his shorts from their view.

They arrived at Boulder Ridge in Kariba at about four that afternoon and organised themselves. After unloading the car the men hurried off on foot down to Andora Harbour, leaving the girls to arrange things at the house the way they wanted. Peter directed Harry through the modern village of Kariba, mimosa, syringa, jacaranda and flame trees lining every well laid out avenue. The leafy canopy for the most part cast a cooling shade along most of their route down the hill. Temperatures here regularly exceeded 40°C throughout the year.

They walked into Johnny Walker's boat yard and in half an hour had the boat organised for their first fishing trip set for two days hence. They both realised that they'd better spend the first full day with the women.

Stopping off at the Kariba Village bottle store where they picked up beers, a bottle of locally produced vodka, coke and other mixers, they arrived back at the bungalow to be greeted with instructions to light the braaivleis (*barbeque*). They were in their element. As the sun went down over Sugar Loaf hill to the west throwing beautiful golden hues into the evening sky, they all sat there sipping sundowners and gazing out over Kariba Gorge with the huge dam wall on their left. Although nearly two miles away, the noise from the water thundering out of the sluice gates was very loud, drowning out all other sounds.

"I'm worn out, Pete," said Harry.

"Well you should kip alright here, if Annie lets you." They all laughed.

"No, I don't mean that," said Harry looking fiercely at all of them, a slight smile on his lips. "I mean the job, I've had enough. I must have averaged no more than two hours sleep a night for the last week."

"Well, why don't you ease up and get someone else to do it all?" suggested Peter.

"I can't. And HQ says they can't spare me anyone else right now. Oh, I meant to tell you, Fischer's skipped the country." He told them about the fruitless search and how the car had been found in its shelter at the fishing lodge near Binga.

"There's a boat missing though and it's been sighted at the Sinazongwe Mission on the Zambian side of the lake."

"Ah, hell, don't worry about him, Pirate, he'll turn up again and then we'll nail him."

"Yeah, I suppose you're right. Anyway as I was saying; I think it's time for a change. There's got to be more to life than working your fingers to the bone day in, night out." Harry got up and fished another 'Castle' beer out of the cooler bag lying on the table near by. He flipped the lid and then relit his pipe. "Are there any other farms for sale in the Karoi area, Pete?" he asked puffing up a storm in his pipe bowl.

"You serious, Pirate?"

"Yes."

"I'll ask around, don't know of anything right now. I did hear a rumour that the old fellow next door to Chris Swan is thinking of packing up and retiring down to South Africa."

"Will you check it out for me?"

"Sure, I'll find out when we get back."

"Shucks; that would be perfect, I might even be able to keep up my flying if his strip is right next door." He turned to Annie. "My darling, do you think you could handle being a farmer's wife?"

"Wild horses wouldn't keep me away, you know that," laughed Annie. "And besides, Barbara will be there after we all get married. It'd be incredible."

The waters of Lake Kariba have many guises. They are sometimes incredibly rough and dangerous when the strong winds, which accompany the common tropical thunderstorms, whip up the surface of the lake into a fierce chop credited with responsibility for sinking many a fishing boat. On other occasions it looks like an ice sheet, the surface is so smooth. Not even a slight swell disrupts the illusion. It was such a flawless day when the two men collected their ski-boat and set out for their first day's fishing. Searing heat accompanied it, but Peter applied full throttle to the 65 horsepower Johnson outboard motor and they seemed to fly over the lake. With the cooling wind in their faces they raced across the lake past Long Island to the Sanyati River gorge. It was so exhilarating not a word was spoken until they cruised into the steep wooded confines of the gorge. The gorge itself is fairly forbidding and the heat hit them as if they were entering a blast furnace. But the water is deep and cool and the fishing excellent.

A pair of Fish Eagles[29], high on their perches, watched their every move. Peter looked at them smiling to himself, they know the score. Rhodesian fishermen made a fetish of throwing morsels to these eagles just to watch them let out their famous cry, swoop down from their lookouts and snatch one from the water.

"Don't worry," he said to them, "we'll throw you some fish to eat in due course." He stopped the engine and they set up their rods for trolling.

The beer started flowing.

Several hours later, sunburnt and washed out from too much beer, they slowly retreated out of the gorge towards Spurwing Island, game viewing along the bank of the lake before commencing their long run across the water back to Kariba. Then something bobbing in the water close to the shore alerted Harry. He jerked upright.

"Hey Pete, look over there," Harry urged, pointing towards the shore, "there's a dead Hippo[30]! Let's go over and have a look. I've never ever been up close to one."

"Go over and have a look be damned," Peter replied while turning the boat carefully towards the huge grey lifeless lump that lay in the water next to the shore, "we're going to get the tusks!"

"Well, that's OK with me," said Harry. "Let's face it, it been a pretty boring trip so far. I thought this lake was just full of fish waiting for me to arrive and catch them." Harry didn't realise what Peter had in store for him. But, anything to relieve the monotony. After they'd all spent the first day on a guided tour around and under the dam wall, the girls had elected to go up to the club for the day, play some tennis, swim and generally relax. The men had collected the boat at 5:30 am and had been fishing all day. All they'd caught were three small tiger fishes, the largest about 6 pounds. Peter had actually insisted that they all be thrown back into the water. It was hot as Hades and both men were looking forward to the high speed trip back across the lake with the cooling wind in their faces.

This distraction was just what was needed.

Peter steered carefully through the petrified trees that had been drowned as the lake rose, after they finished the dam. These dead trees were treacherous and could easily put a hole into the hull if one wasn't careful. Harry sat in the bow searching the water carefully as they drifted in towards the shore. He occasionally shouted, 'left', 'right', and 'straight'.

They got right up to the dead hippo. The bank was just a foot or so above the water, grassed and stretching away to the tree line about 100 yards inland. A small group of magnificent waterbuck[31] were grazing just along the way, their white tipped tails swishing and drawing attention to the distinctive white ring of hair around their rumps. As they approached the buck stopped grazing and looked at them warily. They didn't run off although the alpha bull placed himself between the approaching craft and his herd. He stood there alert, ears pricked and huge horns held high. The boat bumped into the dead hippo, rocking it slightly in the water and that seemed to act as a signal to the waterbuck bull. Turning on his heels, he snorted, threw his tail straight up into the air, and the whole herd turned and cantered off into the trees.

"Jesus, he's a big bugger isn't he?" Harry said taking his eyes off the disappearing herd and peering closely at the Hippo. "Something's been having a go at it; see those bloody wounds in its neck."

"No, I think it's just keeled over as a result of a fight with another Mvuu *(hippo)*. Look at the size of the gouges in its side there. Yeah, I reckon a fight." said Peter, "Go on, in you go, Pirate; here's my knife," Peter ordered, tossing over a huge sheath knife at the same time.

"You must be mad in the head, Pete. I'm not getting into that manzi! (*water!)*' Harry cried, 'It's as dangerous as shark infested custard!"

"No, go on, Pirate, harmless, I'll keep the flat dogs *(crocodiles)* away," Peter laughed, "besides, there aren't any around."

OK, so what do you do when your best friend is just looking for an excuse to bate you for not having enough courage? Harry thought. It was a typical blazing hot day in the Zambezi valley and they were burnt to a cinder. The beer had all been drunk, and despite copious quantities of water out of the lake, Harry felt dehydrated and was ready to beat it back to Kariba. They were in an uncleared[32] area known as Hydro Bay off the Matusadona Game Reserve. They were probably about 20 miles, as the crow flies across the water, from Kariba, but really only about 3 miles from Spurwing Island. Harry had heard that the hotel on the island had a great pub. The thought of an ice cold "Castle" made his mouth water. But he could just see Pete telling the boys how he wouldn't go into the water because he was too scared of flat dogs.

"You're on!" Me and my big mouth, he thought. He grabbed the knife and gingerly lowered himself over the side leaving his veldskoens[33] on. You don't go stomping around in these waters without your shoes on, he thought; you'll cut your feet open on something in a hurry. The fact that he'd forgotten his pipe and matches in his pants pocket annoyed the hell out of him because when he found bottom and a sound footing, the water was up to his chest. For a moment, it felt ice cold and was very refreshing. He waded over to the dead Hippo. That wasn't particularly easy as there were patches of sodden floating Kariba weed[34] in the way, which were difficult to push through, while he tried to keep his footing in the slime and mud underfoot at the same time. All the while, Peter was shouting instructions.

"Just you concentrate on looking out for flat dogs," Harry shouted back. He reached the dead animal and started on the lower jaw. The stagnant water around the beast came up to his waist and the hippo, which had obviously been dead for a while, was soft and stank to high heaven!

Within minutes he was being worried by hundreds of flies and mosquitoes but continued to hack away. Cutting away the lips and gum around the tusk was easy and he had the first one loose within a few minutes. He jabbed the knife into its neck, and started working the tusk backwards and forwards using both hands. While he was doing this he noticed that Peter had started moving the boat around, using the motor, randomly, first this way then that.

"What the hell are you doing, Pete? You're making waves!"

"Don't worry about me, you just get those tusks!" Peter shouted back, so Harry did just that. The first tusk was out in about 8 minutes and as Peter came past, Harry tossed it into the boat.

"I say, Pirate H. Andrews, that's a great bit of ivory," Peter laughed using Harry's nickname as only he could. Peter leaned forward and picked it up, "it's all of 16 inches long and 3½ inches thick."

"Great, you want to do the next one?" Harry responded, "It's bloody filthy in here, and I need a smoke!" He extracted the knife from the Hippo's neck and started on the other side. More difficult, this one, he thought, because it's under the water. He had to do it by feel, the water was so full of gunge, and he couldn't see a thing. By now his chest, arms and hands were covered in gore and above the water, also covered in flies and mosquitoes. Below the water he could feel the small fish nibbling away at his arms and fingers as he gouged around with his hands and the knife. I'm surprised I haven't cut myself, he thought.

"Just you watch out for those bloody flat dogs, Pete." He shouted out, lurching up and down as he cut away, constantly looking up and as far as he could around him. He couldn't really see too far, being so close to the surface of the water.

"Nah, nothing, they'll keep away while I'm zooming around in the boat," Peter called back. At that moment Harry actually saw one, not 60 or 70 feet away.

"Oh, no! Well, what's that?" he asked, pointing off to one side with the knife. Me, Mr. Cool, I'm shitting myself, he thought to himself. But I'm not going to give Mr. bloody Templar the pleasure of seeing me give in. Suddenly cutting those tusks out had become a little more urgent as doubts as to his safety started to creep into his mind. He went at it with renewed vigour. The second tusk went much slower than the first one, and he was concentrating more on the flat dog, convinced that there must be others by now. He'd never been through this sort of situation before. Also, deeper down in the water, larger fish were starting to nibble away at his legs, nothing serious, he knew, but he was really starting to get jittery.

He thought, No, bugger this, I'm out of here. He put the knife, handle first, into his pocket as far as it would go and turned to make his way back to the boat, only to find that Peter was now about 30 or 40 feet away, going round in circles.

"Come on Pete. Get me out of here!" he exclaimed not wanting to go into deeper water. He was up to his chest as it was.

"What's the prob? You giving up?" Peter teased, but thankfully, turning towards Harry at the same time. No flat dogs were visible, so Harry relaxed and for a moment actually thought of going back to the hippo and finishing the job.

"You'd better hop in," Peter said, "There are a few of them around now.'" Harry couldn't see any, probably hidden amongst the weed, but as Peter drew the boat up next to him, he did a pretty good imitation of a baboon shooting up a tree. As he leapt into the boat and rolled over the gunnels, the water erupted behind him as a massive set of jaws came out, opened wide, and full of teeth, and then snapped shut. The flat dog lunged at his leg, but it was a no go, it was too late. Peter gunned the motor at the moment 'critique', and the beast missed taking Harry's foot by inches.

"Thanks a lot, you shithouse. Do you think you could have cut it a little finer?" asked Harry. Peter just laughed.

"Not even close! But that's the least of our problems, look over there." he said looking towards the shore. Harry turned round, and there, coming out of the trees, were two armed game rangers, about 100 yards away. They beckoned to the two men in the boat to come in, shouting 'Boya kunu! (Come here!)'.

"Not a bloody chance," muttered Peter, "we're getting out of here!" He turned the boat and started moving away. One of the rangers menacingly unslung his rifle, and beckoned frantically. Within seconds though, they'd started moving into clear water, and for a while Harry stood up and waved at them. Seeing this, Peter applied full throttle and

Harry nearly fell into the water again. They both doubled up in laughter. As they set off back across the lake towards the dam wall out of sight in the distance. Peter sighed,

"Oh well, we got one tusk anyway."

"What do you mean, 'we' got one?" shouted Harry over the noise of the motor now at full throttle. He was laughing at the sheer exhilaration of it all. "I must tell you Pete, that's the best most exciting thing I can recall having done for years."

"It's the life, hey?"

"Beats the hell out of endless work." Harry moved further back towards the stern of the boat so that he could talk to Peter without having to shout. "Pete, do you know, since I arrived in Rhodesia in January nineteen seventy one, I haven't had one break. It has been all work and no play and I'm fed up."

"Pirate, don't think that if you go farming, it'll be any easier."

"I don't, but at least if you want to take a short break, you can. I mean, I haven't done any of this before, it's bloody wonderful. And hell, am I sunburnt? It's going to hurt like hell tomorrow. But I've had more fun today than I've had since I arrived."

They arrived back at Andora Harbour just before dark and Annie and Barbara were on the dockside to greet them. Annie took one look at Harry, smelt him, put her nose in the air and said,

"Harry Andrews, you're walking. There is no chance in the world that you're getting in that car with me. You stink! What have you two been up to?" Peter raised the tusk,

"Look what Harry caught," he said, "a bloody huge great hippo; killed it with his bare hands and then he braved the crocodiles and tiger fish and the game rangers to get in the water and salvage one of its tusks."

"I thought you went fishing," said Barbara. "And you too, Peter Templar, you stink of beer. You're obviously both drunk. You two have been naughty little boys today and deserve a spanking."

"I'll sit on the roof," offered Harry.

"Can my hiding wait until I've had a shower," said Peter They all burst out laughing and not withstanding the protests from the women, the men climbed into the car as well and, windows all down, free air fan blowing as hard as it could, they went home.

The extended week went too fast and before they knew it they were on their way back to Salisbury.

Brod and Marie Volker, under the alias Brad and Marie Fischer, moved into the manager's house on the edge of the golf course at the Lusaka Country Club and were an immediate hit with the members. Brad was courteous, efficient and obviously knew his trade. Service picked up, various items such as beer and whisky seemed not to run out so frequently, the club maintenance and cleanliness improved and the staff seemed to be better turned out and less sloppy. And most important to the members, the beer was cold, served in frosted glasses.

But what everyone was talking about was the improvement in the food. Marie had taken it upon herself to sort the kitchen out and did a good job of it. New dishes and variations on the usual fare started to appear on the blackboard behind the bar and after a week a proper menu was to be found in an imitation leather folder on each dining table. And the food was good. You got a medium rare steak when you asked for it.

White table cloths made a re-appearance; the old boys in the club couldn't remember when they'd last seen them. The quality of the club breakfast jumped to new levels, they even got served cold fresh orange juice without being charged extra.

Turnover increased rapidly and Marie started doing proper afternoon teas for the ladies. White tablecloths were laid out on the veranda and the ladies started to gather there each afternoon to hear and tell of the latest scandals. Tea was served with light sandwiches followed by pastries, hot tea-cakes and scones. Where Marie got the strawberry jam they couldn't fathom.

"She's very common," was the whispered consensus, "but she certainly knows how to do things. And those tea cakes, toasted to perfection, just like those we used to be served at the Crathorne Hotel in Cleveland near Teeside."

Their whispered comments and everything that was said by the men in the bar did not go unnoticed. Hovering ever-attentive waiters reported every word they overheard back to Fischer. And the folio of notes locked in the bottom drawer of the desk in his office began to get quite thick.

CHAPTER 12

The chills, sweating and headaches started about four days after they got back. Within the week Harry was back in hospital in Salisbury, only this time he was admitted to the fever hospital tucked away behind the Lady Chancellor Hospital on Moffatt Street extension. His clever antics butchering the hippo in the water of Lake Kariba had exposed him to the bites of the female anopheles mosquito. He had contracted malaria.

"You bloody arsehole, Pirate," was all Peter could say to him, in reference to the fact that Harry obviously hadn't been taking his Daraprin anti-malarial prophylactic regularly.

"Oh my darling, are you alright?" was about all Annie could say to him.

"Time for your next jab," was all that the nursing sister ever said to him, or so he thought. He overheard her commenting to the other nurses that if his skin got much more yellow from all the quinine they were pumping into him, he could pass as Chinese and change his name to Harry Lee. He wasn't amused but after the headaches passed and he was able to think cogently, he began to value the quiet times when he wasn't the centre of attention.

After days of gazing out of his window at an unkempt Pride of India bush, which blocked out his view of everything else outside, he came to the most momentous decision of his life.

"My mind is made up, my love," Harry told Annie as she walked in.

"No hello? No how are you? Are you losing your sensibilities towards me, my darling?" said Annie putting a bunch of flowers into the basin in the corner of the room. "Well don't worry about it. I'm fine and if you're always going to be this difficult when you're sick just give me a warning so I can get someone else in to look after you."

"I'm sorry, Annie, you're right, but you should know that I love you very much."

"Then show me your love, don't just lie there being scratchy. You're not the first person to get malaria you know."

"Annie, you've got me wrong. I'm not complaining again. I'm happy."

"You are?"

"Yes, yes, yes! I've made the most important decision of my life." Harry looked at her appealingly. "Please sit down, my love, I want to talk something out with you." Annie pulled the room's one chair to the side of the bed, sat down, folded her arms and looked grimly at him.

"Remember the countryside we came through on our way back to Salisbury? Remember as we moved through that spectacular scenery?"

"Yes."

"Well that was what finally got me thinking. And now I've decided, provided you approve of it."

"What?"

"I'm going to buy a farm and turn you into an honest working woman."

"When, Harry?"

"If Pete can get the information I need on this farm he mentioned, I will resign the day I buy it."

"What happened to make you become so keen all of a sudden? You've never had this massive hankering to go farming before." Annie was positively sceptical. She sat there, slightly breathless and leaning forward in credulous wonder.

"My darling Annie, I have for the first time in my life really come to terms with my own mortality, and I've woken up to the fact that life is too short to live out one's days slogging away and never enjoying yourself. Nearly losing you was an abject lesson in how workaholics end up in the divorce courts and that I could not bear. I've told you this before."

"So?"

"Well, that, coupled with the freedom and excitement I experienced at Kariba, and now this. Being stuck in bed with malaria, sick as a dog; life is passing me by, or I'm wasting it. I've realised that I have to move, change the course of my, our lives. All I've really done so far is work in between bouts of drinking and partying. That isn't life; it has no meaning, no substance. I want to create something with you, live a joint life with you. I want us to share our joys, our anguish and pains. You don't know what I'm doing at the moment, and even if you did, I wouldn't be allowed to tell you anyway. I don't know anything about nursing and it doesn't really mean anything to me either. So what I'm trying to say is that if we're to be together, I want us to be together in everything. Work, play, dreaming, eating, loving, sleeping, everything! Do you understand?"

For a moment Annie just sat there, almost open mouthed. She'd never heard him enunciate any of his ideas so honestly and clearly before. In fact, she'd never heard him speak at such length before. She stood up and came close to him, taking his hand.

"Yes, my darling, I do understand and it makes me very happy."

"Will you go farming with me, Annie?" He lay sweating in the bed, looking incredibly vulnerable. "Are you prepared to take the risks with me and the hard work?"

"Of course I am, you old Pirate." She leant over and kissed him. "Your breath is very smelly, Harry. Don't they let you clean your teeth?" She turned away and walked over to a basin of water to soak a flannel so that she could cool his brow.

"Yes, but it's the drugs apparently. You should smell it from this side of my mouth, it's awful." They both laughed and she hugged him.

"Miss you," she said, gently wiping the sweat away from his forehead. She ran her fingers back through his hair.

"Miss you too. However, I'll be out in a few days and I'm not allowed to go back to work for another three weeks."

"Good. That'll give me a chance to fatten you up again. If you were looking scrawny before, you should see yourself now."

The young South African golf pro was impressed. The new manager of the Lusaka Golf Club hadn't ever played golf before but within weeks he was striking the ball further and straighter then most of the old boys who played in the Wednesday school.

"Mr. Fischer, I think it's time you played a game."

"Ach, no, Jannie, I'm not good enough yet." Fischer smacked another ball straight down the range.

"Look, Sir, you are and I'll tell you, you're better than most of the old boys who're going out to play this afternoon. So I've asked the club captain to come out today so that he can play with you and give you a starting handicap."

"You're sure?" asked Fischer dropping his 5 Iron back in his brand new bag.

"Yes, and you know all the etiquette now. You've got all the kit. It's time that you went out and played, even if you don't shape the first couple of times."

Fischer appeared cagey and reticent but, under the seemingly embarrassed exterior, he was delighted. Here was his chance. He knew that if he was ever going to get close enough to the members of the club, then there was only one way to do it; on the golf course. That was where the intimate discussions between the players took place and he had to be accepted by them as a golfer before he'd really find out what they were thinking and what they were up to.

So the transformation from being the strange new manager into one of the guys, an intimate, was rapid. Within weeks Fischer was being invited to join the players for a beer or two. They found him so congenial and entertaining. He had obviously spent time in the bush hunting and fishing and was able to keep them enthralled with amusing tales of mishaps and dangerous escapes in the wilds.

He got to know most of the members on first name terms and found that most of what they had to say about politics was seditious.

"Bloody government doesn't know its arse from its elbow," said Colonel Arlott, "bloody lot of them should be lined up against the wall and shot."

"Yeah, but these Rhodesian so-called freedom fighters are even worse. Especially that idiot Mtundwa, bullet's too good for him. Shit, now he's spouting on about wiping out the Barotse, calls them vermin. Don't know about you guys, but I like the Barotses, great guys. Hell he's not even a Zambian," said Patrick Kursten. "Remember what he said in Dar es Salaam[35]. Shit, next thing, he'll be talking about having all us ex-pats shot."

Fischer leaned back in his chair and looking at the two men through squinted eyes over the top of his beer tankard as he drank. He thought, carry on like this you capitalist arseholes, and you will be.

Then he met Chester Templar, introduced to him by a Captain Derek Miller. Mien Gott, he thought, this is that bloody policeman's father. He steered the conversation very carefully worried that Templar would recognise who he was. But he needn't have worried. Chester Templar never even had an inkling of the connection. But Fischer's mind raced ahead. This is how I can get that arrogant bastard. Teach him to fuck with me. Fischer's face gave nothing away and indeed his manner was positively gushing. He accorded both men expansive hospitality and even remarked on them to Col. Arlott.

"I must say, James, that man Templar, he's a good man."

"Good golfer too," huffed Arlott, still smarting after losing a game of snooker against the two. "But don't bet against Miller either, his golf is deadly, three handicap."

"Yes, he is also a fine fellow. But how do they get to be such good golfers? I don't think that I'll ever have a single handicap."

"A lifetime of hanging around clubs like this. Too much time on their hands, and too much money," mused Arlott.

That's rich coming from you, you old fart, thought Fischer. You never seem to spend any time anywhere else. Always nestling up against the bar huddled with your mates. I wonder what you're up to.

Fischer met with Motswadi towards the end of March and handed him a carefully fabricated dossier. They were sitting in relative discomfort in a Land Rover overlooking the Kafue River. Fischer was supposed to be out fishing having taken the day off. He had driven down to the river in his own car positively bristling with fishing rods and gear. The guys at the club had waved him away with a laugh.

Motswadi said nothing for a while, reading carefully through the report and the dozens of notes attached to it.

"How do you know that Miller is the conduit?" he asked eventually.

"Well it's obvious, isn't it? Every time he flies back to Rhodesia, he first clears a post box at the Lusaka Post Office. It's Box 391."

Motswadi continued questioning Fischer for over two hours, going backwards and forwards through the papers on his lap repeatedly. Finally, he sat up straight and sighed, seemingly satisfied.

"These disclosures, if they can be verified, are very serious, Mr. Fischer." He closed the file and then reaching down, slipped it into the briefcase lying on the seat between them. "You've done well. Leave this with me. I'll contact you if I need anything else. In the meantime you'd better get out and do some fishing, or you'll be the laughing stock at the club." Fischer got out of the vehicle and picking up his rod, bid farewell. Motswadi leaned across and spoke after him through the open window. "And, Mr. Fischer, forget about those spoons, they don't work with these bream. Squeeze some bread into a small ball, stick it on a small hook and just dangle it the water, you'll catch plenty." With that he started up the diesel engine and reversed away from the bank sending up billows of dust all over Fischer.

Three months after coming out of hospital Harry was the proud, but very much poorer owner of a tobacco/maize farm 5 miles north of Karoi, which was only 15 minutes drive from Pete's place. He moved onto the farm on the 31st January 1973, some three months before he was due to go to England to get married. Those three months were the busiest he's ever had, but he had never been happier. His body filled out again and became work hardened. His skin lost its yellow tinge as the sun darkened the exposed parts of him. Annie loved it also. She came out to stay every time she had a few days off duty until she and Barbara, both of them relieved to get away from the back breaking work, left at the end of March to prepare for the weddings in England.

When even that does not prove to be the syrup
needed to fulfil life's needs, to take another yet again?
To throw aside the accepted,
the ways expected of the protégé and set out on that new course?
Please give me the taste, the ordeals to test my feet,
So that in trial I might know.

So that I may break out, extend beyond the mediocre,
allow me to reach a balance, a harmony, an arrangement of strings
so that I may play my symphony.
Not only for myself, my peers, but also, in care for another.
Give me the strength to learn the notes, the power to love,
so that in realisation, I do know.

BOOK 2 – LOVE

CHAPTER 14

*T*he dog was soaked and so was he. He got the key into the lock, jammed his foot in the door, leant down to pick up the dog and dropped the plastic shopping bag onto the front step. The plastic quart milk bottle came flying out, hit a concrete flower pot, the cap flew off and milk sprayed all over the path.

"Shit!" he exclaimed. The dog escaped his clutches and leaning as far as he could to grab her as she bounced away lapping at the milk that now formed a big puddle on the pathway leading to the front door, he fell over, landing on his right shoulder in the puddle of milk and dirty rainwater.

"Oh what the hell!" he burst out laughing and getting onto his hands and knees, he knelt there in the rain his body jerking he was laughing so much. "You bloody arsehole, Andrews," he said to himself and with a mixture of tears, milk and rain covering his face, he looked up straight into the eyes of his mother now standing just inside the front door peering out imperiously. He burst out laughing again saying "Sorry, Mum, don't know what happened. I just lost it." He climbed to his feet looking very sorry for himself and started to clear up the mess of soggy bread rolls, a plastic pot of margarine, tomatoes, cheese and a bottle of pickles, "Thank God that didn't break," and the now three quarters empty milk canister.

"Do you know, Harry?" The rain was pelting down now as he looked up at his mother, "that's the first time you've laughed in the six months you've been here."

He smiled, looking at her with not a little discomfort. "Have I been that bad, Mum?"

"Welcome back, Henry Andrews. Now if you continue standing there you'll catch a death, come on, don't worry about the carpet, it can always be cleaned."

Her use of the name Henry signalled approval, he knew, so he walked in, started stripping off his parka and then remembered Bonnie. Laughing again, he pulled the parka back up over his shoulders.

"Sorry, Mum, it's not over yet, I've gone and forgotten Bonnie." Handing Bunty the soggy bag of groceries He went out the front door again calling the dog. It took him ten minutes to find her cavorting around with a cocker spaniel on the Methodist Church lawn down on Reedley Road.

"Bonnie, come here," he shouted. She saw him and ran immediately to him. He knelt down, ruffled the wet hair around her neck and picked her up in his arms. Trudging back up the road to the house he looked up into the sky and shook his head. He yearned for the sunny hot blue skies of Africa.

"Come on, you rubbish, let's get you indoors and dry you up." Ten minutes later he was sitting in front of the gas fire in Bunty's lounge sipping the hot tea she'd made for him. Bunty had resumed doing her 'Telegraph' crossword.

"This weather does carry on doesn't it?" he said.

"Wait a few weeks, Harry, and you'll then see and remember what England is all about. When the spring really starts, it is the most beautiful place in the world." She looked out the window. "The weather report says that we can expect more rain until Thursday, then some cool fine weather going into the weekend. Nine letters, middle letter C, 'Tory writing to soldier who's drafted'?" she asked.

"Conscript," he immediately answered nonchalantly.

He infuriated her with his ability to whip through crosswords.

Then he suddenly started, sitting up and looked out of the window. The rain was pelting down, driven down almost horizontally by the stiff south westerly.

"What's the matter," she asked, "you're not getting a chill are you?"

"No Mum, I'm all right. I just had a sudden thought flash through my mind."

"Oh, what's that?"

"Well, remember the wedding, how it rained like this? Do you remember how beautiful she was?"

Bunty filled in the clue and then put her crossword and ballpoint down on the side table next to her. She then kept very still, she knew what was coming, and knew also that these sessions were good for him, acting as a catharsis. Linking her hands in her lap, she let him talk.

They woke on the Friday morning, dazed.

"Do you know," said Peter from his bed, "it's a heck of a long way from Karoi in Central Africa to.., where, the hell in England are we?" Harry laughed, leapt out of his bed and put his running shoes on.

"We're in Somerset just outside the village of Wedmore. It's a little village near Cheddar that is only a slightly bigger village near a town called Weston-Super-Mare, which is just south west of a city called Bristol. Any the wiser?"

"No! How would I have ever have heard of.., what's it called?"

"Wedmore, and you should have heard about it."

"Oh, why's that?"

"Well, in the year eight hundred and seventy eight, King Alfred the Great and a marauding Dane called Guthren signed a peace agreement here. Today it's called the 'Peace of Wedmore'. That agreement brought an end to all the wars that racked Britain almost continuously since the Romans left. It led to nearly two hundred years of peace and the creation of the United Kingdom of England. This island has been invaded only once since, in the year ten sixty six by William the Conqueror. Coffee or tea?"

"For coffee, I killa da bull. Thanks, but shucks, its cold here."

"Cold? This is not cold; this is spring, its lovely."

Peter pulled the duvet up even tighter around his head. "Don't wake me, I'll wake you," he said disappearing completely.

Harry trotted downstairs into the kitchen. There was a pot of coffee already brewing. As he picked up the phone to call Annie, he looked out into the back yard and through the steady rain could see his mother, cloaked and wearing wellingtons, bending over next to the chicken run. No sign of his father or brother; probably out in the pastures, he thought.

"Hello, my darling," he said.

"I knew it was you, you yummy man," she replied. "Isn't this rain horrid?"

"Welcome back to England, Annie. I like these new fangled press button phones though. Beats the hell out of breaking your fingers on those old black wheel diallers we still have back in Rhodesia. How's it going?"

"Well Mummy is all of a dither. Thank goodness for Mrs. Forester, she's really calm and organised. Barbara's so lucky."

"Nonsense, love, remember the brunt of the ceremony is on your Mum's home turf. She's bound to be nervous. How are the dresses?"

"Oh Harry, they're so beautiful, you'll love them."

"Hope I can get it off quickly afterwards," Harry laughed.

"Harry Andrews! My body, that's all you want. I knew it all along!" They chatted together for a few more minutes.

"Look, lovee, I must run, got to be in Bristol in an hour, Dad's out on the farm somewhere, Pete's not even up and Mum's just getting some eggs."

"OK darling, give everyone my love; see you at four."

"OK lovee, enjoy your day. Love you!"

He poured a mug of coffee for Peter, climbed the stairs and put the coffee down next to Peter's head.

"Pete, we've got to move buddy. Bristol's half an hour away and we're due to get our wedding suits at ten thirty. I'm going out to find my old man. That'll be a giggle, putting him into tails. I've never seen him in anything other than overalls, or occasionally, an old tweed jacket when he goes to the pub. Listen you lazy bastard, I've left Barbara's phone number under the phone in the kitchen. See you just now." A grunt emanated from under the covers and a head emerged.

"Thanks, Harry, see you."

In those days the newly formed British Airways had already started flying international flights in and out of Terminal 3 at Heathrow. Harry and Peter had arrived the previous afternoon, worn out. Two days prior to that, Harry had picked Peter up at Mount Hamden aerodrome northwest of Salisbury, flown him to Bulawayo where, after clearing customs they caught one of Jim Leonard's Dakotas to Jan Smuts, Johannesburg. From there they boarded a BA 707 which then flew them over night to London. The reception party to greet them at Heathrow was most un-English. Their two fiancés with their parents were there, with Harry's parents and his brother Richard, and Peter's sister Gail and her husband Joss who lived in West Malling in Kent. Hugs and kisses, oohs and ahs, introductions all round, relinquishing baggage to eager hands; it all went by in a haze. What made things worse was that both the men had really tanked it up in their own small en route party somewhere over Africa.

Next, came the long haul back to Wedmore. The Whitworths and Foresters went on to Taunton after a quick cup of tea. Gail and Jos had gone back home from the airport. They were only coming down two days hence on the morning of the wedding after fetching Peter's mother from the airport that morning. Peter's Dad, Chester, was unable to get off work and was in the Republic of Zambia on urgent business for his Company. That afternoon, now in Harry's father's car, Harry and Peter drove down to Annie's home.

Coming into Halse from the southeast is sudden. One moment you're in the country west of Taunton in Somerset, much of it hidden by hedgerows, the next moment you rise out of the Vale of Taunton Dean and you're in the village. Most of the buildings are old, built of stone and have thatched roofs. Harry drove slowly and carefully up the rise and to the right around a blind corner into the village. The men could see the old stone tower of St James church up the hill to their left as they drove past.

"Annie says the gate to their place is just along here, it'll be on our left. I think she thought we'd be coming the other way. Look for the signpost to Fitzhead. The gate to the Manor House is right next to it."

"There it is," Peter said too late. They'd actually gone past the entrance. Harry stopped, checking his rear view mirror as he did so and then reversed 10 paces or so to be able to make the sharp left turn into the gate. They drove up the drive.

"Crikey," said Peter, "They do all right for themselves."

"No, they don't actually. It's a listed building and they can't afford to maintain it all," said Harry. "Annie says that they've actually shut up several rooms, and are leasing out flats over the old stables, that'll be that lot over there on the left. The old man is seriously considering selling the whole damned place, as he calls it. He's already had to lease off a lot of the land to other farmers and so on."

"Well it's very nice all the same."

They approached slowly up the driveway and admired the gracious old rock Manor House. Someone must have seen them because all at once there were people pouring out of doors from all directions. Harry stopped the car and leapt out just in time for Annie to throw herself into his arms.

"Hello you," he said hugging and kissing her fiercely on the lips.

"Wow, careful, Harry," she said coming up for air, "you'd better not bruise me." She laughed into his face, still hanging onto his neck.

"That's better, you looked terrible yesterday," she said. Harry pouted, put her down and turned to say hello to everybody else. Peter had gone through a similar sort of greeting from Barbara. Formalities over with they went in to the house where tea had been laid out in one drawing room or another. It didn't take long however for the subject of the pub to be broached and the four of them, taking advantage of a break in the weather, beat a retreat down the hill towards the village.

Chester Templar, Peter's father, had indeed in the meantime flown up to Zambia in the company Learjet for the third time in as many months. At that precise moment he was getting ready to leave the pub at the Ndola aerodrome and go over to the Mine club where he normally spent his evenings when he was in Ndola. The town is one of several towns in northern Zambia, which service a rich mining area known as the 'Copperbelt'. The airport at Ndola is in fact an old Air Force training base. It has a large number of mostly disused buildings on it, which were constructed out of rolled corrugated iron sheeting. There are rows of frangipani and flame trees lining car parks and walkways, lime wash circling the tree trunks at the bottom to ward off the termites. Then there are 'pride of India' and oleander bushes lining every edge in the place. It looks a lot like an American airbase on some Pacific atoll.

Chester had said farewell to his colleagues and had just picked up his kit bag, when the door was thrown open and a half dozen or so Zambian policemen rushed in. A Sergeant came in behind them and ordered everyone to stand still. He was followed by a plump, but well turned out senior police officer.

"Good evening, gentlemen. I am Police Superintendent Motswadi." He smiled pleasantly at the gathering in the pub, notable for its absence of black faces. "I am afraid to advise that I have here warrants of arrest for Mr. C. Templar," he turned and looked at Chester, "and Captain Derek Miller." Derek, the Learjet pilot, was still propping up the bar draining the last of a Castle lager from his glass. "Would you two gentlemen be kind enough to accompany me to the vehicle outside?" All very civilised and pleasant; Chester and Derek had no idea at all as to why they were being arrested. Ignoring the cat calls and advice thrown after them, the two men obediently followed the Superintendent out into the night and climbed into the back of the standard issue grey police Land Rover that was waiting for them.

Hand in hand, the two couples strolled down from the Manor House to the road and turned left out of the gate. Just 50 or 60 yards further on there was a heavy wooden door, unmarked, in the last building on the right hand side before the road swung right and down out of the village. This was it, the door to 'The New Inn'. In fact there was nothing new about it and Peter couldn't believe that it dated back to the 16th Century.

The whole village it seemed was there to greet the women and meet the men and the beer flowed.

"Come on, Pete, try this Courage Best,"

"Yewk! Tastes like horse piss," said Peter, "I'll stick to lager if they've got some." Everyone laughed.

"You've got no chance, pal," said Harry, "this is an English country pub. They only serve natural English beer from a barrel."

"Well, I've got Murphy's," said Simon, the publican, "you might like that, it is rather like a Guinness." The happy band watched as Peter got his tongue around that and seeing that he found it palatable, settled in to find out more about these two lads that were taking off two of their favourite daughters. The only thing that they really established was that these 'fureignerls' could drink copious quantities of beer. Mr. Whitworth arrived sometime later to break up the party and get them back up to the house for dinner. He was however waylaid, managing to gulp down two pints of 'Best', before Mrs. Whitworth was forced to come down herself, much to the amusement of the villagers and farmers there. The most notable thing about the evening is that Peter and Harry were too drunk to drive so Richard had to come down from Wedmore to fetch them home for the night.

Chester Templar woke up not knowing where he was. It was dark and a strong smell of disinfectant, urine and body odour assaulted his nose. For several moments he was weirdly disoriented. Then it all came flooding back as his eyes got used to the dimness and he was able to make out his surroundings. He was in a cell roughly 8 foot square he thought. And it was clean. As he lay there he reviewed what had happened and wondered how it was that he'd come to be arrested.

Generally speaking, he'd had nothing but polite efficiency from the police in Zambia; the few times he'd had any dealings with them at all. He supposed it must have been someone he knew who was up to no good, and by association, he had been implicated. He wasn't too worried about it as the word must have got out and the company would be doing something about it.

He got up off the bunk and noticed that a towel had been draped over the foot rail of the bed. Surprisingly his kit bag was at the foot of the bed as well. He quickly went through it to see what had been taken if anything and noted that only his treasured Swiss Army knife was missing. He thought they must be very sure of themselves because they'd even left his passport and other papers in the bag. He looked around and took the two paces needed to get to the toilet, which was also spotless, and had started to relieve himself when he heard a rattling of keys and the cell door opened. An immaculately turned out police Constable came in.

"Good morning, Sir. Please would you bring your towel and shaving equipment and I will escort you to the shower." Chester pulled up his fly; the flushing mechanism even worked; grabbed his kit bag and the towel and followed the policeman out into the passage. As he walked, he noted that there were only three other cells in the passage. A security door was unlocked and opened in front of him and he was beckoned through before it was locked again. He was taken into a small shower room, containing only three showers and three basins. He was told he had 10 minutes. He quickly stripped off and finding that the water was hot, shaved, showered, cleaned his teeth, put on a clean shirt, underpants and socks and was ready in 9 minutes. He knocked on the door, which was immediately opened, and from there he was lead into another room. The smell here was of coffee.

There were two people in the room, both of whom he recognised. It was a small plainly furnished dining room containing one long wooden table with a four-seat bench on either side. From a hatch on the left as he entered he could hear kitchen noises and after a while the strong smell of bacon came wafting through. One person, short, thickset, haggard and virtually unrecognisable because he'd been beaten up, was standing, cradling a metal coffee mug in his hands, while the other was seated on one of the benches, back to the table. They looked quizzically up at him as he entered.

"Hello old boy, its Chester Templar, isn't it?" the short thickset man asked rhetorically, his words slightly slurred because of the swellings on his face. "I'm Lieutenant Colonel James Arlott. Remember you from the club." He turned slightly towards the other man, "You remember Patrick Kursten, Fisal's fertilisers. Where did they grab you?"

"At the airport pub in Ndola," said Chester. "They've also arrested Derek Miller." Chester's bewilderment was obvious. "Where are we?"

"Mumbwa," said Arlott matter of factly. "What did they arrest him for? He's just a pilot." Arlott filled a mug with coffee and dropped in two lumps of sugar. "Here, have some coffee; you look as if you need it." Chester shivered as he took the mug gratefully. The notorious Mumbwa! His thoughts ran wild recalling all he'd heard about the place.

"Thanks. I don't know why they took him, but I suppose we'll know soon enough. I imagine he'll be joining us shortly. He was brought in with me last night." He looked closely at Arlott. "What happened to you?"

"Well, I was asleep and when they woke me. I told them to fuck off and come back tomorrow. Silly really, but hindsight is always 100%.

"Well, they've got someone else here as well. I overheard the jailers talking about a woman," said Kursten. "But more ominous is the fact that they're saying that we won't be here long. They're waiting for a UNIP firing squad to arrive."

"Oh shit, what's this all about, does anyone know?" Chester felt a cold shiver go down his spine.

"Not a clue old boy, not a bloody clue!" whispered Arlott.

Most of all, Harry Andrews remembered four things about the wedding. The bells of the 12th Century St James' Church, Halse; the way his heart almost stopped when he first saw the brides, especially his, although he wasn't sure who was who at first because of the veils; the rain, and finally the sight of his bedraggled brother Richard running up the hill through the rain towards them. They had been about to get into the car covered in wet confetti, after the wedding reception.

He and Pete, each to be the other's best man, sat there on opposite sides of the central aisle, slightly damp. They were seated on the front pews in the east chapel, in front of the colourful alter. They both listened to the bells. Behind them, when they occasionally turned round, by looking through the fretwork of the heavily carved Screen separating them from the rest of the church they could see the bell ringers moving rhythmically in the ringing chamber. Waiting for their brides to arrive, most of the time was spent looking up at the East Window with its collection of small Flemish and Italian medallions and panels, heraldic shields and Biblical scenes. Peter was quite engrossed studying Patience and Temperance, the two buxom ladies at the bottom.

The church slowly filled up behind them. Harry was occasionally distracted from the window and ran the fingers of his left hand over one of the famed carved bench ends while trying to work out what the carving depicted without looking. He occasionally looked around, recognising few faces. His mother and father, an aunt, some local cousins and their children, and his great grandmother, granny 'Bunnie', came in and sat just behind him. His brother Richard had to stay back in a care-taking role at the farm. Mrs. Whitworth and Mrs. Forester were there, and Peter's Mum, sister and brother-in-law; but the rest of the people in the church, albeit all relations of the brides, were strangers. Just behind them and to the right, stood the 'Eagle' Lectern, carved he'd been told, in 1902. It was so ugly it was beautiful, but Harry was pleased that it wouldn't be in use that day.

Finally the pealing of the bells stopped and there was a lot of scuffling and fiddling around at the door to the church and then the organist started the bridal march. Harry and Peter stood up as they'd rehearsed and turned as one. The pews had been pushed a little to either side to widen the central isle to accommodate four people in a row.

Down the aisle they came, the two brides, their respective proud fathers between them. Harry could remember nothing else. The sheer emotion of the moment almost overwhelmed him. He felt butterflies rampant in his stomach and the tears welled in his eyes. He was barely able to see. He forgot everything that happened after that until the moment the priest declared them 'man and wife'.

Then he kissed her. He forgot about the vows repeated jointly by the two couples, the moment when Peter and he exchanged rings to place on their brides' fingers, and more especially, he couldn't even remember the signing ceremony in the bell-ringing chamber. He remembered only that kiss. He looked down into her eyes and he genuinely felt weak at the knees. Peter and he had decided together that three seconds was about all the crowd would bear so the kiss was not prolonged. He pulled up and looked at her intently and whispered,

"You're so beautiful."

CHAPTER 15

The retreat from the church was a disaster. The rain poured down and a dozen men were pressed into lining the pathway to the east end of the church, with umbrellas over the path. It wasn't much help. The girls' wedding gowns got soaked and Harry dropped his top hat in the mud. Finally they all fell into the limousine deliriously happy.

"Congratulations you guys," said Peter.

"Thanks Pete, same to you." Their wives were already in a huddle working out what they were going to do about the wet dresses.

The retreat from the reception in the Manorial hall was no better. They had just managed to bid good-bye to everybody, both the garters and two bouquets of flowers had been thrown. The village idiots had ruined the limousine with lipstick. Tin cans and streamers were dripping their colours all over the white vehicle. The chauffeur was edging the limo through all the parked cars down to the road, when a bedraggled sight ran up the driveway. It was Richard, Harry's brother. He was panting and water was pouring off his raincoat as he unceremoniously opened the door of the limo and tried to get in. They made space for him wondering what the problem was.

"Bad news I'm afraid, Peter" he said after a few moments catching his breath.

"What is it, Dickie?" Peter leaned forwards, deep concern reflected on his face.

"Well, you'd better read this." Richard undid the top buttons of his raincoat and brought out a copy of 'The Times", refolded to page 5. "This morning's paper." Peter took it from him and read.

Five Europeans Detained
From Reuters

....

In Lusaka, Friday.

Five Europeans were arrested today by Zambian Security Police in a sweep described by Joshua Tiringula, State attorney as a move to rid Zambia of subversive elements.
The accused are Captain Derek Miller, a Canadian pilot of the Mines services jet aircraft known to have flown the President on several occasions and at least one other of the accused, Mr. Chester Templar, a Quantity Surveyor employed by the mines. Two of the others are Lt. Col. James Arlott, also employed by the mines, and Mr. Patrick Kursten, a fertiliser company representative. The identity of the fifth detainee is unknown.
Mr. Tiringula said in a brief press statement, that the five accused were spying for a foreign power and would appear before a Tribunal next Thursday, preparatory to being remanded for trial. He said that the police were seeking a sixth member of the spy ring and were acting on a tip off from an informant "Claude". He said that the six were working under the instructions of the Central Intelligence Office in Salisbury, Rhodesia, and that they had been passing information on troop movements and the activities of the freedom fighters.
When approached and asked to confirm the rumour that the detainees were to be shot, President Kaunda said, "The audacity. Do they think I'm blood thirsty?"
The five accused are believed to have been detained in the Mumbwa Prison, 100 miles west of Lusaka.

THE TIMES SATURDAY MARCH 30 1973[36]

Peter went very still and then after a few minutes passed the sodden newspaper over to Harry. While Harry read he quietly explained to their wives what had happened.

"Sorry guys, this rather messes up our plans." Peter turned around and pulled back the privacy screen separating them from the driver. "Driver, see if you can reverse back up to the house. Something's come up and we won't be leaving just yet." He turned back to the others. "Look, I'm going to have to go in and tell my Mum and Gail and Jos. Harry, this is where we put our thinking caps on."

"I'll come with you, honey," said Barbara climbing out with him.

"You sure? Could be some wailing and gnashing of teeth." Peter sounded grateful. He opened the car door and quickly threw up a brollie. Then taking her arm, they moved quickly into the house. Richard followed them in.

Harry took Annie's hand and looked lovingly into her eyes.

"My darling, I fear that this spells the end of our plans to honeymoon at your folks place in Spain. I think we'll be going straight back to Rhodesia."

"Oh, Harry, who cares? We have to be there for Peter."

"You're right. And I'm buggered if I'm going to stand by while some tin-pot dictator shoots my mate's old man." She felt, rather than saw the cold anger building up in him. He had suddenly gone into himself and she saw only hard resolve in his face.

"Harry, don't do anything stupid, not now."

"Don't worry, darling, we'll sort this out."

"Oh come on, Harry, what can we do?"

"If necessary," he looked up her again, his eyes cold blue, "we'll go in and get him out." She shivered, beginning to understand the steel in this man she'd married only two hours ago. She also began to have doubts and not a little fear crept into her mind. He must have sensed that she was worried because he turned and put both his arms around her and hugged her very tightly.

"Don't worry, Annie, you're safe with me. I promise you we won't do anything unless we have to." He kissed her gently on the lips and lingered there for a moment. Then he drew away and sat upright on the wide seat.

"Mum's the word now, OK? Come on, let's go in and get the ball rolling." He turned to the driver.

"Driver!" The man looked around. "You never heard any of that did you?"

"No, Sir."

"Because if I hear one word," Harry spoke almost in whisper, "you've got a problem, you understand what I'm saying to you?" Like the driver, Annie looked at him, dumbstruck. What she saw was a fighter, sitting there, leaning forwards aggressively, shoulders hunched, and realised then that this gentle loving man was very, very dangerous. The driver obviously did too. With a moment's hesitation he let out his breath, looked away and confirmed,

"Yes, Sir."

"Good, now be a sport and dump all of our luggage back in the house." Harry was smiling disarmingly again, "Someone will tell you where to put it." He felt around in his pocket and found a £10 note. He folded it and passed it over, "this is for your trouble. When you've done, you can go off back to Bristol. Thanks a lot, pal." He took Annie's hand again, "Come on, love."

They ran up the steps and entered the house. There was a quiet buzz to the remains of the wedding reception. People, worried looks on their faces, were milling about, not quite knowing what to do or say. Peter and his family were obviously in the privacy of the study.

"Hey, what's this folks?" Harry called out. Peter had obviously told them briefly what had happened. "Bar's still open and really there's nothing to worry about, Peter's dad will be out in no time, you'll see. Now come on all of you, relax! Grab another drink." In seconds the atmosphere improved and a hubbub started, people firing questions at Harry from all sides. Harry fielded them all with dispassionate ease and slowly the room emptied as people drifted off. Annie again marvelled at the ease Harry handled situations, and her doubts disappeared. This man would kill to protect her. Tears of gratitude and love came into her eyes and she had to leave the room to hide her emotions.

Some time later, the caterers had already packed their stuff away and left and the band had long since gone, Mrs. Whitworth went around closing all the curtains.

"Now the sun decides to come out," she commented, "bit late."

"Good omen, Mrs. Whitworth," said Harry helping her clear up.

"Harry, it's now Mum, or Elizabeth. Don't you dare call me Mrs. Whitworth again young man."

"Yes, Mum." They laughed together relieving the tension somewhat. Harry's folks also helped clean up and then Peter came out of the study.

"Mrs. Whitworth, would it inconvenience you if we were all to meet in the dining room?" She hesitated.

"Mum, we have to have a council of war, metaphorically speaking of course," said Harry.

"Certainly Peter, is your Mum feeling well enough? Would she like to lie down?"

Peter smiled, "She's a tough old lady, Mrs. Whitworth, she's fine. Should we have a meeting of the clans, so to speak, for Harry's so called council of war in say thirty minutes?"

"That's fine," said Harry, taking charge, I'll get everyone in there. With that he disappeared for a while into Mr. Whitworth's study. Annie looked in at him and seeing him busy on the phone, went back to help her mother.

"To start with, Harry, I think that Annie and you should still go off on honeymoon." Peter stood next to the fireplace, a stiff scotch clasped in his left hand, his right arm being held tightly by Barbara. Harry hovered nearby while Annie helped her Mum distribute cups of tea to those who wanted.

"Negative, Annie and I have already discussed it. We're coming back with you, that is final and not open to discussion," said Harry. He looked fiercely at Peter, forcing him to laugh.

"Well, that settles that," said Peter. "Easier than I thought. Right, the second thing is to sort out flights back to Johannesburg."

"Done! I've already phoned BA and we're flying out tomorrow night, flight BA six-seven-two at twenty-one-thirty." Harry looked fiercely at Peter again. "Your Mum's on the same flight."

"Crikey, you have been busy. How did you manage to organise that?" asked Peter in amazement.

"Know a couple of people, besides us aviators stick together." The tension in the room measurably decreased. "Also they're giving us refunds on the Spanish tickets." Harry bent over and slung another log on the fire.

"Anything else I might not know about?" Peter looked at his friend, the question written on his face.

"As a matter of a fact, yes I've also just spoken to Jim. There'll be a Dak waiting for us in Johannesburg on Monday morning. He'll fly us straight back to Salisbury." The whole room was stunned. Harry looked around.

"Hey, what's the big deal, transport's my business, least I could do."

"You're not all going to travel together on a small aeroplane are you," asked Harry's Mum.

"A Dak is the safest aeri flying, Mum, nothing to worry about. Anyway it's a twin engine airliner of which there are more flying than any other aircraft ever built."

Jim Leonard was at Jan Smuts Airport, Johannesburg to meet them. He had received customs clearance for a ferry transfer to Lanseria, another smaller regional airport just completed, on the northwest side of the city. From there, the five of them would be flown directly to Rhodesia.

Harry sat in the right hand seat in the cockpit of the Dakota for the flight up to Rhodesia and once they were maintaining Fight Level 10[37] and on track, Harry was able to talk privately to Jim.

"Jim, will you lend me your new King Air?"

"Sure, what for?" Jim leaned forward and tweaked the rudder trim wheel. His nonchalance didn't deceive Harry one bit.

"Pete and I are going into Zambia to get his old man out." No prevarication, no fudging, just straight out with it. Jim said nothing for a while.

"Why the King Air?"

"It's a twelve seater, it's quiet and it can land and take off in less space than a Charlie two-ten or BE thirty-five".

"Only if I fly you in and out. Any sign of trouble and I'm out of there, OK?"

"Done!" Harry lent over and shook Jim's hand.

"How do you intend to organise communications?"

"Bit of a problem, I don't want to schlep one of those heavy military radios in. Cut down on my fire power."

"Hold it," Jim said, "King Avionics are producing a new aeronautical hand-held, the KN ninety-nine, the size of a telephone hand set, battery life 5 hours continuous. I'll get some and we can use a top end frequency. Nobody will think of listening out for us."

"Thanks Jim. As for arms, I may come back to you. Pete and I are going to try Bill Sturrock at CID first and then Mick Glover. If I have no joy with either of them I'll let you know."

"Be bloody careful, Harry, don't trust anyone to keep their mouths shut, you hear?"

"Yeah, but if the Zambians let them go during the next three weeks then there won't be a need. Now, Jim, do you think one of your ground staff in Lusaka could participate in a small way? Someone like Joseph?"

"Depends, if it will in any way endanger him and his family, the answer is an emphatic no."

"Good Lord no. I may want someone on the ground before hand to distribute some booze to the guards and wardens." Jim burst out laughing.

"Harry Andrews, you never cease to amaze me, you are a bloody pirate, you."

They arrived in Salisbury at almost the exact time that a government spokesman in Lusaka announced that there was increasing pressure from the masses for the detainees to be shot with no further recourse to a tribunal or costly court case. Harry and Pete just looked at each other saying nothing.

They arrived at Peter's parent's house and without further ado, the wives were trundled into Peter's Land Cruiser, advised that the men would be out in two days and sent off home out at Karoi. Peter sorted things out for his Mum who was exhausted after all the travelling and worrying. He put her to bed after a stiff Scotch whisky, courtesy of Harry's time with Trans Afrique Air. She went out like a light.

Harry and Peter sat down and started planning. As usual Peter had his nose put out of joint because Harry had already lined up an aircraft, sorted the thorny problem of radio communication and had already worked out how to get the fire power they were going to need.

"Shucks, Pirate, I reckon your nickname is very apt. You are a bloody buccaneer. All that's missing is the eye patch and your cutlass."

Harry laughed, "That's the second time someone has said that to me today. Well, maybe I'll wear one when we go in, might frighten the warders and guards enough to entice them to lay off."

"Fat chance. Now have you anyone else in mind to come in with us?"

"Yes, Sampson."

"Sampson? Hey, that's not a bad idea. I'll ask him." Sampson, or police Sergeant Ndlovu as he was previously known, had resigned from the police with Peter and now worked on Peter's farm as the 'Boss Boy' or foreman. Harry knew something of his background. At the age of around eight, he had watched his father die after being bitten by a boomslang[38] that he'd dislodged from their chicken coop. He'd taken three days to die, the blood draining out of him through his eyes, nose, mouth, ears, fingernails and anus. Two months later, his mother had been gang raped and murdered by some thugs from Bulawayo. So he had walked through the bush 30 miles to Tegwane Mission, where the Roman Catholic priest, after hearing his story through an interpreter, had taken him in. Sampson learned to speak English quickly and the teachers soon realised they had a really intelligent boy on their hands. Not only that, but he grew big and strong. He excelled in the boxing ring, and by the age of sixteen became the Southern Rhodesian junior heavyweight boxing champion by knocking out the champion, a young white policemen named Peter Templar. However, Sampson was very impressed by Peter's sportsmanship after he regained consciousness. So, four days later on his seventeenth birthday, he had walked the 56 miles to Bulawayo and joined the police force. Since then he had followed Peter around, seeking transfers with Peter, wherever he was posted. They were inseparable, trusting each other implicitly. He had also helped Harry enormously by finding skilled labourers for Harry. The old man from whom Harry had bought the place had employed only a handful of older men on the place because he hadn't in fact actually done much farming at all in these latter years. Furthermore, Sampson's brother[39], Chadrack, was now Harry's foreman.

"Three of us are enough. Besides, if we're to get everybody out, we've got no more room in the aircraft."

"Deployment?" asked Peter who had long since learned that, in these sorts of matters, Harry was so far in front of him, it was better to just give Harry his head. Harry looked at Peter.

"Shouldn't we wait until we have a plan of the prison before we work that out? However I have been thinking of timing and how to catch the warders off guard."

"Yes?"

"Well I think it's got to be an early morning raid, about three am on a Sunday morning. Furthermore I'm hoping to have a man on the ground before the event to get the warders all pissed. I'm thinking of an accident outside the prison gates, scattering African beer all over the show for them to pick up and steal." He hesitated as he thought about it. "No; too much to leave to chance. Anyway I'll work something out."

"I'm sure you will, Pirate, I'm sure you will."

"I'm not finished yet."

"Oh, what else?"

"We have to warn the detainees that we're coming.'"

"And I suppose that you've already worked out how to do that?"

"Yes, you're going to do it," smiled Harry. "You have to establish communication with your father, starting tomorrow. Even if you have to go to Zambia and knock down doors to get to him, you have to. He has to be ready when we hit the gate. Also he may be able to get us a lot of inside intelligence, number of guards, locked gates and doors, where they keep keys etc."

"Ok, I get the message. I'm glad you left me something to do. I'm beginning to understand why Huxley had you promoted so fast."

"Nah, I was letting him screw my sister."

"But you haven't got a sister, Pirate."

"Yeah, that's right!" they both burst out laughing again.

"God, this is fun," said Harry. "My farm for a prison!"

CHAPTER 16

The sun burned down on Harry and Peter as they entered police HQ for their appointment with Detective Superintendent Bill Sturrock CID. Inside the building seemed to be hotter than out in the street. Sturrock, drenched in perspiration, rose to greet them as they entered.

"Congratulations on your promotion, Bill." Harry and Peter said it almost as one.

"Thanks, guys, take a pew," he said gesturing at a couple of straight-backed wooden chairs scattered untidily around. "Tea?" Without waiting for a reply he shouted at a passing duty Constable and then dropped into his chair, slung his feet up on the table in front of him and swore. "Christ, this is the hottest April I can remember. Where's the bloody rain?"

"We've had enough out at Karoi," said Peter. "Just another inch or so and I'll be ready to bring in the tobacco and maize."

"Suppose it pleases someone somewhere," said Sturrock. "What's this I hear you two got married?" Nods and everyone leapt to their feet, handshakes all around, smiles. The commotion attracted the attention of other passing policemen and it seemed that an endless stream of guys came in to congratulate them, or frequently, when the man was married himself, to commiserate. At last it settled down, their tea arrived and

Sturrock leaned back onto the rear legs of his chair. "Ok guys, what can I do you for?" His reversed the word order intentionally. Peter smiled remembering Sturrock saying that once before to him. It indicated that a relaxed discussion could follow, although they were both fairly grim faced.

"The Zambian Government is threatening to shoot the 'seven'," said Harry. Since the arrest of the original five Europeans for spying, a sixth and then a seventh had been arrested. No one knew the identity of the seventh and last person.

"Well there's not an awful lot we can do from this end, Pirate."

"We know that, but you can help us." He looked across at Peter. "Pete and I.., this is off the record hey, Bill?"

"Yeah, sure."

"It's not going to happen," said Peter quietly.

"How do you mean, what can be done about it?" asked Bill.

"Well Pete and I are going in to get them out, even if we only get Chester Templar."

"What? Are you mad, do you know where they are?" Bill Sturrock had dropped his chair down onto the floor with a thud and leaned forwards over the desk-table. He looked at them intently and saw bleak determination written on their faces. "Oh, oh, you are serious."

"Yes, Bill, we are serious. So serious in fact that we know how we're going to do it, more or less when we're going to do it, and with what." Peter kept his voice very quiet. There was a hint of menace there, which Bill Sturrock had seen before during the fraud case.

"Crikey, guys, what can I do to help?" Bill shrugged and despairingly spread his hands palms up.

"You can give us information, Bill, police and troop movements in Zambia, what they're armed with, plans of the gaol, which rooms or cells they're all being kept in, and so on. Complete denial is of course totally acceptable to us, and we're both still bound by the Official Secrets Act." Peter sat back and got out his cigarettes.

"Hey I'll have one of those," said Bill. "I gave up but hell, guys, do you know what you're getting into? This could start an international furore." He caught the cigarette Peter threw across to him, followed by the matches.

"We don't give a stuff, Bill," said Harry. "They cannot be allowed to get away with this kind of shit. Can you imagine how Pete's mom feels? She thinks she's never going to see Chester again."

"We also want three machine guns and some stun grenades," said Peter.

"What, are you nuts? How the hell am I going to get my hands on any of that?" Bill Sturrock looked at them in amazement.

"And some explosives and fuses." Sturrock rocked back on his chair again. "Bill, if these people were working for you, then you have an obligation to help us. If they weren't, then there's even more reason. They're Rhodesians, despite what their passports say, they've been detained unfairly, and it is the duty of this government to get them out, come high hell or low water." Harry leaned forward a little more, shoulders hunched, his body language giving great emphasis to what he was saying.

"Shit!" was all Sturrock could think of saying. He turned and gazed out the window for a while and then said to the two men. "Look, I'm going to have to spread the word a little upstairs and get a bit of support for this. There could be some flak. Can you give me a couple of days?"

"Sure, but pass the word that they shouldn't try to stop us, we're going in, with or without help, and they wouldn't want me getting into any gun-running from RSA would they?" Peter sat back askance at Harry's aggressive stance.

"Crikey, Pirate, you do play hard ball, don't you?"

"You better believe it, pal, and I'd be grateful if you'd convince the others too. We're getting Pete's old man out of there, even if we have to blow up the prison to do it, with everybody else inside it!"

"Next stop Mick Glover," said Harry.

"What's he like, I've never met him?" asked Peter. He concentrated on driving while Harry gazed absently out the window.

"Good guy. He also believes like me that this war is bullshit and Smith should end it. But he does his job because he's a soldier and that's what he's paid for."

"I must admit, since the 'Portuguese Empire'[40] collapsed, I've begun to realise that we're wasting time and lives continuing. I s'pose Smithy is trying to get the best deal out of Wilson." Peter didn't sound convinced.

"It's simple mathematics, Pete, we can't fight the world and we certainly cannot defend all these borders on three countries. It's just a matter of time. Better to get it over with and settle down under a new black bourgeois. Things won't be much different."

They drove out on the Hatfield Road and turned left around the airport to get to the Kentucky air base. The long grass stretching off across the open fields looked parched and wilting.

"Good thatching grass that," said Harry.

"Yeah, and easy to put a match to," responded Peter. "You really must put a wider security fence around your house Harry. It's too easy for the guys to get in close and light your roof. They'll hit you, God forbid, before you know it."

"I'm going to. Jim's flying me up some of that new fangled razor wire they've developed down in South Africa. When it arrives I'll extend the perimeter. Until then though, I'll just have to rely on the dogs warning me."

The guard at the barracks gate recognised Harry immediately and didn't even ask them a question. He saluted smartly and raised the boom for them in seconds. They were ushered into Squadron Leader Glover's office without any wait at all.

"Harry Andrews, you bloody Pirate, great to see you." Mick stood up and rushed around his desk to greet his old friend. "And congratulations, I hear you've got yourself hitched."

"Shit, what's a man to do. She put the screws in from day one. How are you?"

"Busy, busy, as you can see. But my Allouettes[41] are falling apart. I'd love to have you back bringing in spares for me. Jim is still battling, but I don't have the same relationship with his guys as I did with you."

"No chance, Mick. I'm a farmer now. Mick, I'd like you to meet a really good mate of mine, Pete Templar." He turned to Peter. "Peter, this is Squadron Leader Mick Glover."

"Hi Pete, Harry's told me a lot about you."

"He's got a big mouth," responded Peter, "he's been talking about you too." They all laughed. "Nice to meet you at last."

They all sat down, tea was served and after a few ums and ahs, Harry began.

"Mick, within three weeks, Pete and I are flying into Zambia to take his father out of Mumbwa Prison."

"God, so it is your father, Pete. I wondered."

"Mick, I need some help, nothing much and nothing that will come back on you."

"Hit me." Mick didn't even flinch.

"I need to know several things. Firstly whether Zambian radar will pick us up and alert the military up there." Mick laughed, took a swig of tea, choked, spluttered and laughed again.

"Harry, they've been without surveillance radar, military or civilian, for years. Nothing to worry about."

"Right, that leads me to question number two. If we go in, a night operation, will you guys let me come back without shooting us down?"

"What do you intend?"

"Depart Karoi plus-minus twenty three hundred hours zulu on a Sunday morning, land there vicinity Mumbwa; we need about two hours max to carry out the extraction, probably six or seven personnel and then we'll be back in the air south bound by three hundred hours. ETA Mount Hamden airport or wherever at plus-minus zero-three-four five."

"Aircraft type?"

"Kingair two-hundred."

"Well Harry, two things; you can't use Mount Hamden, Salisbury tower will be following you in. Better to use some remote strip that you can fly low-level into. Secondly you've got nothing to worry about from us as long as we know what's happening. It's the South Africans you must worry about."

"That was my next question. Can you keep them off our backs?"

"Sure. You just advise me of your final planning and I'll let them know, and you'll have to confirm immediately before departure, OK?"

"Mick, you're a brick. As for a remote strip, Chris Swan might let us use his; I'll let you know. But now my final question. I need somewhere safe to land within a thousand yards of the prison."

"I'm sure we can come up with something, old boy. Best is the road in of course, but that might have problems. There is actually a strip there you know. Why not just use that?"

"Won't it be guarded?" asked Harry. Peter hadn't said a word. He just sat there staring in amazement at the two men and feeling very inadequate.

"Don't be silly," said Mick. "All they've got is an old munt who wields the fire extinguisher and looks after a Jet A[42] Kerosene tank. Lives in a grass hut to the side of the strip. I suggest you pay him off at the time."

"How do you know all this, Mick?" asked Harry.

"Wouldn't be doing my job if I didn't. We watch every airstrip in Zambia like a hawk." Harry sat back well satisfied with what he'd learnt and looked across at his friend. Shit, this gets better and better, he thought. I wonder if…

"You wouldn't be interested in giving us gun-ship[43] back up?" Harry blurted the question out.

"Not on your Nelly, my friend. I'd be crucified if anyone found out. You're on your own and the only reason I'm helping you at all is that I know you well enough, Pirate, to know that when you say you're going to do something, I'm not going to be able to stop you. So I might as well try and make your little exercise a bit easier."

"Thanks, Mick." Harry paused for a moment. "There is something else."

"With you pal, there always is," laughed Mick. "What?"

"Combat gear, helmets, night glasses, black face paint, medical kit, the usual."

Mick smiled. "Those poor buggers don't know what's going to hit them. Sure, I'll see what I can put together."

They sat together for the next half an hour going through details and during that period, Peter sat there watching the two men plan, without saying a word himself. He was somewhat in awe of Harry and he became acutely aware that this slight man that he'd dragged from that aeroplane wreck, was an inventive and very capable person.

Annie was dropped off at the farm by Barbara at about 3:30 that afternoon. After she had said goodbye, Barbara indicating that she needed to press straight on, Annie got out of the car to be greeted by the entire staff of the farm, their wives and their children. They had turned out to welcome back the new 'missus' of the farm. Annie smiled and laughed with them, enjoying the singing and went around shaking hands with the labourers. Chadrack, the foreman, after attending to her bags, followed her around and introduced her to those that she didn't know. He also made sure that the children didn't pester her too much. She climbed the steps on to the porch and turned around to address them all.

"Thank you very much everybody. The reason that Mr. Andrews, Harry, is not back from Salisbury is that he and Mr. Templar have to do some business there first. He'll be back tomorrow. I am so happy to be here and when he comes I will tell him what a wonderful greeting you all gave to me." They all cheered, relieved that this new missus looked as if she was going to be very nice. Annie turned to Chadrack. "Chadrack, where is George?"

"He is here ma'am, putting all your bags in the house."

"Oh, I didn't see him. Is everything on the farm alright, Chadrack?"

"Everything is very good, Ma'am. We have started to harvest the maize now as Boss Harry told us, and the tobacco is not too much, but it is good. We can start picking in four weeks."

"That's wonderful Chadrack. I am going to unpack now and bathe, but can I meet with you and the headmen at five o'clock. I want to do some things and I want to ask you all what you think."

"Yes, ma'am, I will bring everyone to the veranda at five o'clock." With that Chadrack went off and Annie went in to the house. There she found George in the kitchen. He was putting the finishing touches to a tea tray.

"Hello, madam, I have made you some tea and scones. Is Miss Barbara coming?"

"No, George, she had to go straight to their place. Like me she has got plenty to do." Annie went through to the lounge, still very spartan from occupation by 'Harry the bachelor' and looked dully around herself. She was dog tired and flopped down on the couch. She thought to herself that she would have to make a list of things that she had to do. Her brown hair was all in a mess, a large lock hanging over her face, but she didn't care.

She lent over and poured herself a cup of tea and put a buttered scone on a plate. Munching that, she considered the priorities. First things first, get the clinic started and the farm school up and running again. The vegetable garden must be sorted as well as the furnishings in the house. Only then would she start thinking about the curtains and turning this place into a liveable home. She dozed there for the next hour until George come through into the lounge and clearing his throat thoughtfully to wake her, he told her that Chadrack was back with the headmen.

"Good, thank you. George, will you bring them all tea?"

"Yes, madam, straight away."

Prettying herself up a bit in front of the hall mirror and thinking that she looked a complete mess, she went out onto the veranda and sat down on the step. The men all gathered around her.

"Thank you for coming to see me now but I want you to consider some matters so we can meet next week to talk about them again," she said. A general murmur ensued. The men were intrigued. What did this new mistress want to talk to them for?

"I would like to reopen the farm school." The men all looked at each other and whispered wonderingly. "I know it's only got one classroom, but I think it's important that the small children get what we white people call a 'Kindergarten' or 'Nursery School'. I want all the children who are 5 years old to start going to school and I am going to ask Mr. Andrews if I can employ a teacher for the children and also to teach me your language. That's the first thing. I want you to think about this and discuss it with each other and tell me next week if this is what you want." The murmuring was getting quite loud now and because it was all being spoken in Shishona, Annie didn't understand a word. Chadrack was in the thick of the discussion and eventually turned back to her.

"Ma'am, the men say that the old school building is no good, it is not safe."

"What do they mean, it is not safe Chadrack. I inspected it just before I went away, it was fine."

"No ma'am, that's not what they mean. They mean that it is easy for the other people to come and shoot there."

"Oh, you mean it has no security."

"Exactly, Ma'am."

"I see." Annie thought or a moment. "Where would they like it to be?"

"Inside the security fence, Ma'am."

Annie stood up and marched off around the house, all the men followed her. She could see no building, which was suitable for a schoolroom. Nor could she see any place that one could be built, unless it was in the vegetable garden. Arriving back at the steps, she sat down again and looked at Chadrack.

"If Mr. Andrews agrees, I will tell him to put a new fence up to go around the old stables and then we can convert some of those buildings." There was a general murmur, which Annie could see meant that the men liked this plan.

"Ma'am," said Chadrack, "the men are happy with this plan and tell me that you don't have to wait for next week. They are very happy for you to do what you say."

"Well that brings me to the second thing I wanted to ask you," Annie said. "You men do not know, but I was a nurse in Salisbury, at the St Anne's Hospital." More murmuring. "That is where I met Mr. Andrews. I was looking after him when he had a crash in an aeroplane." Wow, this was all news to the men and the hubbub started anew, but this time much more loudly. This was a very exciting bit of information to tell their wives about. Chadrack had to shut them up.

"Well, I want to start a clinic." Nobody knew what a clinic was except George, who explained to everyone. There was an excited uproar and Chadrack again had to shout to get them to be quiet. "I think that we can put that next to the school also," continued Annie, "when a new security fence has been built, if that is acceptable to you all. Will you consider this matter and come back to me next week?"

The excitement was palpable. There were smiles and the older men present took their hats off to say goodbye to Annie. The men put their empty mugs back on the large tin tray George had placed on the edge of the veranda and rushed off in different directions. Wearily, Annie stood up and went inside to the main bedroom.

Throwing her shoes off, she collapsed on the bed in her clothes and fell fast asleep. George came in later, saw her like that and gently placed a rug over her without waking her.

That's exactly how Harry found her at 7:30 the following morning. He and Peter had left Salisbury at the crack of dawn and after dropping off Peter, he had arrived back at the front door at 7:15 am. He opened the bedroom door and seeing her fast asleep, he tiptoed over to the bed and sat down quietly on the edge.

He sat there for almost five minutes just watching her. My God, but she's beautiful, he thought. He leaned over and gently kissed her cheek.

"Hello, my darling man. You're back." She rolled onto her back and stretched out her arms for him.

"How long have you known that I was here?" he asked leaning forwards and giving her a hug.

"Since you opened the door." She hugged him tightly. "I even watched you watching me, through my hair."

"You little minx. I had no idea." Harry sat up. "I hear you've been busy already?"

"Harry, you must do the new security fence first and I want to start converting the old stables into a clinic and a school room."

"Yes, my darling, I know all about it. Chadrack was spluttering he was talking so fast." He smiled down at her. "I'll get it started immediately." He rose and going through to the bathroom said, "Now up you get, George will have breakfast ready at eight. I've got a busy day and it should have started at six this morning."

"Harry Andrews, you're not going to force me out of bed every morning at six are you?"

"Too right my girl, but at five o'clock. This is a farm and the sun waits for no man. Actually, funnily enough, when you're used to it, you'll find that it's the best time of the day and you'll love getting up early." All he heard as he closed the bathroom door was a huge groan disappearing under the blanket.

During a big breakfast of oatmeal porridge, scrambled eggs on toast with two pork sausages, tomato and wild mushrooms, the two of them discussed their plans.

"My darling, I'm going to be largely tied up with Pete's problem for the next three weeks, although it seems to be pretty well sorted out already, if everyone plays their part. So I'm basically going to have to leave supervision of the building works to you."

THE WYVERN REVENGE

"Harry, all I need are the workmen and materials and I'll get on with it."

"That'll be done today. Chadrack knows a couple of good guys in Karoi and I'll go to the co-op this morning to tell them they're to give you everything that you want. Jim should have the new security fencing here next week and everyone is to drop everything and get that up the instance it arrives. Can't have you working all day in an unsecured area." Harry accepted a cup of tea from Annie and spooned his customary two sugars into it.

"Thank you," said Annie almost as if she didn't believe it was necessary.

"No Annie, this security thing is becoming quite serious. The word I get is that the insurgents have started to target the white farmers in order to make the rural areas ungovernable." He looked at her intently. "And I want you to join the Bisley section down at the club and learn how to fire a rifle and a pistol."

"Oh come on my love, it's not that bad."

"It is and it may be more dangerous than we think. The situation has been deteriorating fast since we went to England. Also, if you go anywhere, you're to take Chadrack with you. He will be armed, so get used to it. In fact, he won't let you go without him."

"How long is this going to go on?"

"Until this government wakes up to the fact that they're not going to win."

"That could take years."

"Yes. Oh.., I've just remembered. Please excuse me from the table, my darling, I want to phone Chris Swan and get to see him." Harry got up and kissing Annie on the top of the head as he went passed her, he disappeared into his office. He came out five minutes later carrying a SLR 7,62mm rifle[44] and a 9mm Beretta automatic. He laid them on the table next to her.

"Here lovee, these are for you. First thing's first and that is to learn to strip and clean them like an expert. If I'm not around, ask Chadrack. He can strip and reassemble these weapons faster than I can."

Annie looked at the two firearms with a distaste that within moments turned to fear.

"You're dead serious about this aren't you?"

"You better believe it, Annie. When you know how to strip, clean and reassemble them both, then I'll teach you the basics about firing them. Ultimately though, the Bisley Club have a police instructor who is better than me, so that's why I want you to go there. Also they give courses in defensive techniques, security and so on. It's important that you attend."

He hesitated, "And let me tell you a little about Chadrack. He is one of fifteen children, has never been to school but can read and write English well, all self-taught. He joined the Rhodesian African Rifles when he was 16, was promoted rapidly to Sergeant major, served in Malaya and Nyasaland[45] with distinction and has been decorated three times. If anyone can protect you, he can and he will, with his life. He hates the insurgents and their cause more than we fear them. And he knows this countryside like the back of his hand, so believe me, when he suggests anything, I listen to him very carefully, as you must. See you later." With that he was gone.

CHAPTER 17

Harry's Peugeot 403 Diesel half-ton truck had 150 000 miles on the clock when he bought it. He took it into Pusy and Diss in Salisbury the day he bought it. Two weeks later and a few thousand dollars poorer he drove it out to the farm. They'd said it was good for another 150 000 miles. Whatever, he was very happy with it. The only irritation was the length of time it took for the glow plugs to warm up enough to start it.

He took Chadrack with him into the Farmers Co-op and arranged for all the supplies he needed to start the building works. It all had to wait, however, until Jim arranged the delivery of the 'razor' wire he had ordered from Johannesburg. They could, however, get on with putting in the two-metre high eucalyptus fence poles and the basic diamond-mesh fencing.

Chadrack, in the meantime, went off to find a bricklayer, plasterer and carpenter amongst the local people. He was gone for some hours as Harry expected, so while he was away, Harry went up to the police camp club for lunch with Chris Swan.

"Hello, Pirate! Congratulations and welcome back." Harry was standing at the bar sipping a cold 'Castle', sucking away on his pipe and thinking about his crops.

"Hi, Chris, thanks, and thanks for coming. Hell's bells, how the blazes did you catch onto that handle? Seems everyone knows that Pete has nicknamed me Pirate! Beer?"

"Just the job. It's still very warm for this time of year, but at least the rains have been good," observed Chris Swan. He was a big hairy man, slightly balding with a perpetual smile on his face. People said of him that if he wasn't smiling, 'watch out'!

"Yes, thank goodness. How's it going; how's the family?"

"Brilliant, couldn't be better. Good harvest this year and if the tobacco prices keep up, I should do all right. How are you doing?"

"Annie's well. Gave her a bit of a turn this morning about security, but she'll come through. I've even got small crops of tobacco and maize coming in. The old bugger did me the favour of planting out fifty acres or so after we signed, so I might be able to keep the wolf away from the door for the balance of the year. I will be able to plant out properly in the spring. Lot of clearing to do though. This bush really comes back with a vengeance, doesn't it?" They swigged their beers for a while and then went through to the mess for lunch.

They sat down continuing their discussion about farming and ordered their meals.

"Look, Chris, you know Pete Templar pretty well don't you?"

"Of course, great guy."

"Well can I speak to you in confidence?"

"About Pete? Sure."

"We're going in to get his old man out."

"Shit!" Chris Swan spluttered.

"Exactly! But the point of talking to you is that we're doing a night thing by air and I want to use your strip. Provided you've cut down all the anthills that is." They both laughed.

"The Inspectors have me now, they're there every month. Why my place?"

"Security, the fewer people that know, the safer we'll be."

"Who knows so far"

"Police and Air Force, and they're helping us."

"That right? Well then who am I to say no? Cost you a beer though."

"What a pleasure."

After getting back to the farm with the new artisans riding on the back of the truck, Harry held a work meeting with Chadrack and then for the rest of the afternoon he closeted himself in his office mapping out the raid. He phoned Jim Leonard to further the transportation arrangements and confirmed that the launch pad would be the Chris Swan strip. He also followed up on the supply of the razor wire. Jim advised that he should have the inside information on the airstrip and external guard situation back from his man in Zambia within days. Harry then called Mick Glover and Bill Sturrock, to arrange meetings with them for Friday week. That was when Peter was coming back from Zambia. He created a detailed list of what they needed and a provisional plan of action, subject to obtaining accurate information on the prison itself.

Peter came across, advising that he was flying to Lusaka in the morning, via Johannesburg, to begin the process of trying to see his father and get the information they needed regarding internal arrangements in the prison. The two of them sat huddled in Harry's small office for over an hour before being interrupted for dinner at 6:30 pm.

Annie in the meantime began a regime of work on the farm that she intended to continue into the future. Instead of prettying herself up she gathered her hair tightly behind her head and only put sun cream on her face, neck and arms. She found a khaki shirt in Harry's cupboard, rolled up the sleeves, put on a pair of denim jeans and tennis shoes and then went to work.

She gathered the domestic staff around her and going through the rooms of the house one by one, she explained to them what she wanted done. George, who was in charge of the house, kept in close attendance, nodded approvingly at her explanations and orders. She then sat down with him in the kitchen and mapped out a weekly menu, meal times, arrangements for tea breaks and finally how they were going to organise food supplies and provisions. Whoever went into the village every week would collect whatever orders they had placed with the co-op or chemist or wherever. No trips specifically for the household were to be made. They all had to be farm-related journeys.

She then went out into the garden and this time, with the head gardener in attendance, she inspected every corner of the 2-acre garden, which lay within the existing security perimeter. She went through the vegetable garden and made mental notes of what seeds she needed.

After that, it was into the office, where she spent the next two hours tidying up Harry's mess. Once done, she opened a cashbook she'd found and made a few account entries, so starting a proper accounting system for the farm.

It was only when Harry and Chadrack returned after lunch that she ventured out of the protection of the security fence. With Chadrack and the three new artisans she went through the old stables carefully and devised a plan for the alterations for the new school and clinic, which she knew would be approved by the elders. She left Chadrack to put her orders into effect and she went back to the house. Sitting at the dining room table, she wrote down everything that she would need to buy for later discussion with Harry. Finally she organised accommodation for the building team. By the end of the day she was exhausted.

She flopped into a hot bath and lay there, weary and aching, luxuriating in the steaming water. As she relaxed, she realised that she'd never been so happy in her life.

Peter arrived in Lusaka at 11:30 the following morning. Once through customs and immigration, an exercise that cost him US$20, he hired a car from the second car hire firm he tried; the first had no vehicles left. Driving into the town he was struck by the deterioration in the place. Where previously there had been good roads and well kept verges, there were now potholed tank traps, overgrown verges and seemingly derelict buildings. There was rubbish everywhere and plastic packets, it seemed, were caught on every Acacia thorn and barbed wire fence. So much for President Kaunda's philosophy of humanism, he thought. It occurred to him that this was one thing the Smith regime had got right, Because of sanctions, there was a shortage of plastic, and all packaging was undertaken using bio-degradable brown paper; so the countryside and towns were relatively tidy.

He parked in Cairo Road and went into Kingston's Bookshop, where he purchased a street map of the town and then went directly to the Department of Correctional Services.

"Good morning. I wonder if you can help me?" he started.

"Yes." The plump woman behind the steel grill under the 'Inquiries' sign didn't even look up.

"I want to get permission to visit a prisoner in Mumbwa Prison," said Peter forcing himself to smile broadly.

This seemed to mildly interest her as after a few moments she looked up from the important something she was doing, Peter couldn't see what, and she looked at him.

"You have come to the wrong department." With that she looked down again.

"Can you tell me which department I have to go to?" More forcible this time, Peter started scratching his head with a hand clutching some US dollar notes.

She looked lazily back up at him, saw the dollars carefully exposed in his hand, and suddenly was all smiles and became very helpful.

"Yes, Sir. You must go to Police Headquarters and speak to one of the Superintendents there."

"You wouldn't happen to know who I should ask for?" Peter continued to smile broadly.

"No, Sir, but if you wait I shall find out for you." She leapt up and rushed out and down a nearby passage.

Without waiting for her to return Peter left the building, got into his car and after a few moments of studying his map, he reversed out of the parking bay and set off towards police headquarters.

"Good morning, can you help me?" Broad smile, innocent face; I'm a master of disguises he thought to himself. Only this time he was met with efficiency and politeness.

"Good morning, Sir. Can I be of assistance?" The Constable behind the charge office counter was smart and alert.

"I would like to get permission to visit one of the prisoners in Mumbwa Prison."

"Please would you take a seat, Sir," the Constable said, waving at a row of upright wooden benches along the one wall. "I'll call someone to help you."

Peter sat down between an old man and a young woman carrying a small child on her back, and looked around. Police stations are the same everywhere in the world he thought to himself, green paint, wooden furniture and any number of posters covering the walls. He contented himself with studying a large official notice concerning standing orders for crowd control when in the presence of, or near to the President. His amused concentration was however interrupted after only a few minutes.

"Good morning, Sir. Can I help you?" he looked up and stood immediately recognising the stout man standing in front of him as a police Superintendent.

"Good day, Superintendent. My name is Templar. I'd like to see my father in Mumbwa Prison if it is at all possible." Peter spoke slowly and carefully trying not to clip his words, as Rhodesians are prone to do.

"Do you have any identification?" The Superintendent was quite pleased that the man had recognised his rank. Peter handed over his British passport and waited while the policeman painstakingly went through it page by page.

"Have you ever been to Rhodesia, Mr. Templar?"

"No," lied Peter. He put on his best British accent "I live in the UK. That's why it took me so long to get here. I had to fly via Johannesburg." The police Superintendent was no fool.

"Oh, from your tan I would say that you've spent many years in the tropics Mr. Templar." He passed it off as being inconsequential. But Peter went very still. He knew that he'd better come up with a good answer.

"I have. As a boy we spent many years in Kenya and I go back there regularly on holiday. After school I stayed on in England when my father was transferred to southern Africa." He just hoped that the policeman wouldn't check through the entry and departure dates on the British Immigration stamps in the passport. He'd soon realise that Peter was talking nonsense. Fortunately, the Rhodesian authorities had never put a stamp in it. The Superintendent, however, seemed satisfied and handed his passport back to him.

"Yes of course. I am Superintendent Motswadi. How did you know my rank?" Peter couldn't resist a short laugh.

"Because Superintendent, I am a policeman, also a Police Superintendent, Somerset Constabulary." You bloody liar Peter thought to himself, but that should get his attention.

Superintendent Motswadi reacted as if the Queen had just walked in. This time Peter kept a straight face and thought to himself that this was better than using US dollars.

"Superintendent Templar," he enthused, "please will you come this way. I'm sure we can make arrangements for you; if we may just ask you a few questions first?" He ushered Peter along the corridor towards his office. "Would you care for some tea? Won't you sit down? Please take your jacket off? This won't take long." Peter had to pinch himself on his right thigh to stop himself from laughing or smiling. He kept a severe look on his face and sat down on the visitor's chair facing the desk.

"I must say I am grateful for the co-operation, Superintendent."

"No, no, no! My name is Jackson, Mr. Templar. May I call you Peter?"

"Certainly, Jackson, all my friends call me Pete." Peter stood up again and put out his hand. Jackson Motswadi took it and shook hands briskly, twisting his hand in the latter part of the handshake to catch Peter's thumb.

"No, you must learn to shake hands the African way, you're in Africa now," he beamed. Peter wasted no time in copying his actions.

"Please sit down, Pete. Now do you have any information as to the reason for your father's arrest?"

"No, Jackson, just what I've read in the papers. I am not here to protest his innocence," he added offhandedly. "For all I know he may be guilty as hell. Wouldn't put it past him." Peter thought to himself that this lying came easily. He felt a bit sorry for the policeman sitting in front of him, he seemed like a thoroughly decent man. "I just want to see him, make sure he's alright, and make sure he's properly represented and then I must let the courts have their way."

"Good, Pete, quite right." Jackson Motswadi opened a drawer in his desk and pulled out a pad. Placing the forever requisite three sheets of carbon paper in between the folios he began to fill out Peter's authorisation. After a few minutes of questions; full name; how long will you be in Zambia, etc., he tore off the top folio.

"Here you are, Pete, authorisation for visitation privileges on four occasions for the duration of your stay. I have also made provision for you to be accompanied by legal council although I understand the British Consul has also been active in that department. Will that be sufficient?"

"Wonderful." Peter glanced down the sheet of recycled brush paper. "I couldn't ask for more. Thank you, you have been most helpful, Jackson, and I'll be sure to notify the British authorities accordingly." He stood up to go and Jackson Motswadi smiled again.

"Pete, if you have any problems, please do not hesitate to call me here at Headquarters."

"Thank you, Jackson, good bye." They shook hands again, and this time Peter beat Jackson to the 'African' handshake, demonstrating his newfound skill. He left the office and had to stop himself from running and laughing down the corridor, through the charge office and into the street. He got into the hire car and began shaking in nervous reaction to what he'd just achieved. It was some minutes before he was settled enough to start the car and drive off to the Airport Holiday Inn.

He checked in, had a shower, put a small camera into his trouser pocket and then made his way out of town towards Mumbwa Prison.

CHAPTER 18

That same day saw an increase in the tempo of work on 'Merrywaters Farm' as Harry and Annie had decided to call it. From then on they both worked like mad and most evenings were both so exhausted they went to bed shortly after dinner. Not surprisingly it was Harry who was the most done in; he still hadn't regained all his strength after his bout of malaria. For the weeks that followed they toiled hard and the effect of the hard work, good food and abstinence began to show clearly on him.

So when he went into Salisbury the following Friday to fetch Peter from the airport and attend the meetings he'd arranged with Bill Sturrock and Mick Glover, he already looked like a different person. His body had started to fill out and harden again and he had gained that deep tan only white farmers in the tropics seemed to have. This time Sampson, Peter's foreman, accompanied Harry. Sampson had agreed immediately to be the third member of their raiding party team. Sampson was as excited as punch to be going into the 'big city'. He kept Harry amused the whole trip with anecdotal stories of his prowess with women.

He only stopped when they got to the airport. He couldn't take his eyes off all the beautiful umfazi[46] airport staff. However he did come back to earth when he first set eyes on Peter coming out through customs. His face lit up like a light and he couldn't wipe the smile off it.

"You get all the information we discussed?" Harry wasted no time. Peter ignored him for a moment.

"Mhoro, Sampson, makadii? *(Hello Sampson, how are you?),*" he asked in Shishona, grabbing Sampson's shoulder and hugging him as Sampson reached across for Peter's bags.

"Ndiripo changamire, makadi-ni? *(I'm well, Sir, how are you?),*" Harry stood back and watched the interplay between the two men. They were obviously incredibly close friends. Who said white and black people can't get on?

"Well! Nice to be back, hi Harry, yes I think so, let's get going." Peter rushed it out all in one breath.

"Don't you want some breakfast or anything?" asked Harry.

"You've got to be joking. I've had two breakfasts this morning. One when I flew from Lusaka to Johannesburg and the other, flying north to Salisbury. Zambia have so much trade with us it's ridiculous that you can't fly direct. Now let's go before I run out of steam."

In the truck, the three of them squeezed into the cab, Peter gave them the bones of what he'd found out and Harry heaved a sigh of relief. Thinking to himself, Wow! If it's all I think he's managed, it's more than I could have hoped for. They arrived at the airbase for their meeting with Mick Glover. Harry grabbed a cardboard box out of the back of the truck and then he and Peter went in. Sampson stayed with the truck, ostensibly to guard it. In truth Harry didn't think that he could arrange security clearance for Sampson at short notice.

"Hi, guys." Mick ushered them through into his office. "Well I've got most of what you asked for Harry. How are you going to collect it?"

"Can we put it in my truck now? We've got Pete's foreman out there standing guard." He put the box down on the floor behind Mick's desk.

"Sure thing." Mick did an about turn and disappeared for a few moments. When he came back he asked, "Can you trust your foreman, Pete?"

"Of course, with my life. He was with me in the police."

"Good, then I suggest you arm him immediately, you'll find some pretty nasty goodies in those boxes and I'd hate them to get into the wrong hands. Also there's a chart of the Mumbwa area showing the aerodrome and the road in. What's in that box?" he asked pointing behind the desk.

"Oh, just a thank you, Mick, nothing serious. Just some nice goodies I got Jim to bring up from Johannesburg."

"Hey man, you mustn't."

"Tell that to your wife, there's nothing in there for you; just some nylon stockings, make-up, perfume etc. Stuff you can't get here because of the world economic sanctions against Rhodesia." Harry laughed, "Besides what are friends for?"

"Thanks, Pirate," said Mick.

"Nonsense, it's we who have got to thank you, you've been incredible." They all shook hands and Peter and Harry left.

"Right, next stop, Bill Sturrock," said Harry as they walked out into the car park. "Pete, we'd better take Mick seriously about arming Sampson." He looked towards the truck, some 30 yards in front of them. Sampson was sitting on a box in the back of the truck. "There's a revolver in the cubby hole, give it to him."

Peter nodded and when they got to the truck he called Sampson down and spoke to him quietly in Shishona. He reached into the truck and the pistol changed hands and disappeared into Sampson's shorts without anybody who may have been watching being the wiser.

Sampson climbed back onto the rear and said to Harry, "I'll stay here now, boss Harry. I won't move until we are back at the farm." He settled down and after wriggling about a bit to make himself comfortable he never moved again for the four and half hours that it took them to finish their business in Salisbury and get back to Peter's farm in Karoi.

The visit to Bill Sturrock took longer. Peter and Harry sat in a huddle with him for over an hour pouring over plans, retrieved from archives that dated back to the 'Federation'[47] days.

"Now as to the ordnance you asked for, you'll be supplied from the Police Armoury in Karoi. I've made arrangements for all the stuff you wanted to be delivered there on Tuesday." Bill Sturrock's voice took on a stern air. "Pete knows the C.I. in charge there and he's been briefed to release the stuff to you, against signature, one week prior to your confirmed departure. He knows nothing about your mission; only that it is for a special operation. Harry, we want all of our equipment back and your acceptance receipt will only be destroyed after you return the stuff and have been debriefed by the Anti-Terrorist Squad. So you'd better be able to account for every round that you expend, grenade you hurl, the number and description of any casualties, the lot. You got that?"

"Yes," said Harry. "Bill, how many people are in the loop?"

"Six, as far as I know. Commissioner Huxley's been doing the running so you'd be better off asking him, which you won't. And I know he's been talking to your Air Force man, Glover is it?"

Harry didn't answer, but sat there for a moment, thinking about the risks. The operation still looked secure and he eventually smiled.

"OK, it's a go," he said.

"Fine, now this is what we want from you in return. There is no intelligence yet as to the seventh of the 'Seven'. We want you to try and find out who it is. We believe that he may be the one who shopped the rest, three of whom were actually working for us. I won't say who, but Pete, your dad is not one of them. That's why we've agreed to this operation. We want it nice and clean. No casualties if possible, or a miniMum in any case. With a bit of luck if you're successful, it may even be kept out of the press. Their Government can't afford the embarrassment and they may just say that they've released and repatriated them. OK?"

"You've got our word," said Harry, speaking for both of them.

"Well, that's it then," said Sturrock.

"No," interjected Peter. "There is one more thing, if you can help Bill?"

"Hell, you guys don't give up do you?"

"I was up at Mumbwa until this morning," said Peter, "and I've taken a whole lot of shots." He took a 16mm spool out of his pocket. Handing it over to Sturrock, he asked, "Do you think you could have the police lab develop this and give us copies?"

"You cunning bugger. What's on here?" Sturrock asked, tossing the spool up in the air a few times.

"Silly buggers didn't even search me, when I went in. Superintendent Jackson Motswadi, obviously case officer for the 'Seven', issued my clearance. He seems to carry a lot of weight up there. Either that or they're so confident they're becoming too casual."

"Don't you believe it, Pete," said Sturrock. "Motswadi's a fine policeman and does carry a lot of weight. We think he's next in line for Chief Constable. They probably just jumped when they saw his signature. But you still haven't told us what's on this spool."

"Well, just a whole lot of shots of the outside of the prison and several taken from the inside. On three occasions I was able to slip the Minolta out of my pocket and take pictures. They may not be any use, but they might help and give you some more gen. about the goal as well."

"That's pretty good going, Pete. I'll take these down to the lab right now. You can collect your copies at the Karoi PC tomorrow afternoon." With that Sturrock got up, ushered Harry and Peter out and then disappeared almost at a run towards the back of the police station.

Joseph Ndube had been working for Trans Afrique Air for seven years. His intelligence and application to his work brought him swift reward. Jim was not slow to recognise excellence when he saw it and promotion was steady through the various levels of menial and then managerial jobs, at the Lusaka Airport office of Jim's Zambian operations. Joseph was now the Operations Manager, had a company vehicle for his own personal use, had an entertainment, subsistence and travelling allowance, and generally speaking was the envy of every one of his countrymen that knew him.

Jim had spoken to him about the need to find out all about the Mumbwa airstrip and the Mining Company airstrip at a small town called Kabwe some 100 miles away. He briefed Joseph on the basis that they needed an alternative airport to Lusaka. Joseph was instructed to do it quietly so that nobody knew that their strategic planning included provision for continued operations in the event of Lusaka being shut down for any reason.

Joseph thought about his instructions carefully and had some difficulty deciding how he was going to find out about Mumbwa airstrip without letting anyone know that he was doing it. The solution presented itself as he left the airport that evening. As he drove out he passed the Jet A fuel bowser returning from the tank farm. Fuel, yes, that's the way he thought.

The next day he got to his hangar-office early and at 6:00 am on the dot he phoned through to the airport fuelling depot. Making his voice as authoritative and gruff as possible to disguise it, he asked,

"Is that the Lusaka Airport fuel depot?"

"Yes, Sir, this is Edibiah[48] speaking. Can I help you?"

"Ebidiah, this Mumbwa Prison. We urgently need fuel tomorrow morning."

"Oh, Sir, I must have the requisition," replied Ebidiah.

"Ebidiah, we have no time now because I can't get Lusaka authorisation until tomorrow afternoon. I will send it to you tomorrow. Can you deliver before ten o'clock?"

Ebidiah looked at the delivery schedule hanging on his wall, saw that there were no special flights that needed fuelling in the morning and thought that he could probably leave the on-field fuelling to his assistant while he went off to Mumbwa for the day. Also, he hadn't been to that very good shabeen[49] near Mumbwa for a long time.

"Yes, Sir, I can be there before ten o'clock," he said forgetting about the formalities. There had never been a problem before, why should there be one now?

Joseph parked his Nissan in its customary bay and crossing the parking lot, contrived to nearly get run down by a large Jet A fuel bowser.

"Hey, you, watch where you're going." The truck screeched to a halt barely inches away from Joseph.

"Why don't you watch where you're going?" Joseph shouted back. He stepped to the side and looked up at the driver. "Oh, it's you, Ebidiah, you crazy old man. Where are you going in such a hurry?"

"Howzit, Joseph, sorry about that." The driver leaned out of the window of his truck and looked down. "I am in a hurry actually. The police phoned to tell me that they've had a run on Jet A at Mumbwa and I have to go there now and top up their tank."

"Are you going by yourself?" asked Joseph

"Sure, why?"

"Well it's a long way."

"No, it's two hours there and two hours back, so I'll be back before dark."

"Do you feel like some company," asked Joseph, "I've got nothing to do today."

"Hey sure, hop in, also I know a very nice little shabeen on the way back we can stop at. Nice girls there too."

"OK, Ebidiah, just wait a minute, I'll tell the office where I'm going so they don't call the police."

"OK, hurry. I told the police they will have their fuel by ten o'clock."

"I won't be a minute."

In the two hours it took them to get there, Joseph found out everything there was to know about the Mumbwa airstrip and soon realised that it was not suitable for commercial air operations. Knowing that he was going to just have to play along for the entire trip, he relaxed while Ebidiah drove and talked on about everything. He leant back and enjoyed the scenery. When they got to Mumbwa, they were checked in at a barbed wire gate about 100 yards before the main prison compound and buildings. The guards were friendly and casual and quickly greeted Ebidiah as an old pal. Joseph didn't even need to count the pair of them.

"Ebidiah, did you bring us a special bottle?" one of the guards called out.

"No, not today, brother; I had to leave Lusaka in too much of a hurry. Your boss wants his fuel by ten o'clock. But next time I promise." The guards laughed and lifted the boom. Ebidiah drove through and almost immediately after the gate, turned right onto a narrow track leading off through the woodland. Four minutes later they emerged onto an airstrip cut out of the virgin bush and stopped next to a hut where an old man sat on a paint can puffing away at an old pipe. Ebidiah and Joseph got down out of the truck.

"Hello, old man, how are you?" Ebidiah smiled his greeting to the airstrip manager.

"Hello, young Ebidiah, I have been waiting for you. Did you bring my stuff?"

"Of course, old man." Ebidiah handed him a heavy plastic bag. The old man opened it and peered inside. He seemed satisfied.

"Thank you, Ebidiah, exactly what I wanted." He turned and went into the hut without saying another word. Ebidiah moved around the truck to the only other structure on the field, a lean-to thatched shed, within which was parked a small four wheeled trolley converted to carry a fuel tank. When the tank was full, the trolley was too heavy for the old man to pull out, but as long as the aircraft parked nose in close to the shed, the filler hose could reach the tanks in both wings.

Taking the correct precautions Ebidiah proceeded to refill the trolley tank. When he had finished, but before he disconnected the earthing cable, he bled off fuel from the bottom of the tank checking for water or other contamination. He did this four times, each time pouring what he'd extracted into a one gallon plastic bottle.

"I have to do that and take the sample back to my boss. He says it goes to the laboratory for testing every time." Ebidiah sealed the container and slung it into the cab. He disconnected the earth, rolled it up along with his own hose and checked that everything was properly stowed. He took an invoice book out of the truck and laboriously filled in all the details, checking and then rechecking the meter readings. He then turned to Joseph.

"Right, now we can relax, the job is done."

The next morning, Joseph, head thick with the aftermath of a debauched afternoon and evening with Ebidiah, reported back to Jim Leonard. The call took an hour, for some reason his boss wanted to know every detail of his trip to the prison. He couldn't understand why Mr. Leonard was so interested in what kind of alcohol the guards and the old man drank.

CHAPTER 19

"Good morning, Mr. Fischer, may I have a cup of tea?" It was Wednesday afternoon and as was his custom, Jackson Motswadi was wearing his golf clothes ready to have a round of golf with the British Chargé d'Affairs.

"Certainly, Sir," said Fischer. He turned to a passing waiter and ordered one pot of tea.

"No, order something for yourself and join me," said Motswadi, "I've got half an hour before my tee off time." Fischer changed the order to tea for two and sat down. They were on the veranda of the Lusaka Country Club. The view was spectacular out over the golf course southwards down towards the Kafue River valley.

"You have done well, Mr. Fischer. The case against the six spies is pretty watertight and the President is pleased with all the positive publicity our country is getting because of it."

"Good!" said Fischer. "I'm glad we nailed those people and I hope that you have them shot, particularly that man Templar."

"Oh. Why's that?" Motswadi queried casually. He looked out at the view and thought to himself that life couldn't be better. He'd already been advised that he was next in line for a big promotion.

"His son caused my wife a lot of suffering. She nearly lost her baby." Alarm bells went off in Motswadi's head but he never even blinked.

"I'm sorry to hear that. What happened?"

"Oh, we were involved in an aircraft accident in Rhodesia and Templar's son was the first on the scene. Instead of looking after my wife, who was about to give birth to our child, the sod helped the pilot instead. My wife and I had to stand around for an hour waiting for him when he should have taken us straight into the hospital. Bloody useless pilot was all right. I don't know what the fuss was all about."

The tea arrived and Motswadi waited until the waiter was out of earshot before asking his next question. Fischer leant forwards and began pouring the tea.

"What was Templar's name, can you remember?"

"Yes of course I can. He was Chief bloody Inspector Peter Templar, BSAP, is who he was. I suppose he's been promoted by now. He's an arrogant bastard."

"You don't say," said Motswadi. Well, well, well, he thought. Now I wonder what he was up to coming here under false pretences. I shall have to think about this very carefully. He said nothing further to Fischer on the matter, but instead changed the subject. They chatted a while, then he sat back, cup in hand.

"My sources tell me that the Rhodesians are very keen to learn who the non-existent 'seventh' of the seven is, Mr. Fischer. They seem to think that the 'seventh' is 'Claude' and they're actively searching for him." At that point he finished his cup of tea and stood up. Picking up his golf bag he turned back to a worried looking Fischer and said, "I must get a move on otherwise I'll be late on the tee. But I would watch my back carefully if I were you, Mr. Fischer. I want you to report any unusual interest, any interest at all, about these matters, is that clear?"

"Yes, Sir," said Fischer hastily rising to bid his guest farewell. He was so concerned he forgot to wish Motswadi good luck for his game.

Harry, Peter and Sampson spent the next few days rehearsing the raid, learning the layout of the prison and its surroundings and drilling and practising with their weapons.

Jim arrived in his Kingair two days earlier than Harry had expected and they were amazed to find when he landed at the Swan airstrip, that he'd had the aircraft painted a dark matt green colour. Not proper camouflage, but effective nonetheless.

"Slight change of plans needed, Harry," said Jim Leonard.

"What do you intend to do?" asked Harry. They were sitting in Harry's office drinking tea and had just started to go over the whole exercise.

"Well, I think it'll be better if my flights actually emanate in Lusaka and end there. Let me explain. I suggest I fly up there on business tomorrow, Friday. I'm then going to file a plan for Kasaba bay up on Lake Tanganyika and then take off. There is no search and rescue because Kasaba bay is not in telephonic communication with Lusaka and after you sign off after crossing the Congo border north of Ndola, that's it. There are no further coms with Lusaka until you reappear at the same spot on your return flight. I don't even need to go that way. I'll merely make Ndola think that I'm flying off into the blue when in fact I shall be flying south to come back to this strip. I then pick you lot up, we fly to Mumbwa, fly back here, I drop you and whoever off, and then on Sunday I fly back to Lusaka after advising Ndola that I am returning from Kasaba Bay. I'll orbit Lusaka in order to come in from the north and nobody is any the wiser."

"Shucks that's a hell of a way to go. You won't have enough fuel," said Harry.

"Yes I will, that's the pretext to land at Mumbwa, we're low on fuel. The old boy there will be only too happy to flog us some Jet A, his boss wont even know because Joseph says the trolley tank was overfilled anyway. Those guys have had a scam going for ages. The only other thing is that I would like to go into Mumbwa high and silent just as the sun goes down. With luck nobody will see or hear us and then there's no rush. We can refuel, get the old man loaded with booze, lay out some reflectors along the runway to assist us at take off, and stand by until you're ready to leave."

"Sounds OK, Jim, yes it's solid. Do the guards ever go over to the strip?"

"No, apparently the barracks are the other way."

"Well how do we get the guards all loaded up with booze?"

"Simple, I take the booze up tomorrow, my man Joseph will then take it over by truck. He visited a brothel frequented by the guards and made mates with several of them. The only thing is that he thinks that it's a bit odd that I'm so keen for him to retain his contacts there. He knows nothing of our real intent. I wouldn't dare, not so much because I don't trust him, but more because if he's taken into custody, he has nothing to tell them."

"Makes sense. OK, so now we leave here mid afternoon on Saturday and get back at dawn on Sunday. I'll have to tell Mick Glover and Bill Sturrock immediately. I don't want anyone south of the Zambezi border deciding that we're hostile."

Farming activities also carried on and in between their bouts of training Harry and Peter raced backwards and forwards between their respective farms supervising the harvesting of the maize crops, and tobacco picking. Both Annie and Barbara saw little of their men for two weeks. Harry certainly came into the house most evenings totally exhausted from his exertions; barely able to keep his eyes open at the dinner table.

The basic fencing materials had arrived and the whole farm labour force was seconded from their normal duties to help get it erected. It was tiring work and there were many cut and bruised hands and fingers by the end of the task. After that, the builders began in earnest on their alteration works for the new schoolroom and the clinic.

Superintendent Jackson Motswadi was starting to get a prickly feeling. He couldn't put his finger on it, but he was uneasy. His thoughts kept going back to the discussion he had had on Wednesday afternoon with Brod Volker. After his game of golf he had excused himself early and quickly made his way back to his office. He sat there in the mostly empty building, leaned back in his chair and let his mind wander. Was there anything to consider arising from what now turned out to be quite a reckless visit by Peter Templar to see his father. He thought about it and ultimately came to the conclusion that Templar had been facetious through force of circumstance. The man had clearly been worried about his father's welfare and knowing that the Zambian authorities would not have allowed him into the country knowing that he was resident in Rhodesia, he had hidden the fact and claimed to be from England. But still, what was it that was worrying him? He picked up the phone and called Mumbwa asking to be connected to the Commandant. In minutes he was questioning the man about the welfare of the detainees; what the guard dispositions were; had there been any unusual activities or rumours circulating and so on. He was advised that all was in order and the detainees were secure. But still the sense of unease persisted. He resolved that soon he would take a drive out to the prison and check things out for himself. That decided he locked up his office and went home. He spent the next few days up in Ndola on the Copperbelt investigating the never ending problem of 'copper' theft and spent a lot of time with the mine's security officials.

The issue of the detainees had to be put aside until his return to Lusaka. It was late on the Friday evening that he returned but he wasted no time. First he called Brod Volker and arranged to see him the following morning in his office. Then he called Mumbwa and received confirmation that all was quiet. Finally he turned to the paperwork on his desk and spent the next two hours in peace and quiet going through reports and papers.

He was about to pack up and leave when the last scrap of paper on his desk caught his eye. It was an Invoice from the oil company for the supply of Jet A fuel to Mumbwa airstrip. Now what was this? He couldn't recall having seen the original requisition and set it aside to check on Monday morning. Who ordered the fuel? As far as he could recall there should be at least half a tank of fuel there. The fuel wasn't used that often and then, generally, only by the police helicopters when they were out patrolling the area or on 'Gunja' busts. His sense of unease returned. But there was nothing that he could do about it then, the place was like a morgue.

That Friday evening, Peter and Barbara came around with Sampson and Harry laid on a barbeque. Sampson loved to do the cooking, so he and George were left to organise the meat and sausages while Harry organised beer for all the men and gin-and-tonics for the women. The men stood together next to the fire and spoke quietly about their upcoming trip.

"Don't you worry, Boss Peter, we will fetch your father, no problem," said Sampson. He took a swig from the dumpy bottle of beer he clasped in his left hand while he busied himself turning over the sausages with his other. His hand was so big, the beer bottle looked tiny. George looked at him.

"Sampson, do you know the language that those people speak in Zambia?" he asked.

"No."

"It is important that you and Boss Peter only speak English when you are there, otherwise they will know that you should not be there."

"George, that is a very important thing that you have just said," said Harry. He turned to Peter. "Do you think that you could remember to only speak English? Actually, it's important that I understand what you and Sampson are talking about at all times as well."

"Very good point. Well done, George, I hadn't thought of that," said Peter touching George on the shoulder. "So you're not just a good cook." George beamed with pleasure that he'd made such a valid contribution to the expedition.

"How, George cannot cook. He stands in the kitchen and uses all the special things that the white man uses," said Sampson. "That's not cooking. This is cooking." They all gazed into the red-hot coals of the barbeque fire that Sampson was tending. The delicious smell of the meat and sausages coming off the grill was beginning to make their mouths water. It is an art to make a brushwood fire on a concrete slab, separate out the coals, suspend a grill over it supported by some stones, and then to actually cook a decent meal on it. Sampson was an expert, Harry was not, but he did enjoy the results and so kept everyone well plied with alcohol.

The barbeque was a great success and the first to retire was Jim. He bade them good night and went off to bed. George and Sampson went off and Annie, Barbara, Peter and Harry moved their deck chairs closer to the fire and sat there quietly contemplating what was to come.

"Promise me you won't do anything stupid now, Harry, and you'll look after Peter for me," said Barbara solemnly.

"We shouldn't have too much trouble Babs. The guys inside are expecting us and we don't even have to worry about trying to open their cell doors. Sturrock was able to identify exactly what the locks to the doors all are, from the photos Pete took, and we've got master keys to them." Harry looked across at Barbara. "The prison guards won't give us any trouble; they're prison warders, used to keeping unarmed people in goal. The warders inside aren't even armed, just the external patrols and with a little luck we will have sidelined them enough for them not to give us problems. My hope is that they will be totally drunk by the time we take them on and lock them up in the guardhouse."

"Many a slip between the cup and the brim, Harry Andrews," said Annie. "You just be careful."

"We will, my love, we will."

Peter and Barbara rose and after saying goodnight went off to their guest bedroom at the other end of the veranda. George had already tidied up so Harry threw another log on the fire and sat down again close to Annie. Taking her hand he looked at the flames and told her not to worry.

"I am worried, Harry, and I will be until you get back. But I know you and I trust that you've done everything you can to ensure that it'll go off without a hitch." She shivered a little.

"Are you cold?" he asked. "Do you want to go in?"

"No, lets just sit here for a while, it's seems so long since we were able to have a little quiet time to ourselves." She sighed, thinking of the activities of the last few weeks. "Golly, we've been busy."

"It should quieten down once this is over and we get the crops in. But I'm very proud of you, my darling. You're certainly a hit with everyone here on the farm."

"Oh they're wonderful people, Harry, and they've responded so positively to all the things I've been trying to do."

"Well I must tell you, Annie, they already worship you, as I do." He felt her hand move in his. "With all this work, how do you keep your hands so soft?" She laughed.

"A trick I learned from Emily, George's wife."

"What sort of trick? Maybe I should try it."

"There's a local palm tree..."

"Illala."

"That's it. Well the women collect the palm nuts and then squeeze the oil out of them. It has a beautiful fragrance and Emily told me to apply it every morning and evening."

"Well it certainly works." Harry yawned and stretched. "Gawd my body aches. Come lovee, I'm dog-tired. I must go to bed."

"No, you're going to have a hot bath and then I'm going to give you a massage with Illala oil."

CHAPTER 20

She stood up and without letting go of his hand she led him inside. While she ran the bath she forced him get undressed and led him into the bathroom. After his usual trick of prancing around because he thought the water was too hot, he eventually settled down in the steaming water and let the heat soak away his weariness. Annie knelt next to bath and slowly sponged him down looking carefully at the body of the man she so loved.

"My darling, that's marvellous."

"Stand up, I want to do your back." While he struggled to his feet in the bath, she quickly slipped off her clothes and stepped into the bath behind him.

"What are you doing?"

"Shh.." she said rubbing soap into the sponge. She slowly worked her way over his back and legs and then caressed his buttocks with the sponge. She then rinsed off the soap and turned him around. Using the sponge again she started rubbing his stomach, once again flat and hard from the hard work and saw the effect it was starting to have on him. She gently rubbed the sponge around his growing penis and then dropping the sponge and cupping her hands full of water she poured water over him holding his manhood and stroking him as she did so. He groaned and touched her shoulders.

"Hey, you vixen, what are you doing to me? It's too wonderful; I won't be able to hold on."

"No, Harry Andrews, not yet. Get out and dry yourself, I'll see you in a moment." While he dried himself she quickly bathed and then followed him through into the bedroom. She saw that he was already sprawled out on the bed and almost asleep, his arousal over.

"Don't you go to sleep now; I haven't finished with you yet." She dropped her towel and naked, kneeling next to him on the bed, she took the half filled Coke bottle she'd already placed on her bedside table and poured some of the oil out of it onto his back.

"Hey, that's cold," he protested.

"Shut up and relax," said Annie pushing him down. She began to knead the muscles and nerve centres on his back feeling the knots.

"Oh that's wonderful," said Harry. He lay there moaning as she worked away at him. As he began to relax she could feel the tension drain out of him. She rubbed his legs and then straddling him she began to erotically rub his whole body using her own. She could feel herself becoming aroused and so stopped and kneeling to one side made him turn over.

"Wow, Harry Andrews, what's this you've been hiding from me?" He grinned weakly and closed his eyes feeling her hands roam over his body.

"Well, what do you expect? I can barely prevent myself from grabbing you and doing things to you." He reached out his arms to embrace her but she batted him away.

"Don't you dare!" she laughed. She then started with his arms and pouring more oil on to his chest, she straddled him again and gently massaged his shoulders, chest and stomach. He was so hard by now she could feel his penis instinctively trying to bore its way into her.

"Not yet, my love." She moved her whole body down and sat astride his shins. Leaning forwards she massaged his thighs and then his crotch and his testicles. He was starting to writhe a little and would have sat up and pulled her to him, but she pushed him back. She took his penis in her oily hands and slowly worked them up and down his shaft. She lent further down and took his penis, now engorged and hard as a tree trunk, into her mouth, gripping tightly with her lips and circling the head of it with her tongue. She could feel him begin to lose control and stopped immediately.

Backing away she left his penis for a moment and rubbed his pubes and testicles with her one hand while with the other she began to caress herself. Squeezing and rubbing her breasts and nipples, one then the other, she moved her hand down and began to gently masturbate, catching her clitoris between the first and second fingers of her hand. The exquisite sensation started to bring her quickly and feverishly to a climax. No, not yet, she thought and so gently holding his penis she moved up and over him and rubbing the head of his penis against her vulva she felt the slickness of it as his penis slipped effortlessly into her. He was so big she briefly felt almost as if she was being torn open but almost instantaneously the pleasure came with it. She knew that they were both close to orgasm and she began to frenetically move up and down on him. Her own orgasm started immediately and wave upon wave of unbelievable pleasure hit her. As she shuddered in ecstasy, she gripped his shoulders and crushed herself against his body. She found his mouth and forced it open with her tongue, feeling he taste of him.

The momentum got too much for him too and although she could feel him trying to control it, he couldn't. She felt him convulse and she pushed down hard onto him, forcing him to penetrate her completely. She felt his orgasm overtake him completely as spurts of heat deep inside her took her over the edge again and again. He jerked repeatedly under her and crushed her body to him, driving the air from her lungs. When it quieted she lay there astride him, still deeply penetrated, panting for breath.

Their love making that night was so frenetic, it was almost as if Annie believed that it was for the last time. She didn't move until she could feel him fast asleep under her, his breathing deep and regular. She gently rolled away and studied him for a while thinking to herself that this man better come back to her. Drawing the sheet up over them both she lay back and was almost instantly asleep.

Harry was so exhausted that it was George knocking on the door with their morning tea that woke him. He felt out with his hand and found that Annie had long since gone. The bed on her side was cold already.

"Come in, George." He propped himself up on some pillows and lay there for a while drinking his tea and thinking. When I go into Karoi today I must remember to get the booze for Jim, I must have a Last Will and Testament attested by a Commissioner of Oaths, I must go to the Farmers Co-op and get the Dextrol so that Chadrack can dip the cattle this weekend. Oh, and Dealdron for the termites, I must warn Chris Swan about our change of plans, I must get......

"Come on, sleepyhead, wakey wakey, everybody else is up," said Annie sweeping into the room.

"God, but you're gorgeous, come here, I want to eat you up." Harry looked at her, his heart almost missing a beat.

"No, no, no. You're not having your evil way with me now you yummy man. You're going to get up and greet your guests at the breakfast table in precisely five minutes."

"Goodness, is it five to seven already," he said leaping out of bed.

Motswadi was in his office by 9:00 am. He did his rounds of the police station and inspected the holding cells before returning to his office in time to meet Fischer at 10:00 am. An orderly ushered him in.

"Good morning, Superintendent."

"Good morning, Mr. Fischer, please sit down; there's some tea coming in a moment." Motswadi hung his cap on the hat stand in the corner of his office behind the door and rounding his desk he faced Fischer.

"I hear that you're a bit of a weapons expert Mr. Fischer?" It was a question and Fischer didn't know quite what to make of it.

"Yes, Superintendent." Motswadi looked at him for a while and thought that this idea of his might well work out quite well.

"Are you proficient in explosives, anti-personnel mines, grenade and rocket launchers, light and heavy arms, communications, and so on?"

"Everything, Sir," replied Fischer proudly, "and I was the top in my unit in Insurgency training. I was the senior instructor at my training base in the DDR" *(East Germany).*

"Well the reason I ask is that we are worried about you being identified by the Rhodesians and we think that it is time to get you out of the way, somewhere where they can't find you."

"Agh, don't worry about me, Superintendent, I can look after myself."

"That is as may be," interjected Motswadi, "but we don't want to be implicated if the Rhodesians do have a go at you. And believe me if they become certain that 'Claude' is you, your usefulness to us will disappear immediately."

"What can they do to me here in Lusaka, Sir?" Fischer looked slightly uncomfortable, despite his bravado.

"They can and probably will kill you, Mr. Fischer." Fischer had the good sense to keep his mouth shut and sat there waiting, his mind in a turmoil. 'And now?' was all he could think.

"Yes, it's time we put you to some other safer use." Motswadi watched his visitor carefully. Should I tell him that in all probability a directive from the ruling Politburo would be coming down today ordering the police to hand the detainees over to UNIP Militia tomorrow morning? Motswadi sighed to himself, so much for the rule of law. If that happened, he thought, the detainees wouldn't see out the day. They'd be taken out into the bush where they would be summarily shot. He sat down at his desk as the orderly brought in the tea. "Do you take sugar, Mr. Fischer?" he asked pouring milk into both mugs.

"Yes, Sir, two please. What sort of use?"

But instead of revealing what he thought was inevitable, and the certainty of a Rhodesian retaliation, Motswadi said,

"The Patriotic Front freedom fighters based down in Kafue have asked us if we can help them out with weapons training. They wish to step up their attacks in Rhodesia primarily to make the rural areas ungovernable and haven't got the time or money to send their guerrillas off to your country and others for training. They're based at an old abandoned mission station down there. I'm sure that the accommodation for you and your wife will be quite comfortable."

Fischer didn't know what to think or say. He sat there dumbstruck.

"What about my job at the club? What does my Control say about it?"

"Don't worry about that, I'll sort that out."

"What will people think?"

"Don't worry, you will explain to the committee that you and your wife are due leave and would like to avail yourselves at short notice of an opportunity to go to England for a holiday. The assistant manager, who also works for us by the way, can stand in for you during your apparent absence. You will, of course, not be going back there."

"Are you sure?"

"Yes. You will make arrangements to leave at the end of the month. By the way, there is quite a vibrant little white farming community down in Kafue, so you and your wife won't be totally isolated. Your cover will be that of a teacher, because the camp is disguised as a technical college. Furthermore, every month you will report to me at the Kafue district police camp. I like to know what's going on in these camps, and I know that you speak Shishona well enough to understand what is going on around you."

"Well, if you think it's for the best…"

"Yes I do." Motswadi cut Fischer short. "And besides, I need an informant amongst the expatriate farming community down there as well." He stood up. "Thank you for coming in, Mr. Fischer." Fischer leapt to his feet and made as if to leave. Motswadi waved to him to wait. No, it is important for him to understand what a dangerous position he is in, he thought. So he said,

"By the way, Mr. Fischer, the party hardliners have gone a long way to convincing the President that these detainees should be shot, and the Rhodesians know of this. So you must understand that I cannot take any chances."

"Yes I understand." Fischer's mind was having trouble grasping the implications of this sudden change in his fortunes but he thought it would be better if he talked it out with Marie before he made up his mind, whatever good that would be. He had no choices and he knew it.

"Oh, and before you go there is another question I must ask you," said the Superintendent. Fischer waited while Motswadi gathered his thoughts. He looked again at Fischer, his glance questioning, "Do you think the Rhodesians would try and get their people out of Mumbwa?"

"I doubt it," said Fischer, "they wouldn't risk the scandal. I think they're trying to appear squeaky clean and such a raid would cause more trouble for them internationally than they'd want, including possible military assistance for Zambia." Motswadi looked at him, one eyebrow raised in thought.

"Umm," he said, "no doubt you're right, but I doubt it. Thank you, Mr. Fischer."

After Fischer had gone he stood by the window thinking. *No, I can't take a chance, my career is on the line,* he thought. He instantly turned back to his desk, calling out as he did so.

"Orderly, come here." The orderly appeared at his door immediately.

"Yes, Sir."

"Get the Commissioner of Police on the phone and arrange for me to see him directly and advise him that I wish for both of us to visit the Minister of Law and Order immediately. Then phone the Minister's secretary and advise him that the Commissioner and I wish to see him urgently, this morning if possible."

"Yes, sir." The orderly turned and ran back to his desk.

Fifteen minutes later Motswadi walked into the Commissioner's office.

"Good morning, Sir. Sorry to barge in on you like this but this is urgent."

"Morning, Motswadi, sit down. What's the problem, and why do we have to take this to the Minister, today of all days?" the Commissioner asked. He was a sage old man with white hair. His skin was very dark and it was rumoured that he was of the Barotse[50] tribe, but nobody knew for sure because he only spoke English. In fact he had spent all his formative years in England and had joined the Metropolitan Police in London until returning to Zambia.

"Sir, I have a hunch that the Rhodesians are going to try and mount a rescue mission at Mumbwa."

"What nonsense, Motswadi, what makes you think that?"

"No, hear me out, Sir. Recently a Chief Superintendent Peter Templar..." The Commissioner looked at him sharply. "Yes, Chester Templar's son came to visit him. Templar arrived in the country on a British passport pretending to be in the Somerset Constabulary, whereas he is in fact a Rhodesian, recently retired from the BSAP, I believe, and who is now farming near Karoi." Motswadi shifted his position on his seat. "I can tell you, Sir, that he had me completely fooled. I interviewed him. Well when I discovered that, I began to think, why have the Rhodesians been so quiet about this whole affair? Why haven't they, for instance, made any threats, like to closing the border? They've done that before. And then I have established that they have an all out operation to find 'Claude'. They still do not know who it is, but I am of the opinion that they have an idea. Now why would they be so interested in finding out who this Claude is? It can only be so that they can kill him. And then, Sir, if they are prepared to kill him, why wouldn't they launch a rescue attempt?"

"An interesting hypothesis, Motswadi; but what would you like us to do about it? We cannot shut the stable door on a horse that we do not even have yet."

"I would like to double the guards at Mumbwa with immediate effect, Sir. Or move the detainees to an unknown holding point until the President decides what is to become of them."

"Surely this can wait until Monday, Motswadi? We are supposed to be attending the Queen's Birthday Parade today, and so will half the police force."

"No, Sir. I believe that the Rhodesians will strike soon. It is imperative that we secure the situation before anything that we might regret actually does happen. I would like to go down there today and take one hundred men with me."

"That's out of the question, Motswadi, and you know it. No, the Queen's Birthday Parade will proceed as planned," he looked up, "and you will be in attendance, and then I will support a request to the Minister for you to go to Mumbwa tomorrow and strengthen the guard by one platoon of men. No more, you hear?"

"Yes, Sir. That will be satisfactory Sir."

"Look, Superintendent, the chances are that as of tomorrow these detainees will no longer be our problem. Are you aware of that?"

"Yes, Sir. But what if some of the detainees are innocent? I haven't yet finished building a case against any of them, let alone one. Everything is still circumstantial," said Motswadi looking a little disgusted.

"Ours is not to reason why, Jackson, we must just do our jobs.

Maybe they want to teach the Smith regime a lesson, who knows? But we will do our jobs, is that clear?"

"Yes, Sir."

"Good, well, let's go and visit the Minister then."

Jim Leonard flew over Superintendent Motswadi's house on final to land at Lusaka Airport at the exact moment Motswadi, attired in his full dress uniform, stepped outside to go to the Parade. He looked up and could read the South African identification lettering under the wing. He looked closely at the aircraft as it flew by and thought to himself, yes, and I wouldn't be surprised if the South Africans get in on the act as well. But no problem, I'll be ready for them if they try. I'd rather look a fool doing too much for nothing, than too little for everything. He sighed and got into his car. His sense of foreboding had not left him even though he had arranged to leave for Mumbwa with a platoon of men at dawn the following morning, Sunday. It didn't occur to him that the aircraft that had just passed overhead was carrying camouflage paint.

When it did occur to him it was too late. He found, on his arrival at the airport, after the parade, that the aircraft had already departed for Kasaba Bay. The flight manifesto said 'Passengers on board - 3'.

Joseph was also long since gone. Jim Leonard's instructions to him had been quite precise. He arrived with four crates of Chivas Regal 8 year old Malt Whisky at the shabeen so favoured by Ebidiah at around 4:00pm. He wasted no time getting friendly with two of the prison guards drinking there and soon they were on a roll.

"The reason I came here," said Joseph, "was because Ebidiah, you know him, the man who brings the fuel for the aeroplanes, asked me to stop by and give the old man at the air strip a bottle of whisky. Do you think the gate guards will allow me to go up to the airstrip?"

"Oh, no problem, we can give it to him," replied one of the men.

"Ah.. no. I promised Ebidiah that I would be sure to give it to the old man myself. But I'll tell you, I can sell you a few bottles for yourself, cheap." Joseph watched the men carefully to see the effect of his words.

"Yes, what have you got?"

Joseph could see the anticipation rising in their faces. "I have plenty of whisky. It's that Chivas Regal stuff, very special." The greed was beginning to tell. He could just see their minds trying to get around that, Chivas Regal!

"How much?"

"If you help me, I'll sell it to you for twenty Kwacha a bottle."

"Twenty a bottle, that's very cheap, where did you get it?"

"You promise not to tell anybody?" Both men nodded. "At the Kasani border post. It came off the back of a truck going to Lusaka for the golf club there. Here, let me get you another beer," said Joseph leaving them to think and talk it over. He came back with three more beers.

"Clever." The two guards looked at each other. "How many bottles can you sell us?"

"I've got four dozen, but I must keep some for Ebidiah. He arranged it."

"Four dozen? Come, we go now. Can you take us back to the prison?"

"Of course, I've got my truck outside." They drank up and five minutes later arrived at the gate. The two prison officers got off the back of the truck where they had been sitting on the whisky crates and after a few minutes of conferring with the guards, got back onto the vehicle, and just like that, they were through.

"We must go to the barracks first," one of them said and then following their directions, he drove them to the settlement located just to the south of the prison.

Thirty-five minutes later, pocket bulging with Kwacha bank notes, he drove up to the airstrip and greeted the old man, who as usual was sitting on the upturned paint can in front of his hut, smoking his pipe.

CHAPTER 21

When Jim arrived back at the Swan Strip at 3:30 pm, there were three vehicles parked at the end of the runway. One was a Police Land Rover. Oh-oh, he thought, trouble? He taxied the aircraft into a convenient position and shut down the two Pratt and Whitney PT6A engines, and opened the back door. Harry, dressed like a vagabond in what closely resembled a bunch of dirty rags, was there. He lowered the door, which when open and inverted, converted into several access steps. The retaining cords provide suitable handrails and Jim, a little stiffly, climbed down.

"Wow, quite a reception committee!" he joked. "Do we have a problem?" he asked Harry quietly.

"Not at all. Come, let me introduce you to Superintendent Bill Sturrock. He's our police liaison man." He drew Jim towards the group of people standing to one side.

"Bill, I'd like you to meet Jim Leonard, my ex-boss." The two men shook hands sizing each other up quickly. "Jim you know everybody else except Sampson, the other man in out party."

Jim turned slightly and nearly fell over. The only immaculately dressed person amongst them, a Superintendent of the Zambia Police came forward and shook his hand.

"Hello, Mr. Leonard, I am Superintendent Cedric Mtombe, but my friends call me Sampson because no such person exists." Everybody burst out laughing.

"Well nice to meet you, Sampson. I think you'll make a fine Superintendent. Amazing Harry, who came up with that idea?"

"He did. OK now, Bill has brought us everything we need, and more I might add. What time do you want to leave?"

"Sundown is at six-fifteen and we'll have about eight minutes of visibility after that. Flight time is plus-minus one hour thirty five minutes so we must depart here at four-forty pm."

"Great," said Harry, "that gives us thirty minutes and about ten minutes for pre-flight and take-off checks." He turned around and addressing everybody he said, "Let's load."

Barbara and Peter had gone off to sit in their own vehicle in order to say their farewells. Harry drew Annie to one side and brought her close to him in a bear hug.

"Don't you worry now, we'll be OK," he assured her, feeling her trembling against his body. He kissed her on the forehead and stroked her hair gently.

"My darling, I know now what it must be like for wives to see their men off to war. It's terrible." She spoke into his ear and hugged him back tightly.

"Well this is going to be a short war; we'll be back in time for breakfast."

"I know, but it doesn't make it any better. You watch yourself, Pirate." With that she broke away to hide her tears and ran to Harry's truck, got in and then sat there watching.

"Alright, all aboard who's going," said Harry.

"Hello, old man," said Joseph, I've brought you a present from Ebidiah."

By 5:00 pm the old man could barely stand up, he was so drunk. Joseph took him gently into the hut and lay him down on the single bed in there. Within seconds the old man was snoring his head off. Joseph quickly moved the truck off the runway, backing it into a thicket.

He got out again and swung the backrest of the seat forwards.

Behind it he had stored two large bundles, one a big roll of thin double flex on a spindle and the other wrapped up in an old towel. Working slowly and methodically in the heat and so that he didn't forget anything; he also removed a new 12-volt car battery from the footwell in front of the passenger side of the vehicle. Placing them all on the ground, he unwrapped the towel bundle. It contained two red aircraft rotating strobe lights screwed onto a plank of wood.

Placing these on top of the battery and adding some jump leads to the pile, he carried them to the end of the nearest end of the runway. He placed the battery down on the ground and connected the jump leads to the correct terminals. The two strobe lights came on immediately and began to turn. Satisfied that they were working he disconnected the positive lead again and left it like that.

He walked back to the old man's hut, picked up a short log that served as a stool and then staggered some twenty paces along the side of the runway before dropping it on the ground. Back at the truck he collected the big roll of double flex and then walked back to the log. He untied the ends of the double flex and secured them to the log and walking backwards down the side of the runway, he slowly let out the flex. It was only 200 metres long and by no means stretched even a third of length of the runway, but Jim had told him it was a precautionary step only because they wouldn't use the landing lights until they had enough speed to cool them down. If they used them at the start of their take off run they might burn out.

After that Joseph walked back to the truck and this time opened the fourth whisky crate. This crate however had no whisky in it, just a few carry-bags of small 12-volt light bulbs. He retraced his steps along the runway stopping every 20 paces or so where on each occasion he found a screw-in socket for the light bulbs. If it rained, the system wouldn't work, but looking up at the sky he could see that there were only a few clouds around. Besides he gained confidence from the fact that he couldn't hear any rain birds[51].

That task completed, he walked back to the truck and got back in, leaving the door open. He looked at the sun, getting close to sundown he thought, and then looked at his watch. It was 5:45. Then he waited.

At exactly 6:00 pm he got out, walked across to the strobe lights, reconnected them to the battery, ensured they were both functioning properly and then went and sat down in the truck again. Then he waited.

Jim brought them in from the north against what wind that there was. He adopted 'slow safe speed' with engines at 25% power. The aircraft gradually lost height. I hope I find this field alright, thought Jim. Harry sat beside him peering out the front window looking for the field while Jim concentrated on the instruments.

"Can't you see it yet, Harry; we should be at about one mile?"

"Hang on, I can see the prison vaguely, it's getting a bit too dark. No, yes, there it is at ten o'clock low."

"Great." Jim looked up immediately and turned gently to port. Not too steeply now, we don't want to stall this thing, he thought. They were still high when Jim saw the strobe lights at the far end of the runway.

"Good old bloody Joseph," he said to nobody. "Is that guy going to get a fat bonus or what?"

He immediately cut the engines to 'idle-full feather' and the aircraft started to drop down more quickly but still maintaining 'slow safe speed'. He could make out the runway clearly and said, "Undercarriage down now." Harry moved the appropriate lever to the 'down' position and simultaneously trimmed the aircraft to maintain airspeed. Jim kept his eyes firmly fixed on the runway and flew the aircraft. The aircraft's descent rate increased and Jim judged that he would probably land about halfway down the strip. "OK thirty five degrees of flap now, Harry." Harry complied and again trimmed. He thought that Jim was going to judge it to perfection.

"OK, Harry, I've got it all." Harry sat back and folded his arms.

The aircraft ghosted down with the light fading fast. So quiet was it that Joseph sitting in the cab of his truck didn't realise that they were there until a huge dark-green apparition slewed around sharply right in front of him and came to a halt, nose pointing in the direction from which it had come.

He leapt out of the truck and taking two chocks out of the back of the truck, he ran under the wing from the rear and placed them in front of and behind the starboard wheels. By the time he came out from under the wing and had gone around to the hatch on the other side of the aircraft, Harry had already jumped out. To Joseph, he was like a big baboon standing on its hind legs. The creature was a dirty black colour, virtually unrecognisable as a human being, but Joseph knew that it was because it was pointing an AK 47 assault rifle straight at his stomach and saying "Shhh..".

"Yes, Sir," he whispered. "I am Joseph."

A hand appeared out of the apparition. Joseph took it.

"Hi, Jo, it's Harry; is everything quiet?"

"Yes, Sir," smiled Joseph. "I never recognised you."

"That's the general idea, Jo."

More figures appeared out of the aircraft, including a Zambian Police Superintendent. Joseph nearly turned and ran. He was shaking so much he nearly wet himself. The Police Superintendent put out his hand and whispered,

"Don't worry. Hello, I'm Sampson. Here is my boss, Peter, and here is your boss, Mr. Leonard."

The relief evident in Joseph was palpable. He ran to Jim and shook his hand fiercely and then turned to greet Peter.

But he and the others had gone.

"OK, Jo, bring in the strobes and let's quickly refuel the aircraft. Then you must go immediately. I want you out of here by seven o'clock and back in your bed in Lusaka by nine-thirty."

"Yes, Sir." Jim and Joseph rolled the fuel bowser out from its shed and in no time, Joseph pumping and Jim holding the nozzle, they had pumped 100 gallons of fuel into each tank.

"That should be enough, Jo. Let's get this squared away and then you must go."

Ten minutes later Joseph started up the truck and was gone. He waved to the guards at the gate who by now were sitting on the ground casually sipping away at a bottle of something. He didn't even have to stop, the boom was in its raised position.

After he had gone, Jim connected the battery to the double flex briefly and watched as the lights came on along the runway. He then disconnected them again, climbed aboard, collected a sawn-off 16 gauge shot gun, loaded it with buck shot and then propped himself up against the port wheels, shot gun cradled in his arms. He switched on his portable radio. He ensured that it was tuned into 135,4 MHz, adjusted the squelch and volume and then slung it around his neck. This was intentional; if anything went wrong he'd have to move in a hurry.

Annie and Barbara drove back to Merrywaters farm in convoy after agreeing to meet Bill Sturrock back at the airfield at 5:00 am the following morning. When they got to the house George fussed around them until Annie told him to go home, she'd cook the supper. So she and Barbara sat in the kitchen working steadily through a bottle of South African pinotage and fretted. It wasn't so much that they went on about what was going to happen, those thoughts went largely unspoken. They spoke about the deteriorating security situation.

"Peter has the house upside down at the moment," said Barbara. She was dressed in denim jeans and jacket over a red cotton blouse. "I can't find anything to wear because all our clothes are lying in piles in one of the spare rooms."

"Why, what's he doing?" asked Annie.

"Well, he's got this thing about creating a 'safe' area in the house."

"What do you mean?"

"It's a section of the house which is completely safe from gunfire and attack from the outside."

"But that's silly. You can't make any part of the house safe from outside attack." Annie poured them both out some more wine.

"No, that's not what I mean. It's an area in which to shelter if the house is under attack. Where you can go and no bullets or grenades or whatever can reach. Also that's where he's building a proper radio closet."

"Radio closet?"

"Yes, somewhere where you can sit safely while under attack and call out for help." Annie was silent for a moment and then said,

"So, Peter is obviously very concerned about the risk of attack." She got up and brought out a carrot cake, fetched a knife and cut a few slices. She put a slice onto a side plate and pushed it over to Barbara. Between them, the cake disappeared in minutes, so did the wine. They were both quite mellow after a while but instead of being a lift-me-up, the wine had an opposite effect and they became very morose. Eventually Barbara got up and said she was going to bed. She just made it through the door.

Annie sat there a little longer and then went into the central hallway of the house and began to inspect the walls, opened the hallway cupboards and opened and closed bedroom doors. She went back into the kitchen and found a felt tipped pen. She spent the next hour tying string to windows and stretching the string in a straight line through into the hallway. On each occasion she made a mark on the walls of the hallway. Eventually she stopped and dropped onto the floor in the hallway, her back against the wall. My goodness, she thought, if this house is attacked and they start firing at us through the windows from all sides, we've got nowhere to hide.

She got up from the floor and went through to Harry's office. Barbara found her digging around deep inside the cupboard.

"What are you doing?" she asked.

"Wha..! God you gave me a turn Babs. Can't you sleep either?"

"No."

"Good, because neither can I. You can help me. I'm looking for the plans of the house. I know Harry put one in here somewhere.. Ah, here it is." She stood up with a grubby roll. She pushed everything on the desk to one side and then unrolled the plans and spread them out on the desk, weighting the corner with his tobacco bowl, pipe stand, her Beretta, and a heavy steel straightedge.

"I think that Peter is very sensible and I can't understand why Harry hasn't thought of this himself," she said. Barbara laughed.

"Oh, but he has. It was he who suggested the idea to Peter." Annie looked quizzically at Barbara.

"You're joking, Babs?"

"No, I'm serious. I have been cursing him for weeks. I did hear him say to Pete that he'd get round to it eventually, but that you had more pressing building works to get on with at the moment."

"Typical of Harry. Well, I'm not going to wait. I'm going to start these alterations on Monday. Come let's look at these plans." The two of them spent the next three hours drawing, measuring, and going backwards and forwards between the office and various parts of the house. Barbara looked at her watch,

"My God, look at the time, should I make some coffee? I don't know about you, but I'm not going to be able to sleep tonight."

"Neither am I. What time is it?"

"Two A.M.," said Barbara walking out the door. Annie continued to stare at the plans, but her mind was elsewhere. *I wonder what Harry's up to right at this moment.*

Harry Andrews at that moment was fast asleep. He was stretched out under a hibiscus hedge. Peter Templar lay next to him, fidgeting with his assault rifle and looking out at the front doors of the prison. Sampson sat quietly behind him, an Israeli made Sten light machine gun held lightly in his lap. It was his turn to keep watch. Their attack on the prison was due to start in one hour, at 3:00 am.

Another person was unable to sleep that night. After inspecting his men at the police garrison on Cairo Road in Lusaka to make sure that they would be ready for an early departure the following morning, Superintendent Jackson Motswadi had come home, gone to bed and then, when his wife was asleep, he rose and went through to the kitchen to make himself a cup of tea. He was still sitting there four hours later when the phone rang.

CHAPTER 22

"Time to move, Sir," said Sampson quietly, shaking Harry's shoulder. It was 2:50 am. Harry looked up and across to Peter who was crouching at the ready in the total concealment of the hedge.

"OK guys, this is it." Harry wormed himself out from under the hedge and slowly stood up, weapon cocked and ready. Harry lifted his radio.

"Pirate to Flyboy."

Jim, sitting under the wing of his aircraft, jerked out of his reverie and lifted the radio to his face.

"Flyboy," he answered quietly, "hear you strength five, Pirate."

"The games begin. Pirate," said Harry. He switched off the radio and then secured it again in the grip of the bungee he had looped around his waist.

Each man knew precisely what he had to do. They moved quickly towards the main gate, secure in the knowledge that Joseph had been successful in getting a surfeit of alcohol to the guards on duty there. They split up and approached the gate through the cover of the uncleared woodland on either side of the access road to the prison. Peter and Harry took up firing positions no more than 20 paces from the guardhouse. The guards weren't even visible, but they were to be changed in a few more minutes, so it didn't matter. Sampson hung back and waited for the new guard detail to arrive.

They didn't have to wait long. The two replacement guards strolled along the road casually, firearms strung over their shoulders. They arrived at the guardhouse, called to the others and then burst out laughing. Both the guards on duty had been asleep but before they could stand up, Sampson walked up behind the new guards.

"What is going on here?" he asked, almost shouting. The two new guards swung around flabbergasted, mouths open and fear clearly evident on their faces.

"Corporal, I asked you what was going on here?" Sampson leaned forwards aggressively. The two men sitting on the ground against the front of the guardhouse tried to scramble to their feet.

"Stay where you are," shouted Sampson.

"Ahh.. Superintendent.." stammered the one replacement.

"Shut up. Get against the wall both of you." Sampson gestured with his sub-machine gun. They almost leapt at his command and stood stiffly at attention against the guardhouse wall.

"You are all on Charge. Place your rifles on the ground. You two," he looked at the hapless offenders on the ground. "Lay your firearms on the ground and stand up there next to these other two." The two guards obeyed immediately.

"Now turn around face the wall, hands up, palms against the wall, spread your legs."

That exercise took less than 30 seconds. Harry and Peter came forward and one by one bound the wrists of each guard behind their backs. As each had their mouths taped and were turned around, their eyes bulged in fear as, for the first time, they saw the other two. This was especially so of Harry who despite his blackened face was still clearly recognisable as a white man. Their terror was palpable. It was the effect of the piercing blue eyes scrutinising them from out of a dirty black face that did it. The one man suddenly became incontinent, urine gushed down his legs from below his shorts.

"Relax," Harry said to him. "You keep quiet and you'll be fine." But the man couldn't keep from shaking. Harry pushed him into the hut and instead of making him lie down on the floor so that he could bind his feet together, as was the case with the others, Harry sat him down on the only chair in the small room and then bound him to the chair and then to the burglar bar in the window.

"Sorry about this, old chap, but we can't have you shooting at us now, can we?" Harry patted him on the head and then turned to help Peter with the last of the four guards. Sampson stood stiffly at attention outside, gun at the 'port' position, as if on guard, just in case anyone came along while they were disabling the guards. The last thing they did before moving on was to remove the bolts from the guard's rifles. Harry threw them into the brush at the side of the road. The whole engagement took eleven minutes.

"Flyboy – Pirate." Harry spoke into the radio.

"Go ahead, Pirate," replied Jim.

"Phase one complete, initiating phase two, Pirate."

"Pirate," was all Jim said before settling down to wait again.

"Right, no problems so far; next stop the prison and armoury; let's go." Harry led the way until they got back to the hibiscus hedge. Sampson didn't even break his stride. He walked straight into the open carpark area in front of the prison doors and went totally unchallenged. He walked boldly up to the personnel door, set into the large steel gate and knocked arrogantly. A shutter in the slid back and a concerned voice within said,

"Yes."

"Superintendent Mtombe, I wish to put four men on charge. Take me to the Commandant's office. The door rattled and was thrown open.

"But the Commandant is not here, Sir," said the voice, now frightened.

"He's on his way. Take me straight to his office," ordered Sampson. The man buckled.

"Yes, Sir, straight away." Sampson stepped through the doorway and in one second had the man pinned up against the wall on his left.

"You shouldn't have let me in you fool," he said quietly. "Why didn't you ask for my identification card?" He sniffed closely at the man's breath. "Have you been drinking on duty, Constable? What is going on? Is everyone drunk here tonight? Constable, you are also on charge." The man cowered before him. "Turn around face the wall, hands up, palms against the wall, spread your legs." The poor guard couldn't move fast enough. If he'd been a fraction slower, he'd have observed two hideous figures slip silently into the entrance.

While Sampson tied the man up, Peter ran to his right to the security gate leading into the armoury. It was as he remembered; a heavy wrought iron gate set into a grill in front of the door. He quickly added a heavy steel chain and clasp lock to the existing lock and pulled it to make sure it was secure.

Harry in the meantime had run straight forwards and done precisely the same thing to the gate leading into the main prison courtyard. Any guards inside were now effectively trapped in there until the chain and lock were cut off. There were no keys to either lock.

They then regrouped outside the door on the left, which they knew lead into the prisoner reception rooms, the guardroom with the attendant rest and recreation rooms and then the cells reserved for the political prisoners. This would be the most difficult part they knew, because there were alarms in both areas and there were bound to be at least four guards in the guardroom, albeit asleep, and at least one at the reception desk. Furthermore there were two guards looking after the cells behind, who they didn't want to alert.

"OK, Sampson, you're getting quite good at this. Go do your trick again," whispered Peter. The three of them giggled and the tension was to some degree alleviated.

"Call me Superintendent Mtombe, you malhungu you." They smiled at each other in the dim light and Peter patted Sampson on the back as he turned, opened the door leading into the reception. He strode straight up to the counter. Slapping the unfortunate guard's rifle down on the counter, he glowered at the orderly sitting, feet up, at the desk immediately behind it.

"Stand to attention, Constable," ordered Sampson. The man leapt to his feet and stood stiffly to attention. You don't mess with an angry Superintendent.

"Have you been drinking also, Constable?" The man went an ashen shade of grey. As he spoke, Sampson walked around the end of the counter and approached right up in front of the man. He sniffed and then sniffed again.

"No, Sir, I am on duty sir."

"Is that a fact, Constable?" Sampson lazily waved his AK 47 in the general direction of the duty officer. "Turn around and put your hands behind your back." Before the man had time to protest, Sampson jabbed him sharply in the stomach using the business end of the weapon. Air escaped from the man's lungs in a hiss as he turned away, scared out of his wits.

"Humba gashli[52], Sam," said Peter peering around the corner of the doorframe, "He's just doing his job."

At that moment the phone rang. They stood there frozen. After a half a dozen rings it stopped. They had just let out a sigh of relief and started moving when it rang again, this time for a full minute.

"Come on, guys," said Harry sticking his head around the corner. "We're going to have to move quickly now. I think that the balloon is about to go up."

They quickly tied and gagged the man while Harry stood guard outside the door of the guardroom. Within minutes they were ready to enter and secure the guardroom.

"OK, me first," whispered Harry as he gently but quickly began to open the door. As he did so a guard rushed out. They both got such a fright that both men fell back. It was fortunate that Harry recovered first. It was probably the way he looked that slowed the guard down. But he managed to remove his pistol from his holster. Without even lifting the weapon he squeezed the trigger as Harry moved in. The bullet ricocheted off the floor and, passing just to the left of Harry, embedded itself in the wall behind him. The sound of the pistol shot reverberated loudly through the passage. It briefly stunned them all.

But Harry leapt at the man. Using the steel butt of his own weapon Harry knocked him senseless. It was fortunate that at this stage he hadn't even put a magazine onto the weapon because Sten guns are notoriously sensitive to violent movements and are prone to fire off a burst without any pressure on the trigger. Taking a magazine out of his pocket and clipping it into place, Harry ran into the guardroom to be greeted with three more very sleepy confused looking guards in various stages of rising from their mattresses and getting dressed.

"Don't move," said Harry, menacingly waving his sub-machine gun at them. Peter and Sampson came in behind him.

"Pete, you and Sam take over here, I'm going to press on. Pete, when they're secure, you go back to the main entrance and stand watch. Sam, you follow me when you're ready. Watch out for the other guards as you go out through that door," he said pointing at the guardroom door leading out into the main prison corridor. They'll be alert now."

Then he was gone, literally diving out of the door. He rolled, searched and saw his quarry rising from his seat at the entrance of the Political Wing. Rising to his feet in one fluid motion, Harry began running down the passage towards the man shouting, "Don't do it! Stand still." The man obeyed, totally put off by the apparition running towards him.

It was drunken revelry going on in the prison staff single quarters that eventually caused the Commandant of the prison to get up out of bed and phone the duty officer. His intention was to instruct a detail to go down to the single quarters, some 150 yards from the main prison building and tell them to shut up.

There was no answer to his call. He found that strange but his first thought was that the duty officer was asleep. His anger grew after trying again. When he had let the phone ring for a full minute, he slammed the phone down and angrily put on his clothes. His first action was fortunate. Instead of going to the prison itself, he went to find the party and quieten the revellers down. Everybody was involved and they were all drunk. He shouted and ranted at them and then his eyes rested on one of the bottles they had been drinking. Chevas Regal?

"Where did you men get this whisky?" he screamed at the men cowering before him.

"We bought it from the guards at the gate," came the reply.

Then they heard the shot.

A sense of dread began to take hold of him. What was going on? He put his whistle to his lips and running out into the open he blew it for all he was worth. He was worried that all the guard details would be drunk as well but men started pouring out of their billets. Gathering them around him he told them to get up to the prison as fast as they could and wait at the armoury to be issued a firearm. He ran back to his house as fast as his chubby legs could carry him.

"Superintendent Motswadi?" he asked speaking into the phone. "We have a problem. The guards are all drunk and now there's been weapons fire in the prison building itself. I think they may be trying a breakout. Please send men out immediately." He then unlocked his safe and extracting his own pistol and the keys to the armoury, he ran out the house and up towards the prison.

Jim jerked to attention. Was that a shot? He leapt to his feet and listened. All was quiet for a moment and then he heard the whistle and other sounds coming from beyond the main prison building. He had to protect the aircraft at all cost, so he ran forward towards the prison entrance and arriving there at the same hibiscus hedge he saw men pouring down the road from the south towards the prison. Without hesitating he raised the shotgun high and let off both barrels. The thunderous blasts had the desired effect and to a man, they all turned tail and ran the other way where the first of them then collided with the Commandant who was trying to catch them up. In the confusing melee that followed the Commandant essentially lost control of the men and many of them just ignored him and ran for the shelter of their rooms.

"OK, Jim, I've got it," called Pete running out of the prison door. "You get back to the plane. I'll keep them at bay."

Again Jim was on the move, backwards this time, where through the gloom he found the bewildered old man standing next to the aircraft. Oh my God, was all he could think. The old man has been awakened by the gunfire.

"Come, Madala[53]," he said quietly, "Let's get you back to your hut." The old man saw the shotgun and then looked at Jim.

"Ah, I remember you Sir, you're Mr. Leonard." Jim got such a fright he nearly dropped his shotgun.

"How do you know me?"

"Oh, Sir, I used to work at Lusaka Airport, at the fuel depot."

"Oh, shit!" exclaimed Jim. "Well Madala, you have now created a problem for me. I cannot leave you here to identify me to the police."

It took a few moments but then it dawned on the old man what Jim was talking about. His eyes widened in fear and he started shaking.

"No, Sir, I cannot tell anybody." He looked beseechingly at Jim.

"Well please sit down over there, Madala, I have to think about this for a while." Jim pointed to a spot out in the open near the aircraft. He then sat down again next to wheel and keeping his empty shotgun pointing in the general direction of the man, he contemplated this reverse of fortune. Hell, he couldn't just leave him there to give the game away. But the man is a total innocent, what the blazes do I do? God's truth; and it's me that will jeopardise our security. That is something I can't allow, but I can't just shoot the old fellow. Jim's mind went round in circles until he eventually concluded that he'd have to try to buy the old man off. He felt around in his flying suit and brought out a wad of US$s. Dividing the bundle in two, there must have been $300 or $400 in each hand, he turned to the old man." Old man, you must run now, and you must run far. They must never find you, do you understand, because if they do, they will torture you and kill you. Do you understand what I am saying?"

"Yebo, Bwana" *(Yes, Sir)*.

"Good, now take this American money and go." The old man took the money and ruffled it agilely through his fingers in the pre-dawn darkness, his eyes widened. He had never seen, let alone held, so much money in his long life. It was more than he'd earned in the last 20 years.

"When that money is finished, you find me at Bulawayo airport and I'll give you some more, OK?" The old man shook his head vigorously. "Madala," Jim looked at the old man closely. "If they find this money on you they will take it and kill you, you hear me?"

"Yes, Sir, but I am an old man and I will give it to my daughter. They, these UNIP[54] gundwans[55], will not find me in Barotseland. They cannot swim." Jim realised that this was an allusion to the fact that Barotseland consisted of the headwaters of the Zambezi River. It was, for a large part, an enormous swamp, more than a thousand square miles in extent, which consisted of a myriad of inaccessible islands and channels. He laughed at the joke and turning the old man round he gave him a gentle shove, wondering at the same time how long it would be before he was caught.

"Go! They will be coming to find you soon." He had already searched the hut and knew that there was nothing of value at all in there.

The old man trotted to his hut, disappeared inside, and was out in under a minute carrying his blanket and a knobkerrie[56]. He had placed an old wide brimmed hat on his head. Turning his head as his started trotting off, the last thing the old man said, before disappearing into the bush, was "I am but a leopard in the night, maybe they will know I am there, but they will never find me."

CHAPTER 23

Jackson Motswadi moved as if his life depended upon it. He called the police camp and, shouting at the duty orderly, eventually brought results. To his credit he was underway to meet the armed convoy he'd arranged in less than half an hour. But it was unlikely that they would reach the prison before dawn.

Harry's rapid advance on the guard at the end of the corridor paid dividends. The man fell back on his chair as he tried to rise and draw his pistol. Harry was onto him before he recovered. The pistol dropped from the man's hand and Harry kicked it behind him where Sampson later scooped it up. He rolled the man over onto his stomach using his foot and then knelt on his back while he bound his arms behind him with insulation tape. Turning him over again he stuffed the crumpled centre page of a Penthouse magazine the man had been looking at into his mouth. It was lying on the floor next to the man.

"That's poetic. Now she's in your mouth, instead of you in hers," he remarked, a smile on his face. The man stared at him goggle-eyed.

"Is the guard inside armed?" Harry scowled looking at the man fiercely and prodded him with the muzzle of his Sten gun. It was unlikely, but he wanted to be sure. "Just nod your head."

The guard, now witless, nodded his head vigorously in the negative. Harry unhooked the keys from the man's belt and then pulled him to his feet.

"Come along, old son, you're going to help me." He opened the security gate and pushing the man in front of him, he rushed into the interior of the political prisoners' cellblock. The inner guard was cowering in the corner.

"Open cell three, now!" ordered Harry. The guard dropped the keys in his haste to obey. Soon however he had found the correct one and opened the door to the cell.

"Hi, Mr. Templar, ready to go? Harry said, shoving both guards into the cell with him.

"Hello Pirate, good to see you," replied Templar already clutching his solitary bag. "Nothing further to do here." At that moment there were a couple of rifle shots very close, followed by a burst from what was clearly an AK 47.

"Everything alright, Pirate?" asked Templar looking very worried.

"Perfect. That'll be Sampson keeping the guards in the main prison honest. Right, now lets get these others out of their cells." With that he locked the two guards in the cell and in the space of three minutes had assembled all the detainees in the corridor. All of them were trying to talk at once.

"Quiet!" barked Harry. Everyone stopped and looked at him. "Now I don't want another word from any of you until you're in the plane and in the air, is that clear?" Nods all round. "And I want you to follow my every instruction as if your life depended on it, because it does." He turned on his heel just as Sampson appeared. He handed Harry the pistol he'd picked up in the outer corridor.

"Everybody, this is Sampson. Follow him now and he'll take you to the transport." He turned back to Sampson. "Everything OK, Sam?"

"No problem."

"OK, get going, I'll hold the fort here until you're in the clear. Go on everybody." Sampson and the six detainees were gone into the gloom. Harry backed out of the cell block, locked the door behind him and keeping a sharp look out in front of him, he ran back to the guardroom.

He checked to see that the three men there were properly trussed up and then he ran back into the entrance hall, eyes everywhere looking for threats. There were none. He ran out of the prison and joined Peter next to the hibiscus hedge.

"Right, off you go, Pete, I'll hold them off until I hear the engines running and then I'll come. Peter left without a word. He just touched Harry on the shoulder as he rose and left.

The Commandant managed, in just 5 minutes, to assemble eight armed men and with these he set up an advancing skirmish line, avoiding the road. When they got to the edge of the open area in front of the prison, they could see nothing. He waited a few moments and then rising from his cover he slowly advanced into the open. Harry fired one round from a pistol over his head and forced him back. Then to accentuate it, he moved along behind the hedge and from the corner of the prison he let off a short burst from the sub-machine gun. He then ran quickly back to the other end of the hedge, looked hard to his right and then ran across the track leading to the airfield. This move attracted fire from four or five weapons and he felt the air buzz with passing bullets. He fell behind a mound of earth and rocks, and settling himself, he fired three shots with the pistol, all high and widely spread. He then rolled over onto his back, unhooked his radio and called Jim.

"Flyboy, Pirate."

"Go ahead Pirate."

"How's the loading going?"

"Complete, pre-flight fifty percent. Start in two."

"OK, call when you're ready to shut the door and roll."

"Copy, Flyboy."

"Pirate."

Harry then crawled thirty yards or so through the undergrowth, and changing the magazine on his Sten, let off a short burst into the gravel of the carpark. The bullets sparked and scattered as they hit the ground and again the move attracted return fire,

He looked at his watch. It was 3:55 am; dawn would be in about 35 minutes. We're cutting it fine, he thought, and immediately stood up and ran back to the mound, which offered the best cover. Also, I can't keep firing to miss forever; they'll soon work out that I'm just trying to hold them up. Jim came back on the radio.

"Pirate, Flyboy." Harry brought the radio up to his lips.

"Go ahead, Flyboy."

"Ready to start engines."

"Proceed, Flyboy, call again when ready to roll."

"Will comply, Flyboy."

"Pirate."

The noise of the turbine engine starting up was comparatively deafening despite the firing that had been going on. I'll have to watch carefully now, thought Harry, they're bound to do something now. He was right. A withering barrage of fire started up from the positions taken up by the guards furthest from the entrance to the prison. Harry didn't hesitate, knowing it was the prelude to a rush, and lobbed a percussion grenade into the car park. Four seconds later it exploded, just as the first of three men emerged from the bush opposite him heading for the prison. The blast knocked them flat and after a moment, they started moving and crawled back into the brush. Thank goodness I didn't kill one of them. This is getting a bit hairy now. They'll launch something else now, probably a vehicle that will be far more difficult to stop.

Again his premonition was correct. Over the sound of the second of the turbine engines starting up, he heard the roar of a diesel Land Rover engine. It rounded out of the bush to the south of the prison and rushed straight to the entrance, dropped off two men and then careered to right across the front of Harry, gunfire pouring from it. He held his fire knowing that this was not the charge to stop. The vehicle swung around and disappeared down the road back behind the skirmish line.

"Ready to roll, Pirate."

"Copy, I'm on my way, stand by." He let off another short burst from the Sten and then started crawling backwards. When he was deep enough into the brush he stood up and started running.

But it was all to no avail. He'd no sooner got moving than he heard the Land Rover again coming up behind him. This time it was making straight for the road that led up to the airstrip. It had at least four rifles on board, each of them firing short bursts as it careered along.

Harry stopped and firing low he stepped behind a tree, extracted another grenade and threw it into the road. The vehicle rounded a bend and was thirty feet away from it when it went off. The vehicle careered to a halt and then Harry knew he had to start taking aim and unless he could stop this vehicle he wouldn't have time to get back to the aircraft. Firing low, he sprayed the front of the vehicle with a short burst from his Sten gun. Some of the men in the vehicle leapt out and ran back the way they'd come. But then it moved forward again, a thunderous volley of shots coming from it. It then dawned on Harry that he didn't have a hope of getting back to the aircraft in time to allow it to take off safely anyway. He again showed no hesitation. Lifting the radio, he shouted,

"Go, go, go! Don't wait, they're all over me now, can't hold them. You must go now, I'll run back. Pirate." He then turned the radio off, turned back the way he'd come and started running diagonally back across the track towards the unguarded gate. The Land Rover pressed on and would be at the airstrip within 30 seconds, but Harry heard the revolutions of the engines mount to a screaming pitch and knew that they were gone. He stopped as he approached the gate and turned to hear, rather than see, the aircraft climbing steeply into the dark pre-dawn sky.

He ran out the gate and at a fast trot set off along the road eastwards until he'd put at least a mile between himself and the front gate of the prison, and then he went off the road into the bush. Again he stopped knowing that it would be some time before they realised that there was still someone there and set out to find him. He unhooked the radio, turned it on and was immediately greeted with a repetitious call,

"Pirate, Pirate, come in please. Pirate, Pirate, come in please."

"Hi, Flyboy. I'm OK and on the run; already about one and a half klicks from the gate. Glad you're off. God speed. Do not, repeat, do not disclose my identity to the pax, we must maintain anonymity. I'll see you all in a week."

"Anonymity confirmed. Watch yourself, Pirate. We're out of here. Call every even hour on the hour if you can, I'll have someone listening out. Radio should be good for at least three hours of transmission. Cheers, Flyboy."

"Pirate out."

Superintendent Motswadi and his three truckloads of men arrived at Mumbwa at almost exactly 5:00 am that Sunday morning. Eight minutes earlier and they would have caught Harry running along the road. The prison was in an uproar. Nine men had already been arrested for being drunk on duty and were being held in a cell in the Political Wing. The remaining men outside the prison were on parade in the carpark in front of the prison being shouted at by the Commandant. The locks and chains put on the armoury and inner gates were in the process of being sawn off.

Motswadi's heart sank. This was exactly what he'd feared and he knew, without having to be told that the six detainees held there were gone. He jumped out of his vehicle and after issuing orders as to the deployment of his police contingent; he took the Commandant into his office and made him recite every detail of what had happened.

"How many casualties do you have?"

"None, Sir."

"None? You're telling me that no-one is dead?"

"Yes, Sir. Well, one man has a sore head from being hit by the butt of a weapon when he tried to draw his pistol." Motswadi considered this revelation for a moment. How could anyone organise an escape of seven prisoners and not kill anyone? This was obviously an extremely professional assault, but they had obviously been instructed not to hurt or kill anyone. Incredible, but it pointed to Rhodesian Government operation. Only their troops would have the discipline.

"Now let me get this straight. Your vehicle was being fired upon as you approached the airfield and you had to stop because a percussion grenade exploded in front of the vehicle?"

"Yes, Sir," said the Commandant looking at his feet. He couldn't bring his eyes up to meet Motswadi's penetrating stare.

"How is it that no-one in your vehicle has been hit?"

"I don't know, Sir. All the shots were low." Motswadi was fascinated. Someone firing low and only using percussion grenades; they were clearly determined not to hurt any of the guards; very interesting.

"And when you stopped you could hear the aircraft taking off?"

"Yes, Sir. By the time we got to the airstrip the plane was gone."

"How far were you from the airstrip when you were stopped by the grenade?"

"About two hundred yards, Sir."

"Of dense bush?"

"Yes, Sir."

"Has it occurred to you, Commandant, that at least one of the raiding party must therefore still be here on the ground?"

The Commandant thought for a few moments and then it dawned on him that the person who had thrown the grenade could not possibly have got back to the aircraft in time. He looked up and what he saw in Motswadi's eyes made him flinch. He opened his mouth to speak but no words came out.

"You bloody fool! You are also under arrest." A detail was called in and the protesting hapless Commandant was dragged off to a cell. Motswadi rushed outside again and within minutes a search party began to beat through the bush to the north of the prison looking for signs of the remaining attackers. Going back into the Commandant's office, he then called the other men who'd seen the attackers in to see him one by one. The interrogations lasted for two hours during which Motswadi was able to piece together the entire clever rescue mission. He was standing at the heavily barred external windows of the office, watching the dawn, when there was finally a knock on the door and a Sergeant entered.

"Yes, Sergeant?"

"Sir, you are correct, we have found tracks of one man running away from the scene. He ran out through the gate and along the road. He is wearing veldskoens and from the set of the footprints I think it is a white man shorter than six feet. They are very heavy in the heel. We lost the prints on the tarmac but my men will soon find out where he came off and went into the bush. They are searching for that now. But, Sir, I have to report that the old man who looked after the airstrip and fuel bowser has also disappeared. He has gone north towards the town. He will be much more difficult to follow, Sir, but I think that he will go west, Sir. He is a Barotse."

"OK, Sergeant, form a detail with our best tracker to find him and continue the search along the road. Call me when there is anything to report. Also I would like to know how much fuel there is in the bowser and set a guard there also."

"Yes, Sir."

"Carry on, Sergeant, I have much to do here and when I have finished my report, I must go back to Lusaka and advise the Minister."

"Sir."

On board there was chaos. Everyone was jabbering and jostling for attention from Sampson and Peter and they kept clapping Jim and each other on the back in congratulations and relief. Jim passed along messages for calm, but these went unheeded. So he switched off the autopilot and taking control, did a rapid port then starboard wiggle on the Joystick. The aircraft lurched one way and then the other. Cries of alarm and then silence as everybody froze in apprehension. Jim turned around and shouted backwards,

"Everybody sit down, buckle up, and shut up, we're not out of this yet. Pete, come forward please." Peter sheepishly got up from his seat and stooped his way to the front of the cabin. He was just lifting his right foot over the central control console in order to sit down in the right hand seat when Jim held out his arm and stopped him.

"No, remain in the seat at the back, but I want to tell you something." Peter leant forward.

"Yes, Jim?" Now he was worried.

"No, come closer, what I have to say is for your ears only." Pete stooped further until his left ear was within inches of Jim's mouth.

"We must maintain Pirate's anonymity; we don't want his name splashed all over the papers."

"Oh," was all Peter could think of saying.

"Pete, make sure Sampson keeps his mouth shut and then if any of the pax do know who Pirate is, swear them to secrecy, understand?" The implications of the whole issue dawned on Pete rapidly.

"Got it, Jim, but I think most will know, they'll have discussed it in the prison."

"Well, they're supposed to be spies, aren't they? They're used to keeping their mouths shut. Read them the Riot Act, or Official Secrets or whatever, but ensure that there's not a word, OK?"

"Leave it to me." Pete straightened up and turned to face backwards towards the passengers who were all looking at him in worried anticipation. He scrutinised them all, one by one, his eyes resting briefly on the one woman detainee, a development that none of them had anticipated. His father hadn't told him the sexual composition of the detainees.

"Folks," he started. "As you are aware, we were forced to leave behind one of our rescue party. He is now on the run and no doubt being hotly pursued by the Zambian authorities. I must make it clear that he is the best friend that I have ever had and so nothing had better happen to him." He paused and continued sweeping his gaze over the rest of the passengers. "So please understand, and this is not a request, it is an order for those of you have signed the Official Secrets Act, and it is a warning to those of you who haven't, not one word is to be passed on in any manner whatsoever to anyone as to his identity. Furthermore, the same applies to our own identities, the kind of aircraft this is, how you were rescued, how many there were of us, the lot. Nothing. Is that clear?"

Nodding of heads, murmurs, looks across at each other. "In fact that is to apply from this moment on. No reference whatsoever is to be made to this new situation. We ourselves will deal with this problem as time goes by, just as we dealt with your problem. If the press get a hold of this, we're in trouble, so I'm going to be really forceful on this and say to you that if it is determined that word has got out from one of you, you will have to answer to me, and I will not be inclined to be gentle and kind." A few annoyed looks now, but Peter ignored them. "There is more. We recommend that if the press do get on to you, which sure as nuts they will, that you state merely that you were released, period. Refer the press for further comment to the Zambian Government citing the fact that a condition of your release was complete silence, which it is, on our part. Anyone breaks that silence, and I'll take him back to Zambia myself." He looked fiercely around at them all again and then moved slowly aft to his seat. It was his father that started the clapping, everyone joined in and the applause reverberated throughout the cabin.

When it was light enough to see properly, Harry went back over his track from the road and carefully obliterated what he could find of his passage down off the road. He even carefully cut off leaves that he had disturbed in the visible undergrowth, and then he started to run. His pace at first was very brisk, as he tried to put as much distance between himself and the prison. He ran due south along various footpaths trodden clear of grass and brush by generations of people walking along them through the bush. Where he could, he kept within the woodlands, avoiding villages and fields, but he knew it was only a matter of time before he was spotted and reported. Many times that first early dawn he waded through streams and across soggy inundated flood plains and marshes. Soon he could barely be recognised as a human being, but for the rags hanging about him and the sub-machine gun held across his chest at all times.

He began to encounter more and more people as the sun came up and on each occasion he ducked into the bush nearest to him and hoped he hadn't been spotted. It gave him some comfort to know that other people, animals and cyclists were treading on his tracks behind him. The biggest problems were those caused by the villagers' dogs and he was incredibly lucky that despite being barked at several times, he wasn't seen.

At about 7:30 am, after moving in and out of the bush off the tracks he was following for some two hours he eventually found a suitable looking kopje[57] on which to lie up for the day. Carefully avoiding exposure and watching out for snakes and leopards, he clambered up two hundred feet or so, cleared away some brush and then settled himself under a sizable large-leaved rock fig tree[58]. He took a cartridge out of his pocket and used his knife on the casing rim to loosen the projectile. He twisted and pulled the head of the bullet slowly out of the casing, careful not to spill any of the powder. He then lightly sprinkled that around himself to keep away the ants. Then he examined both his weapons closely, checked his ammunition supply, laid them on the ground next to him and then began to wait.

He gazed out over the countryside, looking left back in the direction from which he'd come. It was a typical African woodland scene. Fertile level land occasionally hand tilled and sparsely planted out with maize, paw paw (*papaya*), ground nuts, mashesh (*an easily fermentable indigenous grain used to produce a coarse milky beer*) and mango trees by the subsistence farmers. Several deep dongas were visible indicating the perennial problem of land management. Scattered about, as far as the eye could see, were other kopjes of all sizes, but all essentially the same as the one he'd climbed. It's so beautiful, but can it be saved, he asked himself? The heat in Africa wastes no time and although it was still early, he could feel prickles of heat down his back, so he leaned forwards and hunched himself over his knees, letting the air cool his perspiration. He turned his thoughts to planning his future course of action.

CHAPTER 24

The Kingair landed at the Swan airstrip at 6:20 am to a huge reception committee. The police were there in force and so was Squadron Leader Mick Glover with two Allouette gun ships. A large tent and a field hospital had been erected to the one side and a latrine constructed. Annie, Barbara and her mother-in-law, Mrs. Templar had set up a bush kitchen, which they left to be manned by George. They then went back and stood next to their vehicles parked to one side knowing that a substantial debriefing was going to take place before they would be allowed near their men.

As the personnel disembarked from the aircraft, the last off was Jim.

"Oh my God, where is Harry?" whispered Annie fighting back the tears. She slammed her coffee down on the bonnet of the truck and ran towards the group of people moving towards the tent. Jim knew they were in trouble the moment he saw her tearing towards them. He gripped Peter by the arm and they both turned to meet her.

"He's OK, Annie." It was Peter who spoke first. She stopped, again casting her eyes over all the people who had come off the aircraft, confusion flooding through her.

"But where is he, still at the prison? Has he been wounded? Arrested?"

"No, none of that, he got away." Peter and Jim took her under the shade of a tree away from the others and explained what had happened and that Harry had a radio and had called them.

"Oh my God!" Her distress was so great she almost collapsed, but the others could see that she was determined to keep hold of herself. Peter grasped her around the shoulders. "So when do you expect the next call?" she asked.

"At eight o'clock," said Jim. "Unfortunately, we won't be able to hear him from here, I'll have to take off again and fly over Kariba to have any chance of being within range. I can be in position in about twenty minutes from here."

"I'm coming with you," said Annie.

"Of course, but first let me explain what's happening to the authorities. We've got ten minutes or so."

Annie couldn't hold back the flood of tears and turned away to go and tell Barbara what had happened, but Barbara was right behind her. She fell into Barbara's arms, sobbing her eyes out.

"Oh, Babs, I knew it, I just knew that something would go wrong." Barbara held her gently as she sobbed.

"I'm sure he'll be alright, Annie. Never give up on Harry. He'll muddle through somehow."

"Barbara, he's out there, a fugitive in a strange country in which a white man is out of place. He's got no food, no one to help him."

"Annie, he's got us and mark my words, we'll get him back. You watch!"

Jim came over to them a few minutes later and told them to get aboard and that Pete and Mick Glover would be joining them to see if they could establish contact.

Harry waited until 8:00 am and switched on his radio. Putting it to his lips and resolving to switch it off after exactly one minute, he looked at his watch and started calling,

"Pirate to Flyboy, Pirate to Flyboy." He had repeated this about six times and was about to give up and leave a blind message when a distant voice came from the radio.

"Pirate, Flyboy reading you strength two, go ahead." Harry heaved a sigh of relief.

"Flyboy, some ten to fifteen miles out. Secure for now, will continue at eighteen hundred hours zulu as arranged, Pirate."

"Confirm ten to fifteen out, secure, will continue at eighteen hundred, Flyboy," Jim called back.

"Affirm."

"Good, all fine at this end. Standby one, Pirate, someone wants to say Hi." In the aircraft, Jim handed his microphone over to Annie who was sitting in the right hand seat next to him.

"Depress the button when you want to speak, Annie," he instructed, "and keep it oblique, we don't want to give the game away."

"Hello, Pirate," she said. Jim had to lean over and lift her finger from the button.

"Hi, kiddo, I'm AOK, no sweat, you relax. Love you and see you in a week."

"Love you," sobbed Annie.

Mick Glover leant forwards and gently pulled the microphone out of her hand. He spoke rapidly.

"Pirate, Chopper Man here, cease calling this frequency from now. Call only one-two-four decimal zero at intervals six, say again, six, starting fourteen hundred hours zulu today, we'll keep a watch and pass on news, Chopper Man."

"Hi, Chopper Man, one-two-four decimal zero, intervals six, first at fourteen hundred, glad all is well, out. Pirate." Harry immediately switched off the radio and hooked it onto his belt again. He lay back, a smile on his lips and thought that things weren't as bad as they looked.

Back at the airstrip, Detective Superintendent Bill Sturrock began the processing of the detainees. First were the identity checks, including photographs, finger printing, checking of next of kin, addresses and so on. After each individual had completed those they were ushered into the medical station for a preliminary medical check up. Thankfully they were all in good health, even Arlott whose bruises and cuts had been properly treated while he was in the prison. Finally he rounded them all up and distributed as many of them as he could into Mick

Glover's helicopters, but had Chester Templar directed to his police Land Rover.

One hour later they were all gathered in the mess hall at the police camp in Karoi. Sturrock came in, several examination pads under his arm and a hand clutching a pile of ballpoint pens. He dumped them on the table placed in one corner of the hall for that purpose, and turned to address them.

"I'm sorry to delay your homecoming and being re-united with your families but you will be held here until I am satisfied that there is not one shred of information left untold that may be useful." A general murmur of agreement greeted him.

"We will start with each of you preparing a written statement in accordance with my instructions as we go along. Please would you avail yourselves of a pad and pen?" He indicated to another policeman standing to one side to distribute the writing material, "And then find a comfortable seat at one of the tables." A few titters at that, all the seats were the same metal-framed hardboard seated chairs found in every canteen in the world. He waited a few moments while they shuffled around, and then began.

"Please write across the top 'This is the sworn Statement of – your full name – aged – whatever it is – given and attested at the Karoi Police Camp at – leave that free." He waited then for them to catch up and then continued slowly. The process took four hours and encompassed two breaks; one for lunch, and the second for afternoon tea. Finally they finished and he suggested that they all take a break, clean up and take a rest.

"Take your statements with you and check them. You may even confer to ensure that the facts are correct. We'll meet back here at eighteen-thirty for drinks and I'll collect them then. At that time I shall have a tape recorder present because I want a more informal 'round table', with all of you at liberty to say whatever you want, which may contribute to our intelligence. OK?" He looked at the only woman amongst them. "Ma'am, a room has been set aside for your personal use, if you'd follow that Constable there, please?" He indicated to his left. "The rest of you are not so fortunate and will have to share a dormitory, but I'm sure you'll find everything you need."

The Zambian Police had started a massive manhunt. Headed by Superintendent Motswadi, a contingent of three hundred men were being used to sweep the countryside around Mumbwa. Besides the old man who had disappeared, they had no idea who they were looking for and having lost the trail pretty well where it began, they didn't have a clue which way to look.

The police interviewed many local villagers and came up with nothing, but Motswadi didn't give up because he knew it was just a matter of time before some snippet of news came in that they would be able to work with.

The gathering at 6:30 was much more cheerful, especially once Sturrock had the bar opened and beers distributed. Sturrock indicated to them to be quiet for a moment and then said pointedly into a microphone placed on the table,

"Please gather around. Can you draw up your chairs and relax." He waited through the clattering of furniture being moved about and the folk settled down.

"This is Detective Superintendent W. Sturrock. I am conducting a discussion session with..", he preceded to name them all, and then gave the time, date and location and the fact that they were all present of their own volition.

"OK folks, I obviously haven't had a chance to go through your statements, but I'll interview each of you separately tomorrow. For now I'm primarily interested in one thing: I want to identify the seventh person arrested, this so called 'Claude'. Please state your surname before you start talking for the first time."

"Ah.. Templar. No, none of us believe that there ever was a seventh person arrested," said Chester Templar.

"Yes, we surmised as much," Sturrock responded, "do you all agree on this?" Everyone concurred. "But, assuming therefore that he is the one that shopped you all, who is he?"

It took exactly 25 minutes of animated and sometimes angry argument before they had worked out that it could only have been the manager of the Golf Club, Mr. Brad Fischer.

"Describe this man." And so the discussion continued. Finally Sturrock stood up. "Thank you very much folks, that's enough for now.

Feel free to help yourselves to another drink. Dinner's at eight, I'll come and fetch you." He switched off the tape recorder, wound the tape back onto one reel, removed it from the machine and left the room. He was so elated he could barely contain himself. There was no doubt in his mind as to whom this man was; none other than Brad Fischer. The depositions so far also served to confirm that the man was not only a criminal, but he was clearly an agent himself, either working for Zambia or East Germany. He surmised this because he knew Fischer was German, or, he thought, Fischer was probably working for both the Zambians and the Peoples Democratic Deutche Republic. That was the most likely. Well we know how to find out, don't we?

Harry marched through the bush for two nights before anyone saw him. He'd even managed to get across two main roads without being spotted. It happened when he was straining water into his mouth through his shirt kneeling at the side of a small stream. He straightened up and looked straight into the eyes of a small herd boy. Even though he'd anticipated this moment for while, he didn't know quite what to do or say, not sure that the boy would understand anything anyway. So he did the obvious, he smiled, stood up, carefully put his shirt back on, draped his equipment and firearms about him, waved, turned around and walked away.

Out of sight of the child, he began to run, knowing that it wouldn't be long before the game was up. So he resolved to work his way farther west into a wilder part of the country and then to make his way south towards the Kafue/Zambezi escarpment. Boot's on the other foot now boyo, the hunter is about to really become the hunted. His mind grappled with his options: run as far south now, or really go quite far west. Where would they put up a cordon? As he moved through the night, his fourth now in Zambia, he came to no solution, but he knew he had to find food soon or he would start to weaken. All he'd managed to find thus far were wild gooseberries and figs. When he got into the valley he knew that there would be more natural food to eat, marulas[59], snot apples[60], mobola plums[61] and other edible plants.

On the other hand the further west he went, the easier it would be to get across the Kafue River, but he would, in any case, have to steal a boat or dugout canoe to do that, so he ceased to think that this was a relevant issue. On the other hand it was much wilder to the west, so that while he might encounter fewer people, the chances of coming across dangerous animals increased, especially as he was moving on the run at night.

He stopped for a while and then realised that it didn't matter if he went west or south, because he would probably be seen from time to time, so he changed his mind. Briefly climbing another kopje and searching carefully behind him for signs of pursuit, he turned south again, thinking that the closer he got to the Zambezi, the safer he would be.

None of this thinking came to any avail, however, because the following morning, sitting high on a kopje, he could see trucks and troops moving around to the north of him. Just ants seemingly spreading out, but through his binoculars the black dots took on a more vertical shape and the occasional glint of metal in the early morning sunlight, gave them away. That day he ran as he'd never run before, keeping to paths and where possible crossing sandy areas, brushing the sand carefully behind himself using a bundle of branches he had broken off for that purpose. He knew it wouldn't fool them, but it would delay them while they cast around looking for his spoor again. He laughed to himself, 'spoor', I really am a hunted animal now.

Motswadi was right and, furthermore, elated. Not only had one of the men on the run been seen but they now also knew he was a white man. Motswadi was convinced that they would apprehend the man. A white man had no chance moving far unseen and unrecognised in black Africa. He recalled all the police he had deployed around Mumbwa and those trying to find the old man, "poor old fellow, he's probably scared shitless and obviously had nothing to do with this whole thing", and then redeployed them further south. He realised immediately from the position of the sighting that the man was trying to go south towards the Zambezi. The fugitive was clearly hoping that he'd get across to the safety of the Rhodesian side of the river. He set up roadblocks and began sweeping the bush south from where the herd boy had seen a strange looking white man.

The three Allouette gun ships came in from the south. Two settled on the 17th fairway, dark figures pouring out of them, while the other, cannon pointing down menacingly, although it could not be seen, hovered over the house. A powerful searchlight bathed the entire dwelling in an eerie light.

The men took precisely 35 seconds to run the short distance from the fairway to the house, break in and secure the three people in the house.

The new manager of the club and his wife had never been so terrified in their lives. They woke to the sound of the helicopters, but hadn't even moved when two men burst into their bedroom, torches on them, blinding the hapless couple staring horrified at them from behind a thin sheet. Sturrock walked in behind the fire force and looked at them.

"Where's Fischer?" Vicious, abrupt. Their eyes only got wider. Sturrock reached forward across the woman and yanked the man up from the bed, holding him one-handed by the neck. The man literally hung there grimly clutching the sheet to his chest.

"I asked, where is Fischer?" slowly shaking the man as he said it. "Or do you know him as Volker?"

The man eventually found his voice and stammered,

"He's not here, Seh, he's gone on holiday."

"Where?"

"I don't know, Seh," said the man, his voice getting stronger as it dawned on him that these people were not after him. Sturrock looked at him, tilting his head slightly and squinting his eyes.,

"Bullshit," he said again shaking the man, but this time vigorously. "Tell me now or I will shoot your wife. He placed the muzzle of his revolver onto the right eye of the woman, following her down as she cowered down onto the bed in terror. The man's reaction was pathetic.

"Please, Seh! No, Seh! I think he's gone to the camps."

"Which one?" Sturrock nudged his pistol against the woman's forehead.

"Please, Seh, I don't know." He was shaking uncontrollably now and the smell of urine permeated the air. Sturrock sniffed and looked at the man closely. No, this man is not lying. He threw the poor fellow back onto the bed and turned on his heels.

"Shit, he's skipped. Come on guys, let's go. Bed time, waste of time, we're too late." Within 60 seconds the two helicopters lifted off and clattered off into the night, followed a few seconds later by the guard ship. The whole exercise took exactly three minutes.

By the time Motswadi found out about it, they were long since back home, the occupants propping up the bar at the Chewore Base back in Rhodesia. But he was delighted.

"One to the good guys," he laughed, chalking up the figure **1** with his finger on an imaginary blackboard.

At his 6:00am call, Harry advised that the Zambian Police were closing in on him and it was Jim, when advised, that came up with the answer.

"Pirate, head due south, tonight. There's a drift across the Kafue River at Lochinvar National Park. Joseph will pick you up there on the north bank one klick west of the Lochinvar drift. Repeat, the north bank, do not cross the river." In fact Jim was very concerned about Joseph because he didn't think that it would take the police long to deduce who had supplied all the guards with booze. He had already shut the office at Lusaka Airport and had stopped operations into Zambia for the time being.

So that afternoon Harry started moving south again, keeping to thick bush and what high ground he could. On four occasions he was forced to dive into the undergrowth, but on each occasion it was an animal. Shortly before sundown he came out on the edge of the escarpment and his first view of the Kafue River, some five miles away. It took him three hours to clamber down the steep slopes leading down onto the floodplain of the valley. At around midnight he came to the Kafue and began to work his way along it in what he thought was the correct direction. It wasn't, and it was only due to unbelievable luck that Joseph, driving slowly along the road, no more than a rutted vehicle track really, glimpsed him as he dived off into the bush on the side of the riverside track, after appearing to be trudging innocently through the dark. He recognised immediately that it must have been Harry, so he stopped and leaving the lights on and engine running, he leapt out of his truck.

"Harry," he called, "its Joseph."

Harry, meanwhile, was frantically working his way backwards on his stomach into the thick bush, Sten gun at the ready stretched out in front of him. He heard the call and almost fainted with surprise. Joseph! His relief was unbridled as he jumped up and ran out. He embraced Joseph in a thankful bear hug.

"God's truth, Jo, am I pleased to see you?" He was almost crying.

"Come, Harry, we must go quickly." He untangled himself from Harry's embrace and climbed up onto the back of the truck beckoning Harry up with him. "There is a road block near to Lusaka and you must hide. He undid a few tie-downs and then pulled aside several logs of firewood to reveal a mattress and blanket hidden underneath. Harry climbed into the space and started to make himself comfortable. When he looked up he could see nothing, Joseph had already replaced the logs and he could hear him tying them down and into place.

"Harry, there is a village near here where we will park for the rest of the night and tomorrow morning I will give some people a lift into Lusaka. You must keep quite so they do not know you are here, OK?"

"Sure, Jo, thank you."

Joseph shone a torch down on the ground. There were tracks everywhere. He carefully gathered some of the long grass next to the track, randomly pulling the long grass fronds straight out of their base structures over a stretch of 30 or 40 yards. Once he had enough to form a scanty brush, he backtracked carefully brushing away the evidence that someone had walked along there and climbed aboard a vehicle at that point. His final action was to open the door and hanging from the steering wheel, feet up on the step, he leaned back and brushed away all evidence of his own footprints. He knew that in the daylight it would take a good tracker no more than a few minutes to work out what had transpired, but they'd be long gone by then. He turned around, speaking through the open rear window of the cab.

"OK, Harry, we go now. Also there is some chicken and milk for you to eat under the mattress." With that the truck started up and began moving off. In the darkness Harry found the chicken wrapped in brown paper and in no time had wolfed it down. Within minutes he was fast asleep lulled into oblivion by the rocking and bouncing of the truck on the rough road.

Joseph drove along the track for about forty minutes. What surprised him was that he had to move partially off the track on three occasions to allow approaching vehicles to get past. Whilst worrying that the drivers might later identify his vehicle he was actually pleased because traffic meant that their hunters would find it much more difficult to work out what had happened to Harry. His tracks would effectively and inexplicably come to an end at the road. He then turned off along a secondary track that led shortly into a small village surrounded by maize fields. He turned the vehicle around and parked it near a hut into which he then disappeared for the two hours that remained of the night. At sunrise he reappeared and calling out to other villagers moving about, he ordered that those who were coming, had better climb onboard for the trip to Lusaka. Many of them, some children, several trussed up chickens and a goat climbed or were lifted up onto the back and settled in on and around the securely fastened down pile of firewood. It was quite festive and after half an hour or so of banter and argument as to whom was going to sit where and so on, they settled down. Harry lay sweating beneath it all clutching his Sten gun and praying, to no one in particular, that they wouldn't smell him. Soon enough though, Joseph started the vehicle and set off.

There was a queue of vehicles stopped at the roadblock. The police gave most vehicles a mere glance and waved them on. They walked up either side of the truck and one of them stopped briefly to talk to Joseph.

"Where are you going?"

"Lusaka." Joseph forced a smile onto his face. "I'm taking these people into the shops and I have some firewood to sell." Joseph well knew that with the villagers on the back, the police would never suspect that there was a white man hidden under the logs.

"OK, you can go," said the policeman waving him on. It was as easy as that. The next Harry knew, Joseph was shaking him gently on the shoulder.

"OK, Harry, it's safe to come out now." Harry shook his head to clear the cobwebs; he'd slept only in fits and starts and he was dying to go to the loo.

"What time is it, Jo?" he asked slowly unravelling himself from his confined quarters.

"Quarter past eight, Harry."

"Dammit, I missed my radio call. Can you phone Jim straight away?"

"Yes. I must leave you here first and go to the post office to call." Joseph looked around to make sure that nobody was watching them, and then quickly led Harry into a small but neatly kept two-roomed house. "This is my house, Harry. I have sent my wife home to her parents in the bush, so as long as you do not go outside or answer the door, nobody will know that you are here. There is food in the kitchen and you can rest."

He went around making sure that all the curtains and windows were closed despite the stifling heat of the place.

"Now I must go to phone and then I will go to town to make arrangements for us to go to Kariba. I will come back at lunch time."

At Merrywaters farm Annie tried to put it all out of her mind showing incredible fortitude. In fact the seemingly continuous presence of Peter and Barbara became a bit of an irritant. She eventually told them that she was OK and that they should go home.

Keeping an eye on what was happening on the farm she spent most of her days supervising the building works. She went into the farmers' co-op and collected the rolls of razor wire for the top of the new fence. Chadrack organised the men and the work and putting the lethal rolls of razor wire in place was commenced. She also visited the doctor, for two reasons. Her period was late and she wasn't felling very well, but more importantly, so she thought, it was to finalise the supply of medical supplies and equipment for her to set up a properly functioning clinic at Merrywaters.

The doctor took a smear and a blood sample and sent her home saying that they'd have to wait for the results to come back from Salisbury before he could advise her of her condition. So, armed with four packing cases of medical supplies and a bottle of aspirin for her headaches, she drove back to the farm.

But the days dragged, each punctuated only by the regular reports she was getting from Jim. She was miserable and the staff and labourers knew it. Showing incredible understanding they uncharacteristically spoke quietly in her presence and literally jumped to do her bidding.

Then Jim came to stay, monitoring the over-border saga on the radio through Sturrock and Glover. It cheered her up some because at least she began to get the up to date reports in real time. But she was frustrated by the knowledge that there was nothing she could do to help. So she continued to feel uncomfortable and listless.

Meanwhile Motswadi was starting to develop respect for this man who had eluded their every effort to find him. They had twice picked up his trail and had twice lost it. His frustration with his men began to show when the trail went stone cold at Lochinvar. He couldn't understand it. They had swept every inch of the ground around there. The man just wasn't there.

He concluded correctly that this was because the man wasn't there at all and began to look at the alternatives. Either the man had gone south though the park in a vehicle or similarly in a vehicle he had gone east towards Lusaka, or west along the track up the Kafue valley. He quickly ruled out south through the park, because no boats or canoes had been reported stolen and the man hadn't crossed the river at the Lochinvar drift. He'd been guarding that carefully for days. So he must have gone east or west. Both options were attractive but east was far more likely.

To the east, there were a large number of tobacco and maize farms owned and operated by white people along the river where a man might conceivably be holed out, or alternatively, actually be living. To cover this eventuality he sent out a hundred men under the command of one Chief Inspector and four Inspectors with strict instructions to search every single white household, including rubbish tips, and to closely question every labourer in their employ.

And then there was Lusaka itself. The balance of his men he concentrated on placing a 'cordon sanitaire' around Lusaka. He felt sure that if the man was in Lusaka and tried to leave, they'd have him. Furthermore he instructed the CID to start a house-to-house visit of every white household in the city. They were to question the domestic staff of each one in search of any clues as to the whereabouts of this elusive raider.

He himself then sat down in his office and began to assemble and analyse all the facts that he had at his disposal. Taking it from the beginning it was not long before he realised that he'd overlooked the fact that there was a third man involved, who must be still in the country. The man who'd sold the alcohol to the guards. Taking a Sergeant and a Constable with him the following morning, he raced out to Mumbwa to interview the guards again.

Jim, staying now at Merrywaters, received the call from his office in Bulawayo at 8:30am, telling him that Joseph had just phoned. He walked through to the kitchen where Annie and George were talking, He could see the drawn out look on her face and knew that she must be going through hell.

"Jo's got him in Lusaka," he announced. Annie turned to him, untold questions in her look. He sat her down and told her what he knew.

"What happens now, Jim?" asked Annie.

"Well, the plan is to drive him out of Lusaka towards the Victoria Falls and then turn off after the Kafue and go down to the lake. Once there, and if his radio is still working, we're to take a boat over at night and fetch him. I can't risk taking an aircraft in there at the moment because they're now on the alert and they'll shoot at anything that they don't recognise."

"When do you think that this'll all be over?"

"Oh, we should have him out in two or three days."

"Well Jim, I'm depending on you. In fact we're all depending on you," she said waving in the direction of George.

"Annie, I understand your agony, but please don't worry too much yet. At the moment we're OK." Jim placed his hand on her shoulder and looked into her eyes. "Be strong," he said. "Look I have to push off to see Sturrock and report what's happened because Harry didn't report in at six this morning. Will you be alright for the rest of the day?"

"Yes. I've got a lot to do around here, as you can see the place is a mess."

Harry knew he stank. He was filthy, all his exposed skin still covered with the remains of the black camouflage paint. His clothes and body were covered in four days of unwashed sweat, wood-smoke odour and dust. He went though into the small bathroom and looked at himself in the mirror above the basin. He didn't recognise himself. But for his eyes and his hair, it would have been difficult to identify that he was white. Only then did he realise that he must look frightening, his Sten gun, binoculars and satchel were still slung around his neck, pistol, radio and sheath knife clearly visible on his hip. All I need now is machine gun and ammunition belt and I'd look like Ché Guevara. He turned away and started to run a bath. When he had about two inches of water in the tub he turned off the watertap and went back into the living room. Sitting down on an easy chair he unslung his weaponry and other paraphernalia and, using an oilcloth from the satchel, he checked and cleaned the firearms. He then lent forward and started to undo the laces of his veldskoens, but then stopped. It had suddenly occurred to him that this disguise might well be useful. Was it wise to clean up yet? What if we have to run for it? He sat back to consider the issues, bath forgotten and promptly fell asleep, his head slowly lolled over onto his left shoulder. Two hours later this is exactly how Joseph found him.

CHAPTER 25

Motswadi arrived at Mumbwa at 7:30am and lost no time setting up the interview room again.

"Who was the man who sold you the whisky?" he asked the first frightened man.

"He is Joseph. He is a friend of the old man." Ah, so the old man was involved. Until now Motswadi had thought that he had run away because he was frightened.

"How did he know the old man?"

"I don't know, Sir, but he was the friend of Ebidiah, the man who brings the fuel for the aeroplanes at the airstrip."

"Where does Ebidiah come from?"

"He lives in Lusaka, Sir. He works at the airport for the fuel company."

Motswadi considered this for a moment and then said,

"Wait here, I haven't finished with you yet." He left the room and went through to the Commandant's office. Picking up the phone he dialled Police Headquarters in Lusaka.

"Get me the Chief Inspector on duty," he ordered briskly into the phone. He waited for a few moments and then he recognised the person answering the other end. "Motswadi here. Issue a warrant of arrest for one Ebidiah and then you are to go out to the airport fuel depot immediately, find him and arrest him. He is the man who handles the refuelling of smaller aircraft from the fuel bowser. You are to take him back to headquarters, put him in a holding cell, in isolation until I return to Lusaka. Is that all clear?" he didn't wait for an answer, but slammed down the phone and returned to the interview room.

"Right, how did this Joseph know the old man?"

"He came here another time with Ebidiah and they came to the shabeen."

"When was this?"

"About two weeks ago, Sir."

"Alright you may go." Motswadi again realised that this had been a very cleverly organised breakout. It clearly had the hand of the Rhodesian regime in it, but how could he prove it? Also, there was the press to worry about. So far all information regarding the rescue had been kept out of the papers, but for how long? They were aware that there was a manhunt on the go, but little else, other than the fact that the police were seeking an individual whom it is thought would be able to assist the police in their enquiries. He knew that he had only a few days to solve the whole case, get the Rhodesian regime involved and then, he thought, 'the shit would hit the fan', either way.

He continued to interview the other personnel who had come in contact with Joseph but learned nothing further. Wrapping it up, he gathered his men and headed back to Lusaka.

"Your husband seems to be causing quite a stir in Zambia," said Mick Glover on the phone to Annie. "They've mounted a huge manhunt around Lusaka and now they're investigating all the farms along the Kafue."

"Will they catch him?" was Annie's only question.

"Well, they haven't got him yet, and each day that goes past his chances increase, because they can't keep this going for too long. Too many embarrassing questions will soon have to be answered."

"How do you mean?"

"Well, there's been no announcement from the Zambian government that the detainees have escaped or been rescued. Initially they probably thought that they would recapture them. That past, I should have thought that they are hoping to capture Harry and then hold him up to the world as an infiltrator from Rhodesia who has caused, at the behest of the Rhodesian government, the escape of the detainees."

"Why, Harry?"

"Oh, they've no idea who he is, yet; otherwise I think we'd already have had an announcement. But it can't go on. They must make an announcement soon before the press find out that there's been a huge breakout of Mumbwa." Jim sat down at the kitchen table with Annie and accepted the cup of tea that George offered him. "But don't worry. Jo is an intelligent, wily little guy and as long as he doesn't get caught being too clever, they'll be alright."

Using his own car, Joseph went from his house out to the airport. He still hadn't had a chance to shut up the office properly. Also he had to advise the airport management that their operations would cease for the time being. At his office, he called the Trans Afrique Air office in Bulawayo and reported the current situation to Belinda. He then put everything into cardboard boxes and stacked them into the back of his car. There really wasn't much to it, the most cumbersome of the articles being the workshop manuals for the Dakotas, which took up most of the space in the boot of the car. Jim had left instructions that they were to be delivered around to the Aircraft Maintenance Operator (*AMO*) at once for safekeeping. Nothing else was important.

Other than that there were just a few files and a pile of invoices and bills; most of which had been paid. One was left, and that was a fuel bill, for which there was a cheque ready for delivery around to Ebidiah's office.

Joseph shut the office, locked it behind him and drove off towards the AMO, on the way intending to stop at the fuel depot. But as he approached, he saw Ebidiah being wrestled into the back of a police Land Rover, hands cuffed behind him. Joseph didn't even slow down, knowing full well that it was now only a matter of time before they would be coming after him.

He delivered the workshop manuals as instructed and drove out of the airport gate only to be greeted by another development. During the two hours or so that he'd been at the airport the police had closed off access to the airport and were now manning a roadblock made up of Land Rovers slewed across the road. They didn't give him a second glance and waved him straight through. Clearly this was measure designed to stop any fugitive from trying to leave by aircraft.

Joseph drove carefully and slowly back to the house. There was clearly now no point in them trying to leave Lusaka by car. They were going to have to walk out. He stopped off at his cousin's house and giving him the keys, he made arrangements for his cousin to drive the car out onto the Victoria Falls road that evening to a rendezvous point, a lay-by on the road about twenty miles out towards Kafue. He told his cousin to tell the police at the roadblock that he was going to Livingston to collect spares from the bonded warehouse there.

Joseph then walked home. He found Harry flopped over in his seat and at first he panicked, thinking that he was dead. But then he realised that the man was merely asleep.

"Harry, we have to get out of here now." The word 'Harry' hadn't even left his mouth before the barrel of the Sten gun pointed straight at him.

"Oh, hi, Jo, sorry about that. I'm a little edgy." He laid down the weapon and stood up. Unthinkingly, he said, "OK, lead the way." Then he considered the situation. Hell I'm slipping, he thought. "But it's still daylight, still two hours till sundown?"

"Harry, we can't stay here a moment longer. They've arrested my contact at the airport and are probably already on their way here. We'll have to risk it. Here, with dark glasses and a floppy hat it will be difficult to tell that you are not one of us. We will cycle, I have two bicycles outside and you will cycle on my wife's bike with your stuff in the front basket."

"Hey, you're on the ball, Jo. No wonder Jim thinks so highly of you."

"And then I will ride in front. You must try to keep about a hundred yards behind me. If I get stopped, I will create trouble and you must continue past and ride on out of Lusaka to the south. If we become separated, there is a vehicle waiting for us at the lay-by on the Kafue road just this side of Chilunga. Do you know it?"

Harry thought for a moment.

"I think so. Is that the one about a mile before the BP service station on the edge of the escarpment?"

"Exactly, but do not use the road; use the paths and tracks all the way. Right, are you ready?"

Harry put on the dark glasses and the hat, folded the Sten gun butt into the barrel and put it, along with his other stuff into his scruffy satchel. He hefted it onto his shoulder and said,

"Gokay, follow me, I'm right behind you."

Unsaid were his concerns for Joseph and his family, but he knew that Joseph had often been based in Bulawayo at the Airlines headquarters and Jo had told him that his wife, taking virtually all their personal possessions, had gone home to her family near Mfuwe in the Luangwa valley. She and the kids were probably safe for the meanwhile.

Superintendent Motswadi arrived back at his office at almost exactly 12 noon. He wasted no time in calling for the prisoner Ebidiah who had now been in custody, and held incommunicado, for two hours. Motswadi judged that he would talk readily enough and he was right.

Within fifteen minutes he had worked out everything there was to know about Joseph's manipulations and realise that Ebidiah in fact was innocent of any involvement in the affair. He also established that the old man was unlikely to have had anything to do with it either. So it was probable that he merely ran away in fear. However, that did not change the fact that he would like to interview the old man.

Instructing the duty orderly to prepare a warrant of arrest for Joseph, he went through to Ebidiah's arresting officer, the Police Inspector that he'd had the telephone discussion with when he was at Mumbwa.

"This man Ebidiah will now give you a statement in the matter of the "six" detainees. When he has completed it, you will take him back to the airport."

"Yes, Sir," was the sharp response.

Turning to Ebidiah, Motswadi said, "Ebidiah, you will now repeat everything that you have told me to this officer who will write it all down. You will then sign and swear to your statement, and then you will be taken home. But you will hold yourself available as a state witness, otherwise I will have you rearrested. Do you understand?"

"Yes, Sir," responded Ebidiah.

"Good." With that Motswadi collected his arrest warrant at the front desk and ordering a Sergeant and two Constables to accompany him, he went off to arrest Joseph.

Adopting the correct procedures, the police, under the command of Superintendent Motswadi, surrounded and broke into the house some 30 minutes after the two had ridden off. As he walked into the front room, he sniffed.

"What is that smell, Sergeant?" he asked, sure he knew the answer already. But his disappointment was beginning to show. This was the second occasion that they'd been just too late.

"It is the smell of a dirty white man, Sir, and he was here no more than one hour ago. There is water in the bath but it is cold and there was this oilcloth lying on the floor under that chair," replied the Sergeant deferentially.

"So he's been here, our mystery white man, interesting." He took the cloth and sniffed it.

"Gun oil," he observed. "So we know for certain that they are armed. Right, Sergeant, five men to question everyone in the surrounding houses. When did they leave, how many, what were they carrying, what kind of car does this man Joseph drive, if possible the registration number, you can get that from Motor Vehicle Licensing, and I want it all yesterday, understand?"

"Yes, Sir."

"And, Sergeant, notify all patrol cars, the road block personnel and the army. I want these terrorists caught and brought to justice."

But again, they were too late. The details of the car only reached the Zambezi River border patrol soldiers 20 hours later. They found the car, abandoned off the road near the old cable pontoon car ferry crossing at the Kafue mouth, just 100 yards from where it flowed into the Zambezi River. They even found the spot on the bank of the Zambezi where the two men had stolen a mokoro *(dug-out canoe)* some four miles east of the confluence. Audaciously, they had taken the mokoro from under the noses of some farm workers right next to a large field of rape, which is grown commercially for its vegetable oil and unsurprisingly for the yellow pigmentation in it's flowers.

Jackson Motswadi had never felt more frustrated. He had deployed virtually the entire available security apparatus of Zambia to catch these criminals, and had failed. But he had his excuses, especially the fact that he had not been allowed to deploy a large guard at Mumbwa.

As it turned out, his boss was fired and to his bemusement, he was immediately promoted to chief Superintendent, charged by the minister to make sure that such a thing never happened again.

History was rewritten with immediate effect.

THE TIMES FRIDAY APRIL 26 1973

Six Zambian Detainees Released
From Reuters
....

In Lusaka, Thursday.
In a brief statement, the Zambian President, Dr. Kenneth Kuanda said yesterday that he had ordered the release of six of the 'seven'. The European detainees, who were arrested for spying in March have been released and deported on humanitarian grounds. He advised a gathering of the foreign press corps that they had been flown to London the previous evening.
He said, "Let this serve as a warning to potential infiltrators, that my Government is always vigilant and we will not tolerate interference from foreign agencies or governments.

"He's out," said Jim to Annie as he ran into the lounge.

She sagged down onto the arm of the chair next to the phone, relief flooding through her.

"Hello, Annie, did you hear me? I said Harry's back."

"Yes, I heard you, Jim. Thank you. Where is he?"

"He's at the Chirundu Police camp having a bath. Look, their phones are down and I got the message via Mick Glover on my radio. He thought it would be best if I broke the good news."

"Oh thank you, Jim. I can't tell you how grateful I am. When will he come home? Why hasn't he phoned?"

"The lines to Chirundu are down, hence the radio call. And well, he'll probably only get home tomorrow. Sturrock's on his way there now to conduct the debriefing. Also, Harry is intent on staying there until Joseph is sorted out."

"Joseph?" She couldn't speak properly; she'd begun crying the moment he had told her, and now she was hunched over sobbing her eyes out, shaking uncontrollably. Jim stood there nonplussed, not quite sure how to deal with this outpouring of emotion.

"Oh, of course, you wouldn't have known about Joseph. He's had to come out with Harry. In fact, it was he who got Harry out. Without his help it might have been a different story. Hey, Annie, are you alright?"

"Well, he's welcome to come here. Of course I'm alright," she snapped. She extracted a tissue from the sleeve of her blouse, wiped her eyes and then blew her nose.

"Why can't Joseph come here then?"

"No, it's not that. It's the asylum issue," Jim explained. "He's got no papers, only his Zambian passport. Besides, when he's free to go, I'm taking him to Bulawayo. He's a valuable man in my operations."

The rest of the day was hectic, and despite her lethargy, she busied herself with George tidying the place up preparing for Harry's homecoming. She phoned Barbara, Harry's parents and her mother and the doctor. That perked her up, and whereas she was going to give it a miss, she went off to the police camp in Karoi for the first of her lessons in the use and maintenance of firearms.

The following morning Harry breezed in, cool as cucumber, Cheshire cat grin on his scrubbed shaven face. She was still in bed.

"Oh, Harry."

"My darling, what's the matter?" he said, his exhilaration turning immediately to real concern. He sat down next to her on the bed. She was crying.

"Nothing you silly man," she said reaching up for him, "welcome home." She hugged him as if her life depended on it and even when he wiggled to indicate that it was time to let go, she wouldn't. Instead she whispered in his ear.

"I'm pregnant."

THE WYVERN REVENGE

And when with that realisation,
I learn to read the score, do my mind and body grasp
the skills to play the melody?
do I play with silvery dexterity, am I well enough intent,
to strain, to make the love work?
I just don't know.

Or do I recline, fall back on old ways?
Ignore my part, both here and there, waiver,
perhaps fail to learn that life must embrace us all?
Or do I play with the orchestra, take my part,
Develop my skills, and enter the refrain for all my worth?
In truth, how can I know?

BOOK 3 - TRIBULATIONS

CHAPTER 26

"*It all actually started in May 1966.*"

Bunty Andrews, distracted by his voice from hanging out her washing on the line strung out across the lawn, looked at her son sprawled out on a deck chair. The day had been surprisingly warm for late February so he had put out a plastic fold-up chair next to the kitchen door, protected from the cool breeze. His head was thrown back, shirt open to the waist as he took in the warming rays of the late winter sun.

"What did, Harry?" she asked.

"The killings," he said, gripping the arms of the chair. He pushed himself up into a proper sitting position. "They killed some people at Sinoa, I seem to remember their name was Viljoen, in May of that year and then a farmer and his wife and her mother[62], a few days later at their farm near Karoi." He put his folded Daily Telegraph carefully down on the lawn next to him, ballpoint pen diagonally across the partially completed cryptic crossword, and looked at his mother. "I knew all about those incidents although I wasn't even in the country at the time. There was an outcry, police and military, the Rhodesian Air Force called out. I don't think they brought the perpetrators to justice. I'm a bloody fool, I should have known it wouldn't end."

She quickly finished hanging up the balance of the washing and sat down on the step next to him.

"Now don't you go blaming yourself." He gave her an enquiring look.

"Well, it's difficult not to. What was I, a bloody Englishman, doing, going and buying a farm in a hot area? I should have known better. Then none of it would have happened."

"That's nonsense Harry, and you know it!" she admonished. "Anyway, you said that it had quietened down."

"Well, it did, after a fashion. The farming communities, right across the country, got themselves organised with radios and defences and so on. It's become far more difficult for the terrorists to operate. So yes, it did quieten down and only from time to time were they successful in breaching defences. But it continued, farm attacks and murders, the burnings, intimidating and mutilating the local people, the laying of mines along sand roads, attacks on motorists, despite the introduction of convoys. Like an idiot I thought it would never happen to us." He paused, fidgeted, ran the back of his hand across and against the short stubble under his chin and gazed up at the branches of the apple tree in the corner of the small garden. "That tree needs pruning."

"Yes, well, don't you touch it. It has got to be done in the autumn; so it'll just have to stay like that this summer. I'll go and make some tea." Bunty got up and disappeared into the kitchen, for the moment leaving Harry to his reverie. He sat there ruffling the hair of Bonnie's neck and back. He looked down at her.

"You're a pain in the butt, Bonnie, you know that?" he said smiling at the dog. "You just can't get enough." The dog turned herself around and presented another area of her body for him to scratch.

"You spoil that dog," said Bunty bending down to place the tray on the step. "She just ignores me." Sitting down, she bent over and poured tea into two mugs, sugared the one and put milk into both. She handed Harry his tea and sat, back against the doorframe, looking affectionately at Bonnie. "What happened to those dogs you had on the farm?"

"Well, only Chollie survived that first attack. He died a few years later of old age." Harry gazed blankly into his tea. "Actually it was the dogs that saved Annie in that first attack."

"But why didn't you move the family into Salisbury, before all that took place?" He looked across at his mother.

"You don't know what it was like Mum. The war was the farthest thing from our minds most of the time. We were more concerned about petrol rationing, getting spare parts for the trucks, tractors, pumps, mills, cars and other things in short supply. By hook and by crook, it didn't matter. One just had to keep things going. The war was being taken to the terr.'s well enough. The military and the police looked as if they had them on the run. But it was insidious, it kept creeping towards one and one didn't realise that it was there, until too late."

"Surely the government knew what was going on, where these people were?"

"Most of the time, yes, but they effectively muzzled the press by just blanking out any news article that they felt gave the game away, so we didn't really know how bad it was. Most of what we knew, we learned at the club, or from our neighbours, and that was innocuous enough, the odd incident here and there, nothing too serious. While we sort of prepared for it, we really didn't think we were under threat." Harry took a sip. "Um, that's nice. Look, I mean, with Annie heavily pregnant, we'd long since sorted the security perimeter. And even then, after the kids were born, Annie ran the school and the clinic in what we thought was relative safety. We felt that all the staff were 100% on our side and Chadrack advised me every time anything funny was going on. Hell, I can't tell you how many false alarms we had, calling out the army, gathering the other farmers, searching fruitlessly, sometimes for days, for nonexistent ghosts. For two years, until the end of '74, I was only engaged in one callout that resulted into a real contact and that was miles away at Makuti." He ruffled his own hair.

"God Mum, I was so confident, I'd had bumper crops and bought the farm next door. We built a whole village for the staff, water-bourne sewerage, a general dealer's store, which I might add, we ran as a non-profit operation for the benefit of the staff and their families. I built a proper football field for them, Annie organised the teams, four of them, kit. She had the doctors at Karoi hold surgeries twice a week at Merrywaters, at my expense. We really did try hard for our people. Shucks I even gave each family a Hereford heifer every Christmas, free grazing rights. Hell Mum, between them they had more cattle on my farms than I did. To put it bluntly, they thought the world of us. The whole thing was coming together beautifully. Money in the bank, a great family, happy crew and a phenomenally productive farm, we had the lot."

"Well, what went wrong?"

"I don't know really. In '74, we thought Smithy was coming to his senses.

John Vorster, the South African Prime Minister, and Zambia's Kenneth Kaunda actually got together and convinced Smith to release Nkomo and Mugabe and others, declare a ceasefire and negotiate a settlement. Remember, they met in a railway carriage parked in the centre of the Victoria Falls Bridge. But that didn't work. There was infighting on all sides and the talks broke down. Both Mugabe and Nkomo left the country forming various other splinter groups in exile, which later joined forces to form the Patriotic Front. But Ian Smith did continue to try. He eventually got two priests, the Reverend Indabaningi Sithole and Bishop Abel Muzorewa to form an interim government with him and they declared an amnesty for all the Patriotic Front guerrillas, as they were known by then. We all heaved a sigh of relief and supposed that the war would end."

"But it didn't."

"No, not by a long shot. Mugabe and Nkomo weren't having any of it and the war escalated. It peaked in 1978 when over 2000 people were killed inside the country and probably twice that number of insurgents by Rhodesian forces raiding bases outside the country."

The turn off to Munze Mission is about 150 south west of Lusaka. It is nothing but a rough track that winds its way through the woodland. It requires 4 wheel-drive most of the year but especially during the monsoons.

The Mission itself lay on a commanding promontory high on the escarpment overlooking the Zambezi valley. Cooling breezes swept up the afforested mountain slopes below, and although obviously tropical, the local microclimate was actually almost temperate. Beautiful frangipanis and flamboyant trees had been spotted about amongst the remaining huge mahogany and other indigenous hardwoods. There was the inevitable Norfolk pine, huge, dominating the turning circle outside the old main administration building, remnant of a bygone age when Scottish missionaries arrived to spread the word of God. They would have turned in their graves had they known what their beloved Mission was being used for now.

It was really a quite pleasing spot, but for the rain; blinding buckets of it fell for five months of the year. It was lashing down at a rate equating to about two inches an hour when the Land Rover carrying the Fischers finally got there. They'd got stuck three times in the 15 miles or so it was from the main road. Fischer and the Special Branch man driving them there were soaked to the skin, sopping and filthy from having to get out and work the vehicle out of the deeper mud and slush.

But cold didn't enter into it. Fischer was actually relieved to be wet. He sat in his seat allowing the water to evaporate off him, cooling him down. Marie sat in the back, sweltering, dry, but for the huge blotches of perspiration on her frock. But she didn't mind, she was used to the heat of working in the kitchen and over open fires, and besides she was fussing over the child who was a little carsick.

But the journey eventually ended and Marie squealed with delight when she was shown into their accommodation. It was a lovely old colonial styled bungalow perched right on the edge of the escarpment. It was simply and coolly furnished. Old hardwood furniture on red cement floors with limewashed walls and a thatched roof that stretched out over a wide veranda giving glorious views out over the valley. You could see forever. On a clear day, the waters of Lake Kariba were clearly visible in the distance. Windows it didn't have, just mosquito gauze hammered onto the old frames.

Broderik Volker, alias Brad Fischer, not even bothering to wash and change, left her to it, surrounded by their boxes and suitcases, and the child, and went immediately to report to the Commandant. To his surprise a welcoming ceremony had been prepared for him. All the trainees, looking forlorn and destitute in the pouring rain, were on parade in front of the admin building. Mein Gott, what a crock of shit, he thought. I'm going to have my work cut out training this lot. The motley lot looked at him as, totally ignoring the torrent falling on him and holding his head up high, he strode arrogantly, muddy water splashing up with every footfall, to the front steps. The Patriotic Front flag, bedraggled, hung limp on the flagpole in front of them.

But he was to be mildly surprised. A man, who had been lounging on the veranda balustrade, also saw him coming, leapt up. As Brod approached the steps, he shouted an order. Like the bristles rising on a Porcupine's back, a snake uncurling itself as if to attack, the three rows of men jumped to attention, AK47's held in the 'port arms' position. It was actually quite impressive and Brod climbed the steps, turned, came stiffly to attention, gave a military salute, and then raised his right arm, fist clenched, and shouted "Freedom".

As one, the men in front of him did the same, the crashing shout of freedom, loud and violent, again and again, the fists jerking up and down in unison.

Showing no emotion, but smiling inwardly, Fischer turned away and saluted the man whom he thought was the Commandant.

"Major Broderik Volker, reporting for duty, Sir." He looked at the man; saw the amused glint in his eyes, intelligent and ruthless, almost animalistic. Not a cat, but more like a wild dog[63]; he saw that the man was as hard as nails, all sinews, despite the flashy heavy gold chain around his neck. His green T-shirt displayed a picture of Mao Tse Tung, the face bisected diagonally by the sling of a weapon casually hanging at his side. But his khaki trousers were clean and neatly pressed. He wore no shoes. He had a nonchalant arrogance about him that said to the observer to watch out for this man. Fischer felt a slight unease but none the less held the man's strong gaze until the man himself broke away, smiling and coming forwards, proffering his hand.

"Relax Major, I am not the Commandant. I am your new Adjutant, Shenje Ndunze. My friends and men call me 'Himmler'."

"Good morning Herr Ndunze, I am pleased to meet you, I have heard much about you."

"Oh,.. I hope it was not all good!" They smiled together and Fischer thought to himself, I am going to get on with this man. "Please follow me Major, the Commandant awaits us within. He does not like the sun and prefers to remain indoors where his delicate skin can be cared for by his concubine." He turned on his heels and agile as a cat padded off bare foot into the building.

"What about the men?" Fischer asked. Ndunze stopped and turned round peering out onto the parade square.

"Leave them, Major," almost uncaringly, "they can stand like that all day if they have to. Besides, you are required to address them in due course."

Fischer was quite unprepared for what he witnessed next. The Commandant, huge and fat, was reclining on an old sofa, his trousers around his ankles while a naked young girl, tiny by comparison, moved her head up and down in front of his groin. Also, he was an albino, which did not aid his looks. While quite grotesque, the man's bizarre appearance was not what really startled Fischer. It was the size of his engorged penis.

He pushed the maiden away and pulled up his trousers, struggling to get his genitals into the fly. Completely impervious to the stares, he stood up, his huge bulk making him clumsy. He patted the girl on the head and said "Later, child, later."

Quite unconscious of her nudity in front of this strange white man, she stood there looking at Fischer, eyes gleaming, her nipples taught and erect, brazen and clearly in a state of heightened sexual arousal. Then she bent down, picked up a sarong-like wrap, threw it around her torso, tucked it in under her armpit and walked out. The Commandant sounded just like Father Christmas.

"Ho, ho, ho, you like my little butterfly?" his voice deep and resonant, quite jolly. He was seemingly very pleased with himself. "You can have her," he said contemptuously waving her out of his mind. He waddled around to the other side of his desk and picked an ivory handled flywhisk. "You Volker?" Not a statement, a question. Fischer barely understood him the African accent was so thick. He looked at Fischer, swishing the whisk rapidly, blowing air into his face.

"Yes."

"Good. I am Comrade Gundwane, I am in charge here, but you are in charge of the training. I am also in charge of discipline. If you have any problems, you bring the man to me. I kill him slowly in front of the brothers. No more trouble." He turned away to look at something outside the netted window.

Fischer felt a slight tug on his sleeve; it was Ndunze indicating that they should leave.

Outside the men still stood stiffly to attention but to Fischer's surprise, Ndunze ignored them.

"Do not cross that man, Major, he will rub you out." He raised his hand and loudly clicked his fingers. "Like that!" he said.

"Phew!" responded Fischer, at a loss for words. His mind was in turmoil. These ignored men maintaining their rigid discipline; the canine danger lurking in this man next to him with his uncaring disregard for the comfort of his troops; the gross scene he'd just witnessed in the Commandant's office and the niggling itch provoked by the vision of that young black maiden. Not even his own superiors would have summarily dismissed him in such a fashion. Ndunze's words brought him back to reality.

"Also, do not take your trouble to the Commandant. You will not like it, the way he kills people. His favourite torture is to tie the man up and then tear off all the clothes. He then cuts a small hole in the man's stomach so there is not too much bleeding," He gestured with his fingers, "and then to pull the man's intestines out and leave them, still connected, spewed out on the ground in front of the man." He bent over and drew a wide circle in the sand. "Then the ants, flies and crows come and eat the man alive. It is not a sight to see and we, including the women, are all required to watch. The crows try to stand on the man's head and peck out his eyes. The ants swarm up his intestines and start to eat him from the inside. And the flies, they get fat on the food and lay their maggots. Sometimes it takes three days for the man to die. When the gundwanes[64] (*giant rats*) come in the night, they start to eat the man from his ass because they are attracted to the shit. Sometimes the honey badgers[65] and jackals[66] come also at night and after they have torn away the rest of his intestines, they start to tear away at his genitals and legs. The screaming and the smell are the worst."

"OK, I get the picture." Horrified, Fischer shuddered and looked down from the veranda at the soaked parade in front of him. "What now?" he asked Ndunze.

"That is for you to say, Major, the comrades are your men now."

Fischer thought for a minute then stepped forward.

"Masikati *(Good afternoon)*, Comrades. Ndini *(I am)* Major Volker, I hope that you can all understand English because my Shona and Ndebele are no good. Stand at ease." An immediate shuffle and nods of appreciation. Fischer continued. "Today things will change. I am going to train you to take the war back into Zimbabwe, for too long we have delayed."

"Eye! *(Yes!)*" The word mouthed in singsong harmony from all the men.

"But today I must arrange my affairs so you will take the rest of the day to clean your rooms and toilets, your clothes and your equipment. Mangwana *(Tomorrow morning)*, at 7:00am I will inspect you. Everything must be clean. I have just met Commandant Gundwane." The implied threat was not lost on the men.

"Aiwa! (*No! [Aye`ee`wah]*)" The men again sang it out as one.

Fischer turned to Ndunze. "You can dismiss the comrades now and then come to my house in one hour to talk, OK?"

"Yes Comrade." With that, as the men were brought to attention by Ndunze, Fischer bounced down the steps and marched stiffly off to his bungalow.

An hour later Ndunze presented himself at the front door of the bungalow. Fischer went out to greet him and to his surprise saw that he had the Commandant's 'butterfly' with him.

"What's this?" asked Fischer, indicating the young woman with a brief wave of his fingers.

"She's yours Major, the Commandant wasn't joking." Ndunze was smiling, almost laughing at Fischer's discomfort. "Major, you have to take her. The Commandant would be insulted if you rejected her and he would probably give her to the men. You wouldn't like that. No woman can stand being raped a hundred or more times. Being forced to crawl naked around the barrack room pleasuring the men when if and if they want it. The last one went insane after only two days so Gundwane cut her throat."

Fischer shuddered.

"Oh shit, alright." He indicated for the woman to follow him and went indoors.

"Marie," he called. She appeared out of the kitchen. "The Commandant has sent us a servant. Find her a bed and use her in whatever capacity you can. She can probably help you cook and clean and do the washing. But for goodness sake, keep her away from the Commandant. I believe he is quite rough with wayward maidens." He changed the subject, the girl forgotten. "Please would you bring two cups of tea to the veranda? I must talk to my adjutant. "

The two men sat down on the veranda and started. They finished several hours later, long after dark; a training programme had been fleshed out and a daily schedule organised to Fischer's satisfaction. Tomorrow they would begin.

The meeting of COOPS (Combined Operations Secretariat) took place at the RLI (Rhodesian Light Infantry) Barracks on the Hatfield

Road, halfway between the Salisbury city centre and the airport. The men involved gathered in a drab vacant room in the officer's mess, its only furnishing a deeply scarred wooden oblong table surrounded by steel and Formica chairs. Each of them nursed a tin mug of tea in the early morning chill. These meetings only took place early in the morning or late in the evening because everyone there had other priorities as well. Sturrock looked up from his position at the bottom end of the table and addressed the august gathering. Before him were representatives from each of the relevant services, Police, Army, Air Force, Customs and Excise, Internal and External Affairs and the Secretary of Defence himself in the Chair. Every joint action initiated by the group relied on his go ahead. He reported to the Cabinet whence all Operational Directives and decisions emanated. None of them took notes; there wasn't a piece of paper, file or a pen in sight

"We missed him," said Sturrock, avoiding anyone's eye, he gazed out the window.

"Why?" asked the Secretary, face passive but a hint of scorn in his voice.

"Too late, by two to three days I'd judge. He's been sent to one of the camps."

"Bloody dangerous and expensive mistake I'd say?" pressed the Secretary. Sturrock knew his head was on the block. It was he who'd pressed for them to go in and get Fischer at the Golf Club in Lusaka. He knew everyone would be angry, they weren't used to failing. Thank goodness no one was hurt and in other respects the operation went flawlessly. Huxley took over the talking, taking the strain off Sturrock.

"Look, we mounted that operation within 36 hours of finding out who 'Claude' was. None of us had any idea that Motswadi was onto us and would react so quickly. Shit, if only we had him on our side."

"Yes quite. Now what are we going to do about it?" The Secretary leaned back and looked around. A few booted feet shuffled on the floor. It was Huxley who cleared his throat.

"I'd say we relax." Huxley winked at Sturrock. "What this exercise has proved is that we are fully capable of carrying out such operations with a reasonable chance of success. It went perfectly, and that was with policemen, not Peter's Selous Scouts or SAS. We'll find him, just a question of watching the camps. And I might say, gentlemen, it was three of our aggrieved civilians who showed us the way with the Mumbwa affair."

"Yes, James, I've been meaning to talk to you about that. A few noses put out of joint by that little escapade. Can't have a bunch of farmers taking the law into their own hands. Shows us up, what? But yes, beautiful. OK, so what do we do then?"

"We bomb the shit out of them," announced Glover. A mystical look came over the Secretary; he obviously enjoyed his control over the actions of these powerful men.

"That, Squadron Leader, is a decision for our superiors," said the Secretary. He then gently led them on. "But I do detect a certain frustration amongst them. They want to take this war to the enemy, now that the talks with the British Government have effectively ground to a halt and Mugabe and Nkomo have as much as told everyone that they will take power, by whatever means."

"Well why don't you let us go in?" questioned the young Army General, "Our SOB's (special operations boys) are champing at the bit."

"Funerals, Peter, funerals. The PM won't have it. Too many Mummies and children around to create a fuss. You'll have to be patient. That's what we're about after all, joint action; reduce the odds and all that. Not letting you loose by yourself without certainty of succcss, and that depends on air supremacy and support and intelligence. We've enough of a problem finding these fellows at home to have your chaps running riot next door. But don't worry, Peter, you can go back and tell your warriors to gird their loins, shine their spears, your time is coming." The young general sat back, his thirst for action not really assuaged.

"OK, then," said Squadron Leader Mick Glover, "let's start by sending in the Hunters and Canberras."

"What did you have in mind?" asked the Secretary leading Glover on.

"Well we know where the camps are. I can have my gun ships follow them in, loaded up with Peter's SOB's, to mop up. We can insert about 30 men at a time, holding one chopper in reserve for casevac duty." It then dawned on most of those present that this is the direction in which the Secretary wanted the discussion to move. They all started to speak, animated at the thought of action.

In forty minutes a plan was agreed.

"Very well gentlemen. I think it is time to coach our great leader into announcing a 'Right to hot pursuit' public policy. Time to turn things round, become proactive, not just reactive. Sends out the wrong signals. To hold the fort, we must stop ducking and start throwing some stones back. May I have proposals from each of you in 48 hours then?" Putting his hands palm down on the table in front of him the Defsec stood up; both a slight grin and a thoughtful frown evident on his face.

Despite the political situation and the insurgency problem, for the Andrews' and Templars, those were halcyon years. Virtually inseparable, both families enjoyed the fruits of their efforts and the labour of their workers, given willingly and to great effect. They, in particular, were the envy of many of the local people. Both farmers and their wives worked hard for the multitude of people who were dependent on them for their welfare. There were moments of excitement too.

Harry sat down exhausted against a large boulder, propped his Winchester .375 in the fork of the tree next to him and fished in his pocket for his pipe.

"Bloody hell Pete," he said, "this cat is moving fast."

Peter stood nearby, leaning nonchalantly against the shady trunk of a Miombo tree[67]. They were quite high up in a range of hills that ran along the western side of Harry's farm. He was looking out over the patchwork of cultivated farmlands, open grazing and woodland stretching east as far as he could see. He could clearly see the dust thrown up by the hoes and tractors a couple of miles away as the labourers ploughed up some fallow land. Also he could just make out the roofs of the main farm buildings in the distance, surrounded by the inevitable concentration of darker green foliage of exotic trees like jacaranda and syringa[68].

"D'you know? You've got a brilliant farm here," he grunted, an unlit Texan waggling in his mouth. He took his Ronson, a birthday gift from Barbara, out of the pocket of his shorts and lit up. "In fact, I'd say you've done bloody well, Pirate."

"Hey, it didn't just happen you know. Shit, Annie and I have grafted like a chain gang to get it right, with a little bit of help from our friends." He looked at Peter affectionately. He was alluding to the fact that at they frequently pooled their labour and machinery. If Peter wanted to clear a new land[69], Harry went over with all his labourers and equipment, and Peter would do the same in reverse. During the tobacco and cotton picking seasons and for the maize harvest, this system proved invaluable to them both. They each essentially doubled their work force at no extra cost at times of need. Also they were both currently active with several other farmers in a Combine Harvester Co-operative. So instead of having to spend hundreds of thousands on capital equipment, they'd got the banks to finance a non-profit company that now supplied at cost the services of ten immaculate harvesters to each of them.

Also they'd put together and equipped a building company, now run by one of Chadrack and Sampson's many cousins, which they, between the two farms, kept gainfully employed full time, building houses for the staff, barns, alterations, repairs and so on.

"Well, I've always said that there was merit in the Kibbutzim system. In fact it is probably the only system that'll get the locals away from subsistence farming and buggering up the land. After my holiday in Israel I actually sent a report suggesting it to Conex *(The Agricultural Conservation and Extension Department)*. But typically, they're too set in their ways and threw it in file 13." Peter sat down, laid his old Lee Enfield .303 carefully on the ground and then sprawled himself out, blowing a smoke ring straight up into the still hot air.

"Why did you suggest it in the first place, very socialistic?" asked Harry, mildly interested.

"Harry," pressed Peter emphatically, rolling onto his side so that he could look at his friend, "it takes the 'ism' out of communism. Everyone would profit. Listen to me carefully Harry. 90% of this country's agricultural and horticultural production is in the hands of white farmers like us. But there aren't enough of us. The black population growth is staggering and unless we can get the black farmers into the market economy we're going to be in deep shit. In the first instance, we will have to stop exporting a lot of our produce because it'll be needed locally, which will mean loss of foreign exchange and less ability to keep up with the rest of the world. Secondly, unless we can get them productive, they're going to start becoming envious, wanting what we've got. When the pioneer column arrived to establish Fort Salisbury in the late 1800s, the indigenous black population was only some 250 000. Now it's about 7 or 8 million, but in 20 years or so, it'll be close to 20 million. There will be more trouble, mark my words. They haven't got the money to buy fertilisers, harvesters and tractors, or Conex skills. Slowly but surely they're going to effectively destroy the productive value of the land they do farm." He sat up. "Hell, Sampson's a bloody good guy, but I battled to get him to understand why we rotate crops; he couldn't understand that different crops take out and put back different things into the soil. To him they were all the same, and soil is just soil, why do we put fertiliser in it? Why do we leave lands to lie fallow every three years? Another thing he still hasn't grasped is why we've introduced Savoury's paddocking[70] for the livestock. All he could say was that it was a pity that we were putting in fences all over the farm. Hell, I battle with everyone all the time, just getting them to close the bloody gates between the paddocks."

"Yeah, I see what you mean."

"I'm not sure you do Pirate. Look, I know this country, I've lived here all my life and I know in my bones what the problems are. You're dealing with an aboriginal, undereducated, superstitious, proud people. Replacing the white government with a communist black one will achieve nothing. That's just about power. What we've got to do is get these people to be economically productive."

"OK, OK, OK, I hear you. But come on, let's go. I want to get this leopard[71] off my farm or I want to shoot it. Bloody thing's taken enough of my calves." Harry stood up, picked up his rifle, checked to see that it was safe and then slung it over his shoulder. "By the way, if we do get it, for Christ's sake, don't tell Annie. She's upset enough that I'm trying to chase it off as it is."

Peter laughed.

"Yes, Sir, and you'd better not tell Barbara. She thinks I'm over here to help you do the dipping." He leapt to his feet, grabbed his rifle as if he was going to throttle it and moved off. Harry left the tracking to him, learning all the time. From time to time Peter pointed out a scuff mark in the soil, a small patch of flattened grass there, the odd broken stem and so on. Occasionally they'd come across a properly formed series of pad prints.

"See there," said Peter squatting down and pointing with a grass stem, "this leopard is a good 150 to 200 pounds in weight, see how big and deep these prints are? It's a big bugger and definitely a male. This spoor is too big for a female. See also that there are no claw marks. He keeps his claws retracted, he's a cat. Also if you look closely you can see that this light breeze has already destroyed a lot of the definition of the prints. Within a couple of hours they'll be indefinable. I reckon he was here no more than an hour ago." He stood up and carried on slowly. After tracking slowly through some thicker bush for about an hour he stopped and sniffed.

"Smell it?" Peter spoke very quietly.

"Smell what? Perhaps a slight smell of urine, and something else, more pungent," said Harry adopting the same quiet tone and turning his nose here and there, sniffing.

"Exactly, Pirate, piss. The bloody thing has had a slash here." He looked around carefully and then moved one pace to one side. "Here look, it's pissed against this bush, just lightly, he's marking out his territory." Harry looked closely and was able to make out a few drops of moisture on the leaves of the small bushwillow[72] and a few spots in the sand below them, still damp.

"Quiet now, Harry," said Peter speaking very softly.

"Why, is he close?" he asked, whispering.

"Never whisper in the bush, Pirate," said Peter quietly, "whispers carry and animals recognise them instantly. Rather just talk very quietly. Yes, this marking is no more than 15 to 20 minutes old."

Then they heard the grunt, right in front of them.

The hair on Harry's neck stood on end, his scalp prickled.

Peter waved to him urgently. "Sit down please, and keep still for a moment, he's close, a couple of hundred yards, no more." Peter moved very slowly into the bush a few yards and then turned and beckoned to Harry who in turn crouching as he went, moved up next to Peter.

"See here, these deep scuff marks," he said pointing with his finger. He was here when he heard us. This is where he turned around to listen," pointing again, "and then he started trotting. See how the soil has been pushed backwards in this print. He's not far away now, stay on your toes."

"Why? Surely he'll just bugger off?" whispered Harry.

"You don't know with leopards, Pirate. Chances are better that he's going to hole up in an ambush position and wait and watch. Flip your safety catch off now and for Christ's sake, don't point that thing at me." He checked his .303 and as slowly and quietly as he could, he pulled back the bolt and slid a cartridge into the breech. The quietest of clicks ensued.

"Even that, an unnatural sound, is enough to alert this critter. Be really careful now, Harry, and no more talking. Keep right behind me."

Peter moved off at the crouch, considering the placement of every step and then stopping to survey around him before taking the next step. Every six or seven paces he brought up his binoculars and carefully scrutinised the bush in front of him. Eventually, after more than half an hour of this slow advance, he straightened up sighing and turned around to speak to Harry.

"He's gone up that Kopje. Come, we'll move to one side now and see if we can spot him slightly from his flank." He wet his forefinger in his mouth and then held it up. "Wind's OK, lets go." After ten minutes and then another few minutes unhooking himself from a prickly thorn tree[73], he crawled through a large clump of bushes and brought Harry up behind a large kiaat tree[74]. There he halted and at a snail's pace, raised himself up into a standing position behind the tree. He propped his rifle carefully against the trunk and then, again moving excruciatingly slowly, he peered around the tree using his binoculars. Several minutes later he moved very slowly back and turned to lean against the trunk.

"Got him. Here take the bino's and move very slowly." Peter seemed to be miming, he was speaking so quietly, but Harry understood him. He crawled forward to take up the position vacated, laid his rifle gently down next to him and raised the glasses. Barely audible, really just mouthing the words, Peter spoke.

"OK, see the kopje, left edge, big rock with a fig tree sticking out of it? About 200 yards." Harry nodded slowly. "OK, right about 20 yards and up about 40 feet. Big Pod Mahogany tree[75], right of centre, horizontal part of the trunk." After a while, another nod from Harry.

"See him?"

"No."

"Look for his tail, its hanging down." Suddenly the picture seemed to clear and there before him he could make out the leopard clearly; beautiful colouring providing incredible camouflage.

"Ah, I see him. He's fantastic." Harry laid the bino's down and brought up his rifle. He adjusted the telescopic sight to 200 metres, brought it up to his shoulder, slowly wiggled his way into a comfortable position and sighted through the 'scope.

"Don't you believe it. That is the most deadly killer in the African bush, Pirate. Unlike a lion, it'll kill just for fun. Wait until I'm in position to back you up." A nod and then he concentrated on finding the animal through the 'scope. At first he couldn't find it, seeing just heat waves in front of him. But then the tail twitched and he had it, clear as if it was right in front of him. The cat turned its head and seemed to look straight at him. He didn't move a muscle. He felt as if he could just reach out and touch it. He could feel his blood pumping he was so exhilarated, probably adrenalin, he thought. The sweat began to pour off him as he lay waiting for Peter to get into position above him.

"OK, I'm ready," Peter said once he'd lined up himself. Harry continued looking through his sight at the beautiful beast.

"Forget it, Pete, I'm not going to kill it, I can't, it's just too beautiful. Let's both fire close to it just to scare it off. If it comes back, then I'll have a go."

"Ninny," said Peter. "OK Pirate, they're your weaners (*calves still suckling*). You aim at the trunk just in front of its nose and I'll put one through the branches above it. You first when you're ready."

Harry adjusted his position and slowly squeezed the trigger.

Crack! Crack!

The two shots, a fraction of a second apart, destroyed the serenity of the bush. Harry saw the trunk open in front of the leopard, spitting out splinters of wood and bits of bark. And he saw also, the almost blindingly fast reaction. From repose, the animal reared instantaneously up onto its hindquarters, snarling, massive fangs bared as it twisted away. Back arched almost impossibly, it leapt straight down onto the ground below and ran. Harry caught only one glimpse of it as it high tailed away and it was gone.

"Wow, that was exciting," he said almost to himself, eyes glistening. He sagged lowering his head down onto his arm, an ephemeral exhaustion coming over him. Clicking the safety catch on, he stood up, creaking slightly from having remained tense and motionless for so many minutes. "I feel quite light headed."

"It's the adrenalin. That's the high that hunters get every time they get something big like a buffalo or a jumbo." Peter was smiling as he removed the magazine from his old trusted rifle and ejected the cartridge that he had automatically reloaded into the breech replacing the one he'd fired. He then replaced the lens covers on the telescopic sight that he'd had custom fitted to his old re-bored rifle. Harry bent down and picked the bullet up, together with the two doppies *(spent cartridge cases)*. "I saw your shot hit the tree, it was perfect; he's probably got some splinters in his snout."

"Well rather that, I couldn't shoot one of those creatures without very good reason," said Harry.

They moved away, Peter briefly throwing his arm over Harry's shoulders.

"Well done Pirate. Your first live leopard hunt and you would have nailed him if you'd wanted, and that's all that's important really. You're a fast learner. Always remember, you have five senses. In the bush you have to use them all, slowly, very slowly."

Embarrassed, Harry squirmed a little and giggled. "That was an incredible experience. It beats the hell out of nailing impalas[76] for the pot from the back of the truck."

"Too right, but I'll tell you what, we'll go down to the valley[77] and do the same thing, I want to get a nice big kudu[78] to make biltong[79]. I was thinking of going down at the end of next week for a couple of days. Actually, I think Annie's going into Salisbury with Barbara and the all the kids in next Friday's convoy, so we'll both have a free weekend." Peter, like Harry, slung his rifle as they walked through the savannah, chattering like children, the four or five miles back to the truck.

"You're on."

"Right, Sampson and Chadrack can go down on Friday to set up camp. I'll fetch you early on the Saturday morning."

The lessons learned on these escapades and hunting trips to the bush were to stand Harry in good stead.

"You and the Comrades are ready," said Fischer. "It is time to go into action. Tomorrow you will lead 15 men on your first mission as we discussed. You will leave from Sinazongwe and enter Zimbabwe via the Sengwa Narrows. From there you will move to the Bumi Road and meet the truck at the grid reference I shall give you. You will take only one Sam 7 missile, one part at a time, from the narrows. When you have carried out the action, you are to establish a base camp near the Charles Clack Mine at the place we have already prepared. You will then start attacking the farms from Karoi to Sinoa. I will use the rest of the men to keep your base camp properly supplied and to deliver instructions. We have been through this many times, but do you have any questions?"

"Yes, Major, but what about the whites we come up against?"

"Ndunze," said Fischer warily, "The Rhodesians call us terrorists. The role of the terrorist is to cause terror. You will kill them. But if you can prevent your men from doing it, the white women should not be raped; it will turn your overseas friends and allies against you. Horrible death, mutilation, yes. But remember many of our supporters are Europeans and they consider rape a very serious offence."

"Zvakanaka *(OK fine)*, Major. It will be as you say."

So the terrorist bush war in Rhodesia took on a more sinister face. Properly trained guerrillas took over from the previously ragged bunch of zealots making up the forces of the Patriotic front, and infiltrated into the country from Zambia, Mozambique *(which opened up to insurgency operations after the collapse of the Portuguese empire)* and Botswana. Surrounded, the Rhodesians were hard pressed to contain the situation; they just didn't have enough troops. The death, pillage, intimidation seemed to worsen and the Smith Regime, as it was now called almost universally, took a long time coming round to the point of view that political expedience could be forsaken in favour of 'Hot Pursuit' into the neighbouring territories.

The HMS Tiger and HMS Fearless talks had proved fruitless as the British Prime Minister, Harold Wilson, under pressure from the Freedom Movements and Commonwealth Countries, moved the goal posts every time Smith offered an advance on a previous position. He was on a hiding to nothing, too genuine and honest, and lacking the guile needed to negotiate with the consummate politician of the age.

When James Callaghan took over the British Government, it was no better and the die was cast. If anything the polemics between all the sides became fiercer. The Smith Regime and the white 'settlers' in Rhodesia were to be brought to heel, on their knees if necessary. Any settlements they might and indeed did come to with the pacifist black politicians within the country were totally unacceptable.

The atrocity that really signalled this new wave was an attack in Salisbury city centre in August 1976. Guerrillas threw two hand grenades into a crowd killing and maiming many people[80].

CHAPTER 27

Life for Annie and Harry was hectic. The kids were a handful, work on the farm hard and furious. Harry found that he had so much to do, although Annie was heard to say to Barbara that he was a workaholic and created work for himself. The results were evident, however.

The Merrywaters group of farms had started to be held up as examples of excellence. The Gwebi Agricultural College started sending students there for training and Harry had to remodel and renovate the other row of stables, turning them into four guest rooms with a communal shower and toilet, so called rooms 1 to 4 of the 'horseboxes' by Harry and Annie. The Merrywaters annual sale of Hereford weaners became one of the great events of the year. Harry had rid himself of all his bulls, who, it seemed to him, spent most of their time breaking down fences and fighting each other. Instead, every year, he spent good money buying sperm drawn from prize government bulls and artificially inseminating his heifers. Within just five years he had built his herd of 500 Hereford heifers into one of the finest in the country. Even Peter, after years of being solicited by Harry for endless advice, began himself to ask Harry for help.

Annie herself sometimes felt that she'd overreached herself, but she loved it. The school, clinic, general dealers store, the vegetable garden, the house and most of all the children consumed her time. Her pet hate, in fact, was Harry's insistence that she maintain the cattle pedigree and age tables, inoculation schedules, crop rotation and grazing programmes and the like. These charts and plans had come to take over the study, covering the walls, the floor and the desk. Drawing pins pegged rotas, name/number lists to the cupboards and boxes of vaccines and other paraphernalia filled what space there was. She could never find her own stuff, the accounts, order books, stock inventories and the like. It all became too much and she eventually reacted, gently at first.

"Harry Andrews, unless you build me a proper new suite of offices where I can separate all our activities into proper order and where I can actually employ people to help me, I'm resigning." She said it quite casually, because she was sitting cuddled up on the couch, concentrating on helping Beverley read one of the Beatrice Potter books

"Why, what's the matter love?" asked Harry, not really seeming to hear her question at all. His mind actually consumed by the piece of Lego he was trying to get Robbie to put in place on the little castle they'd built together in the middle of the lounge floor. He was on his knees and elbows on the carpet, butt in the air whispering into Robbie's ear. Beverley wasn't concentrating on her book.

"Daddy, Mummy thaid you have to build her a new offith." She still had a youthful lisp that inevitably went straight to the core of Harry. He loved listening to her talk.

"Why, my darling?"

"Cauth it'th too thmall." Harry rolled over onto his back laughing silently.

"Come here, pumpkin," he said to her. No second invitation needed, she threw aside the book and leapt onto her father. With delightful ease he held her up in the air, laughing with her, and then hugged her. Of course, Robbie couldn't keep out of it, and within moments they were all in a tangle, laughing and giggling and tickling, Lego flying all over the show. Annie hadn't moved and although she was exasperated, she looked on lovingly at her family. I couldn't ask for anything more, she thought.

"OK, OK I give up," said Harry eventually. "Bev, have you cleaned your teeth? Go on, bedtime." He stood her upright and gave her a little spank on the backside. "Come Robbie," he said leaping to his feet and picking the child up, "I'll clean yours for you tonight. " Taking Beverley's hand in his, the three of them trooped off to the bathroom.

When they returned Annie hadn't moved. Oh oh, thought Harry looking at the intent on her face, I'm in for it. But in fact he already had the answer to her question. While sorting out the kids his mind had been cogitating on the problem. Annie took the children over and after all the hugs, kisses and good nights, she disappeared with both of the children in her arms. Harry flopped down on the couch and then got down on his hands and knees and started collecting up the Lego pieces, tossing them into their wooden box. Then he stood up, forgetting the Lego, and went through to the office. He switched on the light and stood there leaning against the door-frame. She's dead right, he thought, we can't carry on like this. In fact he hadn't been into the office for several months, preferring to leave the paper work to Annie.

"See what I mean, Harry," Annie's cross voice behind him. He turned and drew her forwards next to him, hugging her shoulders. She stood stiffly next to him, dreading the thought of having to operate in there another day. "And besides, it still stinks of your pipe tobacco."

"Yes you're right as usual, my darling. Tomorrow morning I'll get Chadrack to assign us two men. We'll move all the bedroom furniture out of the 'horseboxes' into the tackle barn and after they're repainted you can have them move everything into there." Annie melted against him.

"So you were listening to me you sneaky thing. Thank you, Pirate. Well, we'll move in next weekend, and I don't want you near the place; you'll just get in the way. You and Pete go off and do what you do in the bush for a couple of days. You need a break and besides I want Barbara to bring over her children." Annie knew that Harry didn't have any patience with other people's kids; he uncompromisingly and unreasonably labelled them all noisy and badly behaved.

"Are you sure, my love?" he asked kissing her on the temple.

"Yes. Harry, you've got to take more time off, switch off. You're going to burn yourself out and remember your promise."

"You girls never forget do you," he laughed. "OK, I'll phone Pete and make a plan. I'd like to fly down to Whamira Hills and do some fishing in the Sanyati River there. We could drive down but there are rumours of some terrorists active around Charles Clack. There's a good camp there with some fishing boats and they've got a good strip. If Pete's available I'll call David Sivewright and arrange it."

"Good, and take Chadrack with you, he needs a break as well. Also, when he gets back from Salisbury, tell Pete to take Sampson along. Barbara and I will be just fine for the weekend. In fact it'll be a pleasure not having those two around protecting us and attending to our every whim, guns hanging from around their necks." Harry could have laughed at the way she said it but this was a serious matter.

"My darling, you've got to have protection."

"Nonsense, Harry. The security perimeter is highly effective; a rabbit can't get within 200 yards of the house without tripping the alarms. And besides I'll get George and a couple of the other men to hang around while you're not here."

"Well, I suppose its safe enough for just one weekend and I take your point about Chadrack and Sampson. They do need to get away. OK, it's a deal. By the way, why's Pete in Salisbury?"

"Oh, amongst other things, his folks are going to Vic. Falls for a week. He's taking them out to the airport. I believe he's also going to Gwebi Agricultural College. I understand they've developed a new strain of maize they've called R52. Apparently it produces double the yield of existing hybrids. He's going to give us the gen on it when he gets back."

"Pete's a brick isn't he?"

"Yes, but he owes you plenty, Harry Andrews. If he weren't married to my best friend, I'd say that you're too generous."

"Nonsense, my love. If it hadn't have been for Pete, I'd probably still be a bachelor, still flying for the police."

The infiltrations into Rhodesia were successful. Fischer's group of guerrillas had established their echelon near Charles Clack and then with other groups spread out virtually country wide, intimidating, killing and pillaging wherever any weakness showed.

In February 1977 guerrillas attacked the Roman Catholic Mission near Centenary north of the capital. The whole compliment of seven white missionaries were murdered and several black patients in the mission hospital. One baby was bayoneted and slung up onto the burning thatch roof of the clinic.

Infiltrations from Mozambique into the eastern parts of the country increased and on the 16th May that year President Kaunda of Zambia declared war on Rhodesia, apparently responding to threats by the regime that it would attack guerrilla bases inside Zambia.

Urban terrorism increased too. In one of the worst attacks of the war thus far, an explosion in the H. M. Barbour departmental store in the centre of Salisbury, killed 11 people, wounding a further 76.

Ian Smith ordered his troops into Mozambique and Zambia. British Prime Minister James Callaghan condemned Smith as irrelevant. 16 tribesmen and women were massacred on a white farm near the Mozambique border and Smith increased the call-up of men to include a 'Dad's' army. In November Rhodesian forces attacked a ZANU PF base in Mozambique killing over 1200 nationalist guerrillas.

White Rhodesians were leaving the country in an ever increasing flood, in 1977 alone 16,638 left for Australia, New Zealand, Britain, Canada and South Africa.

But still the Rhodesian Front Party held onto the belief that they could force a settlement retaining some of the political power in white hands. Ian Smith was a little more pragmatic and on the 3rd March 1978 he signed an agreement with Bishop Abel Muzorewa, the Reverent Indabaningi Sithole and Chief Jeremiah Chirau to transfer power to the black majority on 31st December 1978.

But it made no difference, the attacks continued; Joshua Nkomo warned that they would increase. On 15th April Robert Mugabe rejected the settlement and declared that a multiparty democracy was a luxury the new State of Zimbabwe could not afford and that it should have a One Party Marxist Government.

This was like waving a red rag to a bull and raids into Zambia by Rhodesian forces eventually became a reality. They started with an attack on a base near Lusaka, in which 38 guerrillas were killed.

In Rhodesia in the first six months of the year over 1,850 civilians and soldiers had been killed by terrorist actions.

Over 700 of these were British citizens, which is not surprising considering that the large majority of white Rhodesians were either British or were of British descent. In reality, for political reasons, the British Government had turned on its own people.

The whole socio-political structure of Rhodesia was moving out of control, spiralling rapidly into anarchy and it seemed that the politicians were incapable of dealing with it.

The four men loaded up Harry's Baron[81] and flew down to Whamira Hills. His estimate of a flight of 17 minutes was spot on and they arrived at 4:00pm on the Friday afternoon. Chadrack was amazed and both excited and fearful, not having been in a light aircraft before. By truck it would have taken them 3 hours. Sampson, Harry and Peter teased him mercilessly of chattering and behaving like a female baboon.

The Sanyati River at this remote spot is deep, winding its way though the hills before tumbling down a series of rapids into the gorge that takes it into the Kariba dam. The hills themselves are actually an escarpment that drops down off the central massif of Rhodesia, a mineral-rich highland known as the 'Great Dyke'. The untouched Miombo woodland makes them extremely beautiful and the men sighed happily as they sat back, beers in hand, under the huge mahogany trees of the riverine forest on the side of the river.

Their two days of fishing were marvellous; that is, for the periods they weren't fishing and when they were sitting out on the boma deck, drinking eating and talking.

"No bloody fish in this river," announced Peter, laughing. "Can't be, I haven't caught anything."

"Balls! Look at those two Nkupe[82] that Chadrack brought in. One was all of 16 lbs."

"No, Master Peter is right," interjected Sampson who hadn't caught a thing either. "Chadrack went out last night like a crocodile and put them in the water so that he could bring them in today." They all burst out laughing.

"Come on Chad, what's your secret, how did you get those things onto the hook?" More mirth at Chadrack's expense, "Did you tuck them into your lair?" But they soon tired of that and the topic of conversation moved to current affairs.

"Sam," said Harry, "what's going to happen? Will Mugabe and Nkomo accept the new deal between Muz *(Bishop Muzarewa)* and

Smith?" He leaned back, ever present pipe in hand and looked expectantly at Sampson.

Sampson didn't answer immediately, but leaned forward flicking the remains of his hand-rolled cigarette into the flames in front of him. He then picked up a twig and tucked the end of it under the carapace of a small scorpion that had crawled from under the bark of one of the logs and was trying to escape the flames. He flipped it backwards back into the fire watching it curl up and then ignite, exhausted of moisture. When he spoke, it was considered and forbidding, with an edge of fatality to it.

"No. No, he and Nkomo will not accept Muzarewa and Sithole. They will fight on."

"Why? Surely they'd have achieved their aim: the overthrow of the minority white government and freedom." Harry was perplexed. Peter started to answer the question but Harry waved him into silence. "Let's hear what Sam thinks."

"Master Harry," said Sampson respectfully, "this war is not about freedom for the oppressed masses. If it was, Sir, and I thought it would make the lives of the black people better, then we, Chadrack and I, would be fighting you ourselves. It is about power. Mugabe and Nkomo want power. They don't care about the people. I've spoken of this many times with people who have been to the camps *(terrorist training camps)* and I have heard how they are treated, what they are taught. They are taught nothing about creating a new and better future, only words and more words, 'freedom', 'kill the settlers', 'burn their farms'. They learn nothing about how what they must do when it is over. They do not understand that we need the white farmers. It is their skills that produce our food. Look at you two men and your wives. I think that both of you, you employ seven hundred men and women, you have built us good homes, you pay us good money, you feed us, teach our children, give us proper medical care. Our people are happy and then you give us cattle and land to grow our own mashesh, cassava and mealies *(maize)*. I must ask you, Master Harry, do you believe that Mugabe and Nkomo will give us these things?" It was Chadrack who answered.

"No Sir, they will try to take everything for themselves and their friends. Be sure that when Mugabe and Nkomo take power, there will be more fighting, but it will be between Mugabe and the rest."

"Oh, why do you say that?" asked Harry.

"Like two rhinoceros[83] bulls, they must fight for the right to cover the cow." The analogy was not lost on Harry, but thinking that the conversation was becoming a little too serious he laughed.

"Shit, you buggers always reduce things back to sex, don't you?" They all smiled.

"It is true. They will take out their poles and fight to see who has got the bigger one." Peter and Harry were tempted to laugh but they realised that Sampson was serious. "Unfortunately many people will die before there is a victor. It will be Mugabe who wins. Not because he has the bigger weapon; he hasn't. But it is because he is too clever for Nkomo. Mugabe is like a Honey Badger in the grass. He will come from behind and bite off the balls of the buffalo[84] Nkomo."

"All the same, if they do carry on fighting now that there is a settlement of sorts, the government here will do much damage to camps. I have heard that Smith has given orders that the camps must be destroyed," said Peter.

"Ha!" replied Sampson dismissively. "They are like the charging elephant. When they come, they are noisy and throw up much dust. The comrades will skip into the trees like impalas and hide. The elephant might kill some and stamp on them, but he cannot catch all of them, there are too many."

"Wise words, Sampson, wise words. But I fear that our leader does not understand this, nor do his generals. I should tell you, Harry," said Peter turning to look at his friend, "that Bill Sturrock informs me that they're going all out to get Fischer now. They're going to hit the camps in a concerted push to nail him. All to the good if they get a few of the comrades as well."

"This is the bad man from the aeroplane crash?" this, a question from Sampson.

"Yes."

"Ah, we too have heard that there is a white man in the camps in Zambia who knows this country," he waved his arm around him, "and who trains the comrades. He is much feared and respected. So it is he. He is a bad man."

"How the hell do you get this information, Sam?" asked Harry.

Sampson just shrugged.

"I hear things."

"Sam knows everyone in Karoi," put in Peter, "and he's probably bedded every maiden there. Probably pillow talk." They all laughed. Sam's prowess was well known.

"But," started Chadrack, remaining serious. He chose his words. "The war is coming closer to us now. We must be very careful, Master Harry."

"What have you heard?" asked Peter, his scalp prickling.

"That there are comrades in the location at Karoi, they are asking questions."

Harry was tempted to ask what questions, but knew what the answer was anyway.

Shenje 'Himmler' Ndunze set up his ambush with care. They were in the deep bush of the escarpment at least 20 miles from any town. Only the mining settlement at Charles Clack was nearer. He and eleven comrades had been waiting for this day for a long time. It had taken them months, one by one so avoiding detection by the Rhodesian Defence Forces, to carry the parts of the dismantled Sam 7 missile to this point. One of them could have carried it in its launcher bodily from the drop-point in three days of walking. But assembled, even wrapped up, it looked like what it was, a missile launcher. They couldn't risk being caught in the many roadblocks and cordon searches instituted randomly by the Army and Police. 'Himmler' had, himself, lovingly and painstakingly reassembled the weapon. He cursed at the dust, pollen and insects that settled on the spotless parts as he worked. He cursed at the heat, which caused him to perspire so profusely that he eventually had one of his men stay next to him, purely and simply to wipe away the sweat before it dropped onto the weapon. He cursed when he dropped the trigger-locking pin and it took them three hours to find it in the soil at his feet. So much dirt had adhered to the protective covering of grease that it looked like a twig, But most of all, he cursed the settlers and Ian Smith.

Finally it was finished and he made ready.

It was Sunday afternoon and they were due to leave in fifteen minutes or so, bags packed and merely waiting for Harry to finish his pre-flight planning. Peter threw his feet up onto the rough bark of the raw wooden railing, which edged the swept clearing that made up the 'boma' area of the camp.

"Pirate, this was a bloody good idea," he said yawning, relaxed, the tensions of months of hard work drained out of him.

"It was Annie who insisted we all come," said Harry, packing his calculator, clipboard and charts into his flight bag.

"Now there is a wise woman," said Chadrack. "A woman who understands the needs of man. And who are we to disagree?" They all laughed. Harry relaxed for a moment longer before suggesting that they fly home. He tipped far back on the back legs of his seat and looked straight up into the late afternoon sky, hands behind his head, watching an airliner passing directly above him, high overhead.

"Where's that going to?" asked Peter looking up as well as the distant turbine whine changed to a lower tone.

"It's the 3:15 flight from Vic Falls to Salisbury. He's just throttled back to commence his approach descent into New Sarum. Your folks are probably on it."

"And what is that?" asked Peter, alarm creeping into his voice, pointing slightly down to one side. In his heart he already knew. An arching white condensation trail seemed to be rising up towards the descending aircraft. Harry glanced over and went white.

"Oh my God!" He leapt to his feet and ran the few yards needed to take him out of the shade of the trees into the open so that he could watch.

"Shit! That's a missile and it's going...." He never finished the sentence. He didn't need to. At that instance the missile hit the aircraft, there was a flash and the huge aircraft wobbled mightily in the sky. Then it tumbled sideways, seemingly still intact, rolled right over, nose down, righted itself and started dropping, a huge plume of flame and smoke pouring out of one wing. Then the sound of the blast hit them. A long rolling sound, almost like distant thunder. The others were by now standing with Harry, staring up into the sky, opened mouthed as the aircraft started to fall out of the sky. The nose of the aircraft began to rise as the pilot clearly struggled to bring it under control. He obviously had some control because although dropping fast the aircraft was well out of the dive when it disappeared behind the hills.

"Christ, they never had a chance!" Harry muttered under his breath, horrified. He looked at his watch, noted the time, spent a moment orientating himself - plane almost due east, missile from the north east, he said to himself, and then he turned to Peter. Peter looked as if he'd just seen a ghost. His mouth open, head thrown back he collapsed onto his knees, arms spread out as if calling to God.

"Noooo....!" It came out as a wailing cry. He jerked forwards and buried his face in his hands, sobbing uncontrollably. Harry knelt down next to him, made as if to put his hand on Peter's shoulder, but then he drew back. Speaking firmly and slowly, and with genuine concern, he said,

"Pete, we don't know whether they're on that flight." Peter continued sobbing his whole body wracked with grief. Slowly then Harry drew him to his feet and led him back to his seat overlooking the river. Sitting him down, he turned to Sampson, "Stay with him, Sam, there are things I must do."

Then he was running.

"Chadrack, the guns!" he didn't even look round but continued, tearing along the path towards David Sivewright's bungalow shouting, "Dave, Dave!" Sivewright came out onto his veranda pulling on a shirt.

"Whoa Harry, what's the problem?"

"Christ, didn't you hear it Dave?"

"What?"

"An Air Rhodesia Viscount has just been shot down; Sam 7 or something." Harry came to a halt in front of Sivewright.

"Dave we need your Land Rovers, we must go out and help, if we can. Hurry, get your keys and a rifle, come on!" Harry turned away and started running towards his own tent. He stopped and turned only to say, "and bring your portable radio, OK? And a compass if you've got one?" Sivewright nodded. To his credit, he didn't hesitate even though the import of what Harry had said hadn't yet registered. He had heard a lot about Harry Andrews, and Peter Templar had told him that you don't mess about when the Pirate is on a mission. He turned back into his cottage.

Within 10 minutes, most draped with rifles and carrying boxes of ammunition, and Dave's two drivers, they had gathered on the deck.

"Dave, you're staying here with Pete. Try and get through on your ground station and report what's happened but don't let Pete out of your sight, understand?" Sivewright nodded but not understanding.

"Dave, Pete's parents might have been on that aircraft." Sivewright needed no further nudging and was immediately all business. He went to Peter, coaxed him to his feet and almost supporting him as if he were wounded, drew him away towards the bungalow.

Harry directed the remaining men to the vehicle park behind the kitchen hut. They set about climbing aboard the two Land Rovers parked there but Harry stopped them.

"Shamwaris *(friends)*, this is a terrible thing that has happened. It is our duty to help." All the men present, all of them black, nodded in agreement. Harry looked at them searching for any dissention, and seeing nothing but loyalty and concern, he continued. "Longone, you take me and Chadrack to the airstrip, he knows what to do around the aeroplane. Sam and the rest of you take one Landy and head due east and keep the radio on. Sam, use frequency 132,4. I'll find the crash scene from the air and direct you as close as you can get to it. Then I'll come back here and fetch the other vehicle to help you. That aircraft could have crashed as far as twenty miles away so it's going to take me a while to find it, if we find it at all before dark." He paused realising an omission. Then speaking very slowly and almost apologetically, he said, "My friends, do you have a problem if I recommend that Sampson Ndlovu be your leader? He is a man who has much experience in these matters. He was with me when we rescued Mr. Templar's father another time. He is not just strong like a buffalo, and I don't mean on the mattress." They all laughed nodding at each other, "but he has the skill and cleverness of a wild dog. He has done plenty of this kind of thing and knows what must be done."

Sampson fairly bristled with pride but hid his feelings by bowing his head. The men spoke softly to each other in Shona for a moment, throwing the occasional look at Sampson. Then one of them spoke out.

"Mr. Andrews, we will follow your friend, this buffalo, for he is a man that men can follow for he treats with us as equals." Harry let out a sigh of relief.

"Thank you. You will not be disappointed for I trust this man with my life." He turned to Sampson.

"OK Sam," he said, "you are to lead these men. But please be bloody careful. These comrades are not animals, they shoot back!" Turning to Longone, the man he'd selected as his driver, he said, "Longone, after you drop me off, you get some more people, fetch plenty of firewood and light ten fires on both sides of the runway and a bonfire at both ends, because if it is dark when I come back I cannot land unless I can see where to come down." He didn't wait for a reply but said, "OK, let's go!" Off they went careering up the steep track towards the airstrip situated up on the plateau above the camp.

CHAPTER 28

Shenje 'Himmler' Ndunze fired the missile himself. Even before it hit the aircraft he threw the launch tube down, picked up his AK47, watched the missile strike and then called to his comrades.

"Come, we go now." They assembled quickly and then leading his men he started running towards the aircraft. It was a fast trot conditioned by months of mind numbing training and it consumed the ground, up hill and down, at a phenomenal rate, scattering the game, so wild that it was tame, in front of them. Within an hour, barely winded, they had already covered over five miles, no mean feat considering the rough country and thick bush they were moving through.

At the end of the first hour he halted for five minutes at the top of a hill and for a few minutes searched the horizons. He noted two things. In front of him, the smoke from what was obviously the crash site, and secondly a small aircraft circling high in the sky above it.

"So they have already found it," he muttered. "But we will get there first." His only regret was that he didn't have another missile. The second aircraft would be a sitting duck.

Harry and Chadrack climbed into the air, spiralling upwards to get height for two reasons. The first was to give them as wide a field of view in their search for the downed aircraft and the other was to try to get radio communications with someone. Tuned into the police frequency, he eventually got through at 9000 feet.

"BSAP Control, BSAP Control, this is call sign Victor – Fox Sierra Whisky (V-FSW) calling MAYDAY, MAYDAY."

"Fox Sierra Whisky, BSAP Control Sinoa, go ahead."

"Sinoa, - FSW, Air Rhodesia flight Vic. Falls to Salisbury has been shot down at Whamira Hills. Repeat, Air Rhodesia flight, Vic. Falls to Salisbury, has been shot down at Whamira Hills, do you copy? Fox Sierra Whisky." He and Chadrack spotted the smoke simultaneously and in the time it'd taken to establish contact, Harry had already established himself in a circular holding pattern over the site. The details were not too clear because he had to maintain 9000 feet until he'd finished reporting in.

"Sinoa, I copy your report." The operator read back what Harry had said. "Stand by while I patch you through to HQ Salisbury." Harry relaxed. Thank goodness they don't put idiots onto their radios he thought. Three minutes passed and Harry was starting to become agitated.

"Fox Sierra Whisky, HQ here. Is that you Pirate? Confirm report that Air Rhodesia heavy, Falls to Salisbury destroyed." Harry smiled grimly, James Huxley, thank goodness.

"That's affirmative. Weapon used Sam 7, I repeat Sam7. I'm overhead the crash site now at Whamira Hills, I have New Sarum VOR inbound radial 245°, DME at 122 nautical miles."

"I copy Whamira Hills, 245° inbound, 122 miles. Confirm again aircraft shot down?"

"Affirm. We witnessed a missile air strike from Sanyati River."

"Shit. OK Pirate, get out of there before they shoot you down, leave it to us."

"Negative. We think Pete's parents are on board. Putting down at Sivewrights to render assistance, if possible. Cheers and tell the boys to hurry." Harry flipped to his other radio, which was tuned into 132,4.

"Hello Sam, Pirate here, come in please."

"Pirate, Sam here, go ahead."

"Sam, go back to the camp. I'm overhead the crash site, it's much closer than I thought, no more than 12 miles from the camp. I know where it is but I think it's too difficult and dangerous to just direct you in. Wait for me, I'm coming back. This needs to be done very carefully."

"OK Pirate, returning to camp now."

Harry clawed an aeronautical chart onto his lap and looking up frequently as he wound his way down slowly, descending at 500 feet/minute, from time to time increasing the mixture and reducing power, he set about plotting the exact position of the crash onto the chart. It took him no more than two minutes and then setting that aside he concentrated on flying and landing the Baron back at the camp. He'd been in the air just 35 minutes and landed just as the last light of day bled away to night. Dusk is short in the tropics and by the time they climbed down from the aircraft it was dark.

And so within 45 minutes of the terrorist action, word reached the authorities in Salisbury that an Air Rhodesia Viscount had been shot down. It took the authorities a further 45 minutes before the airline would admit that they'd lost contact with the aircraft and to confirm that their Victoria Falls flight had gone missing. Then the counter measures began to be put into effect. The Air Force and the Army were alerted, although they took a while to believe it and begin their planning. They immediately notified their forces in the area, who, within an hour, put four truckloads of troops and four ambulance units onto the road from Sinoa. The police were ahead of them all, sending almost the entire garrison of the Karoi Police Camp down the road towards the crash site.

They were all too late.

The guerrillas ran into the dark, confident of their footing and knowing exactly what needed to be done. It was the stench that they sensed first, the acrid smell of burning rubber and plastic. And then there it was.

The fact that the aircraft had obviously been under control at impact was lost on them. They saw only the supreme success of their mission. They stopped and stood close to the first item they found, a large wheel strut, the two wheels on it pointing vertically into the night sky. They smiled and patted each other on the back chattering like the proverbial gaggle of geese. They walked farther, sweeping to and fro, fascinated by the ruined remains of the large airliner they'd destroyed. The odd flame still licked the smouldering remnants that seemed to increase in number as they crept forwards. Soon out of the darkness came the main body of the machine, lying at 45 degrees to the horizontal, one wing taken off at the root, the other broken in the middle, high up on a pile of rocks, the twisted tip of it pointing upwards as if trying to claw itself back into the air. The enormity of the atrocity they had committed was irrelevant, and it wasn't yet over.

What alerted their leader to the fact that there were survivors were the bodies lying in a row to one side of the hulk. Instantaneously their demeanour changed. They again became predators, and began searching. Within 15 minutes they had found seven women, two young girls and a man. They herded them together in the light of the dying flames coming from an engine lying virtually burnt-out close to the fuselage.

They smiled and promised to help the bedraggled, torn bunch. Satisfied that they had rounded up all the survivors, the leader flicked his fingers. Smiling, laughing to their captives, they lifted their AK47's and mowed them down. After looting money, watches, some shoes and other items off the bodies, at a signal from the leader, "Come, I hear vehicles," they ran off into the night.

When Harry and his party arrived there shortly before dawn, at first all they could find was death. Harry went carefully along the row of torn and mutilated bodies then turned to the heap of women lying next to the fuselage. His heart sank as he realised that these people had been lined up and machine-gunned to death. He looked at the man, lying there, half his face blown away and suddenly knew. Harry fell to his knees, bile rising in his throat. Unable to help himself, he started vomiting.

It was Sampson, strong but understanding, who pulled him away.

"Come, Master Harry," he said gently, "there is nothing you can do here. Come, we have found some people alive." Harry stood up, blinded by tears, wiped his eyes and mouth and allowed Sampson to lead him away. As the new day dawned, they found three sobbing women, torn, bloodied and terrified, hiding in a crevice in the granite rocks of a nearby kopje. Half an hour later the first police contingent arrived. Within an hour Air Force helicopters were ferrying out the survivors, the three women and another five men discovered hiding further away.[85]

The mass funeral and memorial service held in the Anglican Cathedral at the corner of Second Street and Baker Avenue in Salisbury, was a packed and sombre affair. Harry stood there with his wife and young family, Robbie in Annie's arms, Beverley between them. They were next to Peter, Barbara and their children in the third row of pews, with other family members of the slaughtered innocents occupying the rows in front and behind them. But he was having difficulty relating to the proceedings. All he could think of was that somehow there was irony in the fact that they were in a church right next door to the Parliament buildings; the forum in which the courage to accept inevitable change hitherto had been absent. He shrugged, berating himself at the bizarre thought that it was they who were ultimately responsible for this tragedy.

He looked around. The mourners would have read like a veritable 'Who's Who' in Rhodesia; several government ministers, from the Prime Minister down, the heads of all the services and many other dignitaries. He looked at the coffins, 35 of those killed had been Anglicans. Then he glanced at Peter, scrutinising his face for a moment. Peter looked drawn; dark rings below his eyes, which themselves appeared to have sunk into his skull. He had clearly lost a lot of weight. Watching Peter with Barbara holding his arm tightly next to him, Harry searched his mind to find solutions. Should he have driven straight out to the crash site instead of using the Baron first to find it? Would they have got there in time to prevent the shooting? These were questions which had vexed his mind since that fateful day.

Looking up, he gazed at the beautiful stained glass windows high up behind the alter, focussing on the crucifixion scene in the dominant central position and came to the realisation that they would never have made it. They would have floundered around in the broken country trying to break through, going round in circles trying to find the crash site. They'd never have found it in the dark and by then it would have been too late anyway. By knowing where the crash was, he'd been able to guide them along the existing vehicle tracks to a point closest to the scene and from there they'd walked, a mere mile and a half. Even then they'd had to move incredibly slowly and carefully, Sam and Harry out on point patrols searching for evidence of an ambush, coming back time and again to draw the team forwards to the next holding point. Those three hours for Harry had been extremely arduous, most of it spent crawling or crouching low, searching in near total darkness for any glimmer, any glint that might warn them of the terrorists in front of them. Even when they reached the scene, Harry and Sam had taken another two hours to sweep completely around it until Sam found the tracks of men running off into the night, and others, clearly white men in ordinary shoes, going off in another direction.

They had just been too late.

Barbara had arranged a private reception in the Salisbury Club, just one block away, which, as it turned out, was sensible. They left their own cars in the car park and went together, the Templar and Andrews families, in a large black limousine laid on by the undertakers, out to the Warren Hills Cemetery. Peter was supposed to say a few words over the communal grave of his parents, but choked and ultimately Harry recited the short poem Peter had prepared, arm around Peter standing next to him, tears running down his face.

Afterwards, fortified by three stiff whiskies, flown in especially by Jim Leonard, Peter took Barbara's hand and worked his way slowly through the throng of family friends to stand in front of Harry and Annie. He embraced Annie and then surprisingly hugged Harry as well. Then they were all crying; Annie and Barbara embracing each other, the men still in a hug. There was nothing to say, nothing to assuage the grief felt by them all. Eventually Peter broke away and put his arm around Barbara's waist. He looked at Harry and Annie, now holding hands. Harry made as if to get them some drinks.

"Wait, Harry." Peter's voice was broken, a croak, dry. He swallowed and worked saliva into his mouth. "Annie, Harry, you've been the best friends that a man and woman could ever have asked for." He paused and Barbara gripped his hand, squeezing it, forcing him to continue. "But Barbara and I have had it, we're taking the gap."

"Wha..?" Harry was so dumbfounded he couldn't finish the question. "When, where?"

"Shut up, Harry," said Annie quietly into his ear, "let Peter finish. This is difficult enough for him as it is without you trying to bully him." Peter looked down at Barbara who squeezed his hand again and nodded, maintaining eye contact, resolute. He continued.

"We're going to Australia. I've sold the farm and we leave next week."

"Jesus, Pete," Harry couldn't believe his ears, he was staggered. "Why didn't you speak to me about it? Why didn't I know?" he looked at Annie. "Annie you must have known, why didn't you tell me?"

"Because their minds are made up Harry, and you would have just made it more difficult for them, trying to talk them out of it."

"Bloody right I would!" He turned back to Peter. "Jesus, Pete, the war is nearly over; they're on the verge of signing a deal and a cease fire. Hell, there'll be a black led government in place in three months." He had avoided looking directly at Peter, choosing rather to glare into mid air. But then he forced himself to focus, meeting Peter's forlorn gaze. "Oh my God, Pete, why now, after all we've been through?" He slumped down, feeling betrayed, deserted by them all. "Shit, I need a drink."

CHAPTER 29

"*He never spoke to me again Mum.*"
"But that's ridiculous Harry, didn't you see him and Barbara off at the airport."

"No. He never came out to Karoi again. They stayed in Salisbury, wrapping up his parents affairs, and on the due date, they just flew away. I know that Annie and Barbara continued to exchange letters quite frequently and I know that they spoke on the phone many times; I could tell from the telephone account cheque stubs; and Annie used to tell me how they were doing."

"That's very sad Harry."

"Oh I don't know. They did all right for a while. He set up a security company in Perth and then bought a wine farm near Albany, south east of Perth. Apparently he produced a passable wine. Then it all fell apart. I just hope it's not because he was bitter. You know the story better than I do."

"Henry Andrews!"

"Ah Mum, you've no idea what a bitter taste it left in my mouth. At the time, I looked upon us as a team, a successful one at that, and if I'd have known, I'd probably have packed up and gone with them. Same old story, hundred percent vision after the fact. But if we'd gone, maybe things would have turned out differently."

Harry slurped his tea noisily and pushed his chair back.

THE WYVERN REVENGE

"Thanks for the breakfast Mum. Bonnie and I are going down to see Richard today. Would you like to come?" Harry's brother had taken over the farm at Wedmore. Their father had died years before and Bunty had decided to move to Bristol to be nearer her friends. Richard had done well, his brand of Cheddar cheese being highly regarded and his mutton had done well. But now, having gone through the foot-and-mouth epidemic, he was battling to make ends meet. Harry was intent on helping him out.

"No, I've got bridge this afternoon. Well drive carefully, dear; the roads are crowded in Britain. And I think you should leave Bonnie here. No place to take a dog in the middle of this foot-and-mouth crisis. Besides, Richard's dogs might not be too happy about it."

"Yes I suppose you're right. OK, she stays." He looked at his dog lovingly.

"Now you stay with Bunty, you hear?" It was almost as if the dog knew that Harry was going out without her; with a hangdog look and whimpering quietly, she disappeared under the dining room tablecloth.

"Where are the car keys?" he asked shrugging on his overcoat. Spring had arrived but it was still cool.

It was as if he'd never left, but for the fact that there were now strange little children running around and a young beautiful woman greeting him at the door. He'd met Richard's wife Sharon several times when they visited Bunty and him in Bristol, but this was his first visit to the old farm since returning to Britain.

"Come, I'll show you to your room." Harry picked up his bags and carefully avoiding knocking them against the wall, he climbed the narrow stairs after her. Old habits die hard he thought, remembering the number of times his father had clouted him for carelessly damaging the paintwork.

They hadn't touched the room. It was still exactly the same, his stuff everywhere.

"Wow, talk about 'déjà vu'. I've definitely been here before," he said staring wonderingly around him. Sharon laughed.

"Richie said you'd be back. Make yourself at home; you know where everything is. I've got some tea on the boil, so when you're ready come down. Richie knows you're here and he'll be back shortly."

Harry sat down on his bed thinking. Shit, I haven't been in this room for over 20 years and it hasn't changed at all. Then his mind went back. He leapt up and opened the cupboard, slowly at first, almost as of he didn't want to see what was in it, but then swung the door open. He leant forwards and from amongst all his old clothes, he picked one of his old Royal Air Force uniforms off the rail and spread it out on the bed. He couldn't believe it. It was just the same although it smelled a little of naphthalene. Delighted, he thought, I wonder if it still fits. In three minutes, he'd stripped and donned the uniform finding an old air-force-blue shirt in the chest of drawers. He went to the cupboard again and there were his ties, and issue shoes.

"Bloody unbelievable!" he shouted, ducking out the door and down the stairs. He marched into the kitchen, came stiffly to a halt and saluted his brother and sister-in-law. "Squadron Leader Harry Andrews at your service folks!" they looked at him, astounded, and then Richard started clapping.

"You bloody son of a gun. It still fits after all these years." He rushed forwards and hugged his brother. Leaning back, Richard looked at Harry smiling. "Christ, the prodigal son returns. Bloody good to see you, Harry."

"Hey, less swearing in front of the children, Richard," his wife admonished, but clearly she was delighted as well. Like a boarding school boy home for the holidays, Harry spent the next hour and a half going through all his old possessions, delighting in new discoveries of old pleasures. Then dressing in cords and Wellingtons he went down to join Richard.

He spent an exhausting day being dragged around to see everything that there was to see on the farm, and a protracted stint in the office going over the farm books. The two of them spent over two hours talking about the foot-and-mouth crisis and what could be done to protect the farm from its inevitable consequences.

Finally that evening, Harry was able to sink wearily into his father's old armchair, about the only piece of furniture that he recognised after all the years. The room looked newly decorated, more modern, although his mind was blank as to what it used to look like. He didn't recall spending much time in there.

"You may smoke, Harry."

"You're a star," he acknowledged smiling at Sharon and hauling out his pipe.

"My God, but it's good to be home."

"Well it is your home and you're always welcome, Harry. We're sorry that you haven't come before this," said Sharon.

"I'm sorry about that but I've had other things on my mind."

"No, we really mean it, Harry; it is after all half yours." Harry didn't reply immediately but contented himself with filling his pipe. Richard and Sharon looked at each other. Richard knew damned well that something was coming although he couldn't fathom what. He just hoped that Harry didn't have any ideas about coming to work with him on the farm. He didn't think he could handle it. He poured Harry a brandy, walked over and placed it on the side table next to his brother.

"Thanks bro." He said nothing else until he'd lit the pipe, swirled, warmed, sniffed and then taken a sip of his brandy. He lay back relaxed.

"Well, I've been meaning to tell you about that. I've had a 'Deed of Session' drawn up by Mum's lawyer in Westbury. It's all signed and legal. The farm is all yours." He looked at them as they stared at him dumbstruck. "Yes, I've got it upstairs in my briefcase if you'd like to fetch it bro?"

Richard disappeared instantly and Sharon came over to sit on a poof cushion near to Harry's chair. She looked at him solemnly.

"So the warrior not only returns, but after all he has been through, he brings gifts as well," she said quietly, still, looking at him. Tears welled up in her eyes.

"Hey sis, you'll have me crying next. Stop it," he laughed.

Richard came back into the room holding the deed and without saying anything sat down and began to read. Harry interrupted him.

"But that's not all," he said theatrically. "There is only one condition: I want your bank account details so that I can commence transferring £2000 a month into it. In two years, we'll take another look, OK? I'm not going to have you go out and mortgage the bloody place now that you don't need my signature. No bloody arguments now!"

Sharon couldn't believe what she was hearing and looked wonderingly at Richard. He came over and sat down on the floor next to her, the deed dropped to the floor and he held her hand in his. She looked back at Harry.

"Thank you, Harry," she said quietly, her eyes wet. "You will always be welcome here and that room is and always will be yours, whenever you want it."

"Good, I thought you'd see it my way," said Harry lightly. He lifted his glass. "Cheers." They all drank in silence for a moment, Richard and Sharon silently in their own way working out the import of what Harry had done. Harry sat there watching them, quietly chuckling to himself. He'd had this in the back of his mind for a long time and he was now glad that he'd at last done something about it.

"You've shed many skins, Harry Andrews," she said eventually, "but you still haven't told us what happened after your friends Peter and Barbara went to Australia."

"It's a long story and besides, I should have thought Bunty would have told you all about it. She was more in the picture through Annie than I was."

"No, she hasn't, and anyway we've got all night, big brother," said Richard looking up from the document, "and there's plenty of brandy." Calling him 'big brother' indicated the strength of the esteem in which Richard held his elder brother. The fact was that Richard was two inches taller than Harry and although lean from the labour of farming, about 30 pounds heavier. Harry smiled at him, the gentle giant, and then he began.

"Well, it was OK for about three months. Pete's foreman Sampson Ndlovu moved over, lock, stock and barrel to my place. I didn't have any say in the matter. He just arrived in his old Bedford truck, wives - 3 of them, children —14 of them, chickens, impashlah (household goods) and all. He even had his cattle in-spanned behind the truck. It must have taken him all day to get there. Christ what a sight, I'll never forget it."

Harry took a sip of brandy warming to the task.

"Well as you can imagine, I was a bit concerned, I couldn't have two foremen on my place. Anyway, the solution was self-evident. I moved Chadrack, they were so-called brothers you know, into the house on my other farm making him manager there, and employed Sampson as the boss-boy or foreman, on the original Merrywaters farm. It worked out quite well actually."

He coughed, spluttering on his pipe.

"Well, no, it didn't at first. Annie insisted that I build them another classroom to house all the additional kids in the school." Richard and Sharon burst into laughter. "Hell, nothing like doing your mate's manservant a favour, but having to build a new classroom to house his kids. And, I might add," Harry said laughing with them, "another big house in the compound, although that came later."

Shenji Ndunze and his men moved their base camp closer to the heartland. At times variously called the 'breadbasket of Africa' the rich agricultural land some 150 miles in radius around Salisbury, is virtually unmatched anywhere in the world. This high plateau has it all; rich red loams, gentle undulating terrain, good regular rainfall, warm summers and mild winters. It had been cleared of malaria, sleeping sickness and rabies between the world wars, and foot-and-mouth, anthrax, rindepest and locust infestations were only occasional visitors. If it had any drawbacks it was ticks. But farmers soon learned to dip their livestock regularly, keeping at bay the vector born diseases they carried.

It is here that the white farming community was concentrated, growing rich on tobacco, maize, timber, tropical fruit, cotton, ground nut, vegetable, flower, hemp, dairy, beef and mutton production. It is a paradise, so much so that it was a standing joke amongst Rhodesians that 'Moses lost his way to the promised land'.

It is here also that the 'Freedom' fighters concentrated their efforts. Ndunze established his cadre between Karoi and Sinoa and began to undermine security in the surrounding district. Their aims were clear: get the farmers off the farms, create 'no go' zones where they were able to establish de facto authority. They were ruthlessly successful, hitting farm after farm, randomly, cleverly, leaving no trail. The local people cowered. Dissention was dealt with swiftly and viciously, the decisions of the 'peoples' courts frequently resulting in death and mutilation. The police were perplexed and almost powerless. The policy of moving people into 'protected villages', was a failure. Gun law had arrived with a vengeance. He with the gun had the might and was right.

Fear of and acquiescence to 'Himmler' Ndunze and his cadre spread like wildfire. He brought in a political commissar who began the process of turning the people against the white settler 'oppressors'. They sat, content that they were quite safe from the security forces, flaunting their apparent power, their immunity, outside a small house in Sinoa's black township. Ndunze, pragmatic and taking no chances however, sat on his stool leaning against the doorframe of the dwelling. He merely had to reach behind him into the doorway to bring his AK47 to hand.

"Comrade, how does the Chimurenga proceed?" asked the commissar.

"As you can see Commissar," said Ndunze respectfully, no need to get on the wrong side of this politico, he thought, "we now control the minds of most of the people."

He waved around him at the surrounding humble dwellings.

"Three months ago we would have been reported and arrested. Now we are quite safe. A few simple examples sufficed to change the people from opponents into supporters."

He thought of the killings, the savage brutalising, rapes and burnings that had been necessary to achieve this state. He thought also with exaltation of the airliner that they'd, he himself, had shot down. It had been a moment to cherish, to savour, like the body of a plump young maiden.

"And what is the next stage of your strategy?"

"Oh, that is simple. I have been compiling a list of targets. Particularly I have been gathering information about all the farmers in the area. Once we have decided the most appropriate action we shall again attack. But first I must return to Munze mission. I must fetch more supplies and men and I wish to discuss certain aspects of our future missions with our strategist.

Chief Superintendent Bill Sturrock arrived for dinner in the pouring rain. But it didn't matter as he was staying the night and wouldn't be driving back to Salisbury until the following day. Lightning flashes lightened the darkened sky as he scampered from his car onto the front veranda of the house. He turned around shrugging off his poncho and shaking the water off it. Looking out at the immaculate garden, the ordered nature of the homestead and outbuildings, he sighed, "Shit, let's hope that this war ends soon or even wonderful places like this will be lost." He looked for the security fencing and automatic gate further back down the driveway but they were hidden in the sheets of rain that swept down.

"Of what ill wind do you expound dear soul?" said a voice from behind him. Bill literally jumped, and turning he saw Harry standing holding the fly-screen open at the front door, casual, in control and smiling.

"Hi Pirate. Hey, you gave me a hell of a fright."

"Sorry, not much good at coming out with famous quotes, always get them wrong. Poor at English literature," said Harry. Bill laughed.

THE WYVERN REVENGE

"No, you bloody idiot. I've heard it said that you move as silently as a cat. You must learn to make a noise like everybody else so we know you're around." Harry smiled as he took the poncho and threw it over the nearest deck chair.

"Come on in, George will grab your bag when the rain lets up."

Harry ushered him in. Sweeping up Robbie he called out to Annie in the kitchen that Bill had arrived and that she should let the dogs out. He took Bill straight to the bar where the next few minutes were spent unravelling dogs and kids and trying to get Bill a beer out of the fridge. Eventually, dogs in their baskets outside on the veranda, they settled down, Harry in his favourite position behind the bar, Bill on a tall barstool. Annie came through following and guiding Beverley, who marched in with both tiny hands clenching a bowl of potato crisps, concentration absolute. More smiles, kisses and welcomes and finally Harry asked Bill what he'd meant out on the veranda.

"Fill me in first on what he said," said Annie encircled in Harry's arm behind the bar.

"I overheard Bill Mumbling to himself. Something about hoping that the war will end soon or even places like this will be lost." Harry gave his wife a gentle squeeze.

"Yes," said Bill. "I was alluding to the fact that the war is hotting up. Since Smith declared Martial Law in October, things have got worse, not better. Even with us flattening those two camps in Zambia in November and December the influx of guerrillas has increased."

"Well, I hope you got that bastard Fischer," said Harry taking a draught of beer.

"In the back of our minds believe me, but no, I don't think we've got him yet, but he's not the only one we're after." He helped himself to a handful of crisps. "Since the referendum[86], Smith has been forced to capitulate, thank goodness. Muz will be the Prime Minister by the end of March. God I hate my job."

"Why Bill?" asked Annie.

"Annie, I'm not a politician, I'm a policeman, a trained detective. My job should be twofold. I should be investigating crime, collecting evidence and bringing miscreants to justice. Secondly I should be combating crime by infiltrating criminal elements, gathering information so as to stop perpetrators before they commit a crime." He took a sip of his drink.

"Hell, what am I doing now? I'm running around trying to find guerrillas, people who believe implicitly in the justice of their cause, largely because, politically, their views differ from those of our politicians. Sure, it is wrong for them to go around killing and pillaging, but they haven't really had much choice have they?" He paused. "And I might say, a large number of them are nothing but youngsters, indoctrinated by the clever dialectic of communism, socialism, Marxism, whatever 'ism you want to call it. They have no clue what they're fighting for. And I know this because, God knows, I've had to interrogate enough of them."

"So you're one of those guys that torture them Bill?" suggested Annie coldly. Bill looked up sharply.

"That's bullshit, and you know it Annie. Don't believe everything you read or hear. It's part of their overall propaganda strategy to discredit us. Listen, for the most part, these guys are better off in Chickarubi Prison than they were out there. Shit, at least they get three square meals a day, they're clothed, get proper medical and dental care, got a roof over their heads."

"What about these cases of prisoners dying in custody?" Annie was now on a roll. Bill was going to have trouble stopping her. Harry wasn't inclined to stop her either, he knew better.

"Annie, I agree, there have been incidents of overzealous guards overdoing it and actually causing deaths. Where we have been able, those responsible have been brought to boot. But I promise, as I stand here, no one, not one of these detainees has been maltreated while under interrogation by our people. Hell, Annie, do you really think that these poor sods can hold out against intelligent scientifically developed interrogation techniques? They just don't have the commitment to the communist dogma that would stop them from giving information away. Funnily enough, only it's not funny, slapping them about doesn't work. They're tough as nails. The trick is to convince them that there is no way that anyone will ever know what they told us and that we will relocate them to a safe place. Then they sing like canaries. We also play them against each other saying we know because one of their comrades has already told us. Most of them want out anyway."

George came in and announced that dinner was served, so Bill's discourse came briefly to a halt.

"You go ahead and carve, darling," said Annie to Harry as she picked up Robbie. "I'll put the children to bed and join you in a moment." Everything was delayed while Beverley went around kissing everybody good night. Harry grabbed two more beer cans out of the fridge and led Bill through into the dining room.

"I apologise Bill, Annie gets pretty hot under the collar about these things."

"Hell, no problem! Thank goodness there are people around who are genuinely concerned. Power does corrupt and it's important that there are folk out there drawing attention to our own excesses. The opposition's are self-evident." Harry stood while he carved the roast and Bill stood next to him, beer can in hand, taking in the aroma.

"You like the outside or do you like it rare?" asked Harry.

"Wow, I like it all. Haven't had good roast beef and veg for ages. I'm drooling."

Annie came in and after dishing out the potato and vegetables from the sideboard, she sat and the men followed suit.

"Um, Bubble and Squeak and Yorkshire pud too. Brilliant!" said Bill. "And where did you get this English mustard?" They ate their meal engaging in small talk only, but as the meal came to an end, Harry folded his napkin, placed it carefully on his side plate and straightened up, a slight frown on his face.

"Bill, coming back to what you said on the veranda, it's got me worried," he said.

"Look, I don't want to appear alarmist or anything," started Bill, he lent forwards putting his elbows on the table. "But the security situation has deteriorated appreciably in this area in recent months. Sure, we've managed to nail a few of them, but you've seen and heard of all the attacks that have taken place around here. There seems to be a growing support in the local population for Mugabe and there's not much we can do about it. He comes from just down the road you know, near Sinoa."

"Spell it out, Bill," said Harry leaning forwards, almost crouching as if straining at a leash, intent on hearing Bill's very breathing. Bill felt the heat of his gaze and was forced to look at him. He saw the glittering eyes, unwavering, trying to drill into his mind. He thought to himself, shit, everything they say about this guy is true. I'd hate to get on the wrong side of him. He said,

"Get prepared. Whether you think so or not, they're going to have a go at you. It's not a question of 'if'. It's just a question of 'when'." Bill picked up his beer glass, drank, wiped his mouth with his napkin, and said,

"Annie, that is the best meal I've had for as long as I can remember. Beats the hell out of police field kitchen chow, any time."

"Thank you, but thank George. He's the boss in the kitchen," smiled Annie. But he had her full attention also. "When is 'when', Bill?" she asked, not letting go. She reached out and gently covered Harry's hand with hers, almost as if to restrain him.

"I don't know Annie. But you know how they work. They'll start with your labour. Intimidation, threats, the odd beating, hut burning, small hit-and-run stuff, looking for weakness. When they find it, they'll be at your throats. Can't have malhungu's (*whites*) strutting about keeping everybody happy."

Resigned, but with new resolve, Bill sat forwards again, elbows on the table, and continued,

"Harry, Annie, you run a slick operation here. The whole country knows what you've achieved. Your staff and labour are content, the envy of all the other farm workers in the district. You have to look for signs, sullenness, absenteeism, cheek, laziness, theft, especially rustling, things that are normally not the case. Breakages, watch your equipment and machinery carefully. Travel everywhere armed to the teeth, in convoy if possible, even on your own farms. Break usual routines. Try not to be predictable, take different routes.

Most important though Harry is to watch your dirt roads as you travel along them. They're bringing mines in, including those nasty anti-personnel things. In short, this is no longer a distant threat. It's not a case of 'it'll never happen to me'. I cannot impress upon you enough that it will. Having the opportunity to deliver this unpleasant message is one of the reasons I was so keen to accept your invitation out here. Since Smith stuck that medal on your chest for your part in that Viscount affair you've become something of a juicy target Pirate. All I can say is watch it and watch carefully."

"Should I move Annie and the children into Salisbury?" asked Harry.

"I can't advise you on that, Harry. But that's what they want isn't it? They want you to leave, want you to take the gap like Pete and Barbara."

"Hey, leave them out of it."

"Look, you know what the purpose of the terrorist is," continued Bill, "they want people to give in."

"That's as may be. I don't mind being at the sharp end, but I don't want my wife and kids in the firing line."

"That's very admirable of you Harry Andrews, but don't I have a say in this?" asked Annie. "Anyway, don't even think about it. The children and I are staying right here. This war's going to be over soon and besides, I've got too much to do here. I can't just leave these people halfway through what I've set out to achieve. So don't even think about it Harry," she said fiercely. On that note she rose from the table, subject closed.

CHAPTER 30

Ndunze reported to the Commandant the instant he returned to the camp. His hour-long report was thorough, detailing all their activities and providing a list of potential targets. Commandant Gundwane, eyes barely visible through his dark glasses, had not moved since Ndunze had started. For a brief moment Ndunze thought that the man was dead, propped up by his chair, but then he saw a blink. Ndunze found that he was beginning to fear this man and the thought sat uncomfortably on his mind. He finished his report-back and stood perfectly still in the middle of the room waiting for a response from the obese man in front of him.

Still the Commandant didn't move and he questioned the thought as to why he should be fearful of this fat albino. He began to think that the man was far too dangerous. He had absolute and complete power. At the flick of a finger, he could and did condemn people to death; prosecutor, judge and exterminator all rolled into one fat blob in a split second. He took what he wanted and rumour had it that he was now lusting after Marie Volker. Ndunze wondered idly what Major Volker himself would think about it, or more to the point, what he would do about it, if the lust began to manifest itself. Apparently she'd already been ordered to do his house keeping and had been put in charge of cooking his food.

No, I'm not going to let myself be intimidated by this man, he thought, vowing at that moment never to be without his firearm in future. I will kill him if he even looks at me sideways. He straightened up and stared back at the Commandant.

As if he'd broken the spell, as if the Commandant received a signal that his grip on the man before him had been broken, the fat man leant forwards at his desk and placed his hands on the desk.

"Very good, comrade, very good. You have done well. But you will not be here for long. Your orders are to collect what you need and go back into Zimbabwe. You are to concentrate on attacking the farms. We believe that the unholy alliance between Smith, Muzorewa and Sithole is about to collapse. We believe that all it needs now is one final push and we shall be victorious."

"Yebo, Commandant Gundwane."

"Good Comrade. You will now report to Volker with your list of targets." He almost spat the name out. "Finalise your strategies with him. Tomorrow morning you will leave again, the men are ready for you. You may go."

Ndunze gave the black power salute, turned on his heal and left without another word. On the way out he passed Mrs. Volker, looking strained, entering the house. He nodded, scooped up his AK from the veranda floor and continued walking towards the Major's bungalow. He didn't even blink when he heard the scream from the building behind him. He walked onto the veranda of the bungalow, knocked on the door, heard the shout for him to enter and so opened the door.

He doubled up with laughter at the sight that greeted him. Major Volker was sitting on the couch in the lounge, studiously trying to behave as if nothing was happening, seeming to read from some papers. In front of him wiping the floor with a damp cloth, her wrap around her waist with her young breasts hanging free, was his servant the 'Butterfly', as she'd become known.

"Agh, what is so funny Ndunze?" asked Fischer looking up; fiercely, it seemed to Ndunze, feigning innocence.

Ndunze eventually brought himself under control, using his short t-shirt sleeve to wipe away the tears of mirth from his eyes.

"The irony of it. You fucking a black maiden and Gundwane fucking a white matron. Why do black people want to be white and white people want to be black?"

"What do you mean, fucking a white matron?" Fischer leapt angrily to his feet.

"Oh, come on, Major, do you mean to tell me that you don't know that Gundwane is fucking your wife? He's doing it right this minute."

"What?" Fischer rushed to the window, looked out at nothing and then turned, no longer angry, but now cold, calculating.

"Give me your AK," he ordered holding out his hand.

"Don't be mad Major. Who cares? It's quite funny actually, quite poetic."

"I care," insisted Fischer. "She is my wife. Give me the gun."

"Be it on your shoulders," said Ndunze shrugging. He unslung the weapon and passed it to Fischer who, without another word, ran out of the house. Ndunze followed him out and watched from the corner of the bungalow as Fischer sprinted across the 100 yards to Gundwane's office.

Ignoring the two guards outside the front door, Fischer burst into the building, bringing the now cocked AK up before him, and quietly padded into Gundwane's office through the open door without knocking. His wife, her pants torn off, dress up around her waist, was held down on her back on the desk by Commandant Gundwane's huge hand on her throat. Her hands were weakly scratching at the giant albino's arm, divided legs frantically but futilely kicking in the air. Gundwane himself, trousers again around his ankles was wedged between her legs thrusting into her, his huge penis rigid and obscene as it penetrated deep into her.

Fischer never hesitated. He did three things virtually simultaneously. Hearing the guards running along the corridor behind him, he stepped to one side of the door. Then he spoke, voice loud, strained.

"The penalty for rape is death," he said.

Then, as the Commandant turned in triumph, open mouth drooling, to look at him, Volker lifted the AK47 and fired a short burst straight into the gloating face. There was not even time for his face to register that there was a gun pointing at him, let alone that he was being fired at. The sound of five rounds going off in quick succession in the confines of the room were mind shattering and brought the two guards who'd just run into the room, to a numbing halt. They stared horror struck at the Commandant as his face and his head disintegrated in front of them, splattering the gore of it on the whitewashed wall behind him. Almost in slow motion by comparison, the huge body seemed to float up and away from the desk and flop down, crumpling against the wall. Then, leaving a thick lumpy slick on the wall, the remains of Commandant Gundwane slid a short way further down into repose on the floor. The last movement was that of his penis deflating as all the blood drained back into the huge gushing corpse.

But Volker wasn't watching. He moved up behind the guards, struck the first firmly behind the ear with the steel butt of his AK and as the man collapsed, in one fluid movement brought the weapon to bear on the second man, just as he turned to look at him.

"Don't even think of it, Comrade. Drop your weapon," ordered Volker. The guard was only too pleased to comply and the weapon clattered to the floor. "OK, now go and assemble the Comrades. Now!" he barked. The man, relief showing on his face that he'd not been shot, ran out of the door.

Volker moved to his wife's side, his concern overwhelming him as suddenly as he had reacted earlier. He slung his weapon over his shoulder and lifted her sobbing into a sitting position, at the same time pulling her dress, now marked by a fine spray of blood, down to cover her nakedness.

"Meine Schatzie, it is over." He hugged her to him trying to stifle her sobs, rocking to and fro. That was how Ndunze found him.

Volker turned as he entered.

"Ndunze, fetch some women to attend to my wife and then wait for me on the veranda. I will address the men." His look was bleak, commanding, and Ndunze didn't hesitate.

"Yes, Major."

"Comrades," shouted Volker to the assembly in front of him. "Have I ever lied to you?"

"Aeewa *(No)*," shouted the men in unison.

"Have I always treated you with respect?"

"Yebo!" they shouted.

"Have I not taught you to fight like soldiers?"

"Yebo!"

"Have I not taught you that there are certain rules by which to fight this war?"

"Yebo!"

"Well your Commandant is dead! He is dead because he violated the most basic of these rules. He raped another man's wife: mine!" Strong murmuring broke out amongst the men, each looking at another, quizzical and worried. But Fischer was not worried despite what he knew was the traditional African way, a woman is a woman, a chattel, to be used when and how a man wanted. But he knew also that the men were scared to death of the Commandant and hated his power over them.

"Silence!" he continued. With instant obedience, they looked at him expectantly. "Let this be a lesson to you. I don't care if your political commissars encourage you to rape your victims. While I am in charge of you there will be no such thing, understand?"

"Yebo."

"Good. Now I will assume command of this camp until the Party provides us with a replacement Commandant. Until then, the routine will carry on as before." Volker turned to Ndunze. "Ndunze, form a detail and place a guard around this building. No one is to enter until I can get Motswadi down here to investigate the matter. From now on I will use the office in my house," he said pointing his thumb behind him. "Then dismiss the men to carry on whatever they were doing. I will be at my house attending to my wife. Report to me in one hour."

"With pleasure, Major." He hesitated and then clearing his throat, he said, "Major, you did us all a favour here today. The Gundwane was a bad man. He was a disgrace to our cause and the comrades are very pleased that you have done what you have done."

"Very well..., and by the way Ndunze," he said softly so that the assembled men could not hear him, "despite what you may think, I am not fucking the Butterfly. I am a married man. That is the way she likes to wear her wrap when she works."

An hour later Ndunze handed Volker the list of the farmers in the Karoi area.

"Ah, and who is this man, this Mr. Andrews?"

"He is a very successful farmer five miles north of Karoi."

"No, I mean who is he? What is his other name?"

"I don't know, but he is very popular with the people, he and another farmer who has now left the country. They have done much to improve the lives of the people who work for them, and their families."

"Oh, who was the other farmer, is his name here?"

"No, Major. He has gone. It is said that his parents were killed when we shot down the indegi[87], so he sold his farm and went. I think that his name was Templar."

Volker sat back, exultant, his heart thumping. He breathed out slowly. The coincidence was too great. I have him, he thought. He knew that one of the people they had killed in the aircraft was the same man that had been rescued from Mumbwa and now he knew two more things. The man's son, that bloody arrogant policeman, now gone, had definitely rescued him. Why else had he come under false pretences to Zambia but to check things out? But more important, Mr. bloody Harry Andrews must have helped him and was now also a farmer in the same area. He looked at Ndunze and without revealing his true thoughts, he said,

"I want you to attack the farm of this man Andrews."

"I do not think that this would be wise, Major. The man, Andrews, has done much for our people and it will not be a popular action."

"Ndunze, that is precisely why he must be attacked, wiped out. We cannot have popular farmers, protected by the people. They, more than any other, undermine the purpose of our cause. No, when you return, you will make this farm your top priority, understand?"

"Yes, Major." Ndunze couldn't work out why, but he felt uneasy. Was there more to this man Andrews than he understood or knew? He put the thought from his mind. Orders were orders.

"Yes, Major," he repeated. "But it will not be easy, he is well organised and has a faithful and loyal workforce."

"Well, kill some of them. Make an example of them. No allegiance to a white farmer is acceptable. The Party demands complete obedience. The people are either with us or they are against us. If they are against us they must be dealt with."

"Yes, Major."

"Good. Now I am going to Munze post office. I must use the phone to report this affair to Lusaka. You will wait here, in command, until I return. We have many more things to discuss and I expect that Motswadi will want to hold an enquiry."

Annie Andrews arrived back at Merrywaters at dusk. It had taken her all day driving in an incredibly slow, armed convoy, to get back from Salisbury. She was exhausted, the children were fractious and they were all grubby and in need of a bath. She ushered them off to their bathroom.

Robbie, big enough now, refused to bath, but always showered despite the fact that he could barely reach the shower taps. But he loved imitating his dad, so there was no longer a fight as to who got the bath first; also Beverley had suddenly become conscious of her body and refused to bath with Robbie any more. In fact, the only person allowed into the bathroom when she was in there was Annie herself.

She greeted Emily, George's first wife, and after asking for tea, retired to her bedroom to recover before going on her rounds of the clinic, school and the homestead buildings.

Harry was only due back at the farm the following day. He had flown his plane down to Johannesburg for its annual MPI (*Mandatory Performance Inspection*), and was flying back on a civilian aircraft. He was due back in Salisbury on the SAA 7:30pm flight, an hour hence, and was staying with Mick and Biddy Glover out in Hatfield. The Glovers and Andrews, and especially their children, had become strong friends over the years and frequently stayed in each other's homes. She knew that he would phone the instant he was back.

Annie hated it when he wasn't there. Not because she was scared, but because once the children were asleep, she hated being alone in the large rambling house. Harry seemed to fill the place when he was home, warm it up, there was always something going on. Or, she laughed to herself, it was just his smell, that mixture of pipe tobacco and his aftershave or deodorant. And the fact that he was so untidy, something, his shoes, jacket or a hat were forever strewn somewhere.

She lay in her bath and forced herself to think about what needed to be done now and tomorrow, but couldn't keep her mind focussed. In moments she began to dream about a holiday. They'd been talking about it for over a year, but there always seemed to be just too much to do. She resolved to start setting dates and to get Harry to commit to a trip to the seaside. Robbie could swim like a fish already. He and Beverley and their friends spent most of the weekends in the pool, continually coming in to ask for cokes and biscuits. She smiled as she thought of them and how she'd been forced to ban them from coming into the house without drying off and putting their shoes on. Poor old George had been at his wits end trying to keep up with the trails of water, grass and mud that ran through the house, either to the cookie jar and fridge in the kitchen, or the toilet. So yes, she thought, a holiday. Neither of the kids had ever been to the sea.

Thirty minutes later she emerged refreshed and ready to roll. Emily had laid out the tea and the children were sitting on the carpet already watching Fred Flintstone on the tele. She sat quietly watching them as she drank her tea thinking just how lucky they all were. Then she rose and went out through the kitchen to see what mishaps had demanded attention in the clinic during the day. George, busy preparing the supper, didn't even look up at her as she passed through. It didn't even occur to her at the time, that that was odd. The heat of the day had not yet dissipated as she walked the short distance across the quad behind the house and entered the clinic. She looked up at the sky; a huge cumulus cell building up in the west, eclipsing the sun. The multicoloured hues refracted from the jagged edge of the cloud seemed to make the centre of it seem darker, more menacing. She berated herself for being so ill at ease.

Temperance, George's second wife and a qualified nurse was there, fussing over a man swathed in bandages and lying on one of the three beds. She heard Annie come in.

"Oh Miss Annie, I am so happy you have come. This man is Jeffrey, one of the tractor drivers. He has been attacked." Annie felt the hair on the back of her neck start to rise.

"Hello, Temperance. What happened?" she asked picking up the patient chart that Temperance had started. She ran her finger down the list of injuries. Before Temperance could answer she asked another question. "And have you called the doctor?"

"Yes, Ma'am. But the doctor said that he can only come tomorrow morning and if the man has to be put in the hospital then I must call for the ambulance. So I called the ambulance, Ma'am, but both of them, they have been called to Sinoa and cannot come until tomorrow also."

"Where's Sampson, couldn't he have taken Jeffrey in?"

"No Ma'am. Sampson is at the other farm helping Chadrack with tobacco planting. He will only come when they finish in the fields and also he is staying there tonight."

It didn't concern Annie that Temperance had failed to pursue a means of getting Jeffrey to hospital. She was used to the African way. The man wasn't going to die, so what was there really to worry about. What did concern her was how, why and by whom Jeffrey had been beaten up. And where was Sampson? She knew that at planting time the men frequently worked through the night. She suddenly felt the cold shiver of vulnerability slice up her spine. Was it starting?

"OK," she said, continuing her inspection of the dressings, "he seems comfortable enough. Now Temperance, where did this happen?"

"Jeffrey, he was ploughing in the main road lands ma'm."

"How did he get back to the clinic?"

Before Temperance could answer, a slightly muffled voice came from between the dressings on Jeffrey's face.

"I drove the tractor back, Madam. The master, he will fire me if I leave the tractor, Madam." Annie lent down.

"Who was it, Jeffrey, do you know?"

"Yes Madam. It was the comrades, Madam."

Hiding the alarm within her as best she could, she thanked him and told Temperance to report to her if his condition changed. She left the clinic and broke into a run going back to the house.

"George, George!"

"Yes, Miss Annie," said George coming out of the dining room.

"George, we've got a problem." He looked at her blankly as she sat down at the kitchen table and started to help Emily peel potatoes and prepare the vegetables for dinner. Annie, marshalling her thoughts, turned to George standing patiently for her to continue.

"George, the comrades are here."

"Yes, I know Miss Annie."

"Why didn't you tell me?"

"Miss Annie, you were tired and you always go to the clinic after you come home," he shrugged moving his eyes away. Alarm bells rang loudly in her head.

"What? Have they got to you too George?"

"They have taken two of my daughters, Miss Annie," he said passively.

"Oh shit!" muttered Annie slamming the paring knife she'd been using down on the table. "George, go now with Emily and Temperance, and go to your family. Send two men, by themselves, not on the same path, to fetch Sampson and warn Chadrack. Tell all those that want to come to the house for protection to bring their things. They may use all the horseboxes and the other beds in the clinic, and when those are full, they may come into the house. And before you go, make sure that the generator fuel tank is full of diesel and the generator house is properly locked. Go now, hurry!"

She stood and leaving George and Emily looking at each other, she went through to the study.

"Robbie, Bev," she called walking past the lounge, "TV off, in the study, now, right now!"

She hauled her keys out of her hip pocket and went straight to the gun cupboard. Unlocking it, she started putting various weapons onto the desk. The pyjama clad children walked in.

"Robbie, go round the house now and close all the shutters and windows as Daddy showed you. Then stay in the passage den. Now go!" Harry had schooled his children well about this eventuality, and they knew exactly what they were expected to do, reacting positively every time they practiced it, making a game out of it. It was to Robbie's credit that he didn't hesitate, but turned and ran out the room immediately.

"Bev, get some sun-chair cushions out of the hall cupboard and some blankets and lay them out in the passage den and stay there. I'll be there in a moment." Bev, older and wiser than her brother, realised that something was wrong and so like him, turned and ran.

Annie took the breach blocks out of the weapons she'd not selected, slipped them into a canvas bag and locked them into a separate safe, locked the gun cupboard, gathered the weapons she had selected and followed the children. Dumping the bundle of weapons on the radio desk, she sat down and first picked up the phone.

There was no one on the line so she turned the dialling handle, giving two long twists, two shorts and two longs. Within seconds she heard the clicks as phones were picked up along the line. She waited a moment and then as they'd rehearsed, she said,

"Merrywaters, the comrades are here." Ignoring the clicks as phones were slammed down, she said, "Exchange, notify the police at Karoi and put me through to Salisbury 62 3117." She waited as the exchange dialled the Salisbury number, then the phone went dead. She took the hand-piece away from her ear and looked at it before replacing it on its cradle. Yes, she thought, it's started. She turned to the children.

"Listen you two, you are to stay together and not move from here even if I am not here. This is not a practice. The terrorists are here and I think they are about to attack us, understand?"

"Yes Mummy," answered Bev for both of them.

Annie called the dogs from the lounge where all three of them were curled up in their baskets, pretending they weren't there. There was always a fuss when Harry put the baskets out every night and then pushed the dogs out. Annie was happy they were still inside.

"Chollie, Shaka, Smuts," she said emphatically, pointing to where the children were curled up, "stay!" No second invitation was needed as the three of them literally leapt onto the children and blankets, licking, panting and snuggling up. Despite her agitated state of mind, Annie smiled with her giggling children, knowing how much fun it was for them all. Shaka and Smuts were ridgebacks and were really quite obedient. Chollie, a powerful pitch black chow-collie cross, hence his name, had a mind of his own and whilst he was the de facto leader of the pack, he was also the most lovable, continually seeking out affection. The children loved his long soft hair.

CHAPTER 31

Ndunze and his men had the farm buildings bracketed. He kept the men away from the compound but had made his point already by taking the two girls. He sat straddled on a farm gate watching the homestead some 400 yards away. He saw Annie and her children return and then a while later watched as the floodlights came on. They were blindingly bright and illuminated a wide area around the main buildings. As the darkness deepened a gentle drizzle started and the light cast by the floods became quite eerie, haloes forming around each light unit. His eyes were attracted to the occasional spark appearing at random from a wide area around the main buildings. Ah, so they have got an electric fence in operation, he thought. Clearly Andrews himself was not there, but that was all to the good, it would make things easier. He told one of his men to go and cut the telephone wires and continued to watch the house, dark behind the white light. He thought he saw a light go out in one of the windows and wrongly assumed that the inmates were retiring.

Biddy Glover picked up the phone just as she heard a car arrive outside. That'll be Mick and Harry, she thought.

"Hello, Biddy Glover here."

"Good evening, Ma'm. This is the Karoi exchange, I have a call from Merrywaters for you." Biddy waited while she was connected, becoming agitated as the time dragged on. A full minute passed before the operator came back on the line.

"I'm sorry, Ma'm, the caller has rung off and I can't get through."

Biddy knew all about party lines.

"Is anyone using the line?"

"No, Ma'm, the line is not in use, it is open for only emergency calls, Ma'm."

"What kind of emergency, operator?" She was becoming a little exasperated, thinking to herself, it's like sucking blood out of a rock.

"There was an SOS call from Merrywaters, Ma'm. The madam; she said," he quoted, "The comrades are here." Hearing the men coming into the house behind her, Biddy slammed down the phone and ran through to the entrance hall. She ran full belt into Mick as he entered the passage. He caught hold of her,

"Whoa there, Biddy, what's up?"

"Oh Mick, is Harry here?" Not waiting for an answer, she continued. "Mick, I've just put down the phone. Annie has put through an SOS, the comrades are there." She put her hand into her mouth and Mumbled, "Oh my God."

Mick let go of her so suddenly she almost fell. He swung around and looked at Harry, who'd heard every word.

"Come on, Harry, let's go!"

"Let's go where?" said Harry, not expecting an answer, "We'll never get there in time. It'll take at least three hours even if we don't get stopped on the road, and by then it'll be too late."

"No it won't, we'll be there in less than an hour by chopper. If she got that call through on the phone, then it's only just starting." He grabbed Harry's arm, turned him round and forced him back out of the front door, calling out to his wife behind him at the same time. "Call ops, Biddy. Chopper stand-by crew to be ready to go, go. Destination, Karoi north. Arms for two on board and MAG (belt fed 7,62mm calibre machine gun) mounted. Hold the fort, love." With that the men were gone, door slamming behind them.

Annie checked to see that the two heavy-duty vehicle batteries that provided stand-by power for the radio and the one lamp in the passage den were fully charged. She knew that the first thing the attackers would do, would be to try to take out the power. She then turned on the radio, checked the frequency, adjusted the squelch and put in a call.

"Karoi Centre, Karoi Centre, Merrywaters, test call, do you copy?"

"Reading you 5, Merrywaters, standing by for further coms. Help now being assembled. Call again in 15 minutes."

"Call again 15 minutes, Merrywaters out." She put the radio on stand-by and then turned to wait. She busied herself checking her weapons thinking, thank God Harry made me go through all this so many times.

Ndunze set up six snipers on three sides of the house and a machine gun pointing straight across the beautiful garden at the front door. Furthermore, he'd sent four men, with incendiary grenades to each of the three tobacco barns and the farm workshops. They were to all wait for him to commence the attack. He himself carried two grenades reserved specifically for the house, once they got close enough. He'd sent two more men to the back of the main buildings, more complex than the front and sides. Their role was to merely stop and kill anyone trying to get in or out the back way, so isolating the farmstead from the compound.

It was these men who stopped and then murdered the two men that George had sent to find Sampson and Chadrack. The two farm workers were only found at midday the following day, flies and other scavengers already busy at their throats, cut wide and gaping from ear to ear. Their eyes had been gouged out, their testicles and penises, symbols of their destroyed manhood, stuffed into their open mouths. A side-striped jackal ran off with some of these hanging from his mouth as the bodies were discovered.

Men and their guns and dogs stood around amongst their 4x4s, talking bravely to each other while their wives dispensed copious quantities of tea, coffee, rusks and biltong, gathered at the police camp in Karoi awaiting the order to go. There was no sense of urgency - they'd been through it all before.

The police Inspector in charge of them looked on in despair. They look like the Ku Klux Klan going on a duck shoot, he thought. He climbed up onto the mudguard of his Land Rover and blew his whistle to attract their attention.

"Gentlemen, we roll in five minutes and this is how it's going to happen. He looked at the sorry bunch in front of him. Not one of them was less than fifty years of age. There were rumbles from some of the men at the back.

"Probably another bloody false alarm," he heard.

"Nevertheless, we're going out to give support at Merrywaters, and we'll do it by the book, the way you've been instructed. Understand?" He looked around sensing that was really no heart in these men. Most of them couldn't wait to get back to their firesides and the television. "Look, if any of you want to go home, go now and don't delay us any longer." A few fidgets, scratching of ears, but that was about it.

"OK, you, you, you and you in your trucks with me. The rest of you follow my Sergeant and his men. Two separate convoys. As we approach Merrywaters, the Sergeant will break left off the main road and take the old road into the farm. You will follow his instructions because he and I have practiced this manoeuvre on Merrywaters Farm and know where to de-bus and which way to go in, in the event of the farm being under attack." Not waiting for any questions, he jumped down, climbed in and started his engine.

It took another five minutes whilst the vehicles sorted themselves out before they started off.

Annie gasped.

"Oh my God, I've forgotten the staff, and Jeffrey." She looked at the children: Robbie was already fast asleep, the excitement having been too much for him. She told Beverley quietly, but firmly, that under no circumstances was she to move without being told to, and then rose, checked that she had her pistol, picked up an SLR[88], pulled back the block and slid one of the rimless 7,62mm cartridges into the breach.

She then lifted the sling over her head and curled it once around her left wrist.

"Dogs, stay!"

She went quickly, out through the kitchen and onto the back porch. Looking into the quad she saw that the light was on in the clinic and shivered. It was quiet, too quiet; not even the sound cicadas or the crickets could be heard. Putting her head down, she ran, not stopping until she got to the door of the clinic. In one move she swept it open. She stared in amazement. Jeffrey was gone. Wasting no time, she switched off the light, opened the door and went quickly and silently along the row of rooms known as the horseboxes. All were empty.

Now it hit her. It is happening and all of the staff have run for cover. She started shaking, almost uncontrollably, and was forced to lean against the wall.

"Get a hold of yourself," she whispered to herself. "Harry said that this is probably what would happen." She stood there in the shadows steadying herself for a few moments and then started running again, this time heading back to the house.

Then all hell broke loose. The sudden loud staccato of a machine gun opening up at the front of the house gave her such a fright, she fell heavily onto her hands and knees, the rifle clattering onto the concrete blocks below her. Her fall saved her life because almost instantly an AK47 opened up from somewhere beyond the workshops and the bullets buzzed above her like angry bees, slapping into the wall of the house in front of her. She heard the repeated crump, crump of grenades going off.

That got her moving.

Sobbing, and scared almost witless by the noise, she crawled as fast as she could, dragging the rifle along the ground with her, trying to get out of the glare of the floodlights. Her knee throbbed dreadfully from her fall, but she forgot all about the pain as bullets started to ricochet off the paving all around her. She felt a tug on her buttocks and a burning sensation, but ignored it.

She scrambled onto the back porch and dived through the door. Slamming the door shut behind her, she climbed to her feet, pulled the bar down to lock it, and hobbled into the passage. She reached the den, collapsed in the chair, and covered her ears to keep out the almost continuous 'splat' of bullets hitting the walls of the house. Frequently, a bullet hit one of the steel shutters giving out a loud clang, accompanied by the sound of glass shattering. This noise was amplified enormously as it echoed around the house.

She heaved out a frail cry, "Harry, oh Harry, where are you?" sobbing almost uncontrollably. She buried her face in her hands.

Harry, at that moment, was trying to check the firing mechanism of a machine gun mounted on the floor of the tilted, bucking metal deck of an Allouette Mk 2 helicopter. It was making its best ground speed of about 120 knots through the night towards Karoi, but they were still thirty minutes away.

Mick Glover climbed forwards into the left hand seat and, dialling up the emergency frequency, he put some earphones onto his head and started to call.

Sampson and Chadrack were running as they'd never run in their lives. Sampson carried a Sten gun like a toy in his huge left hand, using his right as a shield to stop his face from being struck by branches and anything else as he ran. Chadrack followed him, feet almost instinctively landing in exactly the same spot as where Sampson's had been a fraction of a second before.

They had been squatting next to their supper fire watching the flames and chatting, way out on the second farm. Sampson and Chadrack had heard the percussion of the incendiary grenades go off and knew instantly. Without a word to each other, they gathered up their weapons and started running, taking the direct route through some kopjes and through some thick bush. They both knew this land well and realised that by road in a vehicle it would take them well over an hour. All they had were tractors, still hitched to heavy sodbusters and it would take them at least forty minutes just to get to Sampson's truck. This way would take them about 20 minutes.

It was Chollie alternatively whining and licking her hands that brought her out of her swoon. Patting him affectionately, she pulled herself together, and then drawing her hands back through her hair, she shook her head as if to clear her thoughts and looked at the children.

Beverley and Robbie sat wide-eyed, hugging each other and shaking with terror in darkness under their blanket in the furthest nook of the den. Shaka and Smuts were no longer lying on them, but now, alert, looking first one way then the other, both ways down the passage, they sat, ears pricked, on either side of the children. Thank God, thanks to Harry, they're not gun shy, she thought. It was Beverley who stuck her head bravely out from under the blanket and spoke.

"Mummy, you're bleeding."

Annie broke briefly into hysterical laughter and ignoring the pain in her knee and the powerful throbbing ache emanating from her backside, she knelt down, hugging the children to her.

"Oh, you little darlings."

Rocking with them for a moment she gradually took complete control of herself once more. She looked round at the rifle lying next to the chair and thought, fat lot of good I was with that. But looking at it gave her new resolve. She released the children.

"OK kids, this is it. Time to start fighting back. Stay here." She picked up the rifle and a light machine carbine, slung that around her neck, picked up two magazines for it and moved quickly to the front of the house and despite her orders to him not to follow, Chollie followed on her heals. She had no way of knowing it, but the delay between the start of the attack, and when she eventually started to fight back, was going to stand her in some good stead.

Opening up the welded flap in the steel shutter of the hall window, she peered out. Initially she could see nothing as her eyes adjusted to the glare of the floodlights, but after 20 seconds or so she began to spot a few muzzle flashes a long way out in the dark. She raised the rifle and taking aim, she fired two shots at the last one she'd seen.

Her mind was functioning properly now and the first cogent thought that came to her was that none of the alarms had been tripped yet. She realised that meant that the perimeter had not yet been penetrated.

She closed the flap and, leaving the rifle lying there on the floor, she ran to the other end of the house. She went straight to her own bathroom, guided only by the faint glow of light coming from the den, and opened the flap there.

This time she didn't even look. She poked the muzzle of the light machine carbine through the window, halted only momentarily by the noise of the window pane breaking and then pressed the trigger, twice, giving two short bursts, which she skewed around trying to spray a wide area while keeping the barrel of the weapon depressed and horizontal, just as she'd learnt at the survival course. Leaving the weapon on the stool next to the bath with the two spare magazines, she ran back to the den, scooped up two more weapons and more magazines, and repeated the process at the other end of the house and out of the kitchen door, in that instance, angling the shots to go out through the entrance to the back courtyard. It was looking out from there that she first saw the nearest barn burning and she could see smoke pouring out of the windows of the main workshop.

From then on, only once stopping to tell the stupid fuckers on the radio to hurry up, she ran round and round through the house smiling grimly to herself at her choice of language. Each time she moved, she did so randomly, firing a few shots from each window, trying to give the impression that there was more than one defender within. After a while she began to tire and she started to despair, her mind playing the inevitable tricks that it does in situations like that. Was she was running out of ammunition? Where was the help she'd called for? Where was Sampson? Why wasn't Harry here? How much time had she got before they rushed the house? Thoughts were going through her mind in flashes, slowing her down, eating away at her confidence, causing the fear well up inside her again.

Ndunze and his men kept up the sporadic barrage for almost exactly twenty minutes and then he noticed that the return fire was becoming more ragged, fewer shots being fired. Were they running out of ammunition? Had some of the defenders been killed? He was elated because he could hear all of his men were still firing, taking it in turns to fire shots into the house, which meant that not one of his men had been hit.

He was wrong in two respects. He thought that their shots were going into the house, raking and destroying the interior. They were not. Not one bullet had penetrated the house itself, except the occasional shot that went through the thatch roof and after striking one of the massive eucalyptus timber rafters at an angle, failed to lodge in the wood, but ricocheted down onto the floor. Over the passage den there was a thick concrete slab, so the children were quite safe, as long as this was all the attackers continued doing. Furthermore Ndunze hadn't worked out that there was only one person defending the homestead.

Neither error had any relevance; Ndunze had no intention of rushing the house. The rain stopped and, almost as if using that as a signal, he halted his fire and started moving forwards. His men, out of sight, heard that he'd stopped the fusillade and ceased their firing. All he wanted to do now was get close enough to get at least one of his incendiary grenades up onto the highly inflammable roof. The comrades were under orders to withdraw the moment they saw the main house burning. They had effectively destroyed the farm as a functioning unit and after setting fire to the house he and his men would disappear, melting into the bush from whence they'd come.

The two 'dads army' convoys, now bunched together had come to a grinding halt. One of the trucks had broken down and, despite all the kicking of wheels and swearing, the two farmers in it just could not get it started again. Eventually, precious minutes having been lost, the police Inspector walked back and told them to stay and fix the vehicle, the rest of them were moving on. He could almost see the relief in their faces. Disgusted at their cowardice and without saying a word, he spat on the ground as he turned away and waved everybody on. Once again they started moving: it was now an hour since the SOS call. He knew that they were going to be too late. What a fuck up.

At last Mick got through. He turned around and beckoned Harry, holding out the earphones and mouthpiece. Harry reached forward, grabbed them, put them on and them found the speak button along the cord.

"Annie."

Annie slumped down in the den chair. How had Harry got through on the radio, he was in Salisbury?

"Annie, come in, please."

"Oh Harry," she sounded exhausted, almost in despair. "Where are you?"

"Five minutes away in a chopper." She perked up. Five minutes away. He got my message. Her spirits rose immediately.

"Oh Harry hurry, I don't think…." She never finished her sentence. At that instant the wailing siren of the perimeter alarm went off effectively blocking out all other noise. Harry jerked as the wail screeched through the earphones.

"Annie," he shouted. "Annie, the dogs, put the dogs out! Annie can you hear me? Put the dogs out, they'll hold the bastards."

Annie only heard the words 'dogs'. She was terrified. Clearly the terrorists were now coming in. She dropped the microphone and ran. Peering out through two firing hatches she saw nothing, and then it dawned on her. Dogs. Of course; Harry was telling her to let the dogs out. She blindly fired a short last burst out of the lounge window and then turned calling the dogs.

"Dogs, Chollie, here, here, come!"

In seconds the dogs were at her feet, tails wagging, expectant, waiting for what she was going to do next. She took them into the hall and unlocking the door, she swung it open just enough to let them out.

"Get 'em, go on, get 'em." The three of them, barking and falling over each other in the rush to get out, shot out of the door. Annie swung the door shut and relocked it and now worried that if she fired, she might hit one of the dogs.

Ndunze shot open the main gate lock, smashing it with bullets. He never touched it, but picked up a long stick he'd brought along for this purpose. He wasn't going to get himself electrocuted. As he swung the gate open at the end of the stick, the siren went off and a bright red beacon on the peak of the roof turned on and began turning, its bright red strobe flashing above the flood lights. But he wasn't worried, this would only take a few moments, then his job was done. Supported by four of his men five yards behind him, he advanced carefully towards the homestead. He felt in his parka, feeling for the grenades snug at the bottom of his right hand pocket.

He never even saw the dogs until too late. Chollie flew at him, head height, and he only had time to get his arm up to protect his throat. It wasn't enough. The impact bowled him over hard onto his back. His intent for the moment forgotten, he fought for his life, the huge black beast worrying at him, snarling and biting. Within seconds, blood was gushing from his hands and arms and one of his shoulders. The snarling teeth snatched at his head giving him a deep gash.

The men behind him were surprised and slow to react. They saw their leader collapse under the attack and were hardly ready as the other two dogs leapt at two of them. A flailing steel rifle butt hit Smuts even as he leapt, knocking him senseless. All the same the dog hit the man, knocking him off his feet. He jumped back up, turned the AK47 and sent a long burst into the quivering dog. Shaka was not much luckier, although more successful. His attack ripped the throat out of a third man. Blood spurted out as the man collapsed backwards trying to fend the dog off. Shaka changed his grip, but he was doomed. The fourth man took a swing at him with his foot sending Shaka head over heals over behind his prostrate comrade. The second man had recovered enough by now and coolly turned his AK onto Shaka and put five bullets into him.

The dog's head disintegrated as it flew away under the force of the impact of the bullets.

The fourth man then ran forward to help Ndunze and let out flying kick that hit Chollie in the chest, knocking him off his quarry. At this point, Chollie, deciding enough was enough and ran off whimpering, chased into the dark by a barrage of bullets spraying around him. As he disappeared a bullet hit him, tossing him upside down. But he got up, and limping fiercely, one of his back legs totally lame, he continued around the house to safety.

The men helped Ndunze get to his feet and they staggered back to the downed man. Looking down at their comrade illuminated plainly in the floodlights, they saw blood pumping out of his throat. Ndunze didn't hesitate. He pulled his trigger, the man jerking as the bullets hit him in the chest and then the blood stopped pumping out. He was dead.

"Fuck!" was all Ndunze could think of saying. He dropped his AK and ripped off his own parka. He and his four men spent the next few minutes, standing out in the open, trying to stop the blood from pumping out of him.

CHAPTER 32

The pilot saw the homestead first.
"There it is, at 11:00 o'clock, the beacon's flashing," he pointed briefly then got his hand back onto the collective. He pushed forward on the stick and the helicopter picked up speed as it dropped down towards the building. The three of them looked, searching and identifying, and then slowly began to make out the devastation. Harry groaned when he saw that his three tobacco barns were burning and there was a fire next to the house.

"That must be the workshops," said Harry pointing.
"At least the house is in one piece," shouted Mick.
As he said it a fire started on the roof of the house.
"Oh no," muttered Harry.

"Indegi!" announced Ndunze to his comrades. They stopped talking and listened. They heard it coming in from high to the southeast.
"No, it is a helicopter," said Ndunze, correcting himself. "Quick," he said taking a grenade out of his pocket, "throw this on the house and then we must run. Help has come for the settlers."

Sampson and Chadrack caught the two men to the west of the house completely unawares. They never stood a chance. Sampson and

Chadrack fired virtually simultaneously into their backs as they lay there aiming at the house. Sampson looked up listening, pointed to the sky from where the sound of a helicopter came.

"Master Harry comes." He then turned and ran towards the rear. Chadrack went the opposite way.

As he approached the fence at the front of the house he saw a man in the middle of the lawn swing his hand and a split second later, with a loud crunch, the roof erupted into flame. Without stopping he ran to get closer and then stopped and took aim at the man running away from the house, diagonally towards him. He steadied himself, breathed out slowly as Master Harry had taught him, and fired. The man crumpled as he ran hitting the grass at full tilt, slid a few feet and then was still.

Ndunze heard the shot and saw his man fall. He whipped around and caught a glimpse of Chadrack running along the outside of the fence. He waved his men down next to the pool pump house and waited. Chadrack rounded the gate and slowing down began to stalk carefully along the driveway.

The bullets hit him, stitching him from his right shoulder to his left hand. His left wrist disintegrated. He felt no pain but looked at it, not quite able to comprehend what had happened. He then dropped to the ground, as everything went black.

Ndunze signalled and the three remaining attackers started to run.

Annie heard the explosion of the grenade as it hit the roof as she ran back to the den. Looking back and up into the rafters she saw that a huge gaping hole in the thatch had appeared over the bedroom wing. Flames raged in and around the hole as the roof began to break up and collapse.

She ran into the den and under the protective barrier of the concrete slab, slamming the door behind her. She went across to the other door and shut that too, effectively sealing herself and the children into a tomb.

She turned back to the children, crawled under the blankets with them and drew them to her breast. Robbie was crying uncontrollably, shaking violently, Beverley, wide eyed just clutching him fiercely to her tiny chest.

"Alright my darlings, this is it, we're safe now. The attack is over." she said trying to comfort them, but she shivered knowing that at any moment the terrorists could burst through the door and shoot them all. She took her pistol from its holster and shifting back into the corner, both children clutched to her left breast, she raised the pistol above the blanket. She pointed it, unwavering but for the jerking induced by Robbie's sobs, at a point midway between the two doors. Her chin jutted out with resolve. They will not take us alive.

Sampson almost bumped into another two attackers running away through the compound, some three hundred yards from the main house. He was running flat out, all caution gone, when they opened fire on him. It was only the fact that they were running hard themselves that saved him and enabled him to dive head first behind a brick and mortar pigpen.

He hit the ground rolling and, almost in one fluid movement, was on his feet running, rifle pointing in more or less the right direction, his finger pressing the trigger repeatedly. He silently cursed the fact that the SLR he was carrying was not an automatic weapon.

Reaching the end of the low wall of the sty he stopped, crouched down and peered around the corner. The two men he'd seen had gone to ground and could only have gone up the pathway leading into the dwelling directly in front of him. In a moment he realised that there was only one way into these houses and opened fire again on the windows of the small house.

"Throw down your guns and come out with your hands up," he called. For his trouble all he got was a barrage of misaimed shots splattering across the alleyway. Then he heard the sound of a heavy machine gun firing from out of the helicopter.

Staying where he was he wondered what to do. Keep them penned in there or leave them to go to help closer to the house. It then went quiet. He looked up and realised that he could no longer hear or see the helicopter and correctly assumed that it had already landed in front of the house. So, he elected to stay where he was. And besides, the comrades were running away. Obviously the fight was over. He stayed there, covering any escape from the house, for thirteen hours until the police found him the following day.

Harry lined up the machine gun on the men on his lawn as the pilot jockeyed the chopper into a close steep left hand arc over the fence, and then let loose. He saw the bullets kicking up grass and dust as they swept towards the running men and he saw two of them fall. The third disappeared into the dark but it was too late, Harry could no longer bring the weapon to bear as the helicopter tilted nose up and then settled down onto the lawn.

It had no sooner touched down than Harry was out and running. He ignored the men lying squirming near the pool and headed straight for the house, panicking that he was too late. He raced onto the veranda opened the shredded screen door and began pounding on the door, shouting for all he was worth. The roof to his right was aflame and smoke was pouring across the veranda. He couldn't begin to imagine what it was like inside.

For a few moments he was stunned and stood there, helpless, realising that there was no way he'd batter the door down in time to save his family.

"The key," he shouted to himself. "You fucking idiot Andrews." He dropped his weapon on to the concrete floor of the veranda and scrabbled around in his pocket, fetched out his keys started to try and open the door.

He nearly dropped them, he was shaking so much and the smoke was so thick, he couldn't see much either. Eventually though, it seemed an age to him, yet it was really only a few seconds, he got the correct key into the lock, only to find that it wouldn't go the whole way in. Annie had obviously left her key in the lock.

"Oh, Christ!" he swore. Then he stopped, took a deep breath and immediately went into a paroxysm of coughing. Stooping and coughing, he backed off to the edge of the veranda where the air was clearer, he brought his coughing under control, took another few deep breaths and then ran forwards again. "Bloody fool," he said to himself as he started tapping the end of his key in the lock in an attempt to dislodge the other key. After a few seconds he felt the other key give way and he was able to slip his in and turn it.

Back at the main road the cavalry had arrived and suddenly

everything changed. Spotlights darted everywhere; 4x4s criss-crossed the lawn, getting dangerously close to the rotating blades of the chopper. Just as he opened the door to enter the house, handkerchief held to his face, Harry saw one enthusiastic idiot drive his truck mindlessly straight into the swimming pool. It was chaos, and, of course they were too late.

Harry carefully walked forward, almost totally blinded by the smoke. He ran his hand along the wall of the hall until he reached the passage door and then turned right making for the den, the only safe refuge in the house. He reached the door, threw it open and collapsed on the floor, having the foresight to push the door shut behind him with his foot.

Now it was his turn. Annie swung the pistol to the left and fired. The bullet scorched across his back, ricocheting off his ribs and nicking his shoulder blade as it passed out of his body to lodge in the wall behind him. He went down again, thudding into the linen cupboard door. Annie adjusted her aim and started squeezing the trigger again. Harry in the meantime had gulped in a huge breath of relatively clear air. He screamed,

"Stop, Annie! It's me!"

Annie, completely exhausted, stared at him momentarily, but as the adrenalin rapidly left her system and she realised what she'd just done, she passed out.

Beverley jumped up and ran forwards. Harry, face down, lay there stunned, but her voice registered and he rolled to face her.

"Daddy, Daddy!" she cried and threw herself into her father's arms. Robbie, now caught in Annie's bear hug, the blankets and Annie's clothes, burst out crying.

Harry, pain filling his entire being, gingerly lifted Beverley off him.

"Alright pumpkin, Daddy's here," he said gently holding her at arms length. "Beverley, we have to go now so just wait here for a moment." Letting her go, he crawled forwards to the corner.

"Alright my son, alright, you're alright now. Daddy's here." He threw aside the blanket, kicked away the pistol and scooped up the child. With his other hand he grabbed the blanket and covered the boy with it. He ignored the white-hot agony searing across his back. With his other arm, he then picked up Beverley and kissed her on the forehead.

"Bevie, pull the blanket right over you…, that's right, there. Now when I tell you I want you to hold your breath and count to twenty, OK?" She nodded her head, staring into his eyes from no more than 6 inches away. "Bevie, you must promise me not to take a breath until you reach twenty, no matter what. Can you do that?"

"Yes, Daddy."

Harry felt for the door handle, keeping his arms tightly around them both, and then spoke to her.

"OK, one, two, three, now, and keep your eyes shut."

Beverley took a deep breath and pinching her nose with her fingers started to hold her breath. He opened the door and swung around it pulling it shut behind him. The heat was appalling and bits of smouldering thatching were dropping down from above. He moved as quickly as he could, guiding himself along the passage by trailing one elbow along the wall, found the hall door and ran out onto the veranda. He jumped the steps onto the pathway below and put the children down.

Mick picked up the children as the police Inspector from Karoi sprayed water at Harry using the garden hose. He turned instantly and feeling the cooling spray on his back raced back into the burning inferno. He felt his skin starting to scorch but he ignored it and in 6 seconds was back in the den. He took a few breaths and, picking up his unconscious wife, as if she was a sack of wheat, he opened the door and ran. He collided with the door into the hall, dislocating his right shoulder. He screamed again, nearly passing out. He turned into the hall and raced forwards again, just as a huge part of the roof collapsed behind him. A great shower of sparks flew up and settled on him and Annie, but somehow he took the five or more remaining steps that he knew were necessary to get them out.

They emerged, smouldering, from the smoke of the inferno, Harry staggering drunkenly. Taking a deep breath, Mick ran up the steps and literally lifted Annie off him just as he collapsed down onto the pathway leading to the veranda. Mick turned and ran to the blanket he'd left on the ground when he'd taken the children to the safety of the helicopter. He lay her down gently and then turned to help Harry.

But there was no need. The policeman, now assisted by one of his askaris, had already lifted him up. With Harry between them, they carried him out of harm's way.

Mick turned back to Annie. The abandoned, gushing hose was now snaking back and forth across the lawn drenching her at each flick, but the water revived her. Spluttering and sodden Annie looked at him, and slowly began to register. Mick caught the end of the hose, doubled it back to stop the water flow and then knelt next to her. Her eyes cleared and then she panicked again. She caught hold of his shirt, pulling him down.

"My children, where are my children?" she screamed breaking frantically away and trying to get up. Mick pressed her back onto the lawn.

"They're fine, Annie, they're fine. Harry brought them out first." She searched his face for a moment and then for the second time that night, she fainted.

Chaos ensued until Mick and the police Inspector eventually brought some order. The house was lost and the policeman banished all the volunteer farmers, sending them home. The ambulance and the doctor arrived, he under his own steam, which was very brave of him, considering the number of attacks taking place on vehicles travelling by themselves on the roads.

It was one of the 'dad's army' that found Chadrack alive and very nearly shot him on sight, thinking that he was one of the attackers. Fortunately his triumphant shout drew several men to him and one of them recognised the bloodied heap as Chadrack. After the doctor had done what he could to stabilise him, Mick had him airlifted by helicopter to hospital in Salisbury.

Harry's shoulder was relocated; his arm bound to his side and his few burns treated. The huge gouge across his back was staunched and dressed. He remained unconscious throughout. Both he and Annie were then taken into the Karoi hospital. The police set guards for the night and Mick took the children into his care. He hitched a lift to the hospital and spent the rest of the night sleeping on an outpatient's bed hugging both the children to him.

The army moved in and commenced a hunt for the terrorists who had escaped, but after twenty-four hours gave up. The tracks went cold at a bus stop a mile away on the main road. Of the captured terrorists, one, very badly wounded, was hospitalised under an armed guard. He was one of the two men hit by Harry from the helicopter. The two who were cornered by Sampson were taken to the high security cells in Salisbury, called alternatively 'canary alley' or the 'sweat shop' by the police officers employed there.

Detective Superintendent William Sturrock took less then two hours to break them. He admitted that he did treat them a little more roughly than he would normally. But as he pointed out to the chief of police, "This was personal Sir."

By keeping the comrades apart and playing them against each other, he had them singing, as the nickname of the cellblock inferred. The first thing that they revealed was that it was they who'd killed the two men sent by George to call Sampson. The two bodies had only just been found.

But in addition, a great deal of intelligence was gathered which was to keep the security forces busy for several days. They raided the terrorist bush camp near Charles Clack Mine finding and taking possession of a huge cache of arms. However, only two of the group were found there. They were both killed trying to defend themselves. It was here that George's daughters were found, bound together in a chicken coop. Bedraggled and filthy, their tiny feet bloodied and torn from being force marched over thirty miles through the bush, they were otherwise unharmed.

Very important however was that Sturrock found out about Shenje 'Himmler' Ndunze their leader, and that they had a mysterious white instructor called Major Brod Volker. Sturrock realised that it was Fischer in a matter of seconds. He also extracted information on where their training and supply base was located.

Munze mission was attacked three days later. Seventy-two insurgents were killed in the action. But whilst the camp was effectively destroyed, interrogation of Fischer's wife Marie revealed with certainty that he wasn't there, but was in Lusaka. As she was found to be pregnant and already had a small child, the forces left her there. She alone with her child, were left alive as the helicopters clattered away. Clutching her baby to her breast, she stood there in the middle of the parade ground, surrounded by the ruined and burning buildings. In front of her, lying in jagged rows were the shattered corpses that were all that remained of her husband's guerrilla army.

After three days and able to move without too much pain, Harry was discharged from the hospital. Annie, still limping heavily herself, carefully helped him into their sole remaining road vehicle, his old Peugeot 403 truck. She placed a pillow in the small of his back so that his upper back and shoulder remained clear of the backrest of the seat.

They hadn't spoken of the attack at all. During the many hours that Annie had sat with him, their conversation concerned only the aftermath. The remorse in both of them was too great: he for not being there, for not having taken the threat of an attack more seriously. She, because she had actually shot her man, nearly killing him. They each shed many tears, but it was if an opaque screen had come down, dividing them.

The children, excited and talkative, sat between them. Other than making sure that they didn't press into his bound up arm and shoulder, they behaved as if nothing had happened and certainly had no idea of the strain between their parents. They were too delighted to be with their daddy again.

How's Chadrack?" asked Harry as they drove out of the hospital gates.

"Lucky to be alive. Five AK bullets hit him. Fortunately four just went through and out. You know about him losing his left hand. More dangerous though is that his rib cage is shattered and one of his lungs collapsed. ICU at the Salisbury Gen won't let anybody in to see him yet." A few more questions and Harry learned that although critically injured, Chadrack's prognosis for life was good. He continued to skirt their problems.

"And George's two daughters?"

"Still in bed in the clinic but they're fine and being pampered by Emily and Temperance. They'll be able to get up in a day or two." She laughed sounding brittle and not really amused.

"I reckon they've both put on 10 pounds, they're eating so much."

But then Annie put a stop to his questions.

"Harry, relax, you'll find out everything in good time. You'll no doubt be going into Salisbury as soon as you're allowed to see Chadrack, but in the meantime, for God's sake take a day or two off. I've had Chadrack's house converted for our temporary use an I've taken all the linen and whatever else we could salvage out of the Horseboxes for us to use." Harry turned and looked at her, a smile on his face; Annie, ever practical, always organising everybody. He tried to reach her.

"Thank you my darling." They reached the turn-off and Annie drove carefully along their access driveway. When they reached the security gate, there was Sampson Ndlovu, his great big face split by an enormous smile, waiting to greet them.

Harry slowly and painfully climbed out of the passenger seat and walked forward. Without saying any thing he hugged Sampson to him using his good arm. He leaned back and looked at his foreman, tears in his eyes. He already knew the details of how Sam and Chadrack had run through the bush, shot three of the terrorists and captured two more.

"How?" questioned Sampson. "Is this my master who cries like a woman while hugging another man?" Harry couldn't help it; he just burst out laughing and then immediately regretted it as more pain shot through his body. He released Sampson and staggered, arching backwards, seeking relief from the agony that shot through his shoulder blade. Finally he straightened again, eyes glistening as he focussed, and smiled at Sampson.

"You bloody rascal," he spluttered. He looked towards the house again and there, hopping towards them with his tail wagging, his hindquarters covered in white bandages in stark contrast to his black coat, came Chollie. Harry knelt down and they nuzzled each other, Chollie licking furiously, Harry crying unashamedly.

After a while he turned as the children came and surrounded him and the dog.

"Chollie's a brave dog, daddy," said Beverley patting his head.

"I know, my darling, I know." Sampson came forward and took each of the children by the hand as Harry walked back to Annie standing next to the truck.

"Come, let's go and look," he said gently, wiping his eyes on his shirtsleeve. He reached out and ignoring the brief resistance, locked her arm under his and walked forwards. Sampson and the children were already 50 yards away. Harry tensed and was about to call them back.

"Leave them be, Harry. George and Emily have set up a temporary kitchen in the horseboxes. The outside pantries were undamaged except for one bullet through the door which half emptied a 25litre can of cooking oil. The bullet went in, but didn't come out the other side so it's still in there, I suppose."

Harry stopped next to the pool and drew Annie close to him. He surveyed the burnt out ruins, the roof gone, everything blackened from the firestorm that had destroyed it. Inside the forlorn shell, the den stood intact, a pile of burnt out roofing material lying on top of it. Its doors had gone. He looked at the mess of the front garden, deep vehicle tracks across the lawn, the flattened flowerbeds, the ruined swimming pool, debris everywhere. His attention was attracted to two small mounds of earth at the corner of the lawn. Two freshly hewn wooden crosses stood over them.

"Shaka and Smuts?" his eyes started to mist up again and he turned away.

"Yes."

He then turned his eyes to the closest barn. One of its high walls had collapsed. It was a complete right-off. He studied the workshops. Again the roof was gone and, in all likelihood, the tractors that weren't out, his stored farming implements, his car, Annie's 4x4, tools, and their equestrian tackle. He sighed.

"The other barns? The cattle?"

"The cattle are OK, those that are left! Oh Harry, you don't know." She put her hand to her mouth and tears started rolling down her cheeks as she said it. "Sampson had to shoot sixty two of them. Most of them were the workers' cattle. We haven't done a final count, but I think we personally lost thirteen. The terrorists apparently went around before the attack and slashed their hindquarters. Thank goodness they were spread out and a lot of them were over at the annexe. All the others have been rounded up and are in the compound kraal. But the barns are gone, bailing and bagging equipment, all the maize and stored tobacco burned, finished." Annie felt her husband slowly slump down next to her, and when she looked, she saw defeat in his face.

"All for nothing," whispered Harry. "Years of hard work and investment, all for nothing." He looked down at Annie. "The staff?"

"Only 15 labourers left. The rest have run. Surprisingly, it's the women who have shown the most resolve to stay. Even the teacher has stayed. The school is open as we stand here," she said cheerfully, trying to cheer him up.

"The annexe?"

"Untouched. And of course there are the two tractors with ploughs and discs that were there"

"Well it doesn't matter really, everything that was worth anything was here and now it's all gone." He stuck out his jaw, looked around once more and then looked closely at her. He momentarily clenched his teeth, his nostrils vibrating as he inhaled sharply through his nose. He puffed out and said, "Annie, what do you want to do? Do we take the gap like Pete and Barbara?"

Annie looked back at him, saw his searching look and knew that what she said now would probably be the most important decision she ever made. She looked into his eyes and saw nothing but his love and concern for her and as if a mist cleared, she knew that everything would be alright.

"Annie, you did the right thing, shooting. What if I had have been a terrorist? I should have shouted, warned you. It was me who was stupid." He said it all gently, no malice, no regrets, only heartfelt love.

She straightened her shoulders and gripped his good arm firmly. Standing on her toes she reached up and kissed him hard, her arm curled behind his head, pulling him to her. She broke off and leaned away.

"Thank you, my darling," she said, standing clear of him but still gripping his left arm. She took another look around at the ruins. Typically, a huge storm cell was brewing in the west. It'd rain soon.

"We stay," she said after a long pause. "We stay and we rebuild Merrywaters, Harry." Her voice choked as she realised the enormity of the problems facing them. A lot of their wealth had been wiped out in one foul night.

Harry said nothing, but he started to smile and crushed her arm against him again.

"Also, your breath's smelly, you need to clean your teeth!"

Harry laughed, he couldn't help it, despite the pain.

"Oh boy, back to normal!"

That day, October 18th 1979, Mugabe and Nkomo signed the Lancaster House Agreement, accepting a draft constitution for a new and independent Zimbabwe-Rhodesia. The following month the patriotic front accepted the British proposals for interim rule during the transitional process.

Four days before Christmas, exactly two months and six days after the attack, Bishop Muzorewa, the Prime Minister, Mugabe and Nkomo signed a ceasefire and the war was over.

Shenje "Himmler" Ndunze was never caught. He escaped into the bush and despite his wounds, he made it back to Zambia, where he spent two weeks in the Sinazongwe Mission Hospital recovering. He returned to Zimbabwe three months later under the amnesty and immediately began work in the party apparatus, preparing for the general election.

Brod Volker appeared before a tribunal convened by leading commissars of the Patriotic Front, wherein it was found that his conduct was found to be "just and equitable" in the circumstances. The tribunal placed heavy reliance on the sworn statement given by Ndunze from his hospital bed at Sinazongwe. The Patriotic Front released him from duty, his services for the meantime no longer required, with no more than a nod of the chairman's head that he could go.

He was immediately instructed by his control to continue his liaison with Commissioner Motswadi, as attention was now beginning to turn to bringing down the apartheid regime in South Africa. As an interim measure Motswadi arranged for him and his wife to manage a rundown Government owned tourist lodge called Kudu Cabins on the Zambezi River, just upstream from the Victoria Falls.

THE WYVERN REVENGE

For when all about fails to accord
Others with much louder harsh notes to destroy my faith,
All out of tune, coarse, vicious and with no reason,
Will I survive, prove that I too can play,
With alacrity and purpose to see it through?
How could I know?

And when the notes are found, the tune sweet,
Am I serene, content to languish in newfound harmony,
And then when a string, a reed, breaks,
Have I the tenacity, the faith in its beauty,
To dig down deep, to rise again?
Only then, I will know.

BOOK 4 – JUSTICE AND RETRIBUTION

CHAPTER 33

"So we started rebuilding." Harry threw back the last of his brandy and fetched out his tobacco pouch.

Richard stood up stiffly. Other than leaning forwards to replenish Harry's glass, he hadn't moved from his position on the floor next to Sharon for over two hours. He had been completely engrossed and enthralled by the saga. He hadn't even noticed Sharon get up and go through to the kitchen to make coffee.

"Jesus Christ, Harry, why didn't you pack up and leave?" he spluttered, horrified with what his brother had told them.

"Shit, Bro, we thought it was over. And in fact it was, for the white man anyway."

"Why, what do you mean?"

"Well, as Sampson predicted when Pete's folks were killed, they then turned on each other."

"Who?"

"Mugabe and Nkomo."

"Oh.."

"It was only much later that they started their campaign to get rid of the white farmers. And like the rest of them, history repeating itself, we never thought it would happen to us!"

"Why not?"

"Well, the British Government arranged the peace settlement and then, with the connivance of Mugabe etc., negotiated a new constitution. When Mugabe took over in April 1980 and changed the name of the country to Zimbabwe, we thought we were safe. The British Government supposedly guaranteed the constitution for ten years. Smithy went back to his farm near Selukwe and everything seemed to return to normal," he paused, "except of course, the fighting between themselves."

Sharon came through with three steaming mugs of coffee and resumed her seat on the floor next to Richard.

"What happened?" asked Sharon.

"Well, early in the eighties, I think Mugabe probably started it on some pretext, fighting broke out in Matebeleland. He sent in the army and hundreds of thousands of Ndebele were killed. The word put out was that it was a fight between the national army and the guerrilla forces." He stopped and took a sip of his coffee. "But we all knew that was bullshit. ZAPU, Joshua Nkomo's party, didn't know it, but they were on their way out. Sure enough in '82 Mugabe kicked Nkomo out of Government. The killing went on until the mid eighties. The army had nothing to do with it really, other than being the instrument. It was actually about crushing all opposition to Mugabe. It was a cull: innocent peasants. And most of the killing was done by the guerrilla forces themselves, the so-called war veterans, the comrades!" He paused again, a quizzical look on his face as another thought came into his head. "Look, you can't blame the British or the West for turning a blind eye. Britain still had a massive problem in Northern Ireland, the Yanks had the Contra affair, the Mount St. Helen disaster, the Cold War was reaching a climax with the collapse of communism and the fall of the Berlin wall in '89. There were massive problems in the Middle-East, Yugoslavia, everywhere, and if the world had its eyes on Africa at all, they were on South Africa, watching, waiting and orchestrating the dying throes of the Apartheid regime. Angola was a mess, Nigeria, Uganda, you name it. The world was in chaos. Who the hell was worried about tiny Zimbabwe?" He stopped, stood up and stretched like a cat and sat down. "Do you know, with all the trouble, Barbara kept writing to Annie telling her that we should emigrate to Oz?"

"Oh, what happened to them? You were going to tell us."

"Pretty sad story really."

Richard leapt to his feet.

"Don't move, let me get some more brandy, I want to hear this."

When Barbara received Annie's letter laying out in detail what had happened, she was horrified and immediately got on the phone from Australia.

"Annie, I've just got your letter. It's terrible!"

"Babs, I'm sorry that it took so long, but, like you, we've had a few problems as you know."

"Are you all right, how are the children?"

"Yes, we're OK. Thank God Harry came when he did. He's been unbelievable. How are you?"

"Oh, Annie, Pete's not shaping, we've lost the wine farm because we had to borrow too much to buy it and couldn't make ends meet. He concentrated so much on those problems that the security company is battling and he's very unhappy. So much so, he's chucking it in and he's applied for a job with the Sydney Harbour Police. So we're probably going over to Sydney soon."

"Oh, Babs, I'm so sorry!"

"Annie, he just can't get Rhodesia and his parents out of his mind. When he's not working, he mopes around, no energy, and worst of all he's drinking too much."

"But Pete was never a heavy drinker?"

"Oh, Annie, Annie, you don't want to see it! He goes down to a bar on the waterfront and drinks to all hours with another bunch of Rhodesian losers who're happy to commiserate with him whilst he's doing the buying. I have spoken to him time and again, suggested he get help. But God, he's pigheaded, doesn't want to hear it and just gets angry."

"Is he treating you badly?"

"No, I wouldn't say that. But he doesn't care. Sometimes it's as if I'm not even there. He just takes another six-pack of beers out of the fridge and disappears for hours on end into the garage pretending to be working on the car or something. So it's probably for the best if we move on, maybe it'll click him out of it. There are a lot of other ex-Rhodesians and South Africans in Sydney. Sometimes I think we were mad to come here, but at least the children love it." They nattered on for another ten minutes or so discussing the children and their men.

"I miss you all so much, Babs!"

"Well hopefully when we settle down in Sydney and you've got back on your feet, you can all come for a holiday to Oz and check it out. You could do worse than immigrating here Annie."

"Babs, you know Harry's views on that, and in any case the war's over now and despite the shortages, things are on the up. Anyway, I want to stay. Bev loves Townsend Girls' High and Robbie is really doing well at Plumtree. Harry is flying for Jim again to get extra money. Most of the staff have reappeared and Chadrack's recovering well. Sampson is covering for him on the extension and, while Harry's away flying, he looks after things here as well. The school and clinic are both going well and it's so nice not having to drive everywhere in convoy now. And anyway, we've got two new gorgeous puppies. More Ridgebacks and Chollie is really enjoying lording it over them."

"I'm so jealous, Annie. I just hope that Peter will come right." She was almost sobbing. Annie could hear her breath catch through the line. "Anyway I'm so glad that Bev and Robbie are doing well at school. Pete'll be pleased to hear that. He loved Plumtree, reckons it's one of the finest schools around. And his mom went to Townsend."

"Babs, you won't believe how Bev's coming on. She's beautiful, and clever too. But she's still a bit of a tomboy."

"We could see that from the photos. I haven't got any recent ones for you, but when things sort themselves out, I'll put some in the post."

"Babs, this call must be costing you a fortune. Please give Pete and the girls our love and I know things must be tough, but hang in there. Tell him we're both pulling for him"

"Thanks Annie and keep in touch."

"Will do. Love you, bye!"

"Love you too, bye bye."

Harare, as Salisbury had already been renamed, was abuzz. The heroes of the Chimorenga had returned and were strutting their stuff in frequent rallies and parades through the streets of the capital city. They were exultant, menacing and intimidating. Shopkeepers feared them, local residents feared them, and when you saw them in the street, you were wise to cross to the opposite pavement. They were definitely were on the prod, searching for collaborators of the Smith regime.

This had several consequences. Local authority maintenance of the streets declined, all their efforts to keep the city beautiful during the war years coming to naught. In many places, the city began to look more like a rubbish dump than a used car lot: burnt out and partly dismantled wrecks lay everywhere, along with all the trash.

The only tidy areas were those the new regime were likely to see, and it became a standing joke amongst residents that they hoped the self-declared President would choose to drive past their home or business because then the municipality would come along first and clean up the street.

More insidious however, was the gradual closing down of what were previously vibrant businesses and industries. Everywhere one went one saw vacant premises. The municipality tried, at first, to secure these either with security fences or boarding, but it was to no avail. Homeless or migrant squatters moved in and in time the squalor set in.

In turn, certainly amongst the white populous, people began to emigrate, the Antipodes, UK, Canada or South Africa, anywhere that would take them, no matter that they generally had to leave everything behind. In short the tax base of the country was leaving and it wasn't being replaced. The international handouts after the fall of the Smith 'Regime' had all but dried up. What they had, they spent badly.

Finally, many of the officer class in the various forces, including Mick Glover, were forced out of their posts and replaced in many instances by totally incompetent lackeys of the new regime. Mick didn't mind and walked straight into a senior position in Jim Leonard's company, managing the Harare operation. It was Mick who talked Harry into coming back to fly for Jim on a part time basis.

Jim Leonard himself was delighted when Harry phoned him offering his services as a pilot and his aeroplane for charter. The aviation business in the post-Rhodesian Zimbabwe was brisk. The country was starved of many essentials and the tourism trade and diplomatic travel was booming. Jim was doing his damnedest to get a piece of it.

"Crikey Pirate, good to have you back, and the Baron will be a Godsend."

"At your service, Jim. Bit battered since we last spoke, and a lot poorer. I'm not going to be doing this for love you know!"

"I know what you mean. Well, hopefully it's all over now. Shit, am I glad you're back? Look, buddy, I'll pay US$275 an hour, dry, for the Baron, we can service it here at cost for you, I'm sure one of my engineers is still current on Barons, and I'll pay you US$25 an hour, flying time only."

"Sounds OK, no mark up in the spares?"

"Hell no! I can order parts direct from Beechcraft in Wichita. NAC have granted me an agency even though they're reopening here. They know they won't be able to handle all the Beechcraft machines flying around this part of the world for a while, so it'll work out fine."

"My maintenance log books are with NAC in Johannesburg. Can you organise for them to be transferred to you here?" Harry asked Jim.

"Yeah, no worries, Binny can organise that today. And yeah she's still with me. I'd been a bachelor for so long, I'd forgotten what it was like."

"What do you mean, 'forgotten what it was like'?"

"Oh shit, you wouldn't have known. Binny and I got hitched quietly last April. Must have been mad, but I was so elated the war was over, she must have caught me when I was pissed or something!" Jim laughed.

"Hell, that's great news Jim, I must tell Annie, she'll be delighted. Congrats! But no more bloody ridiculous forays into Zambia for you!" Harry couldn't keep the smile off his face. However, Jim came back a little more serious.

"Might not be so easy, old boy. We're doing a lot of stuff up in Biafra[89] at the moment. Things aren't good up there and I've got a UN contract flying in medical supplies and personnel in and out. Got two Connies[90] flying non-stop, the States, Portugal, anywhere that'll take refugees, let us land, and give us supplies. I'll tell you all about it when I see you. When can you get in? Plenty of tourist work for you, my boy!"

"How about Wednesday? I'll fly in, Annie can drive; we've a bit to do in town."

"Great, just taxi straight over. I'll tell the boys to give it the once over and find a slot for it in the hangar. Then you and I can set up some kind of schedule, OK?"

"Dead right, see you then."

The weight of the physical labour in rebuilding and repairing the damage at the farm was huge. Not only to Harry, who spent ten to twelve hours a day involved in the shovelling, pick-axing, pulling down, putting up, mixing, stacking, brick cutting, curing, baking and laying, lugging, sawing, drilling, erecting, hammering and collecting. But also for his men, most of whom had returned, and who set loyally about the tasks with vigour and cheer, all of them anxious for things to get back to normal. Their lives had been so good, all understanding that they were better off than anyone else they knew. They had been healthy, well housed and fed, their children were being properly educated and cared for medically and they all had been building up their wealth in cattle. Before the attack, Harry's farms had been running over a thousand head of cattle; pampered, bred in one of the finest herds of Herefords in the country, and protected. Harry had owned only 500 of these. He had been delighted, the grazing was there to be used, and because the individual heifers, owned by his labourers and senior staff, were mixed with his own, his own cattle had been given unparalleled attention by the herd boys.

Conex and the Gwebi Agricultural College were fantastic. The Conservation and Extension officers were there two or three times a week, guiding, testing and providing. The college students camped in tents on the front lawn, and all but took over the running of the farm, helping with planting, weeding, irrigating, fence fixing, reaping and dipping.

Annie and the women got stuck into the picking, packing, bagging, drying, husking, feeding, painting, decorating and caring. In short the farm was a hive of industry, everyone with designated tasks. There were no shirkers, the staff themselves saw to that, and Harry's mood began to change, become more positive. He took more notice of what was going on around him but began to realise that his men were working themselves to death. He called them together one evening.

"Manheru varume (*Good evening, men*), it is time to reap some rewards for all your hard work." Harry addressed them in their own tongue. "Today you may select two of my fat heifers for traditional slaughter so that on Friday night in the school courtyard, which will be the 'boma', we will feast until our bellies are full like a lion's after feeding on an eland bull. We will drink until we sway like the nzou (*in'zoo - elephant*) after he has fed on the fermented marula berry. And we will laugh like the mad bere (*ber'ray - hyena*) until we can laugh no more. Then we will sleep for two days. Today also the women may each take five yards of their favourite cloth from the store, together with matching cotton, so that they can make new dresses for themselves and their daughters. Each of the boys, who have helped with the work of men, may have a new knife for them to keep." He paused, looking at the awe and amazement of the men around him. Clearly, they were staggered and immensely pleased and excited. "Finally, on Friday, there will be no work. The women may take the time to prepare for the 'pungwe' (*all-night party*), but all the elders and I will hold an 'Indaba' (*meeting*). Sampson will arrange for this. But at this indaba I wish every man to come prepared to advise me, Sampson or Chadrack on any matters, which might be concerning you. For myself I am worried about the 'war veterans', who are turning into thieves and thugs and I need your help to find a way to protect us all from trouble from these people." There was much murmuring and shaking of heads, an understanding that this indaba was very important. A serious air descended over the men as they moved off. "Sampson, Chadrack, come to the house for supper at 7:00 o'clock after you have bathed. We have much to talk about."

Barbara, Peter and their children arrived in Sydney on a cold, wet, miserable morning after the five-hour Ansett flight from Perth. The low cloud and driving rain obliterated their view of Botany Bay as their aircraft made its approach into Sydney International.

"Shit, how can people live in this kind of environment?" was Peter's first comment on getting off the plane.

"Oh Pete, stop being so negative!" retorted Barbara holding on tightly to the girls as they went through to baggage handling. "Sydney is supposed to have one of the finest climates in the world. Anyway we know it is arguably one of the world's most beautiful cities." Peter's response as they waited for a taxi outside the terminal was to light up a Camel.

"Shit I could do with a Texan," he muttered, alluding to the 16 volt plain cigarettes he'd smoked in Rhodesia, "and a drink." His depression didn't lift much, despite the sun coming out just as they drove through the city, getting their first look at the place sparkling in the winter sun. The overhead monorail fascinated the girls as they passed under it. But not even the view of the harbour and the Sydney Opera House, its grey-white lobster-shell shaped arches glistening starkly against the azure of the bay-water, were able to stimulate him as they crossed the Harbour Bridge. The taxi, which, to Peter's disgust, was driven by a man who looked of middle-eastern origin and could barely speak English, took them into Sydney North where they were to be temporarily housed in a Bed and Breakfast hotel until they could find a permanent place to live. His attitude was so dampening that Barbara had trouble keeping up with the excitement of the girls. Taking the opportunity to put in a word, she said,

"Look, Pete, we're just going to have to put up with it, and make it our home. We can't afford to move again and so you're just going to have to knuckle under. Things will improve even if I have to get a job. I've been looking at the job pages and I think I can easily find a position here as a nurse." That seemed to depress him even further, so she kept her mouth shut for the remainder of the ride.

The 'B and B' turned out to be better than they had anticipated; a lovely south facing converted house high on the bluff to the west of the Harbour Bridge, and from their rooms they had an excellent view of Darling Harbour and the city beyond. His mood lightened a bit and, after settling in, they wrapped up warmly and all went for an exploratory walk. Peter's mood swing continued when he saw a billboard advertising the upcoming Bledesloe Cup match between the Kiwis and Wallabies.

"S'pose I'd better start supporting the Ozzies," he muttered, "now that the Springboks are banned." His love of rugby, it seemed to Barbara, was about the only thing that gave him a lift.

"Well you must see if you can get to the game."

"Yes I'd like that."

All in all, it looked as if things were working out. Peter was inducted into the Harbour Police and after his boat, weapons, customs, fitness and dive training, which he passed with flying colours, despite his smoking, was immediately commissioned as a Police Inspector. They soon found a little semi-detached cottage for long-term rent in Manly, near the Waratah's Rugby Club, bought an old second-hand Toyota Land Cruiser and after the girls settled down at the local secondary school, Barbara got herself a super job at a small local clinic specialising in 'alternative' medicine. It was run by another ex-Rhodesian, a woman who'd immigrated to Australia via South Africa after they failed to make a go of it in Johannesburg. Her girls went to the same school in Manly and soon a strong friendship developed. Even Peter got on well with them, especially the husband, who equally was mad about rugby.

Shenje 'Himmler' Ndunze couldn't care less about the declining state of Harare. His arrival in the city was triumphant! He presented himself in his smartest 'Comrades' fatigues at the outside gate of the President's residence at the corner of Josiah Tongogara Avenue (previously North Avenue) and Fifth Street. Mugabe's guards were nervous and gave him and the selected few who had come with him, a thorough going over. There were rumours of a coup attempt.

To Ndunze, the medals parade was memorable only in as much as when Robert Mugabe pinned his Heroes Medal on his chest, the great man whispered,

"After the parade, you will report to my aide." He indicated a smartly dressed Major to his right. "I want to talk to you." Ndunze said nothing but saluted and returned smartly to his position in the ranks. Major Broderik Volker's drilling at the camp, so long ago, now stood him in good stead.

The aide led him to a well-appointed waiting room, full of Regency styled furniture, which, surprisingly, still had a photograph of the previous Prime Minister, Mr. Ian Smith, hanging on the wall. The Aide said that the President insisted that it stay there to remind everybody that the fight was not yet over. After a few minutes, he was shown through.

"Relax, Comrade Ndunze. Tea?" asked the great man.

"Yes please, Excellency."

Mugabe led him out onto the terrace. The sun had dropped behind the tall Deodars on the western side of an expansive, immaculately kept lawn and garden.

"Sit down, we must talk." Mugabe indicated a seat opposite him and while Ndunze settled down, poured tea into two delicate bone china cups. It was very comfortable, the vinyl covering of the garden chair covers cool against Ndunze's back.

"Sugar?" Ndunze was nonplussed, feeling totally out of his depth, an eerie feeling overcoming him, so different was this environment to the harsh nature of his daily existence. Mugabe seeing this, tried to put him at ease. "My wife, Sally, insists that now the war is over, I must behave like a civilised man." Ndunze sipped his tea, gingerly clasping his saucer in thick work-hardened fingers, scared to death he might spill his tea into the saucer, or even worse, break or drop the cup.

Mugabe regarded his man, his scrutiny hidden by the thick lenses of his spectacles and his characteristic hooded eyelids. This violent man had served the cause well. He was intelligent also. It was time to take the cause a little further.

"My aide told you why Mr. Smith's photograph is still hanging on the wall in the reception?"

"Yes, Excellency."

"Well, the war is not over!" Mugabe was emphatic. "Now that we have the Ndebele under control, a matter in which you have done very well, it is time to move on." He stood up and started pacing, leaning forwards as he spoke aggressively. "The Second Chimorenga[91] is over, but now it is time for the Third Chimorenga to start." He began to wave his arms around. "In the past, threats to our peace and stability have been politically motivated. Today, and because we have succeeded as a country in creating an enabling environment where all Zimbabweans enjoy their civil and political rights, the threats to our peace and stability have become economically motivated." He stopped and pointed his finger at Ndunze. "In particular, a clear and present, real and potential economic source of instability, social chaos and economic hardships today is the unequal land distribution in our country!" He was now starting to shout. "The fact that a political minority continues to be an economic majority in terms of land ownership in a country where land is the economy and the economy is land, has become a threat to peace, stability and the rule of law." Again he stopped and this time, he glared at Ndunze. "Unless the threat is dealt with in a revolutionary manner, the current temporary setbacks in our economy will become worse if not permanent.[92] So, Comrade Ndunze, I would like you to gather your comrades and begin the task of officially taking back the white owned farms. You might enjoy this."

"We will be happy to serve you, Excellency." President Mugabe sat down again and went on at length to describe what he had in mind, logistics, money and tactics. He listened intently to suggestions from Ndunze. Between them, they framed a proper campaign of intimidation, pillage, physical abuse and denial. They decided on a frame of reference for the attacks to come, how they were to deal with resistance and adverse publicity. Mugabe had a slyness, developed through years of cut-throat political intrigue and subterfuge. The shadows had lengthened appreciably; it would soon be dark and Ndunze was amazed he was still there. He frowned.

"What are you thinking comrade?"

"Excellency, my men will be concerned about the dangers. Even though the war is over, the farmers are well armed.

"Leave that to me. I will soon ban weapons of war and the farmers will be brought to heel and made to hand in all their weapons. It is time also to amend this Constitution, forced on me by the British Imperialists led by Mrs. Thatcher, so that I will have the power to take what rightfully belongs to the people."

"And the Police, Excellency?"

"You leave that to me also. They will not trouble you. Go, 'Himmler', and prepare!"

True to his word, in December 1991, Mugabe pushed through Parliamentary legislation amending the Constitution that gave the government powers to confiscate private land at a price that it fixes. Landowners were expressly denied the right to appeal to the courts over the level of compensation. This was carried into law, despite the warning from the British Foreign Secretary, Mr. Douglas Hurd, that seizing land without proper compensation would deter essential foreign investment. Mugabe's retort was notable in its brevity.

"I say to Britain, you mind your own business!"

Harry, after his experiences, was not one to trust any government, let alone Mugabe's. So he took no chances. Near the place where he and Pete had found the leopard, there was a derelict mine, completely overgrown. It didn't amount to much, just a short horizontal tunnel, a few piles of rock and tailings and some broken and rusted bits of metal. Clearly, whatever the ancient miner had thought was there, wasn't, and he had abandoned the diggings very soon after starting. The countryside near the Great Dyke[93], the length of the country, was littered with the workings of the explorer prospectors during the early years of the 20th century.

Over a period of months, not trusting anyone, Harry, by himself and sometimes with the help of Robbie, home on holidays, built a thick rock and concrete barrier across the entrance to the tunnel. The door was the steel safe door, originally the door to the gun cupboard in his burnt out house. The house was rebuilt without such an elaborate secure core.

The tricky parts of doing this work were to ensure that they did it secretly and that they didn't disturb the dense bush hiding the workings. The first was easy as there were enumerable reasons for him to be out on the farm all day, or to have bags of cement in the back of the truck. The second was more difficult and Harry had to settle on taking the truck to the other side of the nearby dwala (*bald granite domed kopje*), and physically transferring the material and tools on his back over the side of the dwala by approaching the mine obliquely along the edge of the ridge it was sunk into. He approached the mine only once in his vehicle, and that was to deliver the safe door, which Robbie and he manhandled onto a wheelbarrow for the last part of the journey. He then spent hours back-tracking, destroying all traces of his vehicle tyre marks. After the first rains the grass and bushes re-established themselves completely. Thus, within three weeks, there was no sign of his presence, even to a good tracker, which he himself now was.

Slowly Harry turned the hideaway into an arsenal, also well provisioned with canned foods and survival gear. The keys he put in a sealed glass jar, which he buried at the base of a large Sausage tree[94] at the back of the dwala. Only he, Annie and Robbie knew where it was.

Another thing he did was to tell Sampson to join the ZANU PF. He wanted to get his hands on a membership card so that he could forge one for himself. He remembered well the difficulties he'd had in Zambia, unable to move openly, having to hide at all times. He wasn't going to take the chance of letting it happen again. He was pretty confident that he could now pose as a man of colour, provided he could hide his blue eyes behind dark glasses.

"Why do you want me to join those beres, Master?"

"It's time we became members of the party. It might be useful in the future."

When the police arrived to confiscate his weapons of war, Harry gave Annie a wry smile that said I told you so. Sampson had warned him that they were coming and how he knew, Harry didn't ask. He got out of bed, put on a tracksuit and running shoes; mid-winter mornings could be close to freezing. Taking his time, he went to answer the bell. Peering at the telecam image of a Land Rover full of policemen waiting outside the electrified perimeter fence, he pressed the speaker button.

"Morning gentlemen, you're out early. Can I help you?"

"Hello, is that Andrews?" snapped back someone. Harry had no regard for the new Zimbabwe police. There had been too many sackings and rapid promotions; too many cases of intimidation and violence; too many occasions where there was a failure on the part of the police to act even where evidence was clear; and too many incidents of police brutality.

"Mr. Andrews to you, mister." Harry responded. There was a pause.

"Mr. Andrews, I have a warrant here to confiscate all weapons of war at this address."

"Show me."

"Well, open the gate and let us through to the house."

"Hold it up to the camera."

"Camera, which camera, where..?"

"Behind the glass panel in the concrete pillar to your right."

"But I will have to get out of the vehicle to do so. You must open the gate." Harry was starting to enjoy this.

"So get out. I'm not letting you in until I see the warrant." Another pause. Eventually, the passenger door of the vehicle opened and a shivering policeman emerged and walked around the vehicle. He removed a document from his bush jacket and unfolding it, held it up to be inspected.

"Six inches closer," instructed Harry, "and keep it still." A muttered expletive, but the policeman complied. Harry took his time. He waited without actually bothering to read the warrant, he was quite sure it was what they said it was. Eventually, he said,

"OK. Now, who are you?"

"I am Chief Superintendent Nduma." The man was becoming exasperated and Harry thought he'd had enough fun.

"A Chief Superintendent, just to collect some weapons. All right, come on in." He pressed the button controlling the electrically operated security gate at the end of the garden. Whilst they were driving up he dragged two padlocked heavy ammunition boxes full of weapons and ammunition out of the hall onto the veranda. He never invited the officers in, but stood leaning against a brick column at the edge of the veranda holding a sheath of papers and clutching two keys. It was 6:30am and the sun was just peeping over the eastern skyline. It was ice cold and the three policemen got out of the vehicle, stamping their feet to get warm. They shuffled around looking up at Harry who said nothing. The Chief Superintendent walked stiffly forward.

"We...."

"Warrant and identification?" Harry barked, interrupting him and putting out his hand palm upwards at the same time. The Chief Superintendent hesitated and then took the warrant out again and also removed his ID card from his top pocket. He handed them both up to Harry.

"Thank you, Chief Superintendent Nduma." He inspected both documents thoroughly, reached down and handed them back, and then opened his own papers.

"Here are my licences, an inventory and here are the keys. You will find all the arms in these boxes," he said, pointing at them. "Open the boxes, check them, and then before you remove them, I want a receipt." He stood back and gestured to them to come onto the veranda. They moved forwards and he watched them impassively as they opened each box, checked every weapon against the inventory and relevant license. There was a bit of a to do when they discovered that there were no breach-blocks in any of the weapons.

"In the sack," said Harry idly. Each were removed and individually identified from the serial number. They could find nothing wrong and after repacking the weapons, they loaded the boxes into the back of the Land Rover. Harry almost heaved a sigh of relief. He'd doctored all the breach-blocks and firing mechanisms so the weapons could never be used again.

"Right, now we must search the premises."

"No," said Harry, "That's a confiscation order, not a search warrant. My receipt, please?" He was almost smiling. By this time the men were shivering with cold. He continued as he scrutinised the standard receipt, "When you get back to headquarters, check what I have given you against all the licences I have been issued and you will see that all I have retained is my Winchester .375 hunting rifle, a Webley .22 Hornet and a 9mm Beretta. These are not classified as weapons of war and are required for normal use on the farm."

"Please will you fetch them for me to inspect?"

"No. Now get going, I have a farm to run." The policeman, to his credit, kept his cool. He peered up at Harry, still nonchalantly leaning against one of the veranda posts.

"Well I have one last question, for which I insist you provide me with an answer." Harry scrutinised his face, leaning towards him.

"Oh, and what's that?" His chin seemed just that much firmer, his stance just that much more menacing. The policeman couldn't help it. Almost as if pushed backwards by sheer force, he took a quick step backwards, but he gathered his wits about him.

"You have had everything prepared for our visit. How did you know that we were coming this morning?"

"I didn't. I was going to bring these weapons into the Karoi Police Camp this morning to hand them in. I don't need them anymore. Now if you don't mind?" He glared at them briefly and then turned away. As he did so, one of the policemen said in his own tongue, Shishona,

"This makiwa (*white pig*) is like a bull elephant. It is time to remove his balls" One of his comrades giggled.

Harry whipped back again and looked hard at the man, responding in Shishona,

"Yeah, but it's going to take more than one of you bveni (*hyena*) to do it." The man's jaw dropped as it dawned him that this white man, an Englishman to boot, had understood every word he had said. Harry continued, "Chief Superintendent Nduma, I hope you put this Constable on charge for making lewd suggestions to a member of the public." And with that, knowing that nothing of the sort would happen and not waiting for a response from Nduma, he turned again and entered the house, closing and locking the door gently behind him.

CHAPTER 34

For a while, it went well for Peter and Barbara. He appeared to be enjoying his new job, she loved hers, and the girls were very happy, for the first time in their lives being able to go down to the beach and swim everyday. Peter got them each surfboards and like the other teenagers in the area, they spent much of their spare time in healthy pursuits on the beach. Living in Manly had its benefits. It was well served by ferry into central Sydney, had a lovely shopping centre, clubs with excellent sports facilities and a super climate. But all was not in fact well.

"Hi Pete, how was your day?" greeted Barbara, kissing him as he slumped down in his favourite easy chair.

"Shit!" he responded rudely. "Do you know, Babs, people are the worst? Give me a dog every time." He scratched his head and sighed, swinging forwards and holding his face in his hands.

"Well, just relax, I'll make you a nice cup of coffee, and you can tell me all about it." She almost ran into the kitchen thinking I mustn't lose him now, that's the first time he's spoken about his job at all. She was soon back with a mug of instant, one and a half sugars, no milk, the way he always drank it. He took the cup and said warily,

"Babs, we found another body, a young man, in the harbour yesterday, he'd been stabbed, his face, neck, chest and arms cut to shreds and he had been robbed,.. well, he had nothing on him. Also his fingers had been cut off. But today we got back the coroner's preliminary report. He had also taken, or been forced to take, an intravenous overdose of heroin. He was actually dead when he was ripped apart. Then someone fed him to the sharks. Only, with the current, his body was washed up onto the shore within what couldn't have been very long. Anyway, forensics took three hours to find out who he was. We went down to his flat in Kings Cross and found a woman in his broom cupboard. We presume she was his girlfriend, people in the area recognised her photo. She had been subjected to multiple rapes, overdosed and also cut to bits." He paused, taking a sip of his coffee. He took a deep breath as if to gather his thoughts. Barbara kept very still, knowing that this was somehow important, getting it off his chest.

"Fuck it, Babs…" Now she interjected,

"You know I don't like that language, Pete."

"No! Fuck it, Babs!" he persisted, "I left Rhodesia to get away from this sort of thing. I thought I'd seen it all; violence, brutal murders, body dismemberment, rape and pillage, gratuitous mutilation. Shit, it doesn't end. There, it was politically motivated, but they're no worse than these swines. Only, here, it's about mafia-like gang warfare, drugs, prostitution, and hell, we're all the same. For all of my adult life I seem to have been at war, dealing with the dregs of humanity. I hated it in Perth, also, dealing with the lowest of the low. I can't handle it any more."

Barbara rose and walked over to him. She settled down on the arm of the chair next to him and took his head against her breast gently rocking. She didn't know what to say to ease his pain. *What can I say?* Barbara thought. *I have no idea what he has to go through.* She made a vow then to seek counselling and to speak to his superiors.

Despite her efforts to comfort him, the drinking started again.

Harry started flying tour charters for Jim, mainly into the Okavango Delta in Botswana, Victoria Falls, the game reserves, and the Zambian resort areas such as Kafue, Lower and Upper Zambezi, Luangwa Valley and Kasaba Bay on Lake Tanganyika. His passengers were mainly in parties of two or four, South Africans, Brits, the odd American and German and occasionally French or Italian.

He loved it, totally in his element.

Often, it gave him a chance to get back into the bush. He took pride in the fact that he was able to give his passengers the benefit of his bush lore and enjoyed being the popular raconteur at the fireside after a day out on safari.

Inevitably, wherever he was, it was one of the local rangers who knew him, that started it going.

"Ah go on, Harry, tell the guests about when you caught that flat dog in the Delta."

"Forget it; you've heard it all before." Harry would smile, knowing what was coming.

"Or about Mbala?" His tormentor would inevitably turn to one of the guests.

"You know, Harry had a close shave with some lions up on Lake Tanganyika."

"Don't listen to him," Harry would always rise to the bait, "anyway it wasn't at Mbala, it was at Kasaba Bay." Typically, he would rise, replenished his beer at the bar, settle back and start one or another story.

"Well, there was one trip; I flew my wife up to Kasaba Bay for a weekend. We arrived there, landing on this incredible tarmac airstrip built for President Kuanda. He had this fantastic holiday lodge set on the shore of Lake Tanganyika, but it's a total ruin now. It even had its own professionally designed, but never finished, golf course. I suppose, that tells its own story." He would lean forwards and throw another log into the flames.

"We checked in, excited as punch, because this is one of the most remote corners of the globe and it looked pretty organised."

"Who owned it?" someone would interject. "Was it government owned?"

"I suppose so, but at that time it was run by a couple called Tim and Mandy Ham, on behalf of a Johannesburg based consortium. The Lodge was built in lime-washed bricks and mortar, each chalet with its own frontage and view of the lake. There was an excellent pub next to the dining room and lounge and Mandy had a pretty good little curio shop up and running.

I must tell you, Kasaba Bay falls well inside the Sumbu National Park in northern Zambia, you can't get there by road. All provisions and supplies have to be either flown in or brought by boat from Mpulungu; that's about 50 miles down the coast. Let me give you an historical fact. Mpulungu is about 25 miles from Mbala, which, during colonial times, was called Abercorn. It is a little known fact that it was in this area that the last battle of World War One was fought, some six weeks after the Treaty of Versailles on the 11th November 1919. It took that long for the news that the war was over to get there. It was here that the German Army in East Africa surrendered to the British."

"You're joking?"

"No, I'm serious, I mean you can just see it, absolute gentlemen, immaculate uniforms, white flags, meeting in no-mans-land, hand shakes. 'I say old chap, I've good news and bad news. The good news is that the war's over. The bad news is that you lost! Now be a good fellow and give me your sword!'" Everyone would burst out laughing. Harry would preen himself and carry on, now getting into his stride.

"Lake Tanganyika itself defies description, it is so beautiful. It is the longest and second deepest lake in the world and is home to the giant Tiger Fish, Nile and Rock Perch, which all grow to well over 100 pounds, and the widest variety of fresh-water cichlids to be found in the world; a fisherman's wonderland. The lake is also home to a myriad of other fish and is, of course, home to giant crocodiles and plenty of hippos. We saw a croc once that was 24 feet long." Harry would stop, pull out his pipe, stoke it, light up, take a puff and a sip of his beer and continue.

"Well, Annie and I were told to be cautious because a lot of wild animals roamed around the hotel grounds at night. They weren't kidding. On our last night there we had already gone to bed when we did hear lions.

The following morning, around dawn, I was awakened by a grunt from what I thought was right outside my window. I sat up and gently lifted the corner of the curtain and peered out into the early morning light. I gulped and gently dropped the curtain because sure enough, on the small veranda, right outside the door to our room were three lions, apparently fast asleep. On the veranda with them was a half eaten impala. Annie was still fast asleep, so I got out of bed and went across to her bed and shook her shoulder gently.

'Come and have a look,' I whispered, finger to my lips.

'What is..' I had to put my hand across her mouth

'Shhh! Some lions on the veranda.' Well, I tell you, that got her attention and in a flash she was awake and listening.

So I said, 'come,' taking her hand, 'but be quiet, otherwise we'll scare them off.' I raised the curtain once more and we sat there, totally naked, on my bed watching these three animals. I could have leaned over and touched the nearest one, they were so close. Now this is the part where I really was a clever dick.

'OK,' I said aloud, I was thinking that it was time for them to wake up and push off, because pretty soon we had to go across for breakfast and I wanted an early start for the flight to Mfuwe in the Luangwa Valley. The buggers just ignored me.

So I dropped the curtain in place again and said to Annie,

'Let's get ready for breakfast and finish packing. By the time we're ready to leave, they'll be gone. Ten minutes later, I was still stark naked on my bed waiting for Annie to finish in the bathroom. When she came out she leaned over me and peered out the window again.

'They're still there Harry,' she told me.

'Golly, they were casual, no bloody fear around humans. I leaned over and in my firm schoolmaster voice said,

'Hey you guys, bugger off!' I got a reaction. One of the lions, a large female, lifted her head, looked at me through the window, her face devoid of any expression, and then flopped down again and went back to sleep.

'Hey you guys, get lost.' Louder this time, very loud. That elicited a twitch out of one ear, I clapped my hands and shouted at them, all to no avail. Annie was getting a little jittery at the stage.

'How are we going to get out?' she asked me. Me big chief," Harry would tap his chest with the tip of his pipe. That always raised a nervous laugh from some of the listeners.

"'Oh, don't worry lovee', I told her, 'push comes to a shove, sooner or later someone will come out along this way and chase them away.' But I didn't want to wait because we had to get moving.

So I looked around the room and my eyes settled on an enormous rubber tree (*ficus*) in the corner. Under it was a large copper pot. I went over to it and discovered that the plant was actually growing in a large plastic container. I lifted the plant out and set it on the slate floor.

Now I needed a beater, something with which to hit the copper pot to make as much noise as possible. I tried a couple of wire coat hangers, and found them too flexible; the noise they made was feeble. My camera tripod was ideal but I wasn't about to damage that. So finally I settled on the toilet brush. It was an ordinary wooden brush, with bristles only on one side and it was quite heavy. I moved over to the door, set myself up and told Annie,

'Annie, when I give you the word, open the door, wait until I get back inside again and slam it shut again.' She was shaking a bit, but she got my drift. I told her to make sure the door was unlocked.

She set herself up and whipped the door open. I ran out onto the doormat clanging my toilet brush as loudly and quickly as I could." Smiling, he would continue, "I felt quite ridiculous. The lions had gone. All I got were peals of laughter coming from Tim Ham and his wife, who were standing about 30 yards away. I must have looked bloody silly, but thank God, I'd actually put on some underpants. They've probably bored everyone in the world with that story by now."

Surrounded by peals of laughter, Harry would inevitably continue with the rest of the story. "Tail between my legs, metaphorically of course, I insisted that we leave Kasaba Bay really early.

'I don't want to get caught up in any weather over the escarpments,' was my excuse. So we left that wonderful spot before 7:00am and within 1hr30 were on final coming into Mfuwe. The Wildlife Camp Land Rover, driven by my old mate Jacko, was there to meet us. Jacko was the best tracker I have ever known and I have known plenty of them.

I met him in the early '70's on my first trip to the Luangwa Valley and had the good fortune to find out where he was, and to insist on him being our ranger on many occasions. Jacko could smell leopards, or so he said. He certainly knew how to find them. I have seen more leopards in that area than on all of the rest of my wanderings through the African bush put together. He also knew his birds and animals and I learned much from him. Finally he never came up with a cock-and-bull story about animals or the bush, something I have heard dozens of times from rangers as they try to impress tourists.

'Moni Jacko, muli bwanji? (*Hello Jacko, how are you?*).' He was a Chinyanja[95].

'Ndili bwino zikomo bwana, kaya inu? (*I'm fine thank you, and you?*).'

'Chabwino (*fine*) Jacko, this is Annie, my wife,' I said introducing them. Old Jacko winked at me and nudged me so hard, it hurt the whole trip. I don't think he really believed she was my wife. Anyway, he couldn't do enough for her. She loved the attention and it was good for me, too.

Mfuwe is about 20 miles from South Luangwa Park but there is a good tarmac road all the way to the bridge across the river into the reserve. Wildlife Camp is just outside the reserve on the river and is in fact owned by the government. I have always found it simple, clean and acceptable and except once when going there on a walking safari deep into the Luangwa North reserve, I have always stayed there.

For two days Jacko took us for drives into the park and we felt we saw all that there was to see, it was wonderful. It would have been better if the Parks Department did something about the secondary forest growth along the edges of the roads. It's become so thick that it is frequently difficult to watch game. This was the case even though most of the roads in the reserve were raised above the flood plain of the river and game viewing was excellent.

Annie and I were given the last hut along the river, that is, the northernmost one and we could sit out under the enormous mahoganies in relative seclusion and watch the evening fall. A wide range of animals was always visible and we spent good hours watching what was going on. Wandering around at night was a no no; it was far too dangerous, especially with regards to lions, hippos and snakes, but everything else wandered around as well.

After our first night there, we woke up very early, hearing a rumbling sound close by.

It was still quite dark and Annie climbed out of her bed, and lifting my mosquito net, crawled in next to me.

'What's the matter?' I asked.

'There's something in the room,' she whispered.

'What?' For some reason I also whispered. She replied, hugging me really tight,

'I don't know but I can hear this rumbling sound and chomping right here. It sounds as if there's someone eating the hut right in here next to our heads.' As she whispered all this, I could feel her shivering with fear and I suddenly came fully awake realising there was a sound. I burst out in silent laughter. Not a time to make a noise now. So I whispered back,

'My darling, unless he's blinking small, and crawled in here on his knees, what you can hear is an elephant right outside. That rumbling sound is his stomach.'

It turned out that there were half a dozen or so around. As the dawn broke we looked out and could see them clearly, chomping away at juicy morsels off the mopane trees. There was one right next to the door with its back to us. I got up quietly, opened the door, reached out and gently stroked its haunch.

'Annie, come here,' I whispered, turning around and beckoning her. I turned back to the elephant and gently touched its tough hide again. I was surprised that it hadn't felt it. Annie came up next to me and reached out and she gently ran light fingers across its haunch.

Gripping my arm, she whispered in my ear, 'it's hard isn't it?'

'Yea it's very tough.' Then I realised that we'd got a first." He would look around at the guests. "Do you realise that it is extremely unlikely that two people have ever done that before?"

"What?" was the inevitable response.

"Stand together, man and wife, and stroke the backside of a wild elephant in the African bush," Harry would smile.

"If you've done it, surely someone else has," someone would deny reasonably.

"Doubt it. Especially since we were both stark naked!" That would usually raise a great deal of laughter. The tourists loved him, and the word got around that the best pilot to get for your safari was this mad guy called Harry Andrews.

Sometimes Harry and Sampson or Chadrack, and occasionally Robbie when he was home, took a couple of days off during quiet periods and went camping in the bush. Harry took these opportunities to learn everything about the bush he could from his two foremen.

Towing the fishing boat filled with everything they needed, they would drive cross-country on little-used tracks down to the Sanyati Hills and set up camp next to the river. The mountain flora was rich and beautiful, the trees huge and shady and river was navigable for about 3 miles in both directions. It was idyllic.

"Master Harry, you tire too quickly, like an 'mbiz' (*zebra*), when you run through the 'shatine' (*bush*). And you make too much noise. This is why you can never keep up with the 'mhara' (*impala*). You must learn to run like me, like a Ndebele warrior."

"How do you propose I do that, Sampson?" replied Harry.

"You must learn to run on the front part of your foot. Look, I show you." He got up gesturing to Harry to follow him. He found a flat sandy stretch of track near the camp and then after explaining to Harry what he wanted, they ran together across the sandy patch. Then they stopped and turned back. Pulling Harry down next to him, Sampson squatted next to their tracks. Pointing with a grass stem, he said,

"Look here, 'Changamire' (*chief*), these are my footprints. You see how the deepest part is the front part of the foot behind my toes. But here is your footprint. You see how the heel part is the deepest. If I were tracking you, before I even know who you are, I would know many things. One, you are a white man, no black man runs like this, two, you are short, below 6 feet, three, and this is most important, you are running light without a gun. A gun will make you lean slightly to one side to balance yourself and one heel will dig slightly deeper. But lastly, I know also that I will catch you, because running like this you cannot run very far. I can run like this all day and not stop."

Harry was fascinated.

"So, you must learn to run like a muntu and I will show you."

So over a period of time, Harry learned so much about these sort of things; the bush, tracking, the trees, edible plants, roots and fruit, how to kill an animal, clean and skin it efficiently, and how to cook the multitude of bush fare. In short, he became a expert on survival in the bush.

Zimbabwe itself was falling apart economically. Inflation was rampant and the social engineering being undertaken by the Mugabe regime, for that is what it had become, was having catastrophic results on exports, tax receipts, food production and health services. Shortages were growing and in virtually every walk of life, hardship was now the norm, not the exception that it had been when it was under the white government, despite the many years it survived under a tight sanctions program.

However, the good times rolled on for Harry and Annie. Because of his ability to earn US dollars through his flying and his farming production, they were able to cover the shortages by buying in South

Africa to cover their needs. In a sense, Harry was back into sanctions busting.

Harry was really enjoying his trips away, and every now and then he was able to take Annie with him. The farms were operating efficiently and profitably. His bank overdraft had long since been settled and they had a healthy bank balance, both in Zimbabwe and, despite the draconian foreign exchange restrictions, outside the country too. The kids were doing well at school and the scars they'd carried from the attack on them at the end of the war, dimmed into the past.

Shenje 'Himmler' Ndunze used the top floor of the once classical 'Colonial' NEM House in central Harare as his headquarters. It had been long since abandoned by its founding insurance company and a law firm whose partners had fled the country and the new regime. It didn't concern him that the neglected building was falling to pieces; its ceilings falling down, paint and panelling peeling off the walls, toilets defunct and windows broken. They all defecated in the sanitary lane behind the building anyway.

Ndunze and his comrades had methodically cleared the whole area around the capital of white farmers. Other groups were doing the same purging in other parts of the country. The President was ecstatic as the process of cleansing continued, believing that it would cement his popularity and his grip on power. He shrugged off the international criticism and pressure being heaped on him and gave orders that party faithful were to be given preference. His close followers and recognised supporters were soon actively seeking to benefit from this largesse. In fact, they soon began to direct which farms they wanted, selecting the very best for themselves, so it was inevitable that their eyes began to turn to the rich farming areas to the north west. Ndunze was directed to relocate his group to Sinoia, now renamed Chinhoyi, as this was the heartland of the ZANU movement and original home of the President.

Before leaving Harare to set up in his new headquarters in Chinhoyi, he called his cadre in for an important meeting. He gave them each a coke, bought over the road at OK Bazaars, and started.

"Comrades, the President is very pleased with your work. Is it not so that your bank accounts are now bulging with money, like a ripe woman?" He was greeted with cheers and clapping as his delighted followers giggled and clapped each other on the back. He knew that the fact was that much of what they'd earned had been blown away on gambling, booze, ganja and women. But they were having the time of their lives, drugged up most of it. Also, the fact was that they were mainly new recruits. Few of them were war veterans at all, but bullying youngsters of the ZANU Youth Wing, for whom a full stomach and the chance to participate in legalised rape and pillage, counted for much. Their indoctrination and training was so good, they were not much use for anything else but creating anarchy.

"So hear me, for we are now embarking on a new and more exciting phase of our Third Chimorenga." Silence. "We are moving to Chinhoyi, but before we go I need information, which we can only obtain here in 'Bamba Zonki!'[96]" He turned to the blackboard behind him and started going through the items he had earlier written down.

"First, I want detailed maps of the whole area. For this we must go to the Department of Surveys. Secondly, we must find out who owns the land, and for this we must go to The Land Registry Office. Thirdly, where the land is company owned, we must find out who owns the company. For this we must go to The Company's Registry. These departments are all in the Milton Buildings in Samora Machel Avenue[97]." He continued his briefing and delegated various activities to the more alert of his followers, half of them were high on ganja despite the time of day, and then sent them on their way.

He sat on the desk swinging his legs as they all rushed off like excited children, knowing full well what was on the foremost of their minds, 'the chance to get into the delights of the capital'. He could just imagine his days ahead while he tried to extricate them one by one from the various bars, shabeens and whorehouses around the city. He smiled. They deserved it. The white settler farmers were being quite resilient, and had put up a good fight in many places. To make them brave, he encouraged them to smoke a weed or two before any action. But sometimes this led to carelessness. Several of his men had been badly injured by shotgun blasts, electrical shocks from the security fencing, guard dog bites, cuts from broken glass, and sadly some had succumbed to resistance from the farm workers themselves. He had taken special delight in dealing with those traitors to the cause.

His mind turned to the job ahead and immediately the image of Merrywaters Farm came into his head. What a raid, so many of his comrades killed that night. He wondered whether that man Andrews and his family were still there, or whether they'd run, taken the so-called 'gap' and left the country. After that night, he couldn't imagine that they hadn't. He and his men had really done a lot of damage. Well no matter, this time they wouldn't be burning the farm down, they'd be taking it, when its turn came.

Ndunze and his cadre planned their campaign against the white farmers with precision. They started with the easy targets, not only in terms of who owned the farm; it was their own people that they softened up first. The first thing was to completely intimidate the local farm workers. This process was simple: beat up the men, maybe kill one or two, and rape the women. After this treatment, the white farmers could expect no support from their workers. They would then begin the attrition, equipment and livestock theft, unexplained fires, forcing absenteeism, and other harassment. Finally, they'd normally wait until the farmer and family were away from the farm, and they'd sack the place, invading the homestead. At this point, they didn't leave, but would wait for the farmer to return only to find that his farm had been taken from him. The police never ever seem to arrive and so it was difficult for the aggrieved farmer to get his possessions back, let alone get the matter into the courts. Once in occupation, the ZANU PF machine got to work, accusing the farmer of everything, illegal possession of arms, harassment and maltreatment of workers, hoarding of essential food supplies and so on. Simultaneously they would move as many squatters onto the farm as possible, taking over all the machinery and buildings. The farmer was generally on a hiding to nothing. The approach worked as more and more white farmers succumbed, or, occasionally, were murdered. Court cases were few and futile, the police deliberately messing up their prosecutions. More and more judges gave in to the regime and were replaced by others sympathetic to the government. The feeling amongst the remaining farmers was frustration and a fatalistic recognition that it was virtually impossible to fight a corrupt government.

But Harry was not resigned to defeat. In fairly typical fashion, he began to track their activities, noting with some concern that they were moving closer and closer to home. He started to take every step he could to ensure that breaking into his farms was as difficult as possible. He also quietly started to plan for their evacuation. He bought a Honda

220 volt generator pack in Johannesburg and this, together with all their important papers and a large stash of US and Zim dollars, he placed in his secret arsenal. He built a carefully camouflaged vehicle shelter behind the dwala and, with Robbie's help collecting and driving, he parked the fully operational Peugeot 403 truck there, leaving the vehicle's keys in the same glass jar as the key to the arsenal. He told Annie, deliberately in front of George, that it had eventually given up the ghost, and he'd been forced to flog it. He figured that the word would soon spread that the truck was gone.

Privately, he got Chadrack to sign the vehicle ownership transfer papers into his name and he kept the licence up-to-date. Chadrack didn't even realise that he was the proud owner of an old, but fully functional Peugeot 403 half ton truck. He just signed, much as he jumped to do everything else the master told him. Annie, at all times knew what he was doing and thought he was being a bit paranoid. But she let it go, thinking she'd never had reason to doubt Harry's devious ways, and besides, it wasn't hurting anyone.

With the advent of the Internet, Barbara, Annie and Biddy Glover maintained close contact with each other, and they did still speak on the phone from time to time. Peter arrived home late one evening after having had quite a few at the rugby club pub, just as Barbara put the phone down.

"Who've you been talking to?" No hello, no hugs or kisses. A man in trouble and the marriage taking the strain.

"Annie." She looked resignedly at him, almost as if she knew what was coming.

"Hell, why do you spend so much of your time talking to her? Surely you've had enough of that Andrews bullshit?" He stood there, swaying a little, dishevelled, spittle on his lips.

"That's rubbish! Why shouldn't I talk to her, she's my best friend. Anyway, you've been drinking again Pete, so go and pick on someone else, and it better not be the girls." That riled him a little.

"Smooth bloody Harry Andrews, why I ever listened to that bloke, I'll never know. And here's my bloody wife consorting with his, getting her mind filled full of his brand of bullshit."

"Peter, she does nothing of the sort, and you know it. And in any case,

I still can't understand why you've got it in for Harry. He's done nothing but be an incredible friend to you."

"Balls, he's a control freak. The great bloody Pirate! That describes him to a tee. He has to have his way, controlling everyone and everything around him. He never bends and he's always right. If I hadn't been taken in by him, I'd have got you and my parents out a long time before anything happened. Besides, I reckon that if it hadn't have been for him sending Sampson and his men back to Sivewrights after the plane came down, we'd have saved Mum and Dad. Sampson couldn't have been too far from the prang at the time. I blame him for their deaths."

Barbara was horrified and didn't know what to say. So this is what was eating away at him, why he had turned his back on Harry. Supportive as ever, and as she thought more about it, she began to see his point. She busied herself with laying the supper table, frustrated and not knowing what to do. She couldn't even suggest that perhaps he should give Harry the benefit of the doubt.

"Well, that's as may be, but Peter, the children will be home shortly, so please go and wash up and get yourself together for supper. You cannot take it out on them!" She moved over to him and laid her hand on his arm, looking searchingly into his face. He said nothing more and disappeared into their bedroom. That night, she couldn't sleep and so long after the rest of the household were asleep, she crept out of bed and went into the den, where she spent the rest of the night at the computer composing a long e-mail to Annie.

CHAPTER 35

It was Friday, and Harry, neatly dressed in his pilot's uniform of white shirt, captain stripes, wings, tie and navy blue slacks, picked up his three passengers at the Harare Holiday Inn at precisely 1:00pm and then drove out to the airport. He left them, with his own lightweight travel bag, in the airport lounge. The whole building was already showing signs of third-world neglect. Advising that he'd back to take them through customs in about 10 minutes, he went back to the car. Parking in the Trans Afrique Air hanger, he quickly said hello to Mick Glover, got a final weather briefing on the phone from the met office and collected his flight bag of obligatory documentation and spare hand-held aeronautical radio. Into this, he slipped his air navigation charts, his flight planning tablet, scale, flight calculator and the filed flight plan to Livingstone in Zambia. He had filed for take-off at 12hr15 Zulu (2:15pm local time). This was no accident. The take-off was timed to ensure that the passengers were well ensconced in their accommodation before sunset. Finally he checked to see that his passport was in his top pocket.

"Cheers guys, see you on Monday."

"Cheers Harry, break a leg." Harry went out onto the tarmac and dumped his flight bag in the cockpit, checked to see that the first aid kit, signal strips and metal mirror were on board, walked around the Baron with his fuel tester in his hand, quickly but carefully doing a pre-flight check. Nothing caught his eye and the fuel he'd drained from the tanks was clear of water, this was a good AMO[98], he thought. He walked to the terminal, arriving back with his passengers almost exactly 15 minutes after leaving them there. Grabbing his bag, he directed them through to passport control and customs. These procedures took a further 15 minutes, and soon they were walking across the tarmac to the aircraft. In 5 minutes he had the baggage stowed and he and his passengers strapped in on board. He put on his baseball cap and Raybans, briefed the passengers about the flight and started up, starboard engine first. Once the two donkeys had settled down at 800 rpm, the electrical charge was positive and temperatures and pressures were in the 'green', he called the tower.

"Harare Tower, Fox Sierra Whisky – taxi clearance for a flight to Livingstone, flight plan reference 9 slash 898, four on board."

"FSW, Tower – cleared taxi holding point runway 02, QNH 1015, wind steady 15 at 10°." He repeated his instructions, adjusted the subscale of the altimeter, calibrated the FSI against the compass, ensured both fuel tanks were showing full, noted which tank he was on, checked around the aircraft and flicked the brake switch to the 'off' position, and let it roll.

Thus, another flawless routine flight started. As they approached the Victoria Falls two and a quarter hours later, they'd had to fly around a couple of heavy storm cells, he got clearance to do a low level orbit for the passengers, giving them an unparalleled view of one of the most spectacular sights on earth. He then joined left downwind for runway 27 and landed. 15 minutes later they were clearing customs at Livingstone. The airport was well maintained with a shady Mimosa lined tarmac parking area. The open Land Rover from the camp was waiting for them outside in the shade because even though it was after five in the afternoon it was still baking hot. A good-looking smiling black man in smart khaki bush gear approached them and addressed Harry.

"Good afternoon Sir, guests for Kudu Cabins?"

"Hi, yes. I'm Harry, these folks are Mr. and Mrs. Schneider and Miss Schneider. They are from Germany."

"Good afternoon Madams, Sir, welcome to Zambia. I am David, your driver and guide. May I take your luggage?" With this, he dumped the bags into the back of the vehicle, opened the door so everyone could clamber aboard and seat themselves on the padded elevated game viewing benches. David took them via Mosi-oa-Tunya[99] Road for a quick view of the Falls from the northern bank, and then on to the lodge.

Harry found the pilot's bedroom (all bush lodges had a room reserved for pilots. Often they had to share with one or more other pilots when things were busy). He changed into khaki shirt, shorts and creepers and wandered over to the pub. He was looking forward to two days of idle relaxation, while David drove his charges around sightseeing.

The pub itself was really nothing more than a wooden floor with a railing around it, cantilevered out high over the bank of the Zambezi River. Harry sat down on a deck chair, ordered a beer and sorted out his pipe. Then he sat back to admire the sunset over the river. Even though he'd experienced it many times, he really enjoyed this unique spectacle. The sun filters through the clear air of the upper atmosphere and wisps of altostratus clouds and then descends in a fiery glow over the river, highlighting the Illala palms along the banks in a symphony of colour that lasts for several minutes.

"Beautiful isn't it?" a man said. He'd moved like a cat. Harry hadn't heard him come up next to him as he concentrated on the lovely view. Harry, to his credit, never flinched.

"You're so right and it's really one of the rare views in the world. Nothing, anywhere, ever looked like this," he replied, "and it's something that I look forward to every time I come to the Zambezi."

"Do you come here often?" the man asked, almost from a distance. He was obviously also enthralled by the sunset. Harry turned to look at the man. He was a delightful rotund shiny jovial black man who was joined at that moment by another man whom Harry was to learn was one of the priests from an Assembly of God Mission in Livingstone.

"Yes, as often as I can get away." Harry got up and smiled at the man.

"Won't you gentlemen join me? He waved at the nearby seating.

"And may I get you a drink?' asked Harry. "What about you Father?" he asked turning to the priest.

"Thanks very much, Sir" the priest responded, "I'd like a coke." Harry looked at the black man.

"That's very kind of you. Thanks, I'll have a Zambezi." Harry took the empty glass from the priest and went off to the bar to order the drinks. When he got back, the black man had pulled up a chair and was nattering to the priest. The priest was leaning against the handrail looking out over the water.

"Some of the guests went into the market today to see if they could find some curios," the priest said as Harry sat down. "Oh, uh, this is Jackson, and my name is Lawrence.' They leant over and shook hands with Harry.

"Hi Jackson, Lawrence, I'm Harry." Harry said smiling, "The drinks are on their way."

"Thank you very much, you're most kind. I was telling Jackson that today, some of the guests went into the market in Livingstone to buy some curios. Sadly they thought the place was very run down. There was very little in the way of goods on display at all. They were really quite disappointed." Harry had no comment and didn't know where the conversation was heading. He gazed out over the river for a moment and then turned to Lawrence.

"Sorry, I came into this discussion right in the middle."

"No problem," said Jackson, "we are both concerned because we are unfortunately in a lot of trouble here in the Livingstone area." The drinks arrived and for a few moments his words were cut short while Harry signed the chit.

"How so?" Harry asked.

"Well, all commercial activity in Livingstone has essentially come to a halt."

"Yes, we noticed a lot of shops and buildings shut up." Harry observed.

"Yes, but for the tourists and the trucking traffic, there would be nothing. Most agricultural produce from the local commercial farmers goes straight to Lusaka, so there is not even a viable vegetable market anymore. Only one bank remains operational and that is only because it is supported by the Government accounts."

"What, then, is the problem?" Harry asked.

"AIDS." Jackson shifted in his seat. "In my opinion the incident of HIV-AIDS has now reached the level where normal economic life is no longer sustainable. Our hospital is full to overflowing and they are now just sending people home to die. The Father here will tell you that the situation is now desperate." The priest looked across.

"I'm here with the Assembly of God AIDS mission. We believe that the incidence of HIV-AIDS in Livingstone has reached somewhere in the order of 80% of the populous."

"Good Lord, that's phenomenal!" Harry was staggered.

"It certainly is. Furthermore, it is our belief that these sort of figures are pretty well the norm in all the city areas of Zambia. The country is now in a very bad position."

"But I'd understood that there was some kind of threshold at around 30-35%," Harry offered.

"Yes, we understand that there is," the priest responded, "but that's for the entire population, including the poorer rural areas."

"So you're saying that in the rural areas the incidence is very much lower?"

"Certainly, but therein lies the problem. It is the educated, employed and socially active population that is most adversely affected. The people that hitherto ran the government and worked in commerce and industry."

"Ah, I get the picture," Harry said thinking aloud. "Is this epidemic being brought under control at all?"

"No, it's getting worse and its spreading southwards like wildfire. The situation in Zimbabwe, despite denials by government, is becoming critical, and in Botswana and South Africa."

Harry was at a loss for words. Here it was, from the horse's mouth, so to speak, the people at the coalface. He looked at the others in dismay. He thought to himself how much he loved Africa and how saddened he was that it was falling apart. His thoughts turned inwards thinking about how the problem could be resolved. He concluded that in the short term, it was probably impossible, taking into account the limited resources these countries had. Even if they had the drugs, they'd need thousands of doctors to administer to the afflicted. Also, he couldn't see that it was possible to change the hearts and minds of the people such that it would have an influence on their sexual habits enough to stop the spread of the disease.

It was in this preoccupied frame of mind that he went with the two men across to the 'boma' for supper. He admired the view of the river for a moment, resolved to get Annie to initiate an education process on HIV-AIDS at the farm, sighed and then settled down at his own little table. He stretched out a little and gazed intently into a magnificent fire. He inhaled the rich aroma of the sizzling roasting impala to one side of the fire. It was mouth-watering. He took a sip of his lager and sighed again. What a pleasure. So intent was he that the thumping of running feet never registered on his conscious mind. The scream of, "You! You bastard!" did register, but far too late.

Then his world turned upside down, literally. He felt a blow to his back that sent him forwards into and over the top of his table, soaking his face and shirt in beer. His head hit the raked sand around the fire with a painful thump and in turn, entangled his legs as he landed spread eagled on his stomach trying to catch his breath, the table flew over him and landed with a shower of sparks in the fire, showering the impala with ash and sparks. The speed with which he rolled and jerked his feet away from the edge of the fire was a purely involuntary reaction, but thereafter, the speed with which he rose, pirouetting as he did so to face his attacker, was not. It was the schooled reaction of a born fighter. He crouched, filthy, searching, the periphery of his eyes noting people all around scrambling out the way as he focussed on the enormous man in front of him.

"Mr. bloody Andrews, you've got a fucking cheek coming here!" shouted the advancing man. For a while, Harry couldn't work out what the hell was happening and who this was, but backing rapidly away, sucking in air and trying to take it all in, it came back to him. He hadn't seen the man for nearly 20 years, Brad Fischer or, to be more precise, Broderik Volker. The man had put on a lot of weight but he looked as strong as an ox. His mouth fell open; he couldn't help it. Hell, it's happened again, thought Harry, the memory of the aircraft accident so long ago, flashing through his mind. What a disaster.

Fischer rushed at him again and it was only pure reflex that saved Harry. He dropped and rolled forwards under Fischer's swinging arm. As he rose, he pivoted and whipped out a sharp knuckle punch to the kidney area exposed below Fischer's raised arm. Fischer roared in frustration and pain and turned. Harry screamed at him,

"For Christ's sake Fischer, the war's over! Why the hell are you having a go at me?" Again, almost the same thought as years ago flashed through his mind. If this bugger catches me I'm finished. He flicked his eyes around noting the fact that he was cornered, and then saw Jackson try to hold Fischer, shouting in his ear. Jackson himself was a large man, but Fischer literally shrugged him off as if he wasn't there. As Jackson fell backwards, Fischer advanced again, this time more slowly and whispered menacingly,

"I'm going to get you, you arrogant bastard." His voice was almost drowned in the shouts and screams of the others around the boma, begging him to stop. He ignored them and as he advanced he drew his sheath knife. Harry was horrified, his gaze riveted on the 8-inch blade advancing towards him. The thought struck him that this man meant to kill him. He broke away and shrank back against the wall of the boma behind him, his eyes searching for a way out. He thought of jumping the wall, but realised Fischer would get him long before he made it over. Fischer smiled, now only six feet away, "Come, Herr Andrews, you are not afraid, are you?" He feinted to the left but Harry was already moving. He crouched and swept up the shovel used to gather the coals.

"Stand back, Fischer!" he shouted, brandishing the spade in front of himself. Fischer just laughed and lunged. The knife raked across Harry's ribs, tearing his shirt, blood spewing out as he leapt left and then right again away from the fire. But Fischer leapt back also, trapping him between the wall and the fire again. Flinching at the burning in his chest, he shouted at Fischer again,

"Fischer, STOP! What are you trying to do, kill me?"

"Yes!" he screamed and with that he leapt at Harry again. But this time, Harry was ready for him. He'd shifted the shovel into both hands, blocked the rising knife strike, and without waiting, in one fluid movement struck the side of Fischer's head with the edge of the shovel blade. The impact cut through Fischer's ear, temple and scalp and stopped only when it crushed into his skull. Fischer crashed to the ground like a sack of maize and but for one twitch of his leg, didn't move again.

Harry let go of the shovel and fell to his knees, clutching at his chest, almost sobbing while he gasped to get his breath back. He looked down at the blood seeping rapidly all over his hands and the sand below him and then across at Fischer. Seeing the huge bloody gash in the side of Fischer's head, he realised the man was in trouble.

"Oh my God," escaped his lips as he crawled forwards reaching out to feel Fischer's wrist for a pulse. Fischer was stone dead. "Oh my God, I've killed him," he said aloud. He felt a hand on his shoulder. It was Jackson. He was shouting orders around him and then said,

"Please move back Mr. Andrews and sit down in this seat." He drew up a chair. "I am a policeman Mr. Andrews; please do not move from that chair. I have called for someone to help you with that wound. Just wait a few minutes." With that he turned, shouting more orders to the other staff as he took control.

While Annie read the latest e-mail from Barbara, she became more and more agitated.

'… Pete spends a lot of his spare time down in Kings Cross at a pub frequented by a whole bunch of ex-Rhodesians. Lots of "When-We" maudlin, all of them with some moan or another about what happened to them. I went with him once and couldn't stand it. Even chaps like old man James Huxley and some of the others we used to know back home in Rhodesia have become total bores.' Annie considered this briefly thinking of all their friends that had left. There were so many of them. She carried on and phrases like, 'I can't carry on', 'Pete gets upset when I talk to you on the phone', 'do you find Harry to be a control freak?', 'he blames Harry for the death of his Mum and dad', brought tears to her eyes. Annie poured herself another cup of tea, careful not to spill any on the computer keyboard, shouted through to Robbie to turn the music down, and then turned back to the e-mail. She got to the last paragraph of the mail.

'Annie, I love and miss you so much, but I must listen to Pete. Please don't be upset, but for the moment, I'm not going to write anymore. I have to support Pete, he is my husband, and if he doesn't want me to talk to *"that bloody Pirate's wife"* I have to listen to him. He gets very upset if he catches me talking to you on the phone and he doesn't even want to know how you or Robbie and Bev are.

My darling Annie, we've been through so much together and you've been the very best friend a girl could have, but this will be my last letter to you. Please look after yourself and the children. The papers here are full of what's going on over there and I do worry.' Annie stopped reading for a moment. God, she thought, no mention of well wishes for Harry, nothing. She sighed and sat back sipping her tea. Poor Barbara, she must be going through hell. She thought back to that first date so long ago, when all four of them had met and hit it off so well. Who'd have thought that this is what it would come to. Her mind turned to the concept of hate and the discussions she'd had with Harry. How it eats away at you like a cancer. How you become irrational and in some cases violent. Poor Peter too. He was such a wonderful guy and he had made Babs so happy. She took a deep breath. Well I can't do anything about it, she said to herself. She put down the mug and turned back to the computer screen.

'So Annie, this is the end. And don't you worry about me, I'll be OK. Luv ya, Babs.xxx.'

Annie, her heart heavy with grief and not a little anger, thinking Pete was a bloody fool, sent a brief reply immediately, no sorry that it's come to this, no advice, no nothing. Just, 'I've received your sad mail. Love Annie.'

After saying good night to Bev and Robbie and reminding them to check that everything was locked up and the alarms were on, she went straight to bed but couldn't sleep. For an hour she just lay there gently sobbing for Barbara, then slowly, her thoughts turned to Harry. As she lay there she reviewed everything she could think of that she knew about him. She thought of his pig-headedness but after dissecting it, looked at it rather as steely determination, because she knew that he always listened to people around him very carefully. His rashness, she viewed as a basic fearlessness, a willingness to face problems head on. She'd seen him too often, totally unmoving, sometimes for exasperatingly long periods, contemplating his next move, but when he did, it was always at the double, sure and planned.

But foremost, she thought of his love for her and the children that he'd shown so tenderly so many times, especially after the farm was destroyed, and realised that Peter was wrong. Sure Harry was strong-minded and dominating, but she'd never known him to wish ill of anybody and given the option, he had a tendency initially to walk away from trouble. He was dynamic and energetically continued everything he took on until he was happy it had been achieved properly. She couldn't find any real faults in her man, except that sometimes he was too pedantic. Satisfied, she turned onto her side hugging his pillow and gradually began to doze off.

The beautiful image of Harry and her making love out on deck of their houseboat out in the middle of Lake Kariba dissipated, the incessant ringing, two longs and two shorts of the phone bringing her out of her deep sleep. Still groggy she threw on a gown and swayed into the den. No hellos, no name, just an exasperated,

"This better be important, it's the middle of the night and you've woken me up! Whoever else is on the line, put it down. This is private!" She listened as at least two other receivers on their party line put down their phones.

"Annie, its Jim here." Her heart sank as she sagged into the seat next to the desk. Oh my God he's had another prang.

"Annie, are you there?"

"Is he….?"

"No he's fine, Annie."

"Well?…" Her relief was vast, but she became aware of her heart pumping furiously.

"Annie, Harry's been arrested in Livingstone."

"Oh Jim, what's he done now? Why?"

"Well I'm not a hundred per cent sure, but it appears he got into a fight." She cut him short.

"Jim, you know that can't be. When have you ever known Harry not to walk away from those sorts of things?"

"Annie, I don't know, but it seems he killed Brad Fischer."

"Oh Christ Jim, he couldn't have?" She was close to losing control but shook herself, sat upright in the chair, sniffed and wiped her eyes on the sleeve of her fleece gown. "What do you know, Jim, and what can we do?"

"All I can tell you, Annie, is that we have received a call from the assistant manager at Kudu Cabins asking how we're going to get our passengers back to Harare. FSW has been impounded but the pax are due to return tomorrow. Apparently Harry has been detained in

Livingstone central prison. But leave that to me. I'll get an attorney down from Lusaka tomorrow and we'll see what we can do." He paused and when she said nothing, he continued, " There was something about self-defence, which I can believe because if I remember that arsehole, excuse my French, he probably attacked Harry, I'm flying the Bonanza there at first light to make the pick up and I'll find out everything I can and let you know immediately."

"Thank you Jim, but you could have left it until morning to phone me. Now I'll never get to sleep!"

"Annie, it is morning. I take off in an hour. Besides, I've just flown in from Biafra. Fortunately, I wasn't flying and was able to get some sleep." With that he was gone. She put down the phone as Bev and Robbie came into the den.

"What's happening Mum, we heard you shouting?"

"Good Lord, my darlings. Oh well, come through to the kitchen, and help me make a cup of tea and then I'll tell you all about it."

"Mr. Harry Andrews, good morning," said Jackson. Harry looked at him quizzically.

"Morning Jackson," he answered looking around. "Nice day. Where am I?"

"All in good time, Mr. Andrews." Harry noted the formality, different from yesterday. "Sit down here, please?" said Jackson, indicating a seat. Leaning forwards, he picked up a steel teapot off the tray. "Tea? Here's some fresh toast, butter and marmalade, I'm sure you could do with a little sustenance."

Wary of what was happening, but sure he'd find out soon enough, Harry sat down as directed and tucked into a light breakfast.

"You are extremely lucky that Mrs. Volker was away seeing the doctors in Lusaka with her children."

"Mrs. Volker?.. Oh, you mean Marie Fischer. Why do you say that?" asked Harry.

"That's one seriously strong lady Mr. Andrews. She has been known to pick up an AK47 and she's not scared to use it."

"I see what you mean." Harry immediately went into a moment of deep remorse, questions flooding his mind. What have I done? Killed a man with a wife and children. How are they going to survive? What is to become of them? Could I have done anything else? Tears came to his eyes and his sight blurred. Then with some resolution, he wiped his eyes using his handkerchief and thought, well, if I've got to pay the price, so be it. He looked across at Jackson. The accommodation he had been provided wasn't actually in the prison, but was in fact in a staff house, well guarded by armed policemen, in the grounds of the Police Camp on the outskirts of Livingstone. Harry didn't actually know this, he didn't know where he was. All he knew was that he'd woken up with a searing pain across his chest, which he instantly discovered was neatly and tightly wrapped in bandages.

For a while, he lay there wondering what had happened to his clothes and contemplating his surroundings and his fate He then gingerly sat up on the bed. The lime-washed walls were spotless and the room was pleasant and airy. Even the bed with its kapok mattress was comfortable. He saw his overnight bag placed on an upright wooden chair near the door. Folded on top of it were some neatly pressed khakis and a pair of underpants, which he recognised as the clothes he'd been wearing. He wondered if the shirt had been stitched up. Placed next to the chair on the floor were his creepers and black shoes and his flight bag. He looked out of the window and heard a continuous roar in the background, which, it took him a few moments to realise, was the sound of the Zambezi thundering over the falls. The view was one of neat lawns and pathways under acacia and mopane trees, all with two feet of lime-wash at the base of the trunk to ward off the termites. He got to his feet, and as he moved across the room towards his clothes, he experienced the agony of the stitches pulling at the skin on his chest. But he was cheerful and felt quite good as he put on some clothes.

He then walked out of the door of the bedroom and found the bathroom directly opposite him. His shaving gear, hairbrush and toothbrush were laid out neatly on the shelf, with towels, shampoo and soap by the bath. Half an hour later, pipe and bacci in hand and feeling fantastic despite the pain, he wandered out onto the veranda where he found Jackson reclining in a wicker chair.

So he finished his toast, poured a second cup of tea and leaned back in the chair. He still didn't really know who Jackson was.

"With respect, Jackson, who are you?"

"Ah…. You don't know?"

"Haven't a clue, but you must be important." Jackson thought back for a while.

"No, I don't suppose there's any reason for you to know, but Mr. Andrews, I suspect that you and I have crossed swords before."

"Can't imagine where, or why?" Not aggressively, just a statement of fact. Harry started fiddling with his pipe as if to hide his confusion. Jackson laughed.

"However, you might have heard of me. Jackson Motswadi. When you and I might well have met under different circumstances, I was the PCI who was chasing a man whom I suspect was you, around Zambia." Harry was dumbfounded. Of course, he thought, hence the connection with Fischer. He remembered everything Peter Templar had told him about Motswadi. Now I'm in for the high jump he thought. But his voice betrayed none of his dread.

"Well, well, I have to say everything I've heard about you is very complimentary. But surely you're no longer a PCI?"

Jackson laughed again. "No, I'm a Chief Superintendent now, I'm afraid. I sometimes wish I wasn't. Always so much political interference." Harry sat very still for a moment then stuck his chin out.

"Well, Chief Superintendent, congratulations. But perhaps now that we've got that out of the way, you'll be able to tell me what's going on. Am I under arrest?"

"As a matter of fact, no. Last night was clearly a case of self-defence, and you'll be pleased to hear that I have already taken four sworn statements confirming the fact. However, I'm not going to release you until you and I have had a long chat about all those goings-on so long ago. I really would like to get the record straight in my mind."

"Oh," said Harry. "What goings-on would those be?" Harry was never one to give away much.

"Come Mr. Andrews, I won't beat about the bush, as you would say. This is all strictly off the record. Times have changed. At the time, God knows why, we were at war, and sadly, I'm sure you will agree, the wrong people have taken power in your country. But that is as may be. I have no reason whatsoever to arrest you for what happened then. We do not have a docket and I do not intend to open one." He took a deep breath, a sip of his tea and then turned his smiling gaze away from a rotating sprinkler out on the lawn and looked at Harry.

"Your actions, Mr. Andrews, that is, your efforts at avoiding shooting or permanently injuring any of my guards at Mumbwa, have gained you my everlasting respect even though it nearly cost you your life. And believe me, Harry, if you don't mind me calling you that?" Harry shook his head. "Well, if we'd have caught you, that is exactly what would have happened. It would have been out of my hands. I hope you will appreciate that the decision would have been entirely political; my hands would have been tied. But fortunately it didn't happen, No? You escaped! Ha.., what a goose chase you led us on." He laughed loudly. "I remember it like yesterday and still today can't believe how you managed it. So all I want to do is establish what really did happen."

Harry was increasingly impressed by this man. He was erudite, well informed and straight talking. These were rare commodities in Africa these days.

"However, our chat will have to wait. Your boss, Jim Leonard, is on his way over here to see you and I have some matters to attend to." He got up and leaned over to shake hands. "Harry, you must relax, in any case, the doctor says you cannot fly in your present drugged state, so you're going to be here as my guest for a few days at least. Should we meet again this afternoon, for tea, say at 4:00pm? I'll see you then." Still gripping Motswadi's hand, Harry stood up.

"Thank you very much, Jackson." He shook Motswadi's hand firmly. "Everything I've heard about you is true. You really are a great man and I hope one day you will be able to meet my friend and the foreman of my farm, Sampson Ndlovu. You two would really get on well."

"Oh... Who is this Sampson Ndlovu?"

"He was with me at Mumbwa, dressed as a Police Superintendent. We even gave him the name, Cedric Mtombe, although fortunately he never had to use it. He couldn't aspirate 'Cedric'; it came more like 'Shedwick'. We still tease him about it." Both men stood there looking at each other and then burst out laughing.

With that, Motswadi left, moving with great agility down the steps of the porch. Harry stared after him, sucking his pipe furiously; his mind working at double time. My God, what an amazing turn of events!

CHAPTER 36

"Well, as you can imagine, my relief was enormous," continued Harry. "He debriefed me on every aspect of the Mumbwa breakout and my relationship with Volker. Three days later, after Jackson Motswadi and I had spent hours and hours together, I was released and allowed to go back to Harare, no warnings, nothing. In fact I think Motswadi and I became firm friends in the process. He's a really great guy and I've seen him several times since."

"What about Marie Fischer?"

"Oh, according to Jackson, she really took the whole thing quite stoically. Apparently she intended to return to Germany with her children. Since the fall of the Berlin wall and the collapse of East Germany, she had been keen to get back. She apparently still had family there. And once Apartheid had been put to the sword in South Africa and Namibia, the spy and terrorist business had in any case collapsed, I suppose. Interesting that she turned into a capitalist during her time in Africa," Harry laughed. "That's ironic isn't it?" He looked at his watch. "Hell guys, its nearly five o'clock in the morning. I've kept you up all night with my bullshit and I promised Bunty I'd mow her lawn today! Got to get some sleep."

It was hot, hot as only Africa can get before the rains really set in.

Annie was grateful that she'd had the sense to wear a light billowy summer frock, flat sandals and broad woven hat to keep the blistering heat of the sun off her face and shoulders.

The Doctor at Karoi Hospital was as good as his word. All the information she had requested on the AIDS epidemic was there, nicely bundled into a series of files and slides. There were hand-outs in English and Shishona, and there were several A0 size posters for her to put up in the clinic to lecture from. She was sure Harry would be suitably impressed. She dumped it all in the back of her Land Cruiser, which, surprisingly, they had been able to salvage from the burnt-out barn. Decent vehicles were difficult to get in Zimbabwe and so the cost had been worth it. She then walked the 30 yards or so to the post office.

She collected the mail and put it all in her wicker carry-bag, thinking that she'd start going through it at the club after lunch. Finishing her chores in town she then drove out to the club, air-con on at full blast. She waved at a couple of their friends putting-out on the 7th green as she drove into the grounds, noting that the golf course was looking fairly parched. The rains were late this year. Thank goodness Harry had invested so much in building weirs and putting in a pretty sophisticated irrigation system. They'd be in a pickle if he hadn't. As it was, Merrywaters and the annexe had all the water they needed even though they had over 210 acres under irrigation. The crop sprayers were flying there at the moment and Annie had decided to stay at the club for the day, leaving Chadrack in charge. Harry was away on another camping and hunting trip with Sampson.

Chadrack himself was busy trying to chase off a troop of baboons that were raiding the maize lands. He had managed to shoot four of the buggers they'd caught in calabash[100] traps, but they were persistent, indicating that the wilds were also suffering from the drought. Easier for the baboons to raid well-watered mealie[101] cobs. The trouble was though, they were greedy and would individually strip dozens of cobs off the maize stalks and end up running off with only one. Every time they lifted their arms to place a cob under their armpit, the cob they'd taken from the previous stalk, would fall to the ground. It would be extremely funny to watch them doing this, but for the fact that they were a bloody menace and could ruin a crop in one day.

After a pleasant lunch on the club dining room veranda, nods and natters with the odd person she knew, Annie took her coffee out in the garden under the spreading shade of a large pod mahogany tree (*Afzelia quanzensis*), relishing the cooling breeze that comes before a storm. A beautiful, flowering, purple bougainvillea draped over some lime-washed pillars provided additional shade. She reached into her carry-bag and dumped the pile of letters, bills and junk mail onto the wooden slatted table top, keeping a brown paper packet between her feet for the opened envelopes and papers she didn't want to keep. She started by leafing through them, separating them into letters, identifiable bills, and unknown. The bills she put straight back into her carry-bag. Nothing is going to ruin my afternoon, she thought. Then she turned to the unknowns. A couple were Notams[102] and Aviation advisories for Harry, a notification from Conex and a product list from Levy's wholesalers, all of which she put into her carry-bag. The rest was junk, which she stuffed into the brown paper packet for disposal.

Turning then to the letters, she leafed through these again and was about to open a letter that she knew was from her Mum, when an Australian stamp and postmark caught her eye.

She picked it up and flipped it over. On the back it said,

Sender: James Huxley, Central Police Station, Sydney, Australia.

Goodness, James Huxley, haven't heard hide nor hair of him since he took the gap in '94, thought Annie, very surprised. She sat quietly for a moment thinking of all their friends who'd left. Bill Sturrock had gone to Johannesburg and now ran a security company. God, there are so few of us left. She ripped open the letter to which was attached a newspaper cutting, which she read immediately, with growing horror. She almost fainted and before reading it completely she had to stop and get her breathing under control. She sat forwards shaking, reached for the coffeepot and carefully poured herself another cup. She put in half a sugar, slowly stirred it breathing as slowly as she could and then she slowly took a sip. Only then did she try to continue reading, but at first she couldn't because the tears kept flooding into her eyes.

THE WYVERN REVENGE

THE SYDNEY EVENING STANDARD
FRIDAY SEPTEMBER 28 1998

Policeman found dead.
Own correspondent
....
Sydney, Friday morning.

Sydney Police headquarters disclosed this morning that the body of a man was fished out of Sydney Harbour. The next of kin have been informed and it can be revealed that the man was a member of the Sydney Harbour Police. He has been identified as Police Inspector Peter Templar. He was married and had two teenage children and is thought to have been living in Manly.

It is initially reported that PI Templar had been out having an evening with friends and left at approximately 9:30pm on Thursday evening.

He never arrived home and the police were alerted that he was missing by his family during the night.

It is believed that he fell overboard the last Sydney-Manly ferry, which it is known he boarded. He was well known to the crew of the ferry, who advise that he used the ferry every morning and evening.

Foul play is not suspected and the police are at the present time treating the matter as an accidental death.

Annie read James Huxley's letter in absolute disbelief as he told her that Barbara had decided to leave Australia and go home to England. Her house was on the market and the tickets for her and the children had already been bought and paid for by her father. It was expected that she would be leaving within two months. Annie picked up her mobile phone and dialled Harry's number. No answer, he must still be out of range in the bush, so she left a message for him to phone back and phoned Biddie Glover.

Thirty hours later, Harry, with Mick Glover along to keep him company on the way back, flew Biddy and Annie into Jan Smuts International, Johannesburg. A minibus collected them at the aircraft and took them from the private aircraft parking area, the half-mile or so past a row of a dozen or more airliners of all nationalities, to the main international terminal, where they all went straight into the transit lounge. Harry arranged for the luggage to be transferred and thirty minutes later at 7:30pm, the first call came for the SAA flight 622 to Sydney. Hugs and kisses and final orders from the women to their men, and they were gone.

Harry left Mick in the international departure lounge and spent the next hour and a half going through the tedious process of having the Baron refuelled, confirming his return flight plan lodged in Harare, and getting the weather from the met office. Mick wasn't overly concerned about the time it took because Harry had told him that he didn't want to start back until the engines of the Baron were stone cold. Teledyne Continental IO520 engines were a real bitch to hot-start. Eventually they got away at 9:30, half an hour after the SAA 747 trundled off down the 2 mile long runway on its way to Australia. They were back in Harare half an hour after midnight after an uneventful but beautiful night flight back. Harry was back at the farm by 9:30 the following morning.

Biddie and Annie, comfortable in business class, spent a pleasant night asleep during the Indian Ocean crossing arriving fresh and alert in Perth. After a short stop, whilst the jumbo was refuelled, cleaned-up and replenished, they were on their way again on the five hour cross-Australia flight to Sydney. They didn't stop talking until they got there. James Huxley, looking his now not inconsiderable age, met them in terminal 2 at Sydney International and drove them the 20 miles or so, over the Harbour Bridge to their hotel.

"Barbara is in a hell of a state, Annie. She told me that you two have been no-speaks for some years, and she doesn't know what she's going to say to you both."

"Oh James, don't you worry, I'm sure it'll work out. Anyway, Biddie will keep the peace. But we've got to help her anyway we can, even if its just to comfort her."

"But James, you haven't told us how you're doing?" interjected Biddie. And so they carried on until Huxley dropped them off in front of The Manly Pacific Hotel in North Steyne, Manly. By 5:30pm, the two women had checked in, bathed and were waiting in the lounge for delivery of their Budget Hire car. Huxley had advised Barbara that Annie and Biddie would be at her house by 6:00pm. They were talking about why they weren't feeling jet-lagged while Annie sent a text to Harry, when the concierge brought over the car-hire man.

When Barbara opened the door to them, Annie burst out crying and they just simply fell into each others arms. Everything between them turned out fine and Annie began to realise that she shouldn't have worried. Exhausted, Biddie and Annie only got back to the hotel at four the following morning, much water under the bridge.

They spent the next four days going through Barbara's plight, her plans for the future, getting to know the two girls again, and visiting Peter's plaque in the garden of remembrance at the Anglican Church in William Street round the corner from Barbara's house. The house had already been sold and the women all started sobbing as the movers came to take all the furniture off to the auctioneers. They got through it by helping Barbara clean up the house thoroughly, so that the new owners could move straight in.

Then it was over. Barbara and her children left on the BA flight to London, followed one hour later by Biddie and Annie on the similarly long haul back to Johannesburg.

Sampson and Harry had developed an incredible relationship of mutual like and respect. They stood, leaning against Harry's new Peugeot 404 truck, watching a platoon of women weeding a field of young maize. Harry pushed back his hat, removed a well chewed grass stem from his mouth and dropped it on the ground.

"Sam, I think its time that you and Chadrack bought your own farm."

Sampson thought about this for a moment then said obliquely,

"Boss Harry, does the Reedbuck[103] leave the river and go to the desert?"

"What do you mean, Sam? You really do like your riddles."

"Boss Harry, I would be a fool to leave here. Here, my family and

I have a comfortable house and everything we have ever wanted. My children are being educated properly, we are healthy and I have many fine cattle[104]. I have an excellent job, many concubines, and besides, I like it here with you and Miss Annie. I cannot leave. For Chadrack it is the same. It is also the same for all the other men that work for you."

"But Sam, I don't know how long this will carry on. Many farms have been destroyed. The government is intent on getting rid of the white farmers. I don't know when our turn will come, but it will come. They have even stopped paying for the farms now, so when it happens, I am not sure that I will be able to help any of you very much."

"These people, Mr. Mugabe, they are so stupid. Does the Honey Badger kill the Honey Guide[105]?"

"A riddle again, Sam. As much as I love them, what do you mean this time?"

"Boss Harry, I have heard you talking to Master Peter before about killing the golden goose. It means the same thing."

"Well, that's all very well. Bit it still doesn't answer the question."

"The men, all of us, have discussed this matter and we have decided that we must help you to fight them when they come. For us too, we will loose everything if they take away this farm. They will give the farm to one of the Mugabe people, and we will be chased away. And where will we go? There is nowhere."

Harry didn't say anything for a while, but chose the moment to haul out his pipe. After a while, once he had it going, he responded.

"Sam, you cannot fight them. The army and the police are helping them and you would be stupid to make any more enemies. They will already be suspicious of all of you, because you work for me. No, instead, when they come, I want you all to leave straightaway and my job therefore is to make sure that you and the others do have somewhere to go. Now, there is a farm for sale near Makuti, very cheap. It's on the escarpment overlooking Mana Pools National Park off the Chewore Road. It's a good 20 klicks off the main road, so it will suit our requirements very well. I think it is big enough for you all to go to and make a Kibbutz."

"What is this Kibbutz, Boss Harry?"

"It is a farm that you all work on and share the profits. You do not divide it up into small farms because it is more efficient to run it as one big farm with all the necessary machinery. Even though you and Chadrack will be the bosses, all the people who work on the farm, share in the profit accordingly."

"This is very interesting; I must talk to all the men about it."

"No, not until you, Chadrack and I have spoken for a long time about it. Peter and I have discussed this many times when he was here and Miss Annie and I, we have made a plan of how it will work properly, which I must show you and teach you. You will be able to make everybody sign an agreement that I have had the lawyer prepare. This will make the rules for everybody, how they will be paid, and," he repeated, "everyone will profit."

Sampson was flabbergasted. He could not believe that this man, his friend and boss, had done all of this for the people.

"But back to the farm," said Harry, "it is not well developed because the owner was killed there during the war and all the buildings and equipment were destroyed. All the workers have gone and there are just a few people looking after it for the wife and children of the farmer, who took the gap and went to South Africa."

"How, Boss Harry? We cannot afford to buy this farm."

"Yes you can. Let me tell you how. I have already spoken to the lady in Johannesburg and she is prepared to take her money in Rands. I have enough money in my bank in RSA to pay her cash. What we will do however, is make an agreement of sale here for Zim$50 000 in favour of you and Chadrack…"

Sampson interrupted.

"Chadrack and me, we cannot afford $50 000."

"Wait, Sam, I'll tell you how we do this. You will sell me all your cattle.."

Another interruption, Sam was horrified.

"Boss Harry, we can't do that. It is everything we have."

"Wait, Sam, wait! You will use the money to buy the farm in your names, and then you will take the farm. Chadrack must go there straight away with as many of the labourers as possible, and the women, and we will together rebuild there. We will fix the fences, and slowly over the next few months, we will transfer some of the machines and the cattle to Makuti. You will have to dip them twice a week Sam, there will be many ticks."

"But we will not have the money to buy the mombes[106]?"

"No problem, I think we will lose them anyway and it is better for you to get them than Mugabe's dogs. Here, I want only to keep the maize, tobacco and maybe a few other things going, so when the dogs come, most of it will all be gone and the people will be safe. But Sam, there is much to do, and we must act fast. I do not think that there is much time."

"How, Boss Harry, this is too much for me to understand. I cannot tell the people, because I am afraid that I will not be correct."

"Don't worry about it yet. I have much to teach you and Chadrack and once you completely understand, only then will we advise the rest. Also Sam…"

"Yes, Sir?"

"You must say nothing of these plans to anybody, and when we tell the rest, it will be only the older men, you understand?" Sampson nodded his head. "The reason for this is because women talk too much and young men brag too much. When the old men go with their families, they will say that they are moving to a new job, that's all. This will only work if the Mugabe dogs do not find out about it."

"Yes, Sir!"

"We will call this new farm 'Kiachingwa' (*key'a'ching'waa*), Place of Bread. And guess what?"

"What Master?

"Miss Annie and I, we will be working for and with you! The time of the white man in this country is now finished."

Sampson was sombre, realising that Harry was very serious. Boss Harry was prepared to give everything away to his workers, rather than loose it all to Mugabe's dogs. He looked at Harry and thought, not for the first time, that this was a man to die for.

"That will be wonderful, Master Harry. Chadrack and me, we will find a beautiful place high on the mountain overlooking the valley, and there we will first build you a fine house." Sam knew that escarpment countryside well and although he hadn't yet seen this farm, he had a clear image in his mind what it would look like.

They looked at each other and infectiously and simultaneously, they burst out laughing.

So began the fairly rapid transfer of the wealth of the Merrywaters farms. It just seemed to disappear and the Zimbabwe Government never did work out what happened to it all. The sweep of the white owned farms continued apace, while Sampson and Chadrack were given classes every second evening by Annie on farm book-keeping, livestock healthcare and pedigree lineage, especially how to inoculate against foot and mouth, anthrax, and other nasties that occasionally afflicted the livestock, and how to keep track of it all. She also showed them how to use all the reference books.

If all this stuff staggered the two men, then so did the lectures they received everyday and night with such emphasis and urgency from Harry. The legalities required to put together a Kibbutz type of commune were dealt with carefully with frequent trips into Harare to see the attorneys, and finally Sampson and Chadrack had a clear understanding of their rights and obligations and they were successfully able to impart the generality of it all to the elders amongst the work force.

Then there were Harry's lectures on crop and paddock rotation, contour ploughing, erosion, fertilization, pesticides, the use of cattle dip, and the myriad of other items of farming lore that he believed they should apply. They began to realise that commercial farming took a lot of knowledge and non-stop hard work and more than once threw their hands in the air and almost gave up. But Harry persisted,

"My friends," he shouted at them. "Do you think I am doing this for my health! Well,.." He giggled as the thought struck him that this was exactly why he was doing it, in an oblique kind of way, "perhaps I am. But believe me you two, we do not tell you all these things for your own health. We tell you these things, because these are the matters that you must attend to properly if you want to make money from the farm, and to keep it healthy." He was quite blunt. "These are many reasons why the white farmers do well and the black farmers generally do not. And no, this is not a criticism," he said, noticing that the statement had bridled Chadrack. "I understand that it is easy for you to keep to the traditional ways, but if you do, you will slowly become poor again. You look at the Tribal Trust lands, why do you think they are poor areas? Do you think that they were always like that? No, they were not. The traditional ways have made them poor; soil erosion, over cropping, no crop circulation, chopping down too many trees, not using fertiliser, not spraying or not using vaccines. And where is their irrigation? It's not only because the white men took the best land. I know the people are poor and they cannot afford to do many of these things, and most of them do not know better, but you do and you will be getting off to a good start." It was about the longest lecture Harry had ever given, He thought, God, I'm beginning to sound like Jim Leonard.

Barbara and her children arrived back in England at 7:30am in late November. It was cold and blustery and it was still dark. Oh boy, I'd forgotten about all this, she thought to herself. But she stuck her chin out. We're just going to have to knuckle under and get used to it. Her Mum and dad picked them up at Terminal 3 and four hours later, including an hour spent in the usual traffic congestion at the M4-M5 interchange north of Bristol, they arrived home in North Curry.

Efficient and hard working as always, Barbara set about getting information about local schools, getting the girls and herself registered at the local surgery and applying for Social Security numbers for them all. She walked down to the village shop and post office and picked up the DVLA driving licence application form and the local newspapers and immediately set about finding herself a job.

Within two weeks, after almost every day using her Mum as a taxi driver, her daughters were ensconced at the Badminton School for Girls in Westbury, Bristol, and she'd found a job as surgery nurse at the Westbury Surgery. Within a month, she had put in an offer for and secured, a lovely three bedroom flat, a block away from the zoo, which overlooked The Downs. She thanked her lucky stars, that over the years, at every opportunity, they had salted money away in their Jersey bank account. The only hiccup came when she tried to get hold of the bank to withdraw some of their savings. She found that the British government had changed the banking laws; so the Channel Islands were no longer treated as off-shore accounts and besides, her bank had been bought out by a larger Scottish Bank. It took them several days to find her deposit account and turn it into a current account based at their Bristol branch. In the long run, however, it proved to be a blessing in disguise, as it gave her an almost immediate credit rating, something that most returning ex-patriots battled with when returning to England.

The worry lines on her face started to disappear and as her tan faded, she started to look after herself again. At first, all the National Health Service protocols got her down, but after a few months she got on top of them. Her computer skills really came in handy in this environment and the only fear that she had was that she'd become bored with the lack of variation in primary health care, or angry with the apparent disdain the public had for the medical profession. Medical practice in Africa and Australia was highly respected and had been truly exciting because of the wide range of afflictions they'd had to deal with.

She bought a car and a computer, set up an internet connection and joined the Old Girls Tennis Club at Badminton. She frequently visited her own and Annie's parents and her daughters started to thrive at their new school. It seemed that in no time the elder girl had written her A levels and was gone up to Durham University to read Forensic Science. Their lives really began to take some shape.

Things settled down at Merrywaters also. Beverley went off to Cape Town University to read Medicine and three years later Robbie went off to the Swinburne Institute of Technology in Melbourne, Australia, to take a Bachelor's degree in Aviation Technology. He had messed about for a while working in odd jobs, generally in aviation, courtesy of his father's contacts, from grease monkey to dispatcher, so much so that flying and the aviation industry in general really began to get a hold on him. He then put his head down and got his private pilot's license flying Jim's last remaining V-tail Bonanza. He realised that the long road to a commercial pilot's licence was for mugs and he couldn't see himself earning next to nothing for years as an instructor in order to build up his hours, so he did his homework on career options before he approached Harry with the idea of university. He had selected two options, the Aviation School at Kansas U, or Swinburne. The cost had dictated the final selection, but not by much.

"Christ, I miss the kids," Harry said, putting his feet up on the lounge centre table. "The house seems empty without them, I just can't wait for the Christmas break. Should we go away?"

Annie flicked a wisp of hair off her face and leaned back to look at him.

"Well, it would be nice for us. But I'm sure the kids would prefer to be here. Remember, both of them finish this year and it's unlikely that we're all going to get together very often from here on, especially since Robbie has been accepted as an intern at Bell Helicopters in Fort Worth, Texas."

"Has Bevie decided finally where she's going to do her internship yet?"

"It looks like the Johannesburg General or Groete Schuur in Cape Town. I hope she gets into Groete Schuur. She loves Cape Town."

"Yeah. I don't particularly like the idea of her living in Johannesburg. The crime level is appalling."

"I've been thinking about that. Harry, do you think you can get hold of Bill Sturrock and ask him if she can stay at their place? As you know, it's too big for them anyway and it's out in Witkoppen. Mary runs a riding school out there, and on her time off, which won't be often, Bev can go riding, you know she'll enjoy that. They got riding trail rights over the nearby prison land. Also, it's only about 20 minutes from the Hospital on the Western by-pass and the M1 into the city, so she won't have to mess about in any of the dangerous areas. Oh, Harry, I don't know why I'm telling you all this. You've been to their place umpteen times more than I have."

Harry burst out laughing.

"Oh, you little minx." He leant over and tickled her. "You've worked it all out already haven't you? I can read you like a book."

Annie said nothing and had a hard time trying to look totally innocent.

"But that's fine. I like the idea of someone like Bill being on hand if she gets into any kind of bother. I suppose you've spoken to Mary about it?"

"Harry Andrews, I just can't keep anything from you for long, can I? Yes, it's all arranged, but I promised Mary that you would phone Bill to ask. Even if he says no, which he won't, Mary has already decided that it will happen."

"Ok, it's decided then. I'll phone Bill in the morning. Better still I'll have lunch with him on Thursday. I've got to go down for tractor parts and a new manifold gasket for your car."

"What, there's nothing wrong with my car?"

"My darling, you are the most wonderful wife a man could have, but you wouldn't know if there was something wrong with your car even if it blew up in your face. Thank goodness I take it upon myself to drive it once in a while."

"It sounds serious. Can you fix it? I don't want you to go messing up my car."

"A doddle. I'll do it over the weekend, take about three hours."

"Thank you my darling. You're so clever." Annie was teasing, so Harry tickled her again, and, as usual, one thing led to another.

At breakfast the following morning Harry looked lovingly at his wife.

"When did you say the kids will be home?"

"One of us must collect them from the airport on the 16th December," answered Annie.

"Annie, I am getting worried about the situation. Most of the local farms between here and Chinoyi have been invaded, so we really must be on our guard."

"How imminent do you think it is?"

"It's hard to tell. I've accelerated the transfer of everything to Kiachingwa. Our bungalow there is now ready for occupation whenever we need it. The staff are all organised and George's new house will be finished this week. You've got the school and clinic running properly and all the stock from the shop has been taken over. All the bagged maize has been transferred as well as the last of the tobacco we didn't sell last year. Most of this year's crops will come out of Kiachingwa, but that won't amount to much and we'll have to save it as feed maize for the staff and animals. We've only got two fields planted out with maize here. We are no longer needed here. The sooner we're out of here the better and safer. So I suggest that when the kids arrive, we pack up and go out to Kiachingwa immediately."

"Oh Harry, can't we at least spend our last Christmas here?"

CHAPTER 37

Shenje 'Himmler' Ndunze sat in comfort at the desk in the office in what had once been the lovely homestead at Chris Swan's farm. His men had ransacked the place, searching for booze, guns, women's clothing and food. He had his two senior men with him, both alternately swigging whisky from a looted bottle of Johnny Walker. Laid out on the desk in front of him were the maps and property ownership lists he and his men had obtained before leaving Harare. Ndunze actually didn't drink, not liking that feeling just before total drunkenness. He preferred to be in control of himself. But he kept his views about drinking to himself because he knew he'd be the laughing stock if he tried to control his men.

He put his finger tip on the map at a point where he had inserted a black circle with a marker pen. Under his hand, many of the farms contained a black circle drawn on them.

"We are here. I suggest that we go to this farm here next." He moved his finger up the page an inch. He leaned forwards and read the property description.

"Ahh... I think that I have been to this place before, Consolidated Portion 151 of the Farm Clearwater JQ. Who is the owner?" He looked across at his henchman who took his time looking through the list they'd got at the Land Registry.

"It is owned by a company, Merrywaters Farms (Pvt) Ltd."

"That's right, I remember. Yes, that is Merrywaters Farm. Bring in the cook; I want to talk to him."

Putting the now virtually empty whisky bottle down on the table, the other man rose and left immediately.

While he waited, Ndunze remembered the past.

"When I was a young man in the Second Chimorenga, we attacked this farm. We wiped it out, but the people protecting it were well organised and many comrades were killed. It was not a good night. The helicopters came and killed my Shamwaris (*friends*) right in front of my eyes. The dogs gave me these scars." He pointed to the multiple scars he carried to prove it. "I was lucky to escape." He tapped his forehead with his fingers for a moment, thinking hard. "It was owned by a man named Andrews, an Englishman. Let us see if he is still the owner."

He paged through the list of Company Directors they'd put together, but couldn't find Merrywaters Farms. "This list is useless; we have missed many of the farms that are owned in the name of companies. But we will see if this cook knows who the neighbour is." It took a while, but his aide came back eventually dragging the Swan's hapless cook into the room. The poor man collapsed onto the floor in front of Ndunze. He cringed, shaking as Ndunze picked up his bayonet from the table where it had been holding down a corner of the map. He flipped it in the air and in a flash flicked it into the parquet floor three inches from the cook's hand. The knife stood pegged there shivering for a moment before Ndunze lent over and pulled it up, dislodging the wooden floor tile a little as he did so. He nonchalantly stuck his foot out and pressed the tile back into place.

"What is your name?" he asked turning away and looking at the map again.

"Zephron, Changamire (*Chief/Sir*)."

"Zephron, you are now a free man, do you know that?"

Zephron looked at Ndunze, not really understanding.

"And as a free man, it is your duty to assist the country, do you agree?"

"Yes, Changamire."

"Well first of all, I want to know where the settler who ran this farm is."

"He is on holiday in Azania (*South Africa*)."

"When is he due back here?"

"After Christmas."

"OK,.. Well Zephron, you may go. You no longer work here. Take your family and go back to your tribal area. In fact tell all the workers, they no longer work here and must go. This farm has now been reallocated to the people." Ndunze said all this without once turning to look at Zephron, still grovelling on the floor.

"Yes, Changamire, thank you, Changamire." Zephron got to his feet and started to move backwards towards the door, his hands palms together in front of him in supplication. Ndunze waited until he was nearly at the door and then he swung around.

"By the way, Zephron, who is the farmer next door?" he waved vaguely towards the north.

Zephron, not even realising that he had been manipulated, answered immediately,

"Master Andrews." Ndunze never even blinked.

"He is there now?"

"Yes, Changamire."

"OK, you can go," Ndunze said dismissively. Zephron turned gratefully away and left the room. Ndunze had no intention of letting him go to warn Andrews. He looked up at his aide and gave the slightest of nods. The man got up, picked up the revolver that was holding down another corner of the map and then followed Zephron.

Ndunze didn't even blink when the shot rang out. Instead he leant forwards and scrutinised the map even more closely.

"This man Andrews was responsible for the death and capture of many comrades during the Chimorenga. It is time for us to visit revenge on him for those who fell that day." He turned to the other aide and said,

"Send out a scout. I want to know more about the security and the way things look on Merrywaters Farm. He must report back tomorrow morning and then we will plan our action. But for now, bring me that nice looking young maiden, was her name Emily? Yes that's the one, Emily."

Christmas Eve and Sampson Ndlovu surveyed the ground ahead of him as he cycled along the dirt track inside the Merrywaters boundary fence. He did this once a week to check the fences and to identify what animals, especially baboons and warthogs[107], were coming into or leaving the farm. That day, he was going off to Kiachingwa to spend a week with his family.

It was a fresh, dry morning and he could pick up the spoor crossing the track with such ease from his bicycle, he seldom had to dismount to undertake closer scrutiny. However, that morning he did have to dismount because the spoor he found were human, a lot of them. Furthermore, some effort had been taken to sweep away the signs of the footprints. He found several bunches of branches that had been used as swishes in the bush next to the track. Within minutes he established that they had entered just before dawn. The morning dew had been trodden on. Carefully and slowly following the tracks for about 200 yards through the bush, he missed very little. They had come from the south, which was interesting in itself because it meant that they'd been on the nextdoor farm. Sampson thought immediately of Chris Swan and his family and remembered that they were away in South Africa on holiday. He must remember to tell Boss Harry because maybe they had already invaded that farm.

There were about 30 men, moving fast at the trot, none of them barefooted. Several of them wore boots while the rest were wearing running shoes of one sort or the other which meant that they weren't military or the police. This was a gang. He observed that most of them were carrying something, two using their left hands and in minutes Sampson found a spot where they had stopped. He got down on his hands and knees and slowly worked his way around, crawling, using his knuckles. There is nothing more painful than a thorn or deviljie[108] through the palm of the hand. He counted with certainty, four places where knobkerries had been grounded and two, next to tree trunks, where rifle butts had rested. One man, with new boots, was clearly the leader. He could see this from the way the others had gathered around, most of the other footprints facing more or less to one spot. He got up and back-tracked to confirm this and found that most of the man's prints had been obliterated by others following him. But enough were left for him to note that the man tended to walk on the outside of his left foot. Sampson knew immediately that he would have no trouble identifying this track in the future.

He pressed on, following the gang until he was satisfied, but with growing alarm; he knew where they were headed.

Sampson ran back to his bicycle and raced back the way he had come and, sweating profusely, arrived at the homestead 25 minutes later. He went respectfully to the back door and called,

"George!"

George, in the kitchen, heard him and opened the door.

"Mangwanani (*Good Morning*), Sampson, makadii?"

"Ndiripo (*I am well*). Where is Boss Harry?"

Alerted by Sampson's abruptness, he didn't hesitate.

"I'll fetch him straight away." He turned on his heels and ran into the house calling, "Boss Harry, Boss Harry, come quick, come quick, Sampson is here!"

Harry came through quickly, immediately recognising the urgency in George's voice.

"Hi Sampson, come." He led the way across to the office calling behind him to George to bring coffee and rusks. They sat down and Sampson recited exactly what he'd discovered.

"Shit!" was all Harry could think of saying. He picked up his mobile and after a few moments found Chris Swan's home phone number. No answer, but then, he thought, that tells us nothing.

"If something is going to happen, we're not going to get any help today. Just about everybody will be on holiday." He sat quietly for a few minutes while Sampson waited patiently for instructions. George walked in carrying a tray of mugs and a plate of rusks. That seemed to precipitate a course of action.

"George, don't go, sit," he ordered flicking his fingers towards another chair. He got up. "Sampson, tell George what you've just told me, I'll go and get Miss Annie." He walked out, his mind working at fever pitch. He had no doubt that this was it, it had started again, but this time they had prepared more thoroughly.

In minutes, the four of them crowded into the small office, he held a "council of war". After discussing the ramifications of what they all believed was going to happen for ten minutes, Harry held up his hands,

"Ok, this is what we're going to do. George, you will go and get your family right now, and go to Kiachingwa. Take anyone you can and tell everybody to go now! Sampson will bring the lorry down to the compound in a minute and pick up anybody still around."

"Yes, Master Harry," he said not moving. There was a pause and Harry looked at him.

"Well, what are you waiting for, get moving! And take one of those flack-jackets."

"But, what about the kitchen, I am preparing your Christmas dinner for tonight?"

"Forget about it; it will only be me here to eat it. Now go, run!" George got up and almost tripped as he grabbed a flack-jacket, he was in such a hurry to leave. After he left, Harry addressed Sampson.

"Sampson, take the '2 tonner', collect whoever you find at the compound and take them to Kiachingwa. We have planned for this for years and you know exactly what to do. But..." Harry turned and unlocked the steel filing cabinet next to him. He reached in and removed his Beretta and a box of 9mm cartridges. "Here, it's all I have other than the two rifles. Be very careful Sampson. If they recognise you, it is possible that they will try to kill you."

Sampson stood, picked up his own oversized flack-jacket and took the pistol and ammunition from Harry, shook his hand and without a word ran out of the door.

Harry turned and placed his hand on Annie's shoulder, looking intently into her eyes.

"My darling, you must be quick. You and the kids pack a bag now. I want you out of here and at Kiachingwa as soon as possible. I'll go and get the Cruiser out. Hurry now." He let her go and made to move towards the steel cabinet. She held him back.

"Harry, I'm not leaving you here by yourself, forget it!" she said emphatically. She put her arms around him and drew him close. She turned her face up so that she could speak into his ear and said quietly, "you're my husband and what we built up here, we did together. We always have, and always will face our problems together."

Harry didn't know what to say because he knew that arguing with her would be a waste of time. He hugged her tightly, then said,

"OK, so be it. Go tell the kids to move," Harry handed her the protective clothes for herself, Bev and Robbie, "they can take the Cruiser, Bevie drives, Robbie to sit in the back seat riding 'shotgun'. He can take the 'Hornet'. Go, I'll get the guns and Cruiser organised now."

Within ten minutes, the Land Cruiser was loaded, hugs, kisses and tearful farewells completed. Shrugging into his own jacket, Harry pointed in the direction of the road,

"Now get out of here. Bevie, you don't stop for anyone or anything, you hear? And Robbie, you don't point that rifle at a soul, unless it looks like you're in serious trouble."

"Don't worry, Dad, we'll be fine." With that they were gone.

Harry and Annie, arm in arm, Harry, with the Winchester slung over his shoulder, waved good bye and then turned back into the house.

George died almost instantly. The knobkerrie hit him on the temple, crushing in his skull. He'd had time only to see his first wife Emily and their two daughters lying slaughtered on the floor of his living room and collapsed down next to them in grief. He hadn't even heard the man behind him. The compound had been quiet, but as his house was the closest to the homestead, it hadn't even occurred to him that there was anything wrong. His trusty old Chrysler Valiant was parked where it should be, there was nothing that wasn't as it should have been. He knew that most of the workers and their families were already at Kiachingwa.

Sampson threw his bike and the last of the bagged maize in the barn onto the back of the truck, drew a rope over it all, several times looping it through the tie-downs and made sure it was all tight. He then jumped in, laid the flack-jacket on the seat next to him, the Beretta and box of shells in the cubby hole and started up. He saw Miss Bevie driving off with Robbie in the back, and then reversed out of the driveway, selected first and turned left down towards the compound. Three minutes later, when he drove the big '2 tonner' through the compound, he saw no-one. Thinking that they had probably all gone he almost carried on, but then it struck him that George's car was still there. He slowed down looking around carefully. Sure enough there they were; at least thirty

THE WYVERN REVENGE

men trotting in a tight group, singing and shouting, waving firearms and sticks and knobkerries, appearing behind him from around some of the houses. They came to a halt about 50 yards away, still dancing and leaping up and down.

This is not good, thought Sampson, watching them through the back window of the truck. He leaned back without taking his eyes off them and fished the pistol out of the cubby hole. He fiddled around for a few seconds extracting the cartridges from the box and stuffed them into his left trouser pocket. Leaving the truck running, he then opened the door and leapt nimbly to the ground. Facing the crowd, pistol hidden behind his back, he called,

"What are you men doing here? What do you want?"

One man armed with an AK47 stepped forwards. As if this was the signal, all movement and shouting ceased instantly. Sampson felt the hair on the back of his neck prickle. He scrutinised the man carefully as he spoke, noting his lean, almost casual, posture; AK carelessly held, muzzle down in his right hand. He noted, also, the deference that the men behind him gave him. Here was the leader. Sampson glanced lower at the dusty, but obviously relatively new boots.

"We have come to reclaim this land for the people."

"But why, are not the people on this farm happy?"

"Many people are unhappy, many people need the land and it is time that the white settlers go, so that the people may take what is rightfully theirs."

With this, there was a cheer and a brief chant, "Himmler! Himmler!" So this was the great Ndunze, thought Sampson. He needed to warn Boss Harry, but there was no way he could get back to the homestead. The only way was around the fields and these men could beat him there easily taking the direct track though the compound. He scrutinised the man as well as he could through his half closed eyes.

"Who are you?" Ndunze shouted

"I am Samson, boss boy on this farm."

"Ah, I have heard much about you. You have a much famed weapon amongst the umfasis (*women*). Why do you work for this white man?"

"Because my master, Harry, he is a man, but he is gentle and good for our people. He has given us many cattle and built our homes, fed our families and educated our children. Why do you not go and leave us alone?" This entire discussion took place across the space between them, but Sampson noted that they were slowly but surely edging nearer. This is now getting very dangerous, he thought . He leapt up onto the running board of the truck, right hand clutching the pistol out of sight under the upper doorframe of the vehicle. He shouted to all the men, this time waving his left hand in the air to get their attention.

"You people must go. The workers on this farm do not want you here. We do not need your help, you are not welcome. Go now and we will forget this matter!"

Ndunze held his men back with a wave of his left hand.

"So you are with this white man?"

"Yes, he is a good man." Sampson shouted back, "Now you must go!"

"No, Shamwari (*friend*) Sampson, it is too late for that, it is you who must go, you are a traitor." He threw his hand forwards, and shouted, "Bamba (take him)!"

The mob leapt into the air in a frenzy. "Bamba," they shouted and then, weapons pointing to the sky, they started running. But Sampson had been anticipating this. He whipped around and jumped into the truck firing two shots into the air as he did so, judging correctly that the firing would slow the mob down for a moment, slammed the truck into gear and started off. The frenzy behind him increased and the mob made a mad dash to catch him. One man leapt up onto the running board, swinging his knobkerrie at Sampson. But it hit the doorframe. The man screamed at Sampson, dropped his stick and tried to wrench the door open. Sampson let him, but as the door swung open, Sampson shot him in the stomach at almost point blank range. The man screamed as he was flung back into the path of his comrades. This gave Sampson enough time to get the truck into second gear and accelerate a little more. He glanced in the rearview mirror. The men falling back behind him were in disarray, except one man. He had leapt onto the two foot high bank thrown up by the grader next to the road. This gave him a clear field of fire and Sampson watched him out of the corner of his eye as he took aim and fired.

The .763 calibre projectile had passed through the back of the cab, ricocheted off the large wheel-jack lodged behind the seat, hit the rear of the seat, now somewhat flattened and tumbling viciously, ripped through the springs and rubber foam padding. It passed through the front of the seatback and smacked into his left rear ribcage. Fortunately that's where it stopped, lodged against the two ribs it had broken.

Sampson nearly lost control of the vehicle, more from the sound of the bullet hitting his vehicle, than the impact of the bullet hitting him in the back, throwing him hard onto the steering wheel. But he gritted his teeth and kept focussed. He roared in pain, but immediately heard another loud 'Crummmp!' It was a mark of his strength and his burning resentment that he thought, 'Am I a man?' This is nothing but the bite of a Tsetse fly[109], but I am a stupid man. Boss Harry gave me that flack-jacket. He looked down at it on the seat. Stupid man, he thought, never again will I not listen to the Boss.

He drove on like a man possessed, the truck sliding and bouncing dangerously on the uneven track. He was worried. That had sounded like a grenade up towards the homestead. Then he heard a machine carbine firing and the frantic barking of the dogs. It took him ten minutes to get around the maize lands back to the main access road to the homestead, where he turned left, away from the road back towards the house and was then forced to career to a halt in horror.

The smoking remains of the Toyota Land Cruiser lay on its top blocking the driveway, the whole front of it, crushed like a tin can, steam rising from the destroyed cooling system, oil still running out of it onto the ground. Ignoring his own pain, Sampson grabbed the pistol and jumped down, his eyes searching everywhere for danger. Behind the Land Cruiser there was a huge hole in the road. Landmine, the thought flashed through his mind automatically. He ran forward and tried to see into the vehicle, but the roof had largely been crushed down against the main body of the RUV. By getting down on his stomach he could see in. What he saw started the tears in his eyes. He couldn't help it; he just started sobbing, the pain of what he was looking at and the pain of the wound in his back. He gingerly reached underneath and into the smashed vehicle to see if he could detect any life. It took him five minutes of wiggling around and trying different places to reach in, before he knew. All he could do was to reach in and withdraw the .22 Hornet lying next to the limp body of Robbie on the interior roof of the vehicle.

If the blast didn't kill them, Bevie and Robbie had both been crushed to death by the vehicle landing upside down on its roof.

He was starting to tire, hallucinating a little as his own pain got to him. Nothing I can do here, he thought as the reality struck him, and he looked down. With his left hand tucked back behind him, clutching at his wound, his right holding the rifle, he bowed his head crying unashamedly and made the sign of the cross on his chest, then he turned and got back into his truck. He had to get to the homestead as soon as possible now to see what the firing was about.

Harry, too, heard the blast of the land mine, his head jerked away from the phone on which he had been trying to summons support. His blood ran cold.

"Bevie! Robbie!" he screamed.

He leapt up. Dropping his unanswered phone into his pocket, he grabbed his rifle and ran shouting to Annie,

"Annie, let me out the gate and then switch the fencing and the alarm back on. Try and get help!" He ran out of the front door, jumped out onto the lawn without using the steps and he ran. As he passed the graves of his dogs, now three, for Chollie had died naturally some years before, he thought, if only Chollie were still alive. But his two ridgebacks, Denzil and Magnus, were with him. For a man of 53 years of age, he was still very fit and he was quickly through the gate, which opened in front of him. Then all hell let loose.

The brief chatter of a light machine gun was all he heard before everything went black. In fact it was the dogs that saved his life, because the moment they sighted the two men standing in the driveway, they launched themselves into attack, both going for the same man. They hit him as he tried to reload the AK and sent him flying, Denzil worrying his shoulder while Magnus had a firm grip on his wrist, shaking viciously from side to side. The other man stood there helplessly for a moment not wanting to shoot the dogs for fear of hitting his comrade. So he ran forwards intent on kicking or hitting the dogs. But Magnus saw him coming and turned on him. The man stupidly wasn't carrying his weapon at the port. It was casually hanging from his hand as he ran, so he was not quick enough to defend himself as Magnus leapt. The dog's huge teeth wrapped themselves around the man's nose and top lip, deeply puncturing the skin below his left eye. As Magnus fell away, worrying vigorously, he ripped terrible chunks out of the man's face. The man screamed as he went down in agony, now holding his face in his hands, blinded, blood spurting all over his hands from the gruesome wounds. Magnus now started on his arms, tearing and biting.

The other man by now had managed to kick Denzil away and on rising, he saw what had happened to his comrade. Suddenly his bravery left him and he just turned and ran. They had done what they'd set out to do. He saw the white man too, surely dead, thrown back as the bullets hit him.

The dogs were sitting alert, panting with blood and gore dripping from their mouths, guarding Harry when Sampson got there.

Earlier, as the security gate swung shut behind Sampson's truck, a man, hidden behind a thicket, ran quietly through it and hid, momentarily crouching behind the pump-house. He heard the land mine explode and from where he was, saw Harry and the dogs running across the lawn towards the front gate. When he saw his comrades coming up the track, he merely had to lean forwards and press the 'open' button on the gate control console. This time, they were silent and moved fast.

Ndunze signalled for them to spread out and, pointing to a few men to follow him, they entered the house quietly through the back door. Annie was still trying to get through to the Karoi police station on her mobile when they came silently into the den behind her.

"Mrs. Andrews?" She got the fright of her life and jerked the seat around to face them in terror, her mouth open, stuttering,

"Wha..What do you want?"

He didn't hesitate.

"Revenge, Madam," Ndunze said as he grasped her hair and dragged her from the chair. He dragged her kicking and screaming down the passage towards the main bedroom. He threw her onto the bed and told his men to hold her. Taking out his bayonet, he started at her feet, cutting and ripping off her clothes. He stood back and admired her beautiful nakedness and laughed, thinking, I'm sorry Brod Volker isn't here to witness this. Even he could not resist, and besides, who cared any more? He was not aware that Volker was already dead.

"Now is the time, Mrs. Andrews, to pay for your war crimes." He dropped his trousers, his erection already complete and forced himself between her legs.

When he had finished, he signalled to his men, who, laughing, cruelly invaded her in turn, time and time again, long after she'd stopped struggling and screaming and had passed out. When his man arrived from shooting Harry, his anger knew no bounds. He called the rest of the men into the bedroom and pointed to the dishevelled and bloodied body on the bed.

"Take her, and when you have finished using her, bring me the rings on her finger, and then hang her from the veranda roof as a sign. Nothing will stop us now. " He turned and went back to the den, picked up Annie's mobile phone and dialled a number known only to him.

CHAPTER 38

The dogs wouldn't let Sampson near Harry, so he eventually had to coerce them into the cab of the truck and close the door. He didn't want to do this because he didn't know what danger still lurked.

Sampson, sweat pouring off him in reaction to his own effort to keep going, knelt next to Harry noting where the bullets had hit him. There was very little blood, just some seepage from under his left arm pit. He felt Harry's neck and heaved out a sigh of some relief. Despite being out stone cold and looking dead, his Boss was still alive. He ripped open the Velcro zip of the flack-jacket, worked it off and then tore open Harry's shirt. His chest and stomach were a mass of bruises. Only one bullet had penetrated the jacket under Harry's armpit and that had only ripped through some muscle and exited from his back. Sampson found the bullet embedded on the inside of the back of the flack-jacket. He counted five bullets lodged in the front.

He picked Harry up as if he was a baby and went around to the off-side of the truck, used his elbow to force open the door, was nearly knocked over as the dogs leapt to the ground and then carefully pushed Harry onto the seat. When he got the door shut, he went back, picked up the flack-jacket, shirt and Harry's rifle. He slid the weapon out of sight in between the sacks of maize next to the Hornet and then climbed in behind the steering wheel. He gently moved Harry around using the flack-jackets as cushions, until he was satisfied that he would stay there. He then pulled out the seatbelt and secured him in place.

He wound down the window and as he put the truck into gear, he leaned out through the window and told the dogs, "Up, on the truck." In an instant they were on the back, Magnus nuzzling him and licking his elbow, which was sticking out of the window.

Going slowly he rounded the trees next to the main gate then stopped. He reversed into a turning place and drove back out onto the track facing towards the main road. He got out, ordered the dogs to stay and then walked 10 metres through the narrow plantation of pines along the fence. He stood, stock still in the shade of the last row of trees and looked towards the house, squinting slightly to focus through the 300 yards of heat waves.

He could see men milling about on the veranda and then saw them hang the white naked body up over the front steps. The flowing brown hair left him in no doubt as to whom it was. He saw the body jerk hideously as three shots rang out.

"It is done," he said to himself, "and now there is only Boss Harry." He turned, retraced his steps back to the truck, ripping off his shirt as he went. He flicked it around himself and tied the shirttails together in front of him, making sure it covered the wound in his back. He was starting to stagger now and knew he had to get help as soon as possible. But he knew also that he couldn't risk it. He had to hide Master Harry. If these men knew he was still alive, they would stop at nothing to kill him.

He managed to drive 30 miles, but eventually had to stop. He found a lay-bye and parked in the shade as far off the road as he could. He then slumped over the wheel, engine still running. That's how Harry, totally disoriented as he regained consciousness, found him half an hour later.

He groaned, battling to clear his vision, unclipped the seatbelt and leaned painfully over to shake Sampson's shoulder. Sampson merely slipped to the right and his head dropped to halt wedged between the door, steering wheel and dashboard. In so doing he exposed the wound in his back to Harry.

"Christ!" Harry exclaimed. All attention now as the adrenalin started flowing: he leaned down and looked at the wound. "Bloody hell and damnation!" He carried on cursing as he took a grip on the situation. He switched off the engine, and slowly climbed out of the truck. The dogs greeted him as if he'd been away for months. Head down, he sat on the running board and ruffled and patted his dogs until they'd calmed down and then gingerly lifted his arm. He was very stiff and sore but he was able to feel around under his arm and worked out that he'd been hit but that the bullet had gone straight through. He felt his chest, which was painful with every breath, and looked down at the bruises. He realised that he was very lucky to be alive.

Slowly it all started to come back to him and looked around. He didn't have a clue where he was. He took his mobile out of his pocket, no signal, so he got up.

"Dogs stay," he ordered and then walked slowly out towards the road. The sun was virtually overhead and it took him a while to work out which way they had been heading. Towards Makuti he guessed correctly. OK, Sam, he thought, if that's what you had to do, then that's what we'll do. His concern for his family was overwhelming, but if Sam had put him into the truck and was driving him to Kiachingwa, there was a reason.

After the 15 minutes it took him to get Sam into his own earlier position, he was sweating profusely and realised that dehydration was going to be a problem. They'd have to stop for water as soon as possible. He started up and drove off carefully, conscious that he mustn't faint at the wheel. Once they got going, the wind through the driver's window revived him somewhat, but he knew that while it made him feel a bit better, all it was doing really, was dehydrating him further. The BP station at Miami was shut but he drove to the back of the building and found a tank of water where he knew it would be. He was able to water both himself and the dogs without trouble. He cast around and eventually found a beer bottle lying in the ditch next to the service station, scooped some sand into it and half filled it with water. He gave it a vigorous shake and then poured the muddy water out. He repeated this process a couple of times until he was satisfied the bottle was reasonably clean. Filling it to the brim, he climbed back into the cab and slowly forced drops of water down Sam's throat. After a while Sampson spluttered and slowly came round. He drank thankfully and after a while was able to turn and look at Harry. He could see the anguish in his face and without waiting for the question, he said,

"Boss Harry, they are all dead, everybody. Now it is just you and me."

Harry slumped back, horrifically bereft, an indescribable loneliness and depression coming over him. He'd known, in his heart of hearts that this was what had happened, even before Sampson had opened his mouth.

"How Sam?" he asked quietly, choking sobbing out the words. Tears were pouring from his eyes and there was dribble running down his chin from the corner of his mouth.

"Master, I will tell you everything I know, but first we must get to Kiachingwa, where we will be safe." Harry didn't move. "We must go now, Boss, it is better that we don't get taken by the police. There are many people dead." It was as if Harry had gone into a trance. Sam took 10 minutes changing places with him again. He made sure the dogs were back on the truck and then he started off again. The water had revived him somewhat, he wasn't feeling too bad. The pain in his back had reduced to a steady throb now, so he was able to drive non-stop until they got to the new farm. Harry never moved for the entire hour and a half it took them.

When the police eventually arrived on the 27th December, the place was deserted. It took them three hours to drag the decomposing bodies they found out of the destroyed Land Cruiser. Here the jackals had been busy, being the only scavenger small enough to get into the crushed space.

Then they found the body of the man that the dogs had killed, his AK still lying next to him. Most of his identifying features were gone. There was a huge flock of various vultures[110] fighting to get at him.

Moving on, even the most hardened of them was sickened as they cut down the putrid naked body of what was clearly a middle aged white woman. Surprisingly, she was still, relatively speaking, in one piece. The larger scavengers had been held at bay by the security fencing. There were vultures there, but because the body had been suspended four feet off the ground, they could not find enough purchase to do too much damage to the corpse. But other birds had. Her eyes were gone and the massive wounds in her body had been worked at. One of her fingers had been cut off but was not visible in the excreta and gore lying below her on the concrete floor of the veranda. Hankies tied around their faces, the policemen picked up her and the gore using shovels and tipped her into a body bag.

They all knew exactly what had happened, and, after setting up a perfunctory search, they retired back to Karoi, where they left the body bags at the hospital morgue. These matters were best left alone and whilst they opened a docket, nothing came of it. They made no effort to find out about next of kin, nothing. They even hadn't bothered to go down to the compound, so they didn't know that George and his entire family were lying dead and decomposing in his house.

It was Mick Glover and Jim Leonard, frantic with worry because Harry and his family had seemed to have disappeared, and completely distraught at what they discovered, who eventually got some sense out of the police and were able to establish what had happened. Sickened, Mick claimed the bodies for burial and had them transported back to Harare in a refrigerator truck. It was the two of them who found George and his wife and girls and the man Sampson had killed. They found nobody else anywhere, no cattle, pigs, machinery, nothing. The house had been ransacked, nothing of value to be found in it. The barns were empty; the beds, equipment and drugs that should have been in the clinic were gone. The entire place looked as if it had been like this for a while. They couldn't understand it, so they attended to the burial of the bodies and left, knowing that this wasn't over. The mobs would be there soon to claim the land and the houses and they didn't want to be around when it happened.

Harry was listed as missing and it was assumed that the rest of his workers had fled. No-one knew anything about Kiachingwa.

Chris Swan and his family, on their return from holiday 'down south', were refused entry to their own farm and home. They tried everything but weren't even allowed to go in and get their personal possessions. The place had been ransacked so there was nothing left anyway. They had lost everything. So began a long but futile legal battle that left them all but paupers. With the money he had remaining in his

South African bank account, Chris took a lease on a farm at Kafue in Zambia. They never set foot in Zimbabwe again.

The government duly announced that four more large farms in the Karoi area had been 'acquired' by the State for the people. Of course, they had done nothing of the sort. Furthermore, they facetiously handed over all of them to high ranking members of the regime.

When the Minister of Land and Resettlement, Flora Buka, arrived at Merrywaters Farm to claim her prize, she was at first delighted, it looked fantastic. But as she and her acolytes toured the farm in her black Ministerial Mercedes Benz, donated courtesy of the German government, it became more and more apparent that there was nothing there. Most of the land was lying fallow, there was no livestock, the house had been ransacked and but for one tractor, which for some reason had no distributor and the gear lever had been removed, there was no machinery of any kind. There wasn't even any diesel in the fuel tank, which was full of holes anyway.

She was quick to complain to the Karoi Police Chief, who denied, lying through his teeth, that anyone other than he and his men, had been anywhere near the place. Ndunze was summoned to explain why the farm had nothing, when it should have been fully operational. Ndunze was not easily cowed.

"In this particular case, it is known that the farmer was a traitor. He was responsible for the death of many comrades during the Chimorenga. We also knew that he was well prepared to resist us, so we planned our reclamation very carefully. There was no opportunity for the man to remove anything from his farm. His children and he were killed trying to escape from the farm. His wife resisted our questions and unfortunately she died also. So we were unable to find out where everything had been taken. All the houses were empty, also those on the other farm, and all but a few of the staff had gone; I suspect that the staff have stolen all his equipment and taken it back to their Tribal Trust lands."

Ndunze stood there causally, feigning disinterest, a glitter in his eyes was all there was to indicate that he worried about the outcome of this farm takeover. He cursed himself for not taking more notice of the man, the boss boy, in the truck. Where had he gone? Where was the farmer? His body had been removed before he'd been able to go out and check on it. What happened to the dogs? A feeling of unease overcame him. I am going to see this man, Sampson, again. I have no need to try and find him. He will find me and I must be ready for him when he does.

"Well, Ndunze, I am not pleased," said the Minister. "This farm is to be re-allocated to the peasants. I will arrange this. You, however, Ndunze, will find me another good productive farm in this area, and I want it in pristine condition. If your veterans ransack the place, you are finished, do you follow?"

"Yes, Minister." Ndunze wondered just how much power this woman had. He thought it better not to find out. It was rumoured that the President lusted after her daughter, Sally. He said, "It will be done Minister, and I personally will remain to guard your new farm until you arrive to take control."

"Good, you have two months. Be sure that you do not fail in this. I'm sure the President would not be pleased."

After expensive autopsies - Jim had had to fly in a private pathologist from Johannesburg - Annie, Beverley and Robert were buried in a family grave at the Warren Hills Cemetery on the Saturday the 10th January. The funeral was attended by only three people. There were none of their close friends left in the country. Jim agreed to take on the disagreeable task of writing to the families in England, and as he and Mick were both trustees to Harry's Estate, they spent hours with Harry's attorney working out what the hell to do. Harry had left precise instructions with his attorney in Harare as to the disposal of his estate in the event of such an eventuality but the only thing of relevance was an instruction regarding his aeroplane. This was not his last will and testament as it was by no means certain that he was in fact dead.

"Christ!" said Jim, "it's almost as if he knew this was going to happen!" They were sitting in the Harare Club raising their glasses to their lost friends. Mick's wife, Biddie and his children were away doing an exploratory trip to Australia. They had long since decided to take 'the gap' when they could, and had at last been accepted into Australia. Mick had had trouble putting together enough points to validate his immigration application.

He had decided not to let Biddie know about what had happened until he could tell her quietly at an appropriate moment on her return.

He was now, however, more than ever, determined to leave. So all he had said to Biddie on the phone on New Year's Eve was that she had to decide quickly and finally where she wanted to go in Australia, because as soon as she got back, they were going to pack up and go, forever. He realised also that Biddie was now the only one left who knew how to get hold of Barbara Templar, and he wanted to get his story absolutely right before he told her.

Jim's wife, Binny, sat at a nearby table knitting. She knew that she must let her men, yes, that's how she looked on them, get it out of their systems.

"No," countered Mick levelly, "Harry was just a very intelligent and careful man. Something very peculiar has happened, can't put a finger on it, but I have a feeling that we haven't heard the last of this desperate affair yet, not by a long chalk! I suggest you have his aeri ready to go at all times."

"Bloody right I will! But what the hell happened to all his livestock, his equipment, there's nothing left? Nothing except the house was ransacked. It's as if he spirited it away before any of this happened. Hey Mick, you don't think....?"

"Don't be bloody crazy, Jim. You've seen the autopsy reports." Despite the fact that he had been hardened by years of war, atrocities and bloodshed, he shuddered. "Harry loved his family with a passion I have seldom ever witnessed. He'd die for them. I just hope that he hasn't yet, before he can do something about it."

"Yes, you're right, Mick. And knowing Harry, if he is able, his vengeance will be terrible. I almost pity the bastards who did this."

Harry was at this time in their new clinic at Kiachingwa, heavily bandaged up. For several weeks, He just lay there staring out of the window, his dogs lying faithfully under the bed. The clinic nurse, Temperance, George's second wife and now widow, couldn't get near him at first, but fortunately he was compos enough to tell them to let her near him. Thereafter, she tended him carefully. Despite her own grief, she fed him, washed him and made sure his wounds were dressed properly every day. When Chadrack or Sampson weren't there themselves, which for the most part was only when they were walking or feeding the dogs, she sat, at all times, on a chair in the corner of the room awaiting his orders. Sampson had told her what happened and had ordered her to do everything to help Harry. He also promised to take her as a wife and look after her.

Sampson had discharged himself after one night and immediately called a meeting of the elders. He told them exactly what had happened and swore them to secrecy. If they valued what they had, then no-one was to know that Master Harry was still alive.

"Madalas (*Old men*), you must understand what this man has done for us. He has given up his life to make sure that we are safe and cared for. When he is well, you will see, his anger will be mightier than a raging lion with a tooth ache, his skill will be greater than a leopard in the hunt and his stealth will be like the 'tokalosh', the evil spirit that kills in the night. It will be well to remember this, for no man will escape his wrath. I have seen this man fight, he, like the Honey Badger, is without fear."

Having put the fear of Musiki (*the creator*) into them, he was sure that word would not get out and was now busy with Chadrack repairing and manually repainting the truck. They left nothing to chance. It was possible that they would be looking for this truck with a bullet hole in the cab. They filed and panel beat the hole and then welded another piece of metal into it. When they'd finished, even when inspected closely, the repair could not be seen. They took the seat out and found Harry's pipe on the floor. Chadrack wasted no time getting it across to the clinic. Using hide, cured and softened in a vat of boiling wattle bark, which was rich in tannin, and then polished, they re-covered the driver's seat. No sign of the bullet was left. The registration didn't worry Sampson. Boss Harry had long ago re-registered it in Sampson's name. When they'd cleaned the vehicle prior to repainting it, he'd noted that the back number-plate was caked with dust. It was unlikely that anyone had been able to read it.

There was a bit of a scare when the police arrived one afternoon apparently on a ganja bust. However unlikely that was, they were more likely looking for it in order to use it themselves. Chadrack showed them around explaining that he and Sampson had bought the farm from the estate of the old farmer. He even showed the police captain their title deed. The policeman was extremely impressed and after sharing a tin of 'utwala' (*local beer, brewed from mashesh*), under the 'madoda' tree (*where the old men meet and drank*) he left.

As the policeman drove out of the compound, a 'pickinini' (*small boy*) ran up to Chadrack.

"Changamire, they want you at the hospital."

Chadrack ran. He found Sampson already there.

"Chadrack, it is finished. I have told Master Harry everything that I saw and understand."

"Not quite, Sam." Harry looked at him bleakly, his voice like ice. "Can you identify these men again if you see them?"

"Yes, Master…"

"Stop calling me Master, you no longer work for me, and that goes for you too Chadrack. From now on, I am just Harry."

"Yes, Mas…Yes, Harry." Sampson carried on. "I remember all of their spoor also, what they were wearing and their leader I will always remember. It was Shenje Ndunze, the man they call 'Himmler'."

"So he has come back to finish what he started so many years ago." Harry wasn't addressing anyone in particular. It was almost as if he was musing. "So I will finish it for him. Their work is not yet finished, Sam, there will be other farms and that will be my chance. I tell you now, as the son of my mother, these men are dead. They just don't know it."

Even Sampson, tough as nails and afraid of nothing, shivered. The bleakness in Harry's voice, and the conviction it carried, froze him. He had always been right. This man was now extremely dangerous and nothing would stop him.

"But, first things first; Chadrack, I need a pen and some paper and envelopes, I need to write some letters. Will you write out the addresses on the envelopes for me, and then take them into the Makuti post office and post them? It is important that they appear to have been sent by a black man."

"Of course, Harry, anything." He left without another word.

"Sam, I would like you to help me."

"Harry, I am part of you, I am your eyes, I am your ears, I am your feet and I am your fist. It is done, anything you direct! You are me, I am you, my blood is yours."

Harry turned away from the window and looked intently at Sampson.

"Thank you, Sam, thank you. For I cannot do what I must do without you."

Tears came into his eyes as he grasped Sampson's hand.

"For now, I am going to my house, I must think. If you would have Chadrack send the paper there. Come and see me this evening, we will talk. I want you to think also. Think of how you are going to help me find and trap these men."

They walked out of the clinic together with Magnus and Denzil hard at their heels, Harry clutching Sampson's arm, thankful for the strength and loyalty of this fine man. They delayed only while Harry thanked Temperance for looking after him.

He walked into his house and was immediately arrested by what he saw as he entered the lounge. There were, displayed on a side table, framed photographs of him and his wife on their wedding day and a formal photograph each of Annie, Beverley and Robbie he'd commissioned in Harare after they'd finished university and returned home. Tears started to flow again as he started thinking; they hadn't even attended their respective graduation ceremonies.

He shook his head. Get a grip now boyo, he thought, it's over. Something else caught his eye. It was the hippo tusk that he had extracted so long ago, on that wonderful trip to Kariba. It had been crudely etched and polished in part to depict Pete and himself in the boat and the crocodile that had so nearly taken his foot. After Chadrack had heard the story, he'd taken the tusk and lovingly worked at it on the many nights they'd spent around the 'boma', when they were out in the bush. It had taken him months. Then he'd fashioned and polished up a piece of mahogany into a stand for the tusk.

Harry smiled briefly, sighed and then went through to the bedroom. He stripped and showered, the water cold, they hadn't yet built a 44 gallon drum wood-fired boiler for the house.

Refreshed, he went through and found that someone had put writing materials on the dining room table for him. So he poured himself a glass of water and sat down to write.

His first letter was to Jim, no address, just a note.

> Dear Jim,
> I'm alive, just. All has been lost, but I have things to do and I will have to call on your assistance.
> However you have to do it, please have my aeri re-registered in RSA and then have it on stand-by. When I go it'll be fast.
> My love to Binny!
> Cheers,
> H.

The next was to his attorney.

> Dear Sherwood,
> You have my power of attorney, so this is to give you authorisation to assist Jim in anything he asks and to provide the funds he might need to give effect to what he is going to do.
> I will probably never see you again, so I have to say thanks for looking after us for all these years. I will send instructions from time to time.
> Everything is gone, my loving wife desecrated, brutalised and murdered, my wonderful children rubbed out, but, I'm afraid, the people that did this do not know me.
> Cheers,
> Harry

And finally he wrote to Mick. The light was getting quite dim so he went around the room and lit three hurricane lamps first. He noted that all the silk mantles had already been burned, so all he had to do was pump some pressure into them and then light them. They worked like a dream.

> My dear Mick and Biddie,
> I failed to save my darling family and my world has been destroyed, but now it's my turn to hit back!
> Please explain everything that happened to Barbara.
> I will, in time, write it all down, the horror of it all, and I promise that those responsible will be no more.
> I hope that I will sometime in the future be able to come and see you in Oz.

Love to you all, and thanks for all you ever did for us. Sadly it all looks so futile now.
Cheers,
Harry.

He put the letter to Jim and Sherwood together, and sealed them into one envelope. Then, he did the same to the other letter.

The dogs started growling and a few moments later, there was a knock on the door. He got up, carried a lamp with him and opened the door. Sampson stood there with one of his wives, carrying a covered basket.

"Hello, Mabel, "greeted Harry.

"Good evening, Sir," she replied politely. Telling the dogs to settle, Harry waved them in, a questioning glance to Sampson on his face.

"No arguments please, Harry. Mabel is going to be your cook and do your cleaning." Mabel had already disappeared into the kitchen.

"Oh..." was all Harry could think of saying. "Well, come on in." He led the way into the lounge. "Can't offer you a drink, I'm afraid, just water."

Sampson smiled.

"No, I will have a Castle. There is plenty of beer in your fridge."

"You're joking." He walked through to the kitchen, and there, neatly placed in one corner, was a large paraffin fridge.

"Bloody marvellous." He opened the door and with reverence took two dumpies, ice cold, out of a six pack and walked back to the lounge. He noted on the way that Magnus and Denzil already had their priorities right. They were sitting in the classical begging position just inches from Mabel while she tried to sort out some groceries.

"Also, George gave me two bottles of whisky, gin and cane spirit and some cokes and tonic water. I put them in that cupboard." Sampson pointed. "That fridge makes good ice, no problem." He sat down and cracked his beer.

"Well done, Sam. But this is not the time to get drunk. We have much to do." He sat back, unscrewed the cap off his beer and took a swig.

"Before we start, will you do me a favour?" he asked rhetorically, "Can you have the women make some dog baskets for the veranda.

Time these buggers spent more time outside; they're getting to be a pain in the ass."

"No problem Harry. They will be here tomorrow."

"Good. So let's start."

CHAPTER 39

"*Hi* Mum," he said, walking into the house just in time for afternoon tea.

"Hello, Harry, good time?" Bunty stood at the kitchen door.

"Wonderful, the farm's looking good. Sorry about the lawn, I'll do it tomorrow." Harry started to go up the stairs, shrugging off his coat as he went. He wanted nothing better than to get under a shower.

"You've got a visitor." The classical mid-step stunner!

He turned around gripping the handrail.

"Who…?" His face displayed mixed emotions. He didn't know anyone around here.

"Go and look." She waved vaguely towards the lounge, the dish cloth in her hand, flapping about.

Harry slowly backtracked down the stairs, pulling his coat back on. He felt he looked a mess and ran his fingers through his hair as he passed the hall mirror. He was almost afraid to look, but he steeled himself, and walked briskly into the lounge.

She was sitting there, on the couch, hands held together on her lap. Still incredibly attractive, she looked straight into his eyes.

He was dumbstruck, stunned rigid. He was incapable of saying anything, largely because his mouth was wide open, his chin on his knees. He was sure that he felt his heart actually miss a beat.

"Hello, Harry." She got up and walked over to him, straightening her nurse's uniform as she walked. She put out her arms and held him on the elbows and leaned back to look up at him, a slight smile on her face.

"Barbara, wha…oha.." He couldn't hold them back, it just happened. The tears flooded into his eyes and down his cheeks. This first image threw him back more than twenty years when he woke up after his prang and saw the angelic form of Annie before him

"Oh Barbara…" he put his arms around her and pulled her close to him, blubbing like a baby. They stood like that for an age. He felt he couldn't move, frozen to the spot. His mind starting working at last, at top speed as questions flooded into his mind. What's Babs doing here? What has she been told? His self-guilt rose back up his throat like sour bile. Her children? She was supposed to be in Australia. He didn't know she might have left and come back to England. They'd been no-speaks for so long. Eventually he pulled away trying to hide his tear-stained face. He took out a hanky and blew his nose, wiped his cheeks coughed and turned to face her.

"Barbara…" he started but his voice choked.

"It's all right Harry, I know what happened and I'm OK with it."

"Babs, there is only one person on earth who would understand, have a feel for what happened, for how I feel, and that's you. You were there for so long only you would know."

"It's all right, Harry," she repeated, "relax and I'll get some tea. Sit down, let's talk."

Bunty walked in holding a tea tray.

"Don't worry, I anticipated this." She placed the tray on the lounge table. "Here, help yourselves, I've got some scones in the oven. I'll bring them through in a minute." She was gone.

Harry sat down and watched Barbara pour the tea, idly thinking that she still knew how he liked it.

"Christ Babs, how long is it?"

"Too long Harry, here." She held out his cup, already sugared. He reached across and unthinkingly picked up the teaspoon and began stirring it. Barbara watched for a moment and smiled. "God, some things never change. That used to drive Annie bananas."

"What?" Harry looked totally innocent.

"*The way you stir your tea. She once said to me, 'A couple of turns would do, but Harry stirs for half an hour. It drives me to distraction so I sugar and stir for him. It's a serious mistake to give Harry a teaspoon. He turns it into a weapon.'*"

Harry laughed and looking down, he carefully placed the teaspoon back into the saucer. "Yeah, well I suppose you probably know more about me than I know about myself."

"Well I certainly knew most of your intimate secrets for many years."

"Yeah, you two always skinnered far too much." Harry smiled, leaned forwards and then all the thoughts came in a rush. "How are you Babs? What are you doing in England? How do you know what happened? Where are the kids? I'm so sorry about Pete! Sorry I wasn't there for you. I couldn't leave the farm." It all gushed out, one breath.

"Whoah, Harry, whoah." She threw up her hands and took a deep breath. "I'm fine, live here, have done for years, round the corner. My kids are fine." Her voice softened. "And thanks about Pete. But things had been going wrong ever since his folks were…died." She corrected herself. "And I know all about Annie and Robbie and Bevie, because Jim wrote to me, enclosing copies of the autopsy reports. We spoke many times; we were all so worried about you. Nobody knew where you were, all we knew is that you were alive. We didn't know if you were hurt or what. The police had announced that you were dead, apparently shot while trying to resist arrest."

She had to stop for a while because Harry had started to sob again. He got up and turned to the window for a while, hanky out and busy. She kept very still fully understanding his agony. Eventually he returned to his seat and picked up his teacup, sniffed, and smiled grimly,

"Sorry, Babs, please don't stop."

"Well, we all knew that was nonsense. You, being dead, I mean and since I've been in England, I have in any case been good friends with Bunty. We see each other often. I work around the corner at the Westbury Surgery and live just up the road in Clifton." She looked questioningly at him. "We thought it best that I stay away until Bunty thought you were ready. One thing I don't know, Harry, is why you didn't all leave?"

Harry fidgeted, looked out the window and then looked back at her.

"We, that is, **Annie** and I," he stressed the 'Annie', "decided to stay and try and help our people."

"Well fat lot of good it did. Apparently they were all killed as well." Barbara was dismissive, almost aggressive, scorning.

He looked her, his look so bleak, Barbara shuddered.

"Actually no, no, they didn't," he said very slowly. "Just George and his number one wife died, and their two daughters. The rest survived; three hundred of them and their families and are today alive and doing very well."

"How did you manage that, Harry, how do you know?" Her tone was disbelieving, her face showing denial.

He looked at her mildly thinking, do I tell her or do I tell her to fuck off? I don't have to put up with this shit. He sat back, his face displaying little, but thankfully, his mother had appeared. It was almost as if she knew what he was thinking.

"Tell her, Harry, get it out!"

He glanced at her, saw her scowl, sighed and so reached into his pocket for his pipe. He fiddled around for a few moments. Bunty gave Barbara a withering look as if to shut her up; she had looked as if she was about to speak again. At last he said,

"Annie and I, in secret, bought and set up a completely new farm for the staff, out at Makuti. Everybody except George and Sampson were already out there."

"What? Are you telling me..."

"I'm telling you that we intended to spend our last Christmas at home in honour of Bevie and Robbie who had just finished university, then we were going to abandon the farm and move out to Makuti, for a while anyway. There was nothing left at Merrywaters, they got nothing. Virtually everything had already been taken to Makuti, livestock, machinery, everything. We'd even furnished the new house ready to move in to. Chad and Sam built it for us with their own hands; a slightly smaller version of the house at Merrywaters. Look, we knew the writing was on the wall." He spent a moment stoking his pipe. Barbara sat back in amazement.

"But they caught us by surprise on Christmas Eve. We couldn't get help because there was just nobody around. The Swans' had already been overrun, I knew we were next. What we didn't know was that in our case, they were out to kill us, not just take the farm."

"Where were you when it all happened?"

"At the house, George was cooking our Christmas dinner. I sent him *home, telling him to get the hell out of there. Jim told me later that he and his family were the first to be murdered, in their house. I then sent the kids off in the Cruiser, and Sampson in the truck. We'd just got back into the house when we heard the blast. I grabbed my rifle and ran. That's the last thing I remembered, because I was shot, five times. The flack-jacket saved my life, and once again, the dogs. Sampson found me. He saw everything. It was he who took me out to Kiachingwa."*

"Where?"

"Oh, that's what we called the new farm. That's where I hid until I recovered enough to do anything."

"Well what happened, Harry? Why did you disappear?" Fascinated, Barbara was on the edge of her seat.

"I knew that if I was found, they'd kill me. I knew by then that this was more than a farm take-over. The comrades were after us because of what had happened in the war. So, I suppose you could say I went native. It's a long story."

"I've got all night and I really would like to know exactly what happened, Harry."

"Sam, they know who you are, they saw you!"

"Why, Harry? That is no problem. They are like the vundu[111] that can be snapped in the crocodiles' jaws. I am such a crocodile."

Harry smiled grimly.

"Maybe so, but I don't want you out there for a while. For the moment, Chadrack and some of his senior men will be our public face, OK Chad?"

"Yes, Harry, of course. What do you need?"

"First, we've got to find out where Ndunze and his cadre are operating. It shouldn't be too difficult for you to find this out by talking carefully to some of the people in Karoi and Mangula, I mean Mhangura. I can't remember all these places that have had their names changed. Find people willing to talk at the shabeens, soccer clubs, police camps and so on. Money is not a problem. Buy them a few drinks."

"Ha.., this is no problem. I have a good friend, Leftie Ndomo, at the co-op, he likes to drink. Also he will have all the latest news from the farms."

"Excellent thinking, I remember him. In fact I would like you to go in tomorrow because, while you're there, I need 4 tins of Kiwi dark brown shoe polish and some wrap-round dark glasses. On the way, you can drop Sam and me near Merrywaters, there are some things I need to see and do. After that, when we are ready, Chad, you can take ten of your best men into Karoi, buy them pay-as-you-go mobile phones and then send them out everywhere. You find somewhere to stay in Karoi so that your men can report back to you. Then you can communicate with me twice a day on the radio I'll give you tomorrow. Rig up an aerial by simply tying a small stick to the end of it and throw it up in a tree. Take your time and find these imbwas (*dogs*) for me."

Chadrack was delighted that he'd been given this responsibility and was visibly agitated, keen to get his men organised, but he knew Harry wasn't ready yet.

"I will have to get you and your men some money. Sam and I will bring it back tomorrow."

Chadrack and Sampson had no idea how he intended to obtain radios, where he would get the money or what he wanted the shoe polish for, but they'd learned over many years to trust him.

Harry ran his fingers through his hair and changed the subject.

"But that reminds me that right now I need a haircut, I'm going to shave off all my hair and get really brown. Who cuts everyone's hair around here?"

"My nephew," Chadrack answered.

"Chad, can you trust him to keep his mouth shut? The fewer people who know I'm here, the better."

Chad nodded.

"Good, then send him here with his clippers. We will talk again when you get back from Karoi. Also, another lesson, do not go to town unless you can take something with you, anything: firewood, people - who you must charge enough to cover your fuel cost - some mealies to sell in the market, whatever. And you've got to have stuff to collect and bring back. Diesel is expensive and many farmers are poor because they use too much. Never make a trip unless it is necessary for the farming operations, understand? Also, the police are always suspicious of empty farm trucks. I don't mind if we have to wait weeks for this information. If you've got nothing to do there except drink, then it is better to take the bus."

Harry leaned back and admired the view. Chadrack and Sampson had chosen a magnificent spot to build a bungalow for him and Annie. You could see the floor of the valley 2000 feet below, flat and stretching away towards the Zambezi River, shimmering in the heat. By comparison, they were sitting on the veranda in a cool breeze coming in from the east. A troop of vervet[112] monkeys were feeding in a red current[113] tree clinging to the hillside below them. He could hear them chattering away while they jumped from limb to limb in the tree. The branches of the tree swayed alarmingly as they leapt about. However, his mind was not on the wide panorama or the monkey business before him. He was thinking intently about Mr. Shenje 'Himmler' Ndunze, and all the evil, destruction and death he had rained down on him and his family and friends. Well, we will see, he thought.

"Right, now gentlemen and before you go, Chad, I want you to tell me everything you know or may have heard about this 'Ndunze', and when you have finished, we will go and take a look at the truck you've just repainted. We need to weld in a place where we can put guns so that the dogs cannot find them."

Sampson and Chad passed a questioning look between themselves. Master Harry begins, but how?

"Guns, Harry? We have no guns, except your .375, and the Hornet. Ndunze must have your pistol. And the stock of the Hornet is broken." Sampson sounded confused. "It will take me another week to finish a good new one."

"Guns, Sam?" Harry mimicked with a smile. He tapped his temple as if to indicate he was not so stupid. "We have sub-machine guns, hand grenades, pistols, a MAG .300 belt-fed heavy machine gun, bayonets, search lights, binoculars, kit, rations and liquids, first aid kits, maps, a vehicle, an aeroplane, clothing, camping equipment, everything we need to fight these bastards for as long as it takes." He stopped. "But all in good time, all in good time. Now you tell me about this imbwa, Mr. Shenje 'Himmler' Ndunze."

Ndunze, at the time had ensconced himself in Harry's house at Merrywaters. He made some of his men clean the place up a bit and furnish it to his needs using furniture and bedding found in George's house, which, because of the murders committed there, had not been ransacked. He sat at a dining room table in the middle of the big lounge, planning the next step in his campaign, the words of the Minister for ever in the back of his mind. He turned to his aide.

"Bring the comrades. I want to begin the next phase of our operations."

Within half an hour the men had assembled on the veranda. One of them had taken a water bucket and broom to the mess left by the body that had been left hanging there, so the smell wasn't too overpowering. Ndunze's newly acquired Chrysler Valiant, virtually the only thing left on the farm that was undamaged, stood gleaming at the foot of the steps. His men had just washed it for him and he took a few moments to stand there in silent admiration.

"Shamwaris, it is time now to undertake a new search on behalf of the Minister. She does not want this place because the workers have stolen everything and run away like the beres (*hyenas*) in the night."

"Yebo, Himmler."

"So every stick leader will take two men and undertake a search. We must find a farm for the Minister, which satisfies her needs. You are to take no action against the workers or the settlers yet. All I want is information. Only the best farm in the area from here to Mhangura will do and it is our job to find it. When we have decided which is the best farm, then we will make a plan to secure it from the settlers and save it for the Minister." He drove the point home a bit further. "But we must do no damage. The Minister is not pleased and has warned me that unless we find the correct place for her within two months, she will complain to Comrade Mugabe."

That brought a murmur from the assembled men and few fearful glances at each other.

"Now go. You are not to return until you have found a farm that you think is suitable. Your stick leaders understand what is required."

He scrutinised the men around him. Again several were high on ganja, some on alcohol, but again he thought that this was dirty work and good men were difficult to come by. Abruptly, he turned and went back into the house, leaving them to sort themselves out.

With Harry wedged between himself and Sampson in the cab, Chadrack drove the truck carefully along the dirt road leading to the main road to Karoi. Harry was virtually unrecognisable. He was dressed in scruffy and torn farm workers clothing and, but for his eyes, looked like a person of mixed blood. Using some brown shoe polish they'd managed to find, all the exposed parts of him were dark brown, including his now bald head. Chadrack had found him a pair of dark glasses, so even his eyes were not recognisable as those of a white man.

Leaving the dogs at home because everybody knew them, he'd wandered around the compound at Kiachingwa to test his disguise and no-one recognised him. So successful had he been, his appearance and sliding gait so indigenous, that he had had to reveal himself, when a group of fifteen of his people wielding knobkerries, surrounded him and asked him who he was and what was he doing on their farm. They were really quite threatening and ready to beat him up, until he removed his dark glasses and laughed. He'd spent the next half an hour chatting with them and only left once they understood the threat to their own lives, if they told anybody he was there.

The back of the truck was solidly loaded with sacks of maize and fifty or so bundles of firewood. They had made sure that there was no space in which to fit any people looking for a lift. The roads teamed at all times with rural peasants trying to go somewhere.

Eventually they turned onto the main road and Harry cautioned them.

"Guys, from here on I think the danger of being picked up is very great." Wiggling around in the cramped space, he pulled out his wallet and extracted a ZANU PF membership card. The document was a forgery based on Sam's real one. He passed it to Sampson.

"Take a look at that. Can you see any problems?"

Sampson looked at it with amusement, turning it over in his hands. He got out his own and compared them.

"The only problem is that the one you have given me is too clean." He put his away and then started rubbing and creasing the card until he was satisfied that it was as it should be, then he handed it back to Harry.

"That is better, Harry."

"Good. Guys, from now on my name is Rembrandt Duzi, OK?"

They all giggled.

"Yes, Sir, Mr. Duzi."

Mick and Biddie Glover and their children, departed from Harare on the Saturday 16:30 Air Zimbabwe flight to Johannesburg. Jim and Belinda (Binny) Leonard were the only ones there to see them off. They sat for the hour before their flight was called in the upstairs lounge of the terminal, looking out over the aircraft parking apron. Like the rest of the terminal, the restaurant had become fairly shabby over the years, but the food and 'railway' coffee, were still good. And the beer was cold.

They were all very quiet, even Biddie's raucous teenage kids, despite their excitement about going to Australia. They somehow knew that for their grieving parents, this was not the time to create a fuss.

"I don't know where he is or what he's doing, but Harry's going to make it." Jim said quietly. "Mark my words."

This immediately brought tears to Biddie's eyes. Mick stretched over and gently grasped her shoulder.

"He will, Biddie, don't you worry."

"Oh, I'm sure he will, Harry's one tough cookie. It was Annie and his children I was thinking about. It's so sad, after all they went through. I miss them so much."

"Now, now, my love, lets try and keep ourselves on track. You'll have us all crying again in a minute." Mick moved his chair round a bit and put his arm around her. It brought little comfort but she did cheer up a bit.

"God, what must that poor man be going through?" she said.

Mick was at a loss, realising that there was really no way of changing the subject.

"Well, I'm sure he's probably got his hands full right now, hiding or going after the bastards that did it. Jim?"

Jim tore his gaze away from the SAA 737 just coming in.

"Jim, you're all he's got left now and I feel terribly guilty leaving, especially without saying goodbye to him and making sure he's OK."

Jim said nothing for a moment, taking the time rather to order another round of drinks. When they arrived, He looked across at Mick.

"Harry knows you're going; you know that from his letter. So, don't worry. You'll see him again. For myself, I have already taken his Baron down to Jo'burg, had it MPI'd and re-registered in RSA. Had to use a dodgy clearance certificate, but I've done it. It wasn't that difficult really; one of my old buddies high up in DCA whom they haven't sacked and replaced with some ignorant party acolyte. All it took was a nudge and a wink, and Bob's your uncle. It's even official, so if the manufacturers check to see how the aircraft got from here to RSA, they'll find everything in order."

"What was the point? I can't see why Harry was so insistent that you do it."

"Well, reading between the lines, I'd say Harry intends to scarper at short notice. And that says to me, he's up to something, he's not coming back to Zim and he will probably want to sell the plane down south."

"Won't they catch him when he tries to leave?"

"Unlikely. He'll probably fly out of some remote strip and file a plan with Johannesburg control once he's high and airborne, saying that he had no coms at this end. Jo'burg couldn't care less if he passed through customs in Zimbabwe or not. I've done it dozens of times when I've been in a hurry. That's a thought."

"What?"

"I must stick a note on-board telling him I'll buy the plane. It's in immaculate condition and has another 700 hours to go on the engines, got new blades as well. Harry spent a fortune on it, unnecessarily in my opinion. But he always said if he's flying his family around in it, he wants it one hundred and ten per cent."

The tannoy came alive at that moment, the usual pings and then a pleasant woman's voice with only the slightest indigenous accent.

"This is a first call for passengers on Air Zimbabwe flight 126 to Johannesburg International. Please make sure that you have checked in all you baggage and then make your way through customs and immigration to the international departure lounge. Boarding will commence at four o'clock sharp."

Both men threw back their beers and stood up, the awkwardness of friends leaving each other for the last time evident between them. Biddie and Binny were already up and hugging each other, tears running down both their faces.

"Well I suppose this is it." Mick spoke sadly to Jim, sticking out his hand.

Jim took his hand.

"Much water has flowed and all that, Mick. You and I go back a long way and hey, we've had some pretty remarkable times together, haven't we?" a forced laugh. "We're sorry to see you go."

Mick couldn't hold back his tears and grabbed Jim in a bear hug.

"Cheers, Jim, and thanks for everything. You've been an absolute star. We'll keep in touch." He was almost sobbing into Jim's ear.

"Make sure you do. Who knows, maybe Binny and I will have to follow you in due course."

"Well, you'll always have somewhere to stay if you come to Oz. Make sure you see Harry right, hey?"

"I promise." They separated, turned to each other's wives and the tearful farewells were repeated. Lastly Jim and Binny said goodbye to the Glover children and then moved away leaving them go through to customs.

"That is one hell of a guy, Binny. Sad to see him go, but you can't blame him. Fucking country's falling apart."

She said nothing, but gripped his arm tightly as they walked back out into the October heat.

"Right guys, this is where Sam and I get off, anywhere along here, Chad. Stop when you see that the road is clear in both directions."

Thirty seconds later Chadrack pulled up at the side of the road in the shade of some mimosas planted so long ago by the white roads administration. He had only seconds to say good bye.

"Fumbai zvakanaka (*go well*)." Harry nodded and then he and Sam climbed down, slammed the door and almost immediately started to run, first across the road and after climbing through a fence, through the bush. Chadrack was already up to full speed before he saw another vehicle. It was a Chavanduka bus, filled to the brim with people in the steaming, choking heat, chickens, a goat and piles of umpashla (*personal possessions*) tethered on top. Steam boiling out from under the hood, it crabbed along, out of alignment on broken springs, in the opposite direction. He was grateful that on this occasion he wasn't on it.

Sam and Harry loped along through the bush for some twenty minutes to get well clear of the road, then stopped. Harry climbed up onto a large termite mound and took his bearings and then said to Sam,

THE WYVERN REVENGE

"OK, that way." Not waiting, he started to run again, slightly slower, but at a mile eating pace that he could now keep up for hours. Sampson had taught him well. He had taken his bearing on the hills which bordered the western side of Merrywaters. Leading Sam first westwards and then slowly turning southwards and then eastwards, he approached the farm from the deep bush and broken country to the west of the farm.

Because the land was so broken up by gwashas (*ravines*) and kopjes, it was pretty well useless for any habitation, so they were unlikely to, and indeed didn't, encounter a soul, except once in a while a small herd of female impalas, and once a family of warthogs being stalked by two bateleurs[114]. Eventually Harry stopped as he crossed a faint vehicle track, waved to Sampson behind him to slow down and started to stalk carefully through the thicker undergrowth towards the base of a big dwala. They had been running for two hours and the perspiration was pouring off him.

"Hapana manzi (no water)?" Sampson said.

"Don't worry, we'll get some shortly."

"Where, has this Rembrandt Duzi lost his way?" said Sam jokingly, coming up besides him.

"On the contrary Sam," said Harry pointing to a spot at the base of a large sausage tree at the top of which was a large woody gymnogene's nest[115].

"Use your hands and dig a little hole just here. Keep all the sand you take out in a small pile next to your hole. I don't want anyone to know that we have been here."

Sam looked at him as if he was mad, but shaking his head and smiling, he obligingly knelt down and began to scoop away the sand with his hands. It took only ten seconds before he reached something smooth and hard. His interest quickened and in less than half a minute he incredulously held up a jar with some keys in it.

"How! This Rembrandt fellow is amazing. Perhaps he can tell me what this is doing in this place."

Harry laughed.

"You'll see." He took the jar and extracted the keys, screwed the top back on and gave it back to Sampson.

"OK, now bury it again exactly like you found it. Put all the sticks and leaves back on top so you cannot see that someone has been there." While Sampson was doing this, Harry carefully cut some nearby long grass off near the roots and made a bundle. Then he handed the bundle to Sampson and told him to sweep away all signs of their presence backtracking as he did so. Sampson was beginning to grasp the fact that something very interesting was unfolding.

They backtracked carefully about fifty yards to the track that they'd crossed, with Sampson carefully obliterating their footprints in the soil as he reversed with Harry guiding him backwards holding onto his belt.

"OK, stop. Here is where we stopped running." He walked around on the track a bit, opened his fly and relieved himself and then pointed towards the dwala.

"That way, but clear behind us now."

They worked slowly to the base of the dwala until Harry told Sampson to leave the bunch of grass for them to use when they came back and then set off across the broken rocks along the side of the dwala. After ten minutes they emerged from the bush in front of the derelict mine. Harry carefully removed the dry brush in front of his hideaway.

"Jesus!" was all Sampson could say. He was amazed. "When did you make this?"

"Years ago; there's nothing like being ready for any eventuality. Not that it much matters any more. I've already made the cock up of all fuck ups as it is." He said this quietly, almost to himself. But Sampson heard him and knowing he was alluding to the disaster when Miss Annie, his children and George and his family were killed, he reached out to hold him firmly by the shoulders.

"Boss Harry," he looked Harry straight in the eye, "you could have done nothing, nothing! We were both of us lucky to come away alive. The difference with your farm and others they have taken, is that they came here to kill you, not just to take away your farm. You must not blame yourself."

"You never told me what they actually did to my wife."

"Master, I told you they shot her. I myself saw them do it on the veranda of the house. It is better that you do not to think on these matters. It provides no comfort." Sampson himself was struggling to shut out the images of what he had witnessed and his voice was hoarse with emotion. But he knew that no man and husband could take the reality of what he'd seen without going mad with grief.

They stood like that for a while, unmoving; Harry interpreting Sampson's obvious agitation as sorrow. Then, resigned, he broke away.

"OK, what's done is done. But now we have work to do." He took out the keys, selected the correct one and slotted it into the keyhole of his old safe door. It clicked open smoothly. He pulled open the door and bowing regally, he humorously swept his hand towards the interior of the hideaway.

"I say, you first, Sam."

Sampson walked in, having to stoop as he did.

"My weh, my weh!" he recited, amazed at what he found. "There is everything we need here."

Harry was close up behind him. He opened a pack of bottled water and handed one to Sampson.

"Well, let's take out what we need now and what we can carry. We can always come back for more stuff later. Sam, not a word to anyone! Not even Chad should know where it is. Tell him that I had the stuff buried, but not where or what it looks like. Not because I don't trust him, but because if he doesn't know, then he can't be forced to tell."

Mentally going through his own previously considered checklist, Harry directed Sampson to take various items out and stack them outside.

"Rembrandt, now you are mad. We cannot carry all this," he said surveying the huge pile of weapons and equipment they had deposited outside the cave.

"Stop worrying, Sam, I'll show you."

He then went deeper into the mine to a large rock near the end. He rolled this aside and lifted out a large cashbox. He then stuffed his pockets with several thousand Zim dollars and South African rands[116], replaced the box in its hidey-hole and returned to Sampson.

Satisfied they had everything they needed for the moment, he locked up, and with Sampson, now fully understanding what was going on, to help him, replaced all the brush and cleaned up so that there was no trace of the entrance or the fact that they'd been there.

Taking the same rocky path back to a point near the track, he stopped and lowered everything he carried in his arms and on his back to the ground.

"Sam, leave your stuff here with mine and go back and collect the rest. I know it will take you more than one trip, but I have things to do here."

Sam instantly turned on his heels and disappeared back towards the mine. Harry moved towards a huge pile of dead branches and started dragging them aside.

"Bit dangerous this, there might have been a bush fire, but I had no alternative but to hide this thing," he muttered to himself. With a flourish, he moved a large branch away and there was the old Peugeot 403 truck. He cleared everything away and waited for Sampson to get back.

When Sampson returned, his mouth dropped open, he couldn't believe it.

Harry smiled and climbed aboard. He wound down the window and handed Sampson the crank handle.

"Give it a couple of turns and then wait. I'll tell you when to give it horns."

He switched on the ignition and sighed with relief when he saw the glow-plug indicator light up. As it dimmed he put his foot on the accelerator and called,

"Go!"

He shouldn't have worried, the engine fired on the second turn and throbbed away healthily after just a few seconds. Sampson jumped in, put the crank handle behind the seat and laughed.

"I will not worry about this Mr. Rembrandt Duzi again. I think that he knows what he is doing."

Harry selected first gear and rolled out of the brush cover about twenty yards then parked, engine running, opposite their cache of equipment.

"Right, lets load." He jumped out, loosened the tarpaulin covering the back and pulled it back.

"There is still more umpashla," Sampson said, "I will go and fetch it."

The half ton truck had 20 bags of fertilizer in the back, half of which Harry then took out, carefully. Sure enough he found a rinkhals[117]

tucked away in a corner beneath the bags. He had to leap back off the truck in a hurry to avoid being spat at. He left it alone and a minute later it slithered off the truck into the bush. He was finishing this chore when Sampson got back staggering under the final load. They carefully loaded their equipment in one flat layer and then covered it all with the 10 bags of fertilizer that Harry had just taken out. The only thing that was visible was the carefully tethered generator.

"Just in case someone takes a look," said Harry. "Now Sam, before we leave, please go back towards the mine and sweep where you can see we have been. I'm going to build a bonfire."

Once satisfied that the brush was gathered together with enough kindling to start a proper fire, Harry took out his lighter, sat down against a tree and lit his pipe. He then waited for Sampson to finish obliterating their tracks from the mine. Sampson stood by while Harry lit the kindling and within a few seconds, he had a little brush fire burning and spreading. Harry stood back and watched it grow into an inferno

"Should hide the fact we were here. Right, Sam, let's hit the road."

Fifteen minutes later they reached the main road. Sampson got out and opened the barbed wire and dropper gate, dragged it open and waited while Harry drove through. He looked back and could see a fairly large bush fire developing. He smiled to himself, this man, he thought, is there no end to his magic?

Two hours later they were back at Kiachingwe not realising that they had just missed their best chance of getting Ndunze who was virtually alone and still occupying Harry's house at Merrywaters. Most of his men were gone on his instructions. Harry and Sampson had been no more than five miles from him.

CHAPTER 40

An excited Chadrack arrived back at the farm the following day. Before he reported back to Harry and Sampson, he ran to his house, showered, and changed his clothes. He came out of his bedroom and found Sampson waiting for him in his living room.

"Masikati (*Good afternoon*), Chadrack, my brother. You had a good trip?" Sampson himself was bursting to tell his own story, but it is not the African way to press straight on with business.

"It was most pleasant, Sam, and how was your journey?"

"It was excellent. I enjoyed very much to be with Rembrandt Duzi. He is an interesting fellow." There was a glint in his eye as he said it. "He is very similar in skill to Master Harry. He revealed much to me." Even privately they referred to him as 'Master Harry', such was their esteem.

"Perhaps we can have some tea while you tell me of your journey. I will wait until we go before the Master when I shall tell of my visit to the co-op in Karoi. I can tell you though that I sold all the mealies and the firewood that I took with me and brought back many people to Makuti. We have made plenty money on this trip. Sit, my brother, and Jessica, my first wife, will bring us tea."

"You do not require sleep first, before I tell you of my journey?" teased Sampson.

"Brother, I am like the mbada (*leopard*) who sleeps with one eye open. Even if I fall into a deep slumber, I will hear every word you say." He smiled as the metal mugs of sweet tea were brought in by his wife.

"Masvita (*Thank you*)," he said taking his tea from his wife, "but you may leave us mama, this makulu nzou (*big elephant*) and I have much to discuss." He sat back and listened in complete silence for the next two hours while Sampson, without revealing anything about the whereabouts or description of Harry's arsenal, told him of the amazing things they had done. He politely waited until Sampson had finished before speaking.

"This is very interesting but I can tell you that 'Himmler' is at Merrywaters at this minute. It might be best not to delay any further. I think it is time now for us to go to see Master Harry."

Harry's bungalow was well away from the main compound on the farm and they took fifteen minutes to walk there. On the way there, in the gloom of the evening, they were challenged by the armed guard that they themselves had posted near to the house.

"Gum (*Name*)?" an invisible voice rang out.

Sampson was quite pleased.

"Ndini (*I am*) Sampson, and I am with Chadrack."

"Zvakanaka."

Sampson and Chadrack carried on without even seeing the guard.

"Manheru (*Good evening*), Rembrandt," said Sampson jovially, Chadrack has some news for us."

"Well, go and get comfortable on the porch. I'll grab some beers."

They settled down and Harry deliberately took his time lighting his pipe. He was watching Chadrack and it was clear that he was dying to tell his story.

"So Chad, did you have a pleasant day?"

Chadrack got the message and was forced to play along.

"Yes indeed Mr. Duzi, and yourself?"

"Bit boring really, did nothing much," Harry said nonchalantly blowing smoke into the air and taking a sip of his beer.

"Ha, Sampson tells me you still run like a malhungu (*white man*). You had to stop and find a vehicle to drive back in."

"Ah, he did not tell you that he was tired from digging a small hole and could not carry our umpashla?"

"But it not easy for this nzou (*elephant*), to dig a hole. He is too scared that he will stumble and fall in."

Harry couldn't take it any longer himself and joined their laughter.

"OK, Chad, tell me what you discovered."

"Ndunze is still at Merrywaters."

This bombshell really did rock Harry back a bit.

"Shit, and we were there." He thought for a moment and realised immediately that it would have been the wrong moment. A lot more information was required before he went in.

"No matter, it is not the time yet. Sampson and I must prepare properly first."

As instructed, small groups of Ndunze's cadre went out in all directions to find a good farm for the minister. They casually visited staff compounds, laid on a few drinks and asked questions. From time to time, they even approached the farmers for work. The concept was that they'd get a job, do the necessary reconnaissance and then disappear again. After a week, despite their apparently casual approaches, it became common knowledge amongst the locals throughout the area that the war veterans were looking for a special farm.

This was how Harry found out that something was going on and that Ndunze was indeed very active. At first his men reported only that the comrades had been seen here or there, no pattern apparent. However, he tried, where he could, to identify on his maps from where each report emanated and after a while he began to think that they were looking for something, or someone. His initial thought was that they might be out looking for him, because on several occasions his men advised him that the comrades had asked many questions about the farmers themselves.

Then he began to realise that Ndunze was looking for a prize farm, and he began to work out a strategy. We've got to nail some of these groups while they're apart, he thought.

"Can the men help Sam and me to find these small groups of comrades?"

"I think so. But what can we do? When we have found them, they then move on and by the time you can be there, they are gone."

"Not if Sam and I are there already."

"Ah…"

"Gentlemen, there is something of great importance that you must now know." Harry looked at them watching him intently and his heart swelled. No man deserves such loyalty and trust, he thought. And now I must tell them that it is over. "We are now close to the end. Soon it is my intention to take this fight to Mr. Ndunze. Chad, you must understand that two things can happen. I, and even Sam, might soon be dead. If we are not and are successful, then even then, I must go away. My time in Africa is finished. If the government find out that I am alive, they will again try to kill me. Either way, you will have to carry on running this farm like I have taught you. Do you understand what I am saying?"

Both Sampson and Chadrack nodded their heads soberly.

"I will not be here to help you any more. What happens from now on is up to you and the people. Remember the people, Chad. This farm is owned by all of you and you are the leaders only because the people respect you and expect you to do everything that is good for all of them. Your power is the people's power. If you take power for yourself, you will loose the respect and support of the people."

He stopped, thinking, Crikey, I am rambling on. So he got up and went to the sideboard and busied himself breaking open a bottle of scotch. He brought the bottle and three glasses back with him.

"Before we get pissed, Sam, I want you and Mabel to take Denzil and Magnus. They trust Mabel to feed them and they like you. They are good dogs, but I have never felt the same about them as I did about Chollie, Shaka and Smuts."

"It will be a great pleasure Master Harry. But…" he hesitated, "why can't you stay here in this house? You are safe here. We can protect you."

"Sam, it is time for me to go and to make a new life back where I come from. The white man's time in Africa is finished. People resent us because of our culture and our knowledge, the way we do things and many are jealous. No, but I will be pleased if you keep this house ready for me in case one day I return to see you."

"It will be so, Master Harry," said Chadrack.

Harry rose, turned to face the two men and raised his glass.

"I drink a toast to you, Sam and Chad, you are the best friends a man could ever have had. You have both given me much pleasure in my life and I wish you the very best in the future." He threw back his scotch and reached for the bottle. He couldn't help the fact that his eyes were streaming again.

His groups from time to time came back and reported on this farm or that. He logged the information and then sent them out again to look at other properties.

Eventually Ndunze settled on five options and proposed to view each one before he made up his mind as to which one they would take. Considerations were many, but his primary concern was to be able to take the place without having to destroy everything.

Over a period of weeks thereafter, he visited them all noting the state in which the farm was being operated. Three of them were pushovers and they took them over immediately. But none of those they'd taken over had the quality of Merrywaters, so he notified the RPF (*Relocation of Peasant Farmers Division*), that they could begin re-locating people to these farms.

However, the fourth and fifth farms were excellent operations. He went back to Harare, did a deeds search and found that one of them in particular was worthy of the minister's attention. He really enjoyed driving his new car and preened that he was the centre of attention.

The trouble, and he didn't know it as he swanned around Harare, was that his men were beginning to disappear, one group at a time.

Harry and Sampson set up a camp in a group of rugged kopjes some three miles from the Karoi-Mhangura road. The Roads Department had developed a sizable borrow pit for gravel extraction adjacent to the road, which hid an old hunting track leading off behind it. Coming and going only at night they were careful on each occasion they had to move, to obliterate their tracks leaving and entering the quarry.

They located their camp up a gwasha. It was well hidden from the view of any stray passer-by walking along the hunting track through the bush, by a heavily overgrown tumble of large boulders. With a huge dwala hard up behind the camp, no-one was likely to wander around the rock-fall unless they were specifically looking for something.

Their truck was parked in the back yard of a general dealers store owned and operated by one of Chadrack's cousins, about half a mile down the road from the quarry. The storekeeper had a particular hatred of the comrades, who frequently came into his store and helped themselves without paying a cent. It was he who gave them their first contact.

A dark moonless night and the man felt, rather than saw, a knife at his throat.

"Quietly now, who are you?" the question in perfect Shishona came from just to his left.

"Ndini Phineas, Chadrack's cousin." The man was shaking badly.

"Relax Phineas," said Harry as he stepped out from behind the edge of a large rock. "Come with me, would you like some coffee?" Harry led the way slowly through the blackness, reaching back to steady Phineas.

"Masvita, that would be very nice."

They arrived at the camp and Phineas was surprised to find a small fire going, hidden between a constructed barrier of woven saplings. Sampson was wrapped up in his sleeping bag leaning against a rock.

"Manheru Phineas, did I not tell you to whistle when you approached? You are fortunate that it was Rembrandt who stopped you. I would have cut a little before finding out who you are." He smiled though and lumbered to his feet, found some mugs and with great ceremony made two steaming mugs of sweet coffee. He passed one over to Phineas and squatted down next to the fire. Phineas, for his part, looked around to talk to Harry, only to find that he was by himself with Sampson. His jaw dropped a little in consternation.

"Do not worry, Phineas, if Rembrandt does not wish to be heard, he is like the tokolosh in the night. One moment he is here talking to you, the next moment he is gone. But, come sit and tell me why you have come."

"The veterans are here, at the kraal." Phineas waved vaguely as if to say over the dwala in that direction. Sampson knew exactly what he meant.

"When?" This time the voice came out of the darkness.

"They came on the bus at quarter to five."

"Ahh... You wouldn't know how many and where they are sleeping?"

"Oh yes. These men, they are three and they are sleeping at the headman's house. The headman has to sleep in my house tonight."

"You know where that is Sam?"

"Yes Rembrandt."

"OK, Phineas, thank you for coming. Finish your coffee and Sampson will show you back to the road."

When Sampson got back, Harry was already sorting out equipment and firearms.

"Tell me, Sam."

It took them ten minutes to work out a plan.

"Knives, Sam, no guns, unless we have to. OK, lets go!"

The three men were caught completely unawares. Two of them died without even waking up, but the third woke to find his mouth stuffed with a rag, his hands firmly held in what seemed like a vice grip. His eyes bulged in fear as he became orientated, focussing on the large bloody bayonet Harry held in front of his eyes. The man tore his eyes away from the knife and looked up at Harry. All he could make out in the dim light cast by the paraffin lamp on the table were the dark glasses reflecting the slowly turning knife in front of him. He could feel the heated presence of a man behind him slowly applying an even greater pressure on his arms. In seconds he realised he was been trussed up and evacuated into his trousers.

Harry laughed.

"Scared imbwa? Sadly this is nothing to what you will be." Harry's intonation and fluency in Shishona were so good that the man had no idea that the ghostlike figure in front of him was a white man.

Harry turned to Sampson.

"OK, throw all three of them in the back of the truck, then go and get Phineas." Sam picked the man up by his armpits as if he was a child and carrying him like that, sideways and well away from his body as the defecation flowed down the man's legs and onto the floor, went quickly out of the one roomed house. Ten minutes later he was back with Phineas and showed him where not to tread. While he completed his grisly task of taking the dead bodies to the truck, Harry spoke quietly to Chadrack's cousin.

"Phineas, I am sorry, but we have made a mess here. If I give you a little money, can you fix it up so that there is no sign that the comrades were here?"

"Rembrandt, it will be a great pleasure." His faced positively gleamed in the dim light.

Harry nodded and handed him a bundle of Zim dollars. The man took them and turning towards the lamp, looked down at the large wad of money. He leafed through it, amazed at the generosity, and then he turned back to thank this Rembrandt. His mouth opened. The man had gone as if he had never been there. As he turned to go to the door, Phineas heard a vehicle start up a hundred or so yards away.

Harry and Sampson didn't go back to their camp immediately. Instead, they drove several miles to an abandoned farm and pulled up at the entrance to a derelict tobacco barn. Harry lit a hurricane lamp and hung it up. Sampson heaved the bodies out and one after the other strung them up to a rafter, feet well off the ground. While he was doing this Harry sat down to wait on the overturned half of a forty-four gallon drum and lit up his pipe.

Sampson dragged the live man in and, carefully avoiding touching the fouled parts of the man, similarly strung him up but with his toes just able to grip the ground below him. He pulled the rag from the man's mouth and moved back into the shadows near the gaping entrance. Harry sat for a long time, just staring at his captive and puffing away at his pipe. He was thinking, do I show myself to this man yet, or not? Eventually, he decided not to, thinking that it might be unnecessary, the man was obviously and quite literally scared shitless. He put his pipe away and took a sip of water from his flask, placed that on the ground next to him, and said to the man,

"Comrade, before we leave here, you will tell me everything you know about your cadre; what their names are, where they are right now, what they are doing: everything." He said nothing further but took a small notepad and a ballpoint pen out of his breast pocket and then just waited.

In an hour, he had everything he wanted. He put the pad and pen back into his pocket, placed the water bottle back in its pouch at his waist, picked up the lamp and then signalled to Sampson. They walked back to the truck leaving the man hanging. He was dead before Harry had even started the engine.

During the next two days and nights, Harry and Sampson killed twenty four more of the cadre, leaving them all hanging in the open disused barn, gleaning information from two others as they did their grisly deeds.

Shenje "Himmler" Ndunze arrived back at Merrywaters from Harare in the early evening. He walked into the house and never even heard the man behind him swing the rifle butt that crashed into the side of his head. He eventually came to and found himself tied and cuffed, almost suspended from the huge eucalyptus beam that ran along the front of the homestead veranda roof. His feet just touched the floor. For the first few hours he could see little, but as the gloom of the pre-dawn broke, the first thing he saw was the four dead men hanging from the same beam next to him. He had no idea that besides him, only two of his cadre were left alive, and they were lying trussed up like chickens on the floor in his command room.

There was no-one in sight as he was left standing there, unable to move and alone.

After securing Ndunze and arranging for Sampson to guard the place, Harry took a hurricane lamp and went out the back of the house towards the old stables. He hung the lamp on a nearby wooden fencepost and washed his whole body using cold water and carbolic soap while standing naked on the concrete slab next to the horse trough. The water was crystal clear. It was supplied by a gravity-fed dribble of water through a wrought iron pipe Harry had fitted into it twenty years before.

He was particularly vigorous about his washing, using an old pumice stone he found in the destroyed kitchen, scrubbing more than just the dirt and boot polish off his skin. At last he felt clean and then put on some fresh clothing from his kit bag. His final action was to place the leather thong that he'd removed from Ndunze's neck, around his own. His eyes were bleak. He then got into the truck and drove into Harare leaving Sampson on guard.

It was four in the morning when he hammered on the door of Jim Leonard's house in the leafy suburb of Avondale, some two miles north west of the city centre. An alert old man in pyjamas brandishing a 16 gauge shot gun swung the door open. Before he could remonstrate with the person who had so loudly and rudely awoken him and his wife at this unearthly hour, Harry said quietly,

"Hello Jim."

"What the hell... Harry!" he exclaimed in surprise. He caught the gun as he almost dropped it to the floor and turning, shouted, "Binny, come, it's Harry!" He propped the gun in the corner of the hall next to the door and rushed out throwing his arms around Harry, "You old son of a gun, Christ....! Christ..., come on in. Jesus, Harry, we'd almost given up on you, you bastard!" He literally dragged Harry into the house and slammed the front door shut with his foot.

Harry couldn't get a word in edgewise and then had to endure the adoration all over again as Binny rushed into the hall. Eventually they all settled down and went though to the kitchen where Binny immediately put on the kettle and started laying out eating utensils on the breakfast table. She busied herself making fried eggs, bacon, tomato, toast and coffee, shell-like ears open to every word while the men sat down and talked. Harry said very little of his activities, except to say,

"It is basically finished. I have one more thing to do back at Merrywaters, then I'm gone. But first, where is my family?"

"They're together in a family plot at Warren Hills." Jim, worrying about how Harry would take it, searched his face for any signs of distress, determined to stop in an instant if he had to, then explained how he and Mick had recovered the bodies, and made all the arrangements. He told Harry about the independent autopsy they had commissioned and about whom he had notified, etcetera, and what he'd done with the reports. He explained how he had liaised with Harry's attorney and had kept the Baron on stand-by awaiting Harry's instructions. Finally he told Harry about the departure for Australia of Mick and his family.

Harry never moved through all of this and only showed any animation when the breakfast was at last put in front of him. He ate ravenously and said nothing until he was finished. At last he leaned back and sighed.

"Binny, I can't thank you enough. That was the best meal I have ever eaten, I can't tell you how I've been yearning for a good old English breakfast." He patted his belly, and then as Binny placed an ashtray in front of him he felt for his pipe.

"Jim, if you don't mind telling me exactly where they are buried, I'd like to go straight out there to visit them this morning, by myself."

"Not at all, what are your plans?"

"Well after that, I must see Sherwood and settle my affairs. Will you phone him and tell him to meet me here at, say, around eleven. It's private enough and I don't want to spend too much time in Harare, I might be seen and recognised."

"Of course."

"I'd like to stay the night if I may, but then I'm going back out to Merrywaters to attend to one last matter. I must say good-bye to my staff and then this is where you come in, but I won't be seeing you again, unless you come to the UK. From now on, you will be able to find me through my Mum. "

"Anything, Harry, just say the word."

"I want you to get the Baron ferried to Sivewright's. Do you know that strip?"

"Yeah, of course; Binny and I flew down there a few weeks ago for some R and R."

"Good. Do you think you could arrange to have the aeri there in four weeks time?"

"Done." Jim hesitated and then continued, "Harry, I have left a note on the seat telling you that I'd like to buy it. If you're OK with this, then just fly in to Lanseria and when you've cleared customs, go straight across to NAC and park it there. Leave the keys with the hanger attendant. I'll let the guys know you're coming. I'll send you the transfer documents and wire the money to you, wherever you want them."

"Bloody hell Jim, that's bloody decent of you. One less thing I have to worry about, brilliant!"

"Nonsense Harry, that's a blinking good plane, I should know, we've been looking after it. Anyway, here's Joe's phone number." Harry raised an eyebrow as Jim wrote the number down on a bit of paper. "Yeah, I've posted him down there now; he's running my despatch unit out of the NAC hangar. Anyway, give him a call and I'll make sure he's got wheels lined up for you to use while you're down there. Where are you going to stay?"

"I thought maybe at Bill Sturrock's in Witkoppen."

"Excellent, I'll give him a call to expect you and I'll get the papers sent to his place. You can get the whole caboodle done at the same time." He scribbled some more notes down. "Have you got a ticket out yet?"

"Don't be silly."

"Thought not, leave that to me. When you're ready, phone this number," He took back the note with Joe's number on it and wrote down another. "Just speak to Marion, she'll book you in and have your ticket ready for collection at Jo'burg International."

"Crikey Jim, you're ahead of the game. Fantastic and thanks."

It wasn't until the sun had been up three hours on the third day that an old Peugeot 403 truck appeared through the security gate at the bottom of the garden. More adventurous jackals were already scurrying around, trying to decide whether they should venture up onto the veranda and dozens of vultures had gathered in the trees just across the lawn. Every now and then one would swoop down close to Ndunze, only to lift off again, squawking, when it realised he was alive. Swarms of blow-flies gathered in every crevice of the bodies hanging near him as they started to putrefy, giving up their stomach contents to the floor of the veranda. The stench of it and his own defecation, all made Ndunze gag repeatedly, the smelly bile running down his chin and throat onto his bare, heaving chest. He cramped up agonisingly from dehydration, having just to live through the pain. His body was crippled by the knotted muscles in his legs, arms and back and his thirst raged. Exhausted from having to stand in one place for three days, he was almost delirious, but not quite, and his hope and sanity were revived by the approaching vehicle.

CHAPTER 41

*T*heir intimate relationship started when Barbara and Harry met for lunch at the Prince of Wales in Stoke Lane at five past one on a Friday. Two bereaved souls with so much in common. She only had to walk around the corner. He and Bonnie strolled down from Great Brockeridge in ten minutes. He didn't know why, but he felt a little jumpy, almost as if he was excited. He was really glad she'd agreed to meet him for lunch at the pub, and actually yearned to be in her presence again.

The owner of the pub, Charles Ellis, took his order of a beer at the bar before Barbara got there. Bonnie stood up on her hind legs and put her paws on a bar stool, panting and excited. She loved coming to the pub. Charles greeted her and then she scampered off around the pub to see all her other mates. The regulars in there had grown to know her well and were really fond of her.

"Hiya, mate, your usual Fosters?"

"Yes please." Harry stood around to the left, next to the shorter part of the bar counter, while Charles drew his lager.

"You've been coming in for a while now, but normally in the evening." He stuck out his hand. "I'm Charles Ellis."

"Hi, Charles, Harry Andrews." He reciprocated and shook Charles' hand warmly.

"Someone said you live in Great Brockeridge?"

"Yeah, at my Mum's."

"Oh. You're Bunty Andrews' sprog." He looked a little awestruck for a moment.

"Well, one of them actually. I've a brother, farming down at Wedmore." Harry couldn't believe his reaction to this, what seemed to him, sudden friendliness. Two months ago even, he would have ignored the proffered hand and left the pub. Christ, I must be excited, he thought. "Could I run a tab. I'm meeting someone here for lunch?"

"Sure, shall I have one of the girls bring you a menu when he comes in?"

"She." Harry smiled as he corrected Charles who beamed back at him. "That'd be great, thanks."

They were still chatting when Barbara came in. Charles looked across and saw her.

"Hello, Babs, haven't seen you and Bunty for a while."

"Hi, Charlie, no, been a little busy." She turned to Harry and raised her mouth to be kissed. "Hello, Harry, sorry I'm late."

Harry kissed her and gave her a gentle hug and Charles couldn't resist blurting out,

"You two know each other?"

Barbara gave him a knowing look.

"Yes, Harry and I are old friends, very old friends!"

"Wow, I'll be damned, Harry, you're a lucky man. Every hot blooded male in the village has been lusting after this lady, and here you are, arrived out of the blue, and you've got her."

Harry was going a gentle shade of embarrassed pink, much to Barbara's amusement. He could also see a fair amount of amused interest from several of the nearby punters. He was astute enough, however, to realise that most of them knew who she was, so he stammered,

"Hey Charles, I haven't got her at all, Babs, tell him we're just old friends. What would you like to drink?"

Barbara ignored him.

"Rock shandy thanks, Charlie, and two club sandwiches." She looked questioningly at Harry who nodded. "And don't any of you guys get any ideas now. And Charlie, can we have a bowl of water for Bonnie?" She smiled as she drew Harry away from the bar to one of the little circular tables in the corner. She said quietly to Harry,

"I used to come in here often after work for sundowners with Bunty. But when she told me you were here and had started to come into this pub also, we decided to stay away for a while."

Harry looked at her in amazement. They sat down and he leaned forward, taking her hand.

"You're incredible, Barbara. How could you've known I needed space?"

"Harry Andrews, I've known you for how long? And besides, Bunty and I frequently discussed the state you must have been in. We knew that you would need space for a while, at least until you started to talk it out." She didn't take her hand away from his warm dry grasp.

"So the guys here know all about me?" he said waving in the general direction of the bar."

"Well, they probably know a little, from what they've overheard, especially when..." she paused, "...when it all happened. We used to come in here together for a gin and to exchange news and the bits and pieces we could get out of the papers and so on. It was pretty widely known that Bunty had lost some grandchildren and her daughter-in-law in Africa. In any case, we were both pretty cut up about it, as you could imagine. And then of course we used to worry about what had happened to you."

They were engrossed in their conversation, the sandwiches came, were eaten and Harry finished another beer. The time flew, so intensely did they concentrate on each other, oblivious to all around them. Eventually, Barbara glanced at her watch.

"Good Lord, look at the time, I must fly."

Harry was immediately distressed at the thought of her going.

"When will we get together again, Barbara?"

"Um... I've got to feed the cat. I'll tell you what, why don't you come around to me for supper this evening?"

"I'd love to, are you sure it'll be all right? Should I bring anything? Where do you live?" He was as excited as the young man he was on his first date with Annie.

"Nothing, just you, Harry. Bunty knows where I live." She rose quickly and before he had time to stand up, leaned over and kissed him on the lips. "See you at seven." Then she was gone.

Harry was so flummoxed, he just sat there for another half an hour, his mind going like an express train. His was conscious of the involuntary erection pressing hard against his trousers. Eventually it was Bonnie who brought him back to his senses.

The events of that evening exceeded his wildest dreams. It was almost unbelievable. He arrived on the stroke of seven. No hello, no invitation, not a word. She just flung herself into his arms, sobbing. He hugged her closely, his own eyes wetting, his hunger welling. She didn't pull away but pressed herself closer to him, searching out his heat and hardness, her pelvis arched forwards; her breasts, rigid, hot, crushing into his chest. Finally she got a grip on herself and spoke quietly into his ear.

"Oh, Harry, how I have yearned for you to come to me, for us to be together. You and I can only have each other, there is no-one else in our lives. Come." She led him to her bed, the flowers ignored; the bottle of wine he'd brought, dumped on a table on the way.

The passion between them was real. Mutual loss merging into one mind, the same desperation, identical needs, one synchronised orgasm.

He'd forgotten what it was like. He lay satiated, dreaming of Annie but not really seeing her, old similar sensations in times past, the same electrical currents exciting his nerve ends. Eventually, he opened his eyes and there she was, not Annie, her image waning, but Barbara; promises of a new beginning, a new life, a second chance.

She looked down at him, silently observing him, careless of her nakedness, ignoring his scrutiny, and saw his manhood start to come alive again. She slowly, gently, caressed him back to totality, thrusting herself onto him, rising above him, beautiful, wanton, herself reaching that sublime ecstasy over and over until he collapsed, spent, exhausted, pulling and crushing her to him.

They stood together naked in the brightness of the kitchen preparing the meal. She couldn't keep her hands off the different scars that seemed to adorn his hard body.

"You'll have to learn to concentrate on the cooking, woman, otherwise we've had it, we'll starve to death together."

After the 'spag-bol', made with linguini, not spaghetti, they sat cuddled together on the lounge carpet, leaning against the couch, listening to Beethoven's Fifth. As the disc came to the end she picked up their wine glasses. She forced his into his hand.

"A toast, Harry Andrews, Survival!"

He smiled and repeated her supplication.

"Survival, and now us, safe forever." They drank deeply together. She set aside the glasses.

"And now Harry, I want to hear the end game, as you put it. All of it in every gory detail."

"Well, I've told you most of it."

"No, you haven't. You haven't told me what happened after you left Harare and went back to Merrywaters. What happened in those four weeks before you flew down to Johannesburg?"

"Babs, I don't think you would want to hear about these things, too much savagery. I wasn't kidding when I said I went native. I was insane with grief, bitterness and a desire for futile revenge."

"I don't care, I have to know, I have to know how Annie and Robbie and Beverley were avenged. Even if I have to hate you for it."

"Babs, you know that Sampson took me back to Kiachingwa. He kept me there until I came out of it again and then I left. He drove me down to Sivewright's, I took off and was gone. It's over, finished."

But she persisted.

"No Harry, I'll never talk to you again until you tell me. I want you to get it off your chest. I want to know what you did to him. I want to know how you knew for certain, what made you so sure it was him. She pressed him back against the couch, her voice urgent, demanding.

Resigned, he fingered the object secured to the leather thong hanging around his neck.

Harry parked the truck out in the open, searching for anything that might be out of the ordinary. That is, except the total dereliction of the place, now totally overgrown, and the four figures motionless on the veranda of the house. His mind took in the vultures and briefly noted that there was no feeding activity near the house itself. They were still too scared to approach at all close. That meant someone was still alive there.

He opened the cab door and stepped out, alert and listening intently. There was nothing, just the howling of two jackals fighting somewhere in the undergrowth to his right. He walked diagonally across the lawn and then approached the house carefully, a light machine carbine held across his body. Then he saw Sampson wave from the side of the house and he relaxed. He waved in acknowledgement and continued towards the veranda.

The stench of death and excrement was almost overpowering, so he stopped about ten yards from the steps to wait for Sampson. The sun was already fierce and he had to squint, through half closed eyelids and dark glasses, at the figures hanging on the veranda beam. He then concentrated on the fourth man. The great Shenje 'Himmler' Ndunze, he thought. But there was no elation, nothing, except a chilling feeling in the pit of his stomach. After a while the man opened his eyes and started to scrutinise him. Harry pushed back his hat and took off his glasses. Recognition came to the man in a flash of understanding and he slumped a little, seemingly only held on his feet by the cord attaching his neck to the roof timber. Harry could see the pain in his face being replaced by fear. One minute there was arrogance, a man defying his fatigue and pain, hope. The next instance there was a drawing back, a slight drooping of the shoulders, a widening of the eyes and a slackening of the jaw line. Harry knew then that Ndunze knew who he was. He turned to Sampson who'd come up next to him.

"Give him some water, just enough so that he can talk." Harry turned and sat down in the shade of a stately umbrella tree situated in the middle of the lawn. There he waited while Sampson tried and eventually managed to dribble a little water down Ndunze's throat. That proved to be more difficult than it sounded, because when Sampson drew closer, Ndunze recognised him also and started to wail and thrash around. Eventually Sampson gave him a sharp clip on the head with the butt of the AK47 he was carrying. Ndunze's frenzied fear subsided as he sagged against his bonds, half conscious. In a while he came round and Sampson was more successful the second time.

Harry got up and carried the bench a little closer to Ndunze. He then sat down again and rested the carbine on the bench next to him. He spoke in slow, clear Shishona.

"Mr. Ndunze, you do not need to speak for the moment. You will just nod your head when I speak and don't hurry, we've got all day and you will die before me. Do you understand?"

It took nearly half a minute before Ndunze looked up and nodded his head, in so doing, handing control of the situation over to Harry.

"Good. Now, do you know who I am?"

Another half a minute passed before Ndunze's eyes came alive and again he nodded his head in the affirmative.

"Mr. Ndunze, this is the second time you have attacked me and my family, is this not so? The first time was during the Chimorenga." A statement of fact, not a query.

This time the nod came quickly, almost as if Ndunze wanted Harry to hurry up, get it over with. But Harry was in no hurry and had absolutely no fear that they would be interrupted. If they were, he wouldn't have minded. He was in a killing mood, having decided that if anyone, even the police, tried to interfere, he would kill them also. No-one, but no-one was going to deny him this. Between Sampson and himself, he reckoned, they'd need a bloody army to save Ndunze.

He fished in his pocket, found his pipe and stoked up. He then poured some water from his flask into his mouth, swilled it around for a moment and then swallowed it. He looked at the sky, wondering if it would rain. The rains were late again this year. But he didn't mind, in a month he would be back in England, bracing himself against the January cold, wind and rain. He savoured the brief thought in anticipation. He looked again at Ndunze and said quietly,

"Do you understand, Mr. Ndunze, that you made a grave mistake? You killed my children and my beloved wife, not so? You killed my peace-loving people who worked on this farm. You killed my cattle. Is this not all correct?"

Ndunze nodded his head slowly and seemed to sag more heavily on his rope.

"Throw some water on him, Sam. I don't want him dead yet." Harry sat there and puffed gently at his pipe while Sampson resuscitated Ndunze a little.

"Mr. Ndunze, I believe you are also the man, who, during the Chimorenga, shot down the aeroplane with a Sam 7 missile."

This brought Ndunze fully upright. He peered at Harry and searched his memory for facts about this man. He then remembered that the man was a pilot.

"You were the other indegi?" He croaked out the question, his larynx parched and almost broken into dumbness. "If I had another missile, I would have killed you also."

Harry smiled bitterly.

"Yes, but the problem for you, Mr. Ndunze, is that you then murdered my friend's father and mother in cold blood as they stood by the crash. Because you did this, my friend, also, is now dead." He took another swig from his flask and indicated to Sampson to give Ndunze some more water.

"How is your friend, Mr. Ndunze, the German man, Major Brod Volker?"

This brought Ndunze up again, this time with a twinkling of defiance in his eyes.

"Ha, he escaped from you and your army. He is safe and even now searches for you to kill you." Ndunze's voice was now a lot stronger.

Harry stared off into the distance puffing his pipe. He didn't answer at first, but then concentrated on tapping out the tobacco trapped at the bottom of the pipe-bowl. He tapped it against the bench seat gently until the tobacco dropped out. He put his pipe into his pocket and looked back at the arrogant merciless killer in front of him.

"No, Mr. Ndunze. You see, I killed Mr. Fischer, or Major Volker as you know him two years ago in Zambia. He was also very stupid. He tried to kill me with a knife. But unlike you however, I did not harm or rape his wife. She has run away back to Germany with her children."

Ndunze already had years of reluctant respect for this white settler confronting him, but now he realised that he had been a fool to take him on. But Harry was not finished.

"And your men, Mr. Ndunze, your so-called war-veterans, where are they?"

"They are here, they surround you even now." He smiled, "and when they come, it is I, Shenje 'Himmler' Ndunze, Mr. Andrews, who will kill you slowly."

"I think not, Mr. Ndunze. You see all your men, all thirty of them are accounted for. Twenty eight of them I have already killed, only two poor young men who should have known better, are still alive." Ndunze's mouth lost some of it's arrogance as Harry turned to Sampson. "Bring them."

Sampson nodded and within three minutes came back dragging the two young men with him. Harry indicated to Sampson to show them the dead men hanging from the veranda roof and Ndunze. They were so scared they couldn't stand up and Harry made them kneel in front of Ndunze, looking up at him.

"Umfanas (*children*), look at this man, your great leader, and look at his comrades. See how they have fallen."

The two youngsters, who couldn't have been older than their late teens were now shaking so badly, they couldn't watch. They were also dehydrated and cramping in agony and Harry imagined that they were also probably suffering withdrawal symptoms, not having been able to light up some dope for two days. Harry told Sampson to lift them to their feet and release them.

"Umfanas, I am going to let you go home to your mothers, but before you go there are two things you must know." The young men stood before him shivering, tongue tied and terrified. "First, if you go to the tobacco barns at the Swan farm you will find your comrades. Sam, tell them where to go." He waved, not dismissively, but rather in disgust and the fact that he had momentarily run out of words. He sat back while Sampson gave the boys gruff but precise instructions as to where they should go. When he'd finished, Harry took over the discourse again.

"When you find your comrades you will find all of them. Not one has escaped me and I tell you now, that if you ever do this work again, anywhere, anywhere in Zimbabwe, I will find you and I will do the same things again to you. I will find you and you will die, do you understand?" Harry's heart-fluttering bravado was lost on them. If anything, their fear of this malhungu increased.

"But before you go, you will come with me." He indicated to Sampson to bring the young men. Sampson needed no real encouragement. He grabbed the youngsters roughly by their arms, and almost as if to tear their arms off, and swung them around to follow Harry the few paces he took. Harry stopped and held out his hand, carbine carefully pointing nowhere, its sling slung around his arm tightly for ease to bring it to a firing position. He was a mere five paces from Ndunze. He looked up at the man who had brought so much sadness and hardship to his life.

"Ndunze, you and I have finished our talking. You have destroyed my life and because your comrade, Robert Gabriel Mugabe is a tyrant and controls the police and army, I have been forced to take the law into my own hands. You will go to your death knowing that I speak the truth. You have brought misery to thousands of people, for what? For a dream? For a better life? What? You have achieved nothing but destruction and death; and the brief pleasure of the power of the stick and the gun. You take pride in being called 'Himmler'. If you had any idea how many millions of people that man, no, not a man,... that evil devil, was responsible for killing in the space of ten years, you would consider yourself not worthy to lick his boots."

Harry really had Ndunze's attention, not, Harry suspected, because he was speaking eloquently, but because he was mindful of Harry's reference to the fact that he was going to his death.

"Shenje Ndunze," Harry made a bit of a drama out of it in order to impress and control the mindset of the young men behind him, "you have destroyed many good things, many wonderful people and you are a disgrace, as is your friend, Mr. Mugabe, to your people. May God have mercy on your soul. You shot my wife with three shots, so you shall die."

Using his left hand he took the leather thong from around his neck.

"But today you go to your death for this one person, and one person only, my beloved wife." The tears came into his eyes as he said it. He worked his hand around the thong until it came to the gold object strung on it and then held it up.

"Look Ndunze, look closely." He leaned up, holding the object close to Ndunze's face. Ndunze couldn't do much else but look at it, the small engraved dragon-like image just inches away from his face. "You chose to wear this around your neck. You were stupid, because this is the sign of my family, a sign that has been with my family for a thousand years. I gave this sign to my wife on my knees when I asked her to marry me."

He had to stop for a moment, choking on his own words, his grief welling up into his throat. After a while, after turning his head left and right as if to clear it, he continued.

"You defiled and destroyed the most important thing in my life, more even than my own life, and I promised her, that no man would ever hurt her. But I failed because I didn't know there so much evil in men, in you and in your friends. So now, like them, you must die."

Sampson, so strong and inured to death and hardship, was horrified and fascinated all at once by this drama to the point where he was nearly crying himself. In the two young men he was holding, there was nothing but fear, life-long fear, an experience that they would never forget.

All the spirit had left Ndunze. He stood there, devoid of expression, resigned, cowed, but even as the end came, he didn't really understand the evil in him, so indoctrinated had he been.

Slowly, agonisingly, hesitantly, Harry brought his carbine up to a firing position, checked that it was on 'single fire', aimed almost as if he didn't want to look and then depressed the trigger three times. The .275 maxim bullets hit Ndunze, one after the other, all placed within inches of each other in his chest, already tumbling in the air, their leaded heads split open in order to inflict as much devastation as possible. As Ndunze's body jumped the macabre dance of death, his torso disintegrated, huge chunks of it splattering against the wall behind him. The ragged remains sagged there, bloody and final.

Harry fell to his knees, and, despite his agnosticism, said quietly, almost sobbing,

"God, if you are there, please forgive me, but I have done what I had to do."

He kneeled there for all of two minutes, and then climbed clumsily to his feet, slowly, almost as a old man. He turned to Sampson.

"It is done, let them go."

"In a moment, Master Harry. But first I have something to do."

He dragged the youngsters up to Ndunze's hanging ragged body. Right in front of them, he removed his bayonet from its sheath. Using it, he ripped open Ndunze's trousers. In three seconds he had grasped the dead man's testicles and penis in his left hand, and had hacked them off ignoring the warm blood as it gushed out over his hand. He then stuck the bayonet into the gaping mouth, and forced the jaw even wider. He stuffed Ndunze's manhood into the dead man's mouth and then turned to Harry.

"Now it is finished, Master Harry, now it is finished." For the moment, he ignored Harry, who was at that instance, puking his guts onto the lawn. Instead he turned to the young men.

"Go now to the barn as we have told you and see the wrath of this malhungu and never forget, for if you do, you will die."

He watched the young men hobble painfully off and then wiped his knife and hands carefully on the remnants of Ndunze's shirt. Then he walked over to Harry, put his arm around his shoulder, and said quietly,

"Let us go home now. There is much healing to be done."

Harry looked at his old signet ring, then raising it to his lips, he kissed it. He lifted it over his head and then replaced it on its thong around his neck. Sampson looked at it closely, fingering it as it rested on Harry's chest. He had never seen it before.

"What is it, Master Harry?"

"It is the crest… or sign of my family. It is dragon, a mythical creature called a Wyvern. It is like a flying lion with wings and big claws that breaths fire. It has been the sign of my family for over a thousand years and I have redeemed it."

"For sure, Master Harry, this is strong medicine, you are the same like your sign."

Harry laughed.

"Enough Sam, that's bullshit and you know it. Come on, you drive George's car, it's time to go home."

Glossary

[1] Olio: Aircraft hydraulic shock absorber.

[2] Engine: 285 hp horizontally opposed six-cylinder Teledyne Continental.

[3] Empennage: tail end of an aeroplane.

[4] Mopane: *(ColophosperMum mopane)* Type of woodlands' tree endemic in most of sub-Saharan Africa. Favoured by Elephants, the leaf is a bright green camel-foot shape and the timber is popular for construction purposes and firewood. The famed Mopane worm *(the caterpillar of the moth Gonimbrasiabelina)*, a culinary delicacy in Africa, is found in these trees.

[5] BE 35: International Designation for a Beechcraft 4/6 seat V-tailed Bonanza. The tail consists of ruddervators, which act two dimensionally in much the same manner as a normal tail plane of an aircraft.

[6] Aeri: slang for aeroplane, airplane or aircraft.

[7] Karoi: Small farming town in northern part of Rhodesia (now Republic of Zimbabwe in central Africa) on the main road linking Salisbury (now Harare) to Lusaka (capital city of the Republic of Zambia). Situated ±120 miles from Salisbury.

[8] BSAP: British South Africa Police. Cecil John Rhodes, British

Governor of the Cape Colony, established the police force in Rhodesia in the late 19th Century. It was initially a private police force owned by Rhodes' exploration and development company, the British South Africa Company. It was assimilated into the Crown Government of the Colony of Southern Rhodesia circa 1902.

[9] Bulawayo: Second largest city in Zimbabwe. So named after 'Ubulalawayo'-place of killing. Site of the Kraal of Lobengula, Chief of the Ndebele (Matebele) Tribe, an off-shoot of the Zulu nation of South Africa.

[10] RSA: Republic of South Africa.

[11] DCA: Division or Director of Civil Aviation.

[12] Mirage: the South African Air Force was equipped with French Dassault Mirage jet fighters. At the time these state-of-art fighter jets were a match for anything flying at those times and were used by many Air Forces worldwide including the French and Israeli Air Forces.

[13] Louis Trichard: A small farming town in the northern part of South Africa. It was the northern base of the strategic defence system of South Africa and it is believed that with the help of the Israeli Defence Force, the SAF had built an underground fighter base there.

[14] AGL: Above ground level.

[15] Runway 09 or 27 etc: The direction in which a runway is laid out dictates its universal description by International Convention. A runway which lies at an angle of 90° from magnetic north is thus defined as Runway 09, at an angle of 270° it is defined as Runway 27 and so on, to the nearest whole number.

[16] Time Zulu: Aeronautical equivalent of Greenwich Mean Time or International time. In central Africa local time is 2 hours ahead of Greenwich thus time Zulu is 2 hours behind local time.

[17] Boma: from the Ndebele/Zulu word meaning 'meeting place'. In tourist bush camps, typically a 'boma' is a cleared circular area, open

to the sky and surrounded by a windbreak of wooden droppers, reeds or thatching grass. In the centre of the boma, there is normally a large hearth on which a log cooking-fire is lit every evening. It is the tradition in most of these resorts for guests to gather at the boma at the end of every day to drink their sundowners and discuss the day's fishing, hunting or game viewing, and to eat their evening meal.

[18] Bechuanaland: At the time a British Protectorate, landlocked on all sides by South Africa, South West Africa (Namibia), Rhodesia and Zambia. The country is today a thriving Republic within the British Commonwealth called Botswana. It is famous for its unique tourist attractions, the Kalahari Desert, Chobe [choe-bee] River and the Okavango Delta.

[19] Munt, slang noun, Pl - munts. non-derogatory derivative of the Shishona word 'umuntu' meaning man. Used by whites in Rhodesia at that time to refer to a black man or men. The word is still in use in Zimbabwe and all over the world where ex-Rhodesians or Zimbabweans are to be found.

[20] Gunja: [gun`jah] Shishona word for Dagga: Marijuana, Indian hemp, alternative slang – 'grass'. Use of this drug is common in Africa and police forces throughout the continent have all but given up trying to prevent its propagation and distribution. It grows wild and is also cultivated virtually everywhere.

[21] Location: Residential township designed and built specifically to house black people in the segregated towns in Africa of those times, the so-called 'black ghetto', the most infamous of which is 'Soweto' in Johannesburg.

[22] Malhungu(s): [mahl`oon`goo] non-derogatory Shishona term for white person (people).

[23] Landy: slang for Land Rover, a British made 4 wheel drive utility vehicle.

[24] Shishona: Mentioned several times in this book. Shishona is the most widely spoken local language in Zimbabwe. Used principally by ethnic Mashona tribesmen, but spoken and understood by most of

the indigenous peoples of Zimbabwe.

[25] Umtali: Small town on the eastern border of Zimbabwe, now renamed Mutare.

[26] Batman: Domestic servant employed by the Force to serve a ranking officer.

[27] Casevac: Casualty evacuation, a term used by personnel involved in evacuating civilians or other military personnel in need of medical care.

[28] Valley: To residents of Rhodesia/Zimbabwe, the Zambezi valley is the 'valley'. Readers should understand that the Zambezi valley is no ordinary valley. It is the vast flood plain of one of the world's great rivers, rich in pristine flora and wild fauna, it is trapped within towering wild escarpments, in places over 2000 feet in height. It contains plains and gorges (canyons), the most famous of which is the Victoria Falls gorge. Kariba gorge is another in which the Kariba Dam wall was built during the early 1960's. Kariba Dam itself (known to the locals as the 'lake') is approximately 180 miles long and in places nearly 50 miles wide.

[29] African Fish Eagle *Haliaeetus vocifer*. Beautiful black and white eagle that is at a distance visually similar to the British Sea eagle and the American Bald eagle, common throughout sub-Saharan Africa. Usually observed in pairs over larger rivers, lakes and estuaries, they are conspicuous and noisy.

[30] Hippopotamus *Hippopotamus amphibious*.

[31] Water Buck *Kobus ellipsiprymnus*

[32] Uncleared area: While Kariba Dam was being built, long stretches of the future shoreline were cleared of trees by monstrous bulldozers using huge steel balls on massive chains. Where the shoreline was not cleared, the subsequently inundated hardwood trees died but did not fall over and rot away. Instead, they just petrified in-situ and have ever since represented somewhat of a hazard when one is moving about amongst them in a boat.

[33] Veldskoens: Comfortable crepe soled soft suede boots, popular as casual bush wear.

[34] Kariba Weed *Salvinia molesta*. An absolute scourge, this weed at one time threatened to cover the entire protected shoreline of the lake. It also spread widely, being carried under the bottom of boats being moved from one water resort to another. Wide spread spraying and the introduction of a particular parasite that only feeds on the weed, has brought this rapidly advancing weed under control.

[35] On 4th May 1967 "The Times" (page 4, column f) reported on a rally held in Dar es Salaam - ZANU, through a spokesman, a Mr. Peter Mtundwa, called for the assassination of Ian Smith and Mr. Harold Wilson, British Prime Minister. He said, "We are being turned into murderers by their dealing, and we must kill people like Smith and Wilson. When we see Wilson step into Rhodesia, a bullet must go through his head." The rally marked the beginning of the CHIMURENGA (liberation war) and it marked the first anniversary of the proclaimed launch of the struggle in Rhodesia.

[36] Some years before, 'The Times' of May 12, 1967, did indeed report, much as has been recorded above, that five foreign nationals had been arrested for spying for a foreign power against Zambia. Furthermore President Kaunda is recorded as having made the statement made in the text. However the names of all the parties involved have been changed and earlier and subsequent events related in this book have no bearing on fact and are a pure figment of my imagination. The code name of the informant 'Claude' is the same as was reported and the pilot was a Canadian national. But he was Captain J. G. Warren, the author's father, who died on the 7th January 2004.

[37] Flight Level: Altitude of an aircraft reflected in units of 1000 feet from a datum pressure reading of 1013,2 hecto-pascals (hPa) or millibars (mb). This equates to one standard atmosphere of pressure. 10,000ft to 12,000ft was the operational ceiling of a Dakota, which was not pressurised. Today's airliners fly 3 to 4 times higher.

[38] Boomslang *Dispholidus typus* A widespread shy, bird and chameleon eating, tree snake, which bites readily. It inflates its throat in threat

THE WYVERN REVENGE

with highly potent venom that will cause death from internal bleeding in 2 to 3 days, unless treated immediately.

[39] Brother: Chadrack was by no means Sampson's brother; nor were any of his numerous cousins, real relations. It is the way of 'shamwaris' (friends), however, to take on these relationships. This happens when they form a close relationship with anyone, be it as mothers, aunts, brothers, sisters or cousins.

[40] Portuguese Empire: In the early 1970's Portuguese Dictator Salazar was overthrown. Within months the new democratic government of Portugal withdrew all the Portuguese troops from their various colonies around the world. Mozambique was one such colony in which, until the Portuguese withdrawal, Rhodesian freedom fighters were unable to operate. Thereafter the eastern flank of Rhodesia was exposed to incursions, a border some 700 miles in length (see also endnote 97 below).

[41] Allouette: French built Dassault Allouette attack helicopter. The Rhodesian Air Force operated one squadron of the Mark 2 version of these aircraft. Further information is supplied in footnote 43 below.

[42] Jet A Kerosene: Two types of aviation fuel are in common use in aircraft. Normal petrol, which is stringently filtered and down-graded to 100 octane, is called 'Avgas'. The other is paraffin, also stringently cleaned and purified, is called 'Jet A'. Normal reciprocating engines are fuelled with Avgas, while all turbines, i.e., jet and turbo-prop engines are fuelled using Jet A.

[43] Gun-ship: Prior to the imposition of International punitive sanctions against Rhodesia, the Rhodesian Air Force equipped itself with French built Allouette Mk2 attack helicopters: During the years when Rhodesia was subjected to world punitive economic sanctions, the French government refused to supply spare parts for these aircraft. Many parts were thereafter made locally or where that was impossible, were clandestinely obtained in South Africa. The Rhodesian's turned several of these 'choppers' into greatly feared and very effective ground attack platforms, the so-called 'gun-ships', by mounting a large calibre cannon cross-wise through the passenger

cabin. When these cannons were fired, the whole helicopter would literally jump sideways across the sky in recoil. The concept was later used with great effect in Vietnam by the US forces.

[44] SLR; Self Loading Rifle, the British crib of the Belgian Fabrique Nationale (FN) automatic rifle, but differed in that it was only semi-automatic. It was the standard infantry weapon in use by the British and other armies at the time, and was one of the early attempts to standardise weaponry across the allied forces in Europe utilising a rimless 7,62mm cartridge. The irony is that the AK47 fired a 7,63mm projectile, so while the AK47 could be loaded with SLR ammunition, the reverse was not the case. This provided the Rhodesian insurgents with a distinct weapons advantage, which was decisive on several occasions.

[45] Nyasaland: Now the Republic of Malawi. The country was dragged out of the oblivion of the ill-fated Federation of Rhodesia and Nyasaland by Dr. Hastings "Kamusu" Banda, a benevolent Dictator, who after declaring himself President For Life, eventually died, old and disillusioned without really making any difference. See also footnote 47 below.

[46] Umfazi: [um`fah`zee] Shishona/Ndebele/Zulu word meaning young maiden.

[47] 'Federation' of Rhodesia and Nyasaland: From 1953 to 1963, three countries in central Africa, Nyasaland (now Malawi), Southern Rhodesia (which was renamed Rhodesia, and is now called Zimbabwe) and Northern Rhodesia (now Zambia) were united together to form an ill-fated Federation. It was after the break-up of the Federation that the Rhodesian Front Party, headed by Winston Field and then Ian Smith, unilaterally declared independence from Great Britain (UDI), which in turn led to the so called 'Second Chimurenga', or War of Independence. After many deaths, political negotiations and two interim governments, this culminated in the creation of an independent Zimbabwe on the 4 March 1980 with Robert Mugabe as its first Prime Minister. Now the President, he is still in power and has become a dictator, destroyed the economy, is responsible for the deaths of hundreds of thousands of his people and is determined at any cost to hold onto power.

[48] Biblical names: The Christian, especially Scottish, missionary teachings of many denominations have had a quite remarkable influence on the indigenous populations of much of Africa. For this reason a high proportion of the Christian populous are named after famous Biblical characters. The same may of course be said in respect of the Muslim faith.

[49] Shabeen: [sh'ah'been] Unlicensed bar selling commercial and home brewed alcohol. These are common throughout Africa and are very often frequented by prostitutes. It is the existence of these 'shabeens' along the trucking routes of Africa that is thought to have contributed to the meteoric spread of HIV southwards from its suspected origins in Central Africa.

[50] Barotse tribe: A tribe emanating in western Zambia near the Angolan border, who were, at the time Zambia became Independent, fiercely opposed to being ruled by Lusaka. Several uprisings against President Kaunda were ruthlessly crushed. Kaunda sent in his party (UNIP) thugs and it is said that tens of thousands of Barotse tribesmen were slaughtered in order to bring them to heel.

[51] Rain Bird - Burchell's Coucal *Centropus burchellii* Large and beautiful, but secretive bird that is most often heard just before rain.

[52] Humba gashli: Shishona and Ndebeli, [hum'bah gush'lee] literal-travel carefully. Slang-take it easy. Used most often as a farewell.

[53] Madala: [mah'dah'la], old man, a respectful term of address for any older man whose name is unknown. Used in most Induni languages throughout southern Africa.

[54] UNIP: United National Independence Party, founded by a schoolteacher from Nyasaland (another country now called Malawi) called Kenneth Kaunda. He became the President of independent Zambia. In 1972, he banned all other opposition parties and declared UNIP the sole legal party of Zambia, with himself as its President for 27 years.

[55] Gundwane: [goon'd'won] Induni for 'rat', in this sense, a high insult.

⁵⁶ Knobkerrie: from the Afrikaans, 3-4 ft. long throwing stick carved from the bowl of a young tree. Typically has a large knob at one end. Used as a walking stick, crutch or for beating off attack from wild animals. Contributory cause of death in countless bar brawls, faction fights and inter-Nicene conflicts.

⁵⁷ Kopje: [cop'ee].Pl- kopjies. Taken from the Afrikaans for a small rocky hill, in Africa generally a granitic extrusion rising above the surrounding countryside. Africa is full of them and they are also normally covered in thick bush, ideal for resting on as the rocks provide shelter while the height most often gives a commanding view of the surrounding area.

⁵⁸ Large-leafed rock fig tree *Ficus abutifolia*. Bears a delicious fruit, much fancied by birds and many animals.

⁵⁹ Marula tree *Schlerocarya birrea*. Bares a soft pale green fruit the size of a small plum; abundant throughout tropical Africa below an altitude of 2000 ft. Famous because when the ripe fruit falls to the ground it ferments in the sun and is a favourite with many animals. Elephants especially are known to get extraordinarily drunk through eating this fruit. Now used to manufacture a cream-liquor, usually under the brand name, Amarula.

⁶⁰ Snot apple tree *Azanza garckeana*. Bears a very tasty woody fruit, under the hard skin of which the flesh has the appearance and texture of hardened nasal mucus, hence the name given to the tree.

⁶¹ Mobola plum *Parinari curatellifolia*. Bears small and sour, but edible, fruit.

⁶² The TIMES of Friday 20/5/66 page 1 column g, reports on the killing of the Viljoens at Sinoa the previous Tuesday. Then on 6/6/66, page 8, column c, reports on the murder of Mr. Saint Claire Speldewinde, his wife and her mother, Mrs. Linda Crawford at their farm near Karoi.

⁶³ Wild dog *Lycaon pictus*. Killers in carnival clothes, these fearless hunters, found in packs of up to 30 to 40 individuals, will prey on virtually anything, from large animals to livestock.

[64] Gundwane – Shishona for the giant rat *Cricetomys gambianus*.

[65] Honey Badger or Ratel: *Mellivora capensis*. Widespread in Africa, Honey Badgers are totally fearless. They display considerable aggression and have a powerful bite. They will readily attack humans and vehicles, and have been known to bring down buffalo in the manner described in the text. They are best left alone.

[66] Side Striped Jackal *Canis adustus*. These fox like scavengers are nocturnal, moving around in pairs. Their appearance is thought by many to signal the presence of Lions.

[67] Miombo Tree *Brachystegia*.

[68] Jacaranda and Syringa *(Melia Azedarach)* trees: Indigenous to South America and India respectively, the seeds of these trees, together with many other invasive exotic flora such as black jacks, khaki weed and cosmos, were brought into southern Africa in the horse fodder imported by the British Army from Brazil and India during the Boer Wars. These trees, weeds and indeed a species of small black ant with a nasty bite have spread all over the subcontinent.

[69] Land: Rhodesian farmers referred to their 'fields' as 'lands'.

[70] Alan Savoury: Later a Member of Parliament in Smith's Government, but during the 1960s advocated a paddock grazing system for Rhodesian farmers. He suggested the division of large grazing ranges into small paddocks so that cattle and sheep were forced to eat all the grass in one paddock before they were released into the next. The principle was based on the fact that animals naturally tend to select only the juiciest morsels to eat, hence new growth frequently failed to survive. By adopting this system heavily grazed grasses in empty paddocks were able to recover unhindered for several months before being grazed again. The system is very successful in increasing grass cover, especially in more arid areas.

[71] Leopard *Panthera pardus*. Wrongly assumed to be nocturnal these carnivores have an incredible diet ranging from insects and fish, to birds and livestock. They will hunt at any time and are extremely dangerous. They are partial to baboons and will climb to uppermost

branches of a tree in an attempt to corner one. Impalas are considered to form their principal diet where this species is common. They are not dependent on water, but drink when it is available.

[72] Large-Fruited Bushwillow *Combritum zeyheri* One of several species of Combritum, endemic in Zimbabwe, the largest of which is the famed Leadwood tree.

[73] Prickly Thorn tree *Acacia brevispica*. It has small vicious reversed hooked thorns that must be individually disengaged. Commonly known by its Afrikaans name as 'wag 'n biggie tree' – wait a minute tree.

[74] Kiaat tree *Pterocarpus angolensis* The common teak found throughout southern Africa. Used extensively for furniture and fittings such as doors, window frames and skirting boards.

[75] Big pod mahogany tree *Afzelia quanzensis*.

[76] Impala *Aepyceros melampus* These browser/grazer antelopes are common and widespread. They produce loud snorts when alarmed, which can even frighten elephants. They fight a great deal and preoccupation with this often affects their vigilance and so they are quite easy to get near to and are preyed upon by virtually all the larger predators.

[77] Valley: See endnote 28.

[78] Kudu *Tragelaphus strepsiceros*. Magnificent, large but timid browsing undulates they are most adept at concealment, remaining motionless for long periods when suspicious. Mostly mobile at night, their call is a loud bark, and when the bulls fight, they clash together so hard, it sounds like a rifle shot.

[79] Biltong: Meat, salted and peppered, and hung-dried, that can be made from just about anything from eland *(Taurotragus oryx)* or ostrich *(Struthio camelus)* to mutton or beef. Fairly similar to American 'jerky', it is extremely popular chopped into bite sized morsels as a snack amongst most southern africans. Venison biltong is especially favoured.

THE WYVERN REVENGE

[80] See **Time** magazine, editions of 12th and 23rd August 1976.

[81] Baron: Beechcraft BE58; a six seater light twin engine aircraft powered by two Teledyne Continental IO 520 reciprocating engines. Considered by most flyers to be the ultimate in light twins, powerful enough to maintain 8000 ft altitude on one engine, spacious, capable with full tanks of carrying 350 lbs of baggage in addition to 6 people, and fast, with a block speed of around 170 knots.

[82] Nkupe: *Distichodus mossambicus.* Relative of the Chessa (*D. shenga*) but a deep olive colour, almost black. Abundant small-mouthed fish in the Zambezi drainage system. Delicious to eat.

[83] Black rhinoceros *Diceros bicornis* Browsing round-lipped rhino. Smaller than its relative, the white or square-lipped rhino *Ceratotherium siMum,* but far more aggressive.

[84] Buffalo *Syncerus caffer* Gregarious, shy grazers, the African buffalo is extremely dangerous when pursued or wounded, cleverly hiding in thickets from which they will charge head-on. At short range they are impossible to stop. Preyed upon only by Lions.

[85] 4th September 1978: "Time" magazine on 18th September, and many other broadsheets, reported on such an atrocity (the first of two actually), but it went largely unnoticed by the international community. Its attention at the time was consumed by the death of over 11 000 people in an earthquake in Iran, the Middle East crisis and two other aircraft accidents. In Britain, the population was consumed by the run up to the national elections that then brought Margaret Thatcher to power. In this incident an Air Rhodesia Vickers Viscount, a four-engine turboprop airliner, travelling from Kariba to Salisbury and piloted by Captain John Hood, was shot down, crashing into the thick woodlands of the Whamira Hills. A Sam 7 ground-to-air missile hit both starboard engines. There were 56 people on board. 38 died in the crash. 5 of the 18 survivors went off to find water while 3 of the remaining 13 hid nearby. The terrorists who perpetrated the action arrived, rounded up the 10 survivors they could find, which consisted of seven women, two young girls and a man. It is reported that they then robbed the survivors and then mowed them down with automatic

gunfire after appearing friendly and promising to help. The 5, who had gone off, did manage to get water from a nearby tribal village, but on returning heard gunfire and so, themselves, hid until help arrived the following morning. ZIPRA leader Joshua Nkomo, later Vice-President of Zimbabwe, did, on the 5th October, claim responsibility for the action. All other details of the incident given in "The Wyvern Revenge" are, with sincere respect to the deceased and their loved ones, a figment of my imagination. But this incident, I believe more than any other, can be accredited with bringing the Rhodesian regime to its knees and hastening the election of Robert Mugabe to the premiership of the newly founded Zimbabwe.

[86] Referendum: The minority electorate of Rhodesia, in a referendum held on January 30th 1979, voted, overwhelmingly, to bring the blacks into Government after Ian Smith admitted a few weeks earlier that black rule in Rhodesia was the only way of ending the war.

[87] Indegi: Shishona for aeroplane.

[88] SLR; See endnote 45.

[89] Biafra: Breakaway province of Nigeria, involved in a vicious war of secession, which failed after millions of people died.

[90] Connies: Abbreviation referring to Boeing Super Constellation 4-engined airliners: Powered by Pratt and Whitney radial engines, these aircraft were, until the advent of the "jet" age, the 'ultimate' pilots' dream; beautiful, safe and reliable.

[91] Chimorenga: The First Chimorenga, as history written by the ZANU PF purports, was the war between Cecil John Rhodes' British South Africa Company and the Ndebele peoples (who at the time controlled Zimbabwe) in 1896 and 1897. They then see the Second Chimorenga as the War of Independence, which started circa 1964 and ended with the Lancaster House Agreement in 1979. The ruling elite now cite the redistribution of farmland out of white control and back to the people as the Third Chimorenga. The truth, of course, and as alluded to elsewhere in this story, is that when the whites first came to this land in the late 1800's, it was essentially an empty land, the local black

population, themselves invaders, numbering around 250 000.

[92] This statement is taken verbatim from the ZANU PF's Election Manifesto titled "The 3rd Chimorenga".

[93] Great Dyke: A mineralised dyke, one of the richest in the world, running for hundreds of miles north south through central Zimbabwe. Whilst severely disjointed in places, it is rich in a wide range of minerals, including gold, copper, tin, nickel, lead, iron, vanadium, chromite, manganese, asbestos, semi-precious stones and particularly platinum.

[94] Sausage tree *Kigelia Africana,*

[95] Chinyanja: The Chinyanja people are, these days, frequently called the Chewa.

[96] Bamba Zonki: pr., bum'ba'zon'key. Slang for Harare, meaning 'Place that takes everything'.

[97] Samora Machel Avenue: Previously named Jameson Avenue after Leander Starr Jameson, early pioneer, friend of and working for Cecil John Rhodes, who commanded Fort Victoria (Masvingo) after it's founding in 1890. Samora Machel was the leader of Frelimo, the insurgency movement in Mozambique, and who became the first indigenous President of that country after the collapse of the Portuguese empire in the mid '70s'. Machel later died in an air crash in South Africa, victim of a mistaken 'approach' to Maputo by his drunken Russian flight crew.

[98] AMO: Aircraft Maintenance Operator.

[99] Mosi-oa-Tunya: "The Smoke That Thunders", local name for the Victoria Falls.

[100] Calabash: the large tough pear-shaped pod, 300mm long, of a relative the Sausage Tree (*Kigelia africana*). The trick was to make a circular hole in its side, about 40mm in diameter and clean out the seeds and pith. This was then secured firmly to a tree trunk or fence post by wire or tough string, strung through small holes in the

narrow end. When some chunks of biltong (dried salted meat) were left in these, they were irresistible to baboons, who would squeeze one of their hands into the hole, grab a piece of biltong, but then could not take their hands out of the calabash whilst still gripping the biltong. They were so greedy that they just wouldn't let go even when hysterical at the approach of a human. So they were easy prey for the farmers trying to get rid of them.

[101] Mealie: local name referring to maize or corn or an individual cob. So called after the brand name 'Mealie Meal', which is the cornflour or more accurately white maize flour that is the staple diet of the indigenous peoples of southern Africa. It is boiled with water in a pot to make a thick porridge-like dough called 'sudza'. This is eaten with the fingers after dipping it into whatever stew of meat (nyama) was being cooked with it. 'Sudza ne nyama' is made and eaten everywhere and is both plentiful and inexpensive.

[102] Notams: Notices to Airmen. Official publications sent to all pilots providing air-space advisories, radio frequency changes to navigation beacons and ATC's, accident reports and the like. Zimbabwe stopped producing these and so most pilots subscribed to the South African Notams, which covered most of southern Africa anyway.

[103] Reedbuck *Redunca arundinum.*

[104] Cattle: Wealth amongst rural Africans in Zimbabwe and many other parts of Africa is counted in terms of how many cattle they own.

[105] Honey Guide: The Greater Honey Guide (*Indicator indicator*), one of four like-species, is an amazing bird. Fond of honey itself, by continually using a high-pitched chattering sound, fluttering conspicuously, and by hopping from tree to tree, it will guide a man and/or a Honey Badger to a bee hive. It will then wait until the hive has been broken open and raided, and then come down to feed itself. It is considered good practice to ensure that a big chunk of honeycomb is left where the bird can safely get to it and feed.

[106] Mombe: [mom'bee] Shishona for a steer, bull or heifer.

[107] Warthog *Phacochoerus aethiopicus* Like baboons, these wonderful

animals had a habit of raiding the maize fields and are capable of doing a great deal of damage rooting around amongst the plants. When their numbers build up they really become a pest and getting rid of them is a tedious business, because they do most of the damage at night. A good method is to surround one of their favourite fields with an impermeable barrier of thorny brush. Into this are built a few strategically placed traps consisting of a foot long piece of vertical 16 gauge piping welded in place about two feet off the ground halfway between two metal fence posts. Into this is slotted a shotgun cartridge loaded with buckshot. The pipe is rigged with a metal drop-block held in place by a pin tied to a thin trip wire suspended three or four inches above the ground across the gap between the posts. When the trip wire is triggered by an animal passing through the gap, the drop-block is released. It drops, firing the cartridge into the back of the head of the animal beneath. It is very effective, and of course the workers love them because there is little to beat a spit-roasted warthog.

[108] Deviljie [devil'key]: From the Afrikaans for Devil Thorn (*Dicerocaryum eriocarpum* or *D. zanguebarium*). Widespread flowering prostrate trailing herb bearing hard flat fruit found in sandy or rocky grassland, which has two or more hard sharp spines. These are spread when they stick into the hooves of animals and, very painfully, into human feet.

[109] Tsetse fly: (*Family Glossinidae*) This large fly, similar to a horse fly but more yellowish grey and displays black stripes on its thorax, is an animal blood feeder. It carries a vicious proboscis-driven irritant. A nip from these little monsters is particularly painful. Fortunately they were eradicated from Rhodesia /Zimbabwe between the world-wars but are now making a re-appearance because of the lack of vigilance of the various governments in the region. This fly acts as vector for several deadly deceases, including transmitting sleeping sickness in humans and nagana in animals.

[110] Vultures: The most common vultures in this area are the Whitebacked Vulture (*Gyps africanus*). These normally gather in large numbers on carrion. They are most often seen in the company of the Lappetfaced Vulture (*Torgos tracheliotus*). Less common, these are huge, massive billed vultures that normally operate in pairs dominating all others

at food sources.

[111] Vundu: (*Heterobranchus longifilis*) Found in the middle and lower Zambezi, these are giant olive-grey or reddish-brown catfishes which grow to well over 100lbs. The largest freshwater fishes in the region, they are highly prized in angling and can put up a ferocious fight.

[112] Vervet Monkey: (*Cercopithicus aethiops*) The only common monkey in the region. Light grey with a white-fringed black face, it is a member of the Green Monkey family.

[113] Red current tress: (*Rhus pyroides*). The sour but edible 5mmØ fruit grows in easily accessible bunches. A favourite of vervets, these trees are common high on the rocky escarpment of the Zambezi valley.

[114] Bateleur: *Terathopius ecaudatus*.- A common, but distinctive, bulky looking black eagle with a scarlet face and legs. In flight they appear almost tailless. Voracious raptor with a love for warthog piglets.

[115] Gymnogene: *Polyboroides typus*.- Large grey hawk with black primaries and tail feathers with a bold white band across them. Has bare yellow face and legs. To feed itself, it clambers around in trees or on rocks, inserting its long legs into cavities in search of bats, lizards and other small edible creatures. Frequently raids weaver, swift and woodpecker nests, eating the nestlings.

[116] Rands: With the rampant inflation and devastating devaluation of the Zimbabwe $, South African currency is much sought after in Zimbabwe and is in common use. It is not unusual for local people to carry and trade in Rands, obtained in payment or tips from tourists and businessmen.

[117] Rinkhals: *Hemachatus haemachatus*.- Large, stout nocturnal spitting-cobra readily identifiable by the bands of white on its ventral scales. Feeds on mice and toads. Normally feigns death when disturbed or threatened. Highly venomous, it rears up, hood spread and can spit up to three yards. It is best to keep well clear of these snakes as the venom is potentially fatal.